The Need to Help

D1231211

The Need

to Help

The Domestic Arts
of International
Humanitarianism

Liisa H. Malkki

Duke University Press   Durham and London   2015

© 2015 Duke University Press

All rights reserved

Printed in the United States of America on acid-free paper ∞

Designed by Natalie F. Smith

Typeset in Quadraat Pro by Copperline

Library of Congress Cataloging-in-Publication Data

Malkki, Liisa H. (Liisa Helena)

The need to help : the domestic arts of international
humanitarianism / Liisa H. Malkki.

pages cm

Includes bibliographical references and index.

ISBN 978-0-8223-5912-8 (hardcover : alk. paper)

ISBN 978-0-8223-5932-6 (pbk. : alk. paper)

ISBN 978-0-8223-7536-4 (e-book)

1. Humanitarian assistance. 2. International relief.
3. Helping behavior. I. Title.

HV553.M264 2015

361.2'6—dc23   2015008325

Cover image by author;
cover design by Natalie F. Smith.
Photo credit: Christine R. Choi.

Contents

Acknowledgments

First and foremost, I would like to thank all the Finnish Red Cross people who so generously shared their thoughts and experiences with me. I will always be grateful to them for their time and openness. Helena Korhonen first welcomed me in the Finnish Red Cross at the introduction of Olli Alho. The currently serving secretary-general, Kristiina Kumpula, and her colleagues in Helsinki have been very kind to accommodate me since then. The contributions of the Red Cross people in Tampere are everywhere visible. I am also deeply grateful to the interlocutors I have had regarding knitting and other work of the hand. The help of the research staff of the City of Helsinki Library was invaluable. And I have had the most extraordinary research assistants in Jacob Doherty, Hannah Appel, Arvi Pihlman, and Jess Auerbach. Thank you.

The research first began to resemble a whole during a yearlong Stanford Humanities Center Fellowship (2007–8) and a fellowship from the American Council of Learned Societies (ACLS). I am very grateful for both. Summer research funding from Stanford University has enabled me to spend time interviewing Red Cross staff in Finland. At the Stanford Humanities Center, I was fortunate to find excellent fellow travelers in Gerald Bruns, James Clifford, Babacar Fall, and Richard Roberts, among others.

I thank Sally Falk Moore for her farsighted advice, and for setting me on the path to thinking about mass displacement, and the care and control of people. I deeply admire her intellectual force and critical imagination. There is much in this book of what I was taught both by Sally Moore and Tambi, the late Stanley J. Tambiah. In a 2007 American Anthropological Association panel in honor of Professor Tambiah, I was also fortunate to receive truly insightful comments on my Red Cross research from Engseng Ho. Felicity Aulino and Miriam Goheen made that event possible.

Many friends and colleagues have given me support and advice along the way: Carol Greenhouse, my very first anthropology professor, and, later, wonderful friend and colleague. I thank her for our heady conversations. I thank Jean Comaroff for bringing me a Forward Bear from South Africa, and for her always stunning critical insight. She and John Comaroff have given me much in decades of learning and friendship. Harri Englund read the whole manuscript and gave invaluable comments of the kind only he can give. Thank you. Paulla Ebron I thank for her gentle friendship and our theoretical wanderings; I will not forget our nineteenth-century correspondence about slow-burning book projects. Emily Martin has been there through the greatest challenges, and I am honored to be able to claim her as a friend and colleague. Anwar Faruqi has always seen me through good days and bad. I thank him for his lifelong loyalty and encouragement as a fellow writer. Erica Bornstein, Didier Fassin, Ilana Feldman, Peter Redfield, and Miriam Ticktin have together and separately made me think much better and more subtly about what we gloss as humanitarianism. Their impressive body of work has made mine easier. Miriam Ticktin read the complete draft of this book, and gave truly constructive comments. Lynn Meskell has taught me valuable ways of conceptualizing materiality and much else. Laurie Kain Hart gave me wonderful insights on professionalism and chapter 3. Timothy Mitchell gave excellent and much appreciated taped comments on chapter 3. Clare Cameron and Amrapali Maitra—doctors and anthropologists in process—have given me delightful ideas and encouragement along the way. In Tampere, Anna Rastas, Laura Huttunen, Kaarina Nikula, and the late Ulla Vuorela have been dear friends, imaginative colleagues, and generous listeners. Kaarina gave me valuable feedback on chapter 6. To Laura and her colleagues—Arvi Pihlman, Mari Korpela, Matias Helinko, Mirkka Helkkula, and Anna Rastas—an admiring and humbled thanks for arranging the translation of my previous work into a book in Finnish. (The translations in this book are mine.) I thank Donald Brenneis for inviting me to give a talk at the University of California, Santa Cruz. The graduate students at lunch afterward were impressive. Daniel Linger wrote me a letter full of wonderful insights after my talk there. Elizabeth Cameron gave me a valued reminder about how dolls can matter, for better and for worse, as did Marina Warner. Amanda Moore has taught me to think further with animals. I thank Wynn Furth for the extra dry wit. Both Eric Worby and Zhanara Nauruzbayeva did me the honor of giving chapter 2 very close, critical readings, and Zhanara Nauruzbayeva also contributed to chapter 3. Kabir Tambar gave me an inspirational reading of chapter 6. Peter Geschiere, always gentle and inspiring, read chapters 1 and 3. Conversations with Sharika Thiranagama, my sunny friend and brilliant new colleague, have been full of insight and illumination. Chrisy Moutsatsos has been a generous friend and an imaginative colleague through thick and thin. I truly admire the delicacy and power in Ann Stoler's thought and care. I thank Melchior Mbonimpa for the constancy of his friendship and his intellectual honesty in reading my work. Sylvia Yanagisako has intellectual elegance and an understanding heart; I am grateful for her mentorship. Thomas Blom Hansen produces both trust and laughter; in the midst of his own brilliant writing, he has always made time for listening to me and reading my work. Christina Schwenkel has been a constant companion throughout this project and much else, and she has enabled me to think better, especially about materiality and the visual. Reading drafts of Ramah McKay's brilliant forthcoming ethnography and our conversations about writing have been a delight to me. It was always a high point of my day to listen to Elif Babül's intense thought processes. Conversations with Tanya Luhrmann, especially about affect, have helped me to move forward and explore new lines of thought. Susanna Luoto helped me to obtain "humanitarian dolls." I knew I could count on her. I have deeply appreciated and benefited from lively conversations and warm support from Tania Ahmad, Kevin O'Neill, Michelle Apotsos, Jeremy Benthall, Hilary Chart, Molly Cunningham, Sam Dubal, Bharat Venkat, Melissa Caldwell, Duana Fullwiley, Angela Garcia, Bruce O'Neill, Mark Gardiner, Mari Lautamatti-Alho, Armi Malkki, Timo A. Malkki, Timo T. Malkki, Tomas Matza, Selim Shahine, Marilyn Strathern, Anna West, Judith Wilson, and Thet Win. So many people have given me kindness and help along the way that I know I will inevitably have forgotten to name someone. If you are reading this: thank you. I often think about my department and marvel at my good fortune in being here. Thank you to my colleagues.

Thank you to Ken Wissoker for his insight in choosing the perfect readers for this book, and for his always generous and patient "in-process" support. Thank you also to Elizabeth Ault, Danielle Szulczewski, and the Duke University Press art department for all their work on this book. I truly appreciate it.

Aila Ferguson read and impressively critiqued two key chapters of the book, making them a great deal stronger in the process. Elias Ferguson's insights have been very sharp and imaginative throughout. I thank them both for their patience and understanding. Jim, this book, warts and all, is for you. I don't know how I could even begin to thank you.

Introduction.
Need, Imagination, and
the Care of the Self

The interview in the coffee shop had long since become something else; we had been there for hours. She worked hard to get across how trapped she felt in her hospital work, and just in her ordinary, workaday life as a doctor and a woman in Finland. Her desire for the world "out there" and her love of beauty came across as a deep quaking neediness. "Maybe I really was born in the wrong country." She remembered a late friend who, she explained, just wasn't suited to life in his "own" country. He "blossomed like a rose" in the [Middle East]. Before he was killed, they had talked about how, for each of them, "out there in the world" (tuolla maailmalla) was where they would both thrive. Missions for the Red Cross took her out there.

In a Helsinki yarn shop on a quiet afternoon, an old woman had picked out her selection of yarns and stood at the checkout counter. She talked familiarly with the shop owner about the "Mother Teresa blankets" she was knitting to send to the needy—via the Vaaka ry organization, or perhaps the Red Cross; she had not decided yet. She talked about other things, too, and a conversation ensued. Finally she gathered her bag of yarn, her beige purse, and her walking stick. Then I was the only customer in the shop. The owner told me that the "elder" (vanhus) who had just left had knitted scores of blankets for charity (hyväntekeväisyys). She also remarked that the elder did not seem to have much else in her life.[1]

In recent years, a formidable critical literature has emerged on humanitarianism as a key figure in global politics. Likewise, human rights and humanitarian nongovernmental organizations (NGOs) have come to be recognized as increasingly important, and sometimes valorized, actors that "provide independent voices" in a politically "murky and dangerous" Global South.[2] Much has been written about the ethics, pragmatics, and politics of humanitarian interventions; how humanitarian interventions help or harm; how they may be hijacked by war machines and by ever more sophisticated tactics of terrorizing; how their work and security are compromised by militaries (including that of the United States) waging hearts and minds campaigns through "humanitarian care"; how idealistic moves to relieve suffering intersect with the so-called realpolitik of international relations and corporate interests; how different institutional mandates may have contradictory or unintended effects in the field; and many other themes.[3] This is a very dynamic field and I hope that this book will be a useful contribution to it. But I also want to shift focus a bit, from humanitarian intervention and its effects on the *recipients* of aid to a more intimate set of questions about "humanitarians" themselves—in this case, Finnish Red Cross aid workers sent abroad on aid and emergency relief missions by the International Committee of the Red Cross (ICRC).

Here, I am most interested not in the *effects* that their interventions produce, or how to assess politically either the value of their work or the problems it raises. Instead, I wish to begin with what seems to me a more foundational question, which is: *Who are these people?* Who wants to work in humanitarian aid and emergency relief, and why? What are their motivations and aims? Who wants to help? What conceptions of help and want circulate in these social fields? And what forms of imagination animate and sustain them? There is, across the Global South, an apparently ubiquitous (and mass-mediated) social presence—a *humanitarian subject* characterized by a desire to help. But what do we really know about this subject? What forms of understanding might emerge from a closely ethnographic inquiry into humanitarian motivation? Of course, the answers will always arise from social and historical specificity.

Some of the results of this inquiry were surprising. The Finnish Red Cross "humanitarians" I worked with were highly trained, experienced, and had each been on numerous missions around the world. In many ways they were very strong. They knew what needed to get done. (This fact made it very frustrating for them when technical or other obstacles to their work came up, as they frequently did.)[4] Professional as these workers were, however, one should not be too quick to assume that help and humanitarian aid always come from a position of unilateral strength, or power. What I found was impressive strength and good sense, but also, for many, an undeniable *neediness* that drove people to do their often hazardous work. For them, there was a *need to help* (*tarve auttaa*). Taking that observation seriously meant revising some basic assumptions about who "the needy" are in the humanitarian encounter.

In trying to answer such basic questions—who are they and why do they do what they do?—another, equally vital, set of questions emerged. How did people with such motivations think about themselves?[5] What kinds of relations of *self to self* did they form? How did the self, engaged in work that is often described as "selfless," undergo transformations—in contexts of humanitarian aid and emergency relief in war and violence, and death and grieving? Is there such a thing as selflessness? What does that mean? When is the self undone?

A final question took form: It had to do with the *imagination* in terms of which this humanitarian subject, or self, framed both the world and her place in it. Her subjectivity tended to be strongly internationalist, and a sense of international obligation powerfully shaped her personal trajectory and professional habitus—and her drive to work abroad. Why did the "world outside" (*ulkomaailma*) have such power to enchant my interlocutors? "To be out in the world" (*olla maailmalla*) was a powerful object of imagination for them. This ethical, aesthetic, and affective process of world-making came to matter in a number of ways. The processes and practices of *being in the world* "out there" were also complexly aspirational.

I likewise found that these forms of internationalist humanitarian imagination and practice were remarkably *domestic*—in two senses. In the first sense, key aspects of international humanitarian aid always begin "at home" (as opposed to abroad), *somewhere local and specific, even intimate*, in this case Finland. Finnish histories and contemporary cultural and political formations, as well as people's conceptions of themselves as Finns, mattered in both predictable and unexpected ways in the work they did abroad, and key features of the "home" society provided important motivations for this work.

The second sense of the domestic involves practices of care *de facto* often undertaken by women and/or in a home—prototypically, nursing, cleaning, and caring for the young, the old, and the vulnerable, but also such "domestic arts" as knitting and crocheting "for the needy," or participating in "homemade" craft projects organized as humanitarian campaigns (often for fund- and awareness-raising purposes) by aid organizations such as the Red Cross, the United Nations Children's Fund (UNICEF), and numerous others (see chapters 4 and 5). In these later chapters, the focus will be not the professional aid workers in the international field abroad but rather other social categories of Finns in Finland with a nonprofessional need to help. I will examine what happens to the relation of self to self, and self to the world, where helping occurs, but no traveling is involved. At stake are conditions of isolation and abjection in Finland, most specifically among aged people, where some engage in "humanitarian handicrafts" in order to find forms of "stranger sociality" (Povinelli 2006) and human connection (even if precarious) that help them to feel like real persons (cf. Muehlebach 2012). This is an account of stark social realities that again inverts our usual assumptions about where "need" is located in humanitarian relations of helping and giving, on the one hand, and receiving, on the other.

The domestic, in both of these forms, is relatively invisible in the predominant representation of humanitarian actors as always already "cosmopolitan." While these forms could easily be (and often are) dismissed as trivial, inconsequential, or irrelevant, each can be surprisingly powerful and even dangerous in its capacity to entangle the self both with very close, intimate (sometimes cruel) realities "at home" and with more distant realities that may not only affect it but even invade and undermine it.

Thus, the need to help is perhaps not as "quintessentially cosmopolitan" as some scholars would have it (see, e.g., Calhoun 2008:73–75). The case I studied, at least, suggests that it is not as generic "global citizens," "worldly nomads," or "cosmopolitans" but as specific social persons with homegrown needs, vulnerabilities, desires, and multiple professional responsibilities that people sought to be part of something greater than themselves, to help, to be actors in the lively world. And they found their own, sometimes quite idiosyncratic, ways of doing so at different stages and circumstances in their lives. This sense of the domestic sheds light on how the conduct of the aid workers "out there" reflects their specific culture regions and social contexts—and the way that aid work abroad presents for some a line of escape from the familiar, and sparks urges to self-transformation.

Much of this book, then, is the result of in-depth ethnographic interviews with Finnish Red Cross aid workers who have been deployed internationally, usually with the ICRC (International Committee of the Red Cross). I interviewed them sporadically, when they were in Finland and not on mission, between 1996 and 2012. Most of the interviews became one-on-one conversations of many hours. All translations are my own. As will become apparent, I worked with people in numerous different occupational fields (e.g., transportation, logistics, administration, psychological support), but mostly with nurses and secondarily with doctors. Most were women (like the staff of the Finnish Red Cross more generally), but they tended to refer to themselves in gender-neutral terms as persons or people (ihmiset) (Finnish personal pronouns are also gender-neutral).

The earliest 1996 interviews occurred in the long aftermath of the 1994 Rwanda genocide. As I explain later in the book, my original intent was to focus on interviewing specifically those Finnish Red Cross workers who had been posted to Rwanda with the ICRC because I had myself worked with refugees from an earlier genocide in neighboring Burundi. The people I worked with in 1985–86 had asylum in western Tanzania, and were survivors of a genocide where the regime, dominated by people ethnically Tutsi, targeted the majority Hutu population. This meant in practice that I interviewed Finnish Red Cross staff who worked where the roles were reversed, in a genocide where Hutu were the perpetrators and Tutsi (and "moderate Hutu") the victims. The ICRC was on the scene in Rwanda early partly because it already had teams working in Burundi where another underreported genocidal political conflict was under way in 1993. I was just finishing my first book manuscript when the 1994 Rwanda genocide began. My eventual 1995 book, Purity and Exile: Violence, Memory, and National Cosmology among Hutu Refugees in Tanzania, includes a long afterword on the Rwanda genocide as it was happening.

I was in Finland when I learned that numerous Finnish aid workers had gone to work on multinational ICRC teams in Rwanda and Goma (Congo, formerly Zaire). Since there had been only a few international aid workers in the refugee camp where I had worked earlier in Tanzania, and since I had focused on interviewing the refugees in the first project, I began to think seriously about these aid workers and what it could possibly mean to them to be in the middle of one of the most horrific genocides in modern history.[6] Their motivations were initially opaque to me, except in the most abstract of terms—they were humanitarians. But why did they accept that mission? What, or how much, were they hoping to accomplish? How would they be affected by what they experienced there? How would they fathom the magnitude of the human catastrophe they were working in? How could they? Were they damaged by their professional duties?[7]

I formed my new research project around those questions and specifically around the aid workers, and was fortunate to be able to begin research quite quickly. Officials at the Finnish Red Cross headquarters in Helsinki were welcoming and relatively open to researchers, and the aid workers, when in Finland, generously gave me their time and thoughtfulness. As I had anticipated, it was easy to talk with the aid workers who had been posted to Rwanda, Goma, and Burundi. They needed to talk—just as the genocide survivors in Tanzania had needed to talk. Many aid workers said it was worth talking with someone who had lived and worked in the general region, and with genocide survivors specifically. There was some shared understanding.

In the end, I wound up interviewing the aid workers not only about Rwanda and Central Africa but also about the numerous other missions around the world they had worked on. Many of them were very mobile—"veterans," as people at the Helsinki Headquarters called them, and as they often described each other. I did not have the opportunity to interview anyone for whom one mission had been enough, or too much.

The most recent interviews date from a time when the ICRC, including delegates from the Finnish Red Cross, were (and are) heavily involved in Afghanistan (see chapter 6). It is striking to me that even after so many other missions—and in the midst of the extremely long, difficult, and controversial mission in Afghanistan, where the ICRC has worked for decades—Rwanda still kept coming up as an upsetting experience and as a kind of reference point. As I discuss in chapter 2, it was a limit experience for many who had worked there. One person called it a "breaking point."

Need

War, genocide, mass killings, mass rape, torture, famine, tsunamis, earthquakes, floods. These words (often in this string-like form) have become globally meaningful terms for identifying specifically "humanitarian need," especially by "the West," or the wealthy North. What is specifically humanitarian about these situations—situations that have come to form distinct, mobile, and unevenly globalized social imaginaries and fields of action? The qualifier *humanitarian* makes the need of those to be helped appear simultaneously somehow elementary (basic) and monumental (superhuman) in scale: "basic human needs" (water, food, medicine, shelter, sanitation) have to be supplied by "the international community" to alleviate the "basic human suffering" of the anonymous masses of "humanity." (All this seems straightforward, of a practical urgency and thus politically neutral, but see chapter 6.)

Much important work has been written about needs-based versus rights-based humanitarianism, but for the ICRC need was certainly the more fundamental category, the mandate for action. In fact, one can make the case that this must be so in humanitarian work, where the invocation of "human rights," lacking the sanctioning power of a state, so often struggles to amount to more than a pious wish (as Hannah Arendt [1951] 1973 noted long ago), and where it is inevitably evidence of raw, visible *need* (starving, sick, or injured bodies, dying children) that provides an immediate impetus for intervention (cf. Ticktin 2011). Indeed, for all its very real political problems, the language of need often directs our attention to precisely those material conditions of life that, as Harri Englund has observed (2006), abstract commitments to rights can sometimes sidestep or even obscure (see also Festa 2010:15; Rancière 2011:67, 72).

Yet there is a tendency among some scholars in the Global North—as also among the donor public and the thousands of university students and others who want to be aid volunteers—to imagine ("basic") human need with a surprising degree of uniformity, as I have suggested (Malkki 1996), and to see it as somehow essentially located "over there." The "suffering stranger" is still in the main imagined as "distant" (Boltanski 1993; Haskell 1998), socially anonymous, only "basically" human, and usually only momentarily in the aid worker's or volunteer's life.

The historically resonant logics associated with need, suffering, and humanity in humanitarian discourse can end up making some people more basic (read: simple) than others (see Vaughan 1991:115; Englund 2006; and Fassin and Rechtman 2009:183–88, 228–30). Africa has embodied need on a continental scale ever since its colonization was systematized and rationalized. When it comes to the African continent, there is much "basicness," much "simplicity." In the worst case, such views can lead the "needy African" to be imagined as a sort of specimen of "basic humanity" more biological than political—"bare life," as Agamben (1998) and others have argued, more *zoë* than *bios* (cf. Arendt [1951] 1973:267–302; see also Mbembe 2001:1–3; Petryna 2002; Foucault 2003; Biehl 2005; Redfield and Bornstein 2010:18, 23; Rancière 2011:62–75; and Ticktin 2011:14, among others).

In thinking about the depoliticization of *both* rights and needs, Englund cites Alain Badiou, who suggests how

a universal human subject is split into two modalities. On the one hand, the subject is passive and pathetic, the one who suffers. On the other, the subject is active, the one who identifies suffering and knows how to act[. . . .] "On the side of the victims, the haggard animal exposed on television screens. On the side of the benefactors, conscience and the imperative to intervene. And why does this splitting always assign the same roles to the same sides? Who cannot see that this ethics rests on the misery [. . .] the world hides, behind its victim-Man, the good-Man, the white-Man?" (Badiou 2001:12–13, cited in Englund 2006:32–33)

The needy, sick, dirty recipient and the strong, healthy, clean giver: these charismatic figures draw a certain kind of attention—the principal actors in the ever-expanding imagination, documentation, and mediatization of certain kinds of misery and misfortune. The popularly imagined good doctor (from Albert Schweitzer to Paul Farmer), the ever-giving nurse (from Florence Nightingale to Mother Teresa), and their (ideally grateful and well-behaved) suffering, ever-needy mass of patients.[8]

Yet my research with the Finnish Red Cross aid workers revealed a coeval, co-present neediness on the other side, *the neediness of the helper, the giver*. This suggests the possibility of combating the splitting of the human subject that Badiou describes, not *only* (as anthropologists are wont to do) by recognizing the agency, will, and specific motivations of the "recipient" of humanitarian aid but *also* by insisting on acknowledging the frequent weakness, neediness, and non-universality of the humanitarian "benefactor"—the giver who, no less than the receiver, always sets out from a social and existential position both specific and precarious (Butler 2004). The benefactor's own need to help those in need may generate actions that in fact help the benefactor him/herself in surprising and vital ways (see chapter 5).

Through my research with the Finnish Red Cross workers, I came to think of need in ways previously unfamiliar to me. In "Professionals Abroad" (chapter 1), I saw that some of the Red Cross aid workers on international missions sought in their work a partial escape from national belonging— even an escape from their mundane, workaday selves. The safe, well-ordered, and in principle predictable national home, the welfare society that should have met their social and material needs, had become, for some, burdensome and constraining, and emotionally cold. One nurse described it as *ascetic*. The abroad was described by most as more "full of life" and—this is key— as a site of easier human sociality and conviviality, even in the midst of terrible circumstances. This desire for "the world outside" (*ulkomaailma*) was in some interviews so palpable and urgent that it came across as an unmistakable *neediness*. Finland meant safety, progressive social policies, many good things, but also reserve, restraint, and constraint, and, along with it, experiences of social and sensorial deprivation.

Humanitarian work abroad of course meant encountering people with severe needs on a monumental scale now unknown in Finland. But the interviews I did with Red Cross people while they were in Finland (and not on mission abroad) workers also eloquently spoke of giving and helping as alleviating their *own* neediness, allowing them "to be a part of something greater than themselves." I encountered other nonprofessional relationships to need as well. In "Bear Humanity" (chapter 4), I write about "Aid Bunnies," "Trauma Teddies," and all manner of soft toys as "humanitarian devices" for framing human need for the general *donor public* to imagine. And what is more "human" and "innocent" than a child in need? The child is the "exemplary human" (see chapter 3). The 2006–7 Finnish Red Cross Aid Bunny campaign for volunteers to make and donate hand-knitted bunnies—intended to comfort children hurt by political conflicts and natural disasters, but also used as a domestic consciousness-raiser about the special needs of children caught in complex emergencies—framed the specific kind of need that could be imagined and alleviated. It was a thing the domestic donor could *imagine* "doing something" about; it was particular and of a *humanly graspable scale*, and sensorially pleasurable (see Tsing 2005:58).[9] One could say that the Aid Bunny had "the deep present of physical things" (Mitchell 2001:180) that animated it in an enchanting way (Gell 1988). The social imagination of the Finnish knitters (thousands of them) was often charged by an intimate, personalized link to the imagined "play-age" (*leikki-ikäinen*) child somewhere out there, "out there in the world" (*siellä maailmalla*), who would play and be consoled by the Aid Bunny. The suspension (if not erasure) of the child's parents, siblings, grandparents, and other relatives, and also friends, teachers, and neighbors, was a striking feature in the imagining of the needy child (cf. Bornstein 2001, 2012). The children's own proclivities and desires, subjectivities and social embeddedness, fears and plans, were off-frame. The faraway children's need, as understood from a great distance, in the specific social context of Finland, generated an often bubbly, extravagant online playfulness in the practices that people used in making, naming, animating, blogging about, and sending as gifts the Aid Bunnies they had knitted (cf. Allison 2004). It is as if the bunnies, too, became children for a while, and their makers childlike, or sometimes maternal (see Winnicott [1971] 2005). Although clearly meaningful to their makers in a number of different ways, the bunnies were to other eyes the very embodiment of the trivial, and, worse, the offensive, in the face of "the real needs" of people awaiting emergency assistance (even if it was never, of course, the case that people in dire circumstances received bunnies *instead of* emergency relief). But it has to be said: one need that the bunnies demonstrably answered at home in Finland was to provide badly needed *sociality*—whether face to face or virtual—to what were sometimes very lonely people. The most evident need here—a need for belonging and imaginative sociality—was the knitters'.

In "Homemade Humanitarianism: Knitting and Loneliness" (chapter 5), I focus on a theme that runs throughout the book: again and again, international aid seems to involve the domestic arts such as knitting or other handwork (*käsityö*) (see also chapters 3 and 4). The need to help through international service has, as I mentioned, roots in specific structural features of the "home society," of Finland, that create the deep *need to help*, and to become thereby *connected to something other and greater than oneself*—to be connected to "the world" (*maailma*). It is against a background of unremitting social and affective neediness that the people whom I call "the old women" knit. Many do so in an effort to "keep busy" and "useful" in a world that sees them as useless (or simply does not see them), and to have the *dignity of giving* something to an anonymous person somewhere in the world (*jossain maailmalla*) who may need it—or not (cf. Kelley 2003; Muehlebach 2012). Volunteers who knitted "Mother Teresa blankets" (a project like the Aid Bunny), for instance, accomplished several things: they alleviated their own, possibly keenly felt, sense of uselessness and they engaged in activities that required human contact (in going to the yarn shop, for example, as was noticed by the owners of many such shops). The blanket was a gift *of* the self to an imagined other, but also a gift *to* the self. It is possible, then, to interpret the process—including both the making and then of the giving away—as a form of intimate "affect management" and *care of the self* (Foucault 1986; Mazzarella 2009:298).[10]

The Relation of Self to Self

It is through writing about need that I came to think about the relation of self to self. Humanitarianism is often associated with selflessness and self-sacrifice, but less often with other things that came, in my work, to seem more important: self-escape, self-loss, dehumanization, self-humanization, self-transformation, the care of the self, the relation of self to others, and the relation of self to the world (*maailma*). For selflessness, the simplest initial task was to make a mental list of all the famous humanitarians whom history has dubbed "selfless servants to humanity" and who, some of them, still get fed to elementary school children (Henri Dunant, Clara Barton, Florence Nightingale, Albert Schweitzer, Mother Teresa, among others). This sort of selflessness—selflessness as *self-sacrifice*—the professional Red Cross people had no use for, as I will show throughout (cf. Kester 2004:78; see chapter 6). Indeed, I was often told that an aid worker bent on self-sacrifice was not only foolish and inexperienced but also a possible danger to herself and others on her team in the field.

But selflessness is not entirely irrelevant here, and often figured less as sacrifice and more as a kind of self-*escape*. Self-escape emerged as a good descriptor for many of the international aid workers' motivations. Their personal desires to get a break from the safe predictability and routinization of their work life in Finland, and perhaps especially to find a self-conscious respite from *how they themselves were in Finland*, were definitely factors in their decisions as to whether to accept an international mission or not. This is obviously not to say that the specific nature of the emergency call they received was insignificant to them, or that they did not have highly developed senses of ethical obligation.

If such self-escape could be thought of as a kind of selflessness, it was of a decidedly nonsacrificial kind. *It was not as saints but as experienced professionals that they sought their line of escape.* For many, such selflessness became most powerfully articulated as a desire to lose themselves in the intensity of sustained demanding work. In those moments, they did not have awkward selves to manage or what they sometimes described as an encumbering Finnish self-consciousness getting in the way; they experienced, I think, a kind of pleasurable *self-loss*. I would interpret those as moments of a lithe freedom, perhaps even transcendence. Musicians know what this is; it is when they are "playing over their heads" (see, e.g., Berliner 1994).

Another of the possibilities I saw in the relation of self to self was self-transformation. The most memorable figure in this connection is perhaps a doctor I discuss in chapter 1, whose missions were definitely about work (no mistake about that), but who was also sensually captured by the places to which she was posted and "vicariously possessed" by the people (especially women aid recipients) whom she met there (Piper 1991:735–37; chapter 1). She articulated very clearly how she in fact *sought* continual self-transformation through her missions and even through the *materia* of her ever-changing surroundings. She reminded me of Adrian Piper's contention that "empathy must be carefully calibrated between the extremes of self-loss and self-absorption."[11]

It is, of course, common to be transformed by experience, but in Red Cross work, people's spatiotemporal sequence of presences and absences in/from Finland seemed to make such transformation more noticeable. As I mention in chapter 1, people often returned from missions abroad feeling somehow changed, their hearts full and eager to share their experiences—only to find that no non–Red Cross friends or colleagues were truly interested in understanding, or willing to listen for very long. Everyone had their own lives and concerns to attend to, after all.

Of course aid work is something like anthropological fieldwork in that both can be transformative life experiences that engage affects, the senses, and the imagination—the whole person—for better and for worse. Both can be creative and re-creative (see "The Imagination," below), and both can result in what Foucault and others have called limit experiences, in other words, experiences that "[wrench] the subject from itself" (2000:241). But while in the traditions Foucault wrote and lived from, the limit experience was systematically sought and explored (see Foucault 1991, 2000; Lacan quoted in Evans 1996; Bataille 2000; and Blanchot 1993), I discuss (in chapter 2) limits and impasses from which there was no clear way forward, where there were no good choices to be made, where things had become impossible.[12] The person was transformed by the experience, but in a damaging way that diminished and troubled the self. Maybe this could also be characterized as a kind of self-loss. The disaster zones in which the Red Cross people worked of course involved limit experiences of this kind for the people who were in need of the emergency relief, but sometimes the same kinds of limits were encountered by the "helpers" themselves.[13]

The relation of self to self appears in another guise in chapter 5. Against a backdrop of often stark and dehumanizing social isolation (Biehl 2005), volunteer work, (as I described under the heading "Need," above) often amounted to a kind of "care of the self" in circumstances sometimes verging on desperation (Foucault 1986). Associational life—as toothless as it may seem against some of the bleak scenes to come—made it possible for many people to be part of something other and bigger than themselves, to imagine themselves—through their own handwork and volunteer work—as members of a greater "community of generosity" and help, even as they also gained more mundane forms of intersubjectivity and social connection in the process (see Muehlebach 2012:7). The Red Cross was one socially important and truly nationwide institution that made it possible (even for people in very small towns and villages) to enframe their lives differently and to open themselves to new kinds of social and affective experiences that they might not have found otherwise. Getting training to help others was important to people, and provided new possibilities in the relation of self to self.[14]

The Imagination

The imagination has emerged, in an unanticipated way, as an important element in each chapter of this book. Humanitarianism is an object of imagination, and aid projects engage in many imaginative practices. Consider again the figure of the child. So vital to humanitarian appeals, it always has to be not only seen but also imagined in order to be socially effective, to matter. The historically deep practice of fundraising with the picture of the child in need goes on around the world (Vaughan 1991). One might think it so cliché that it is in danger of losing its life. It is junk mail. One ignores it with a twitch of irritation. But then it turns out (as will become clear in chapters to come) that the postcard of the child in need finds a more generous and considered reception among categories of people who become imaginatively invested for reasons of their own. They may be lonely and/or aged. The child in need interpellates, hails them, as "persons who can help" (Althusser 2007; Evans and Hall 2007). The imaginative work of the child in need is to allow "an ex-person," someone "socially worthless," the dignity of giving (Biehl 2005; Muehlebach 2012). The postcard of the child may do more: it may produce an enchanted child then "made real" through surprisingly involved, affective processes of the imagination.

Danger. The aid worker in the field suddenly senses that she herself is in danger, and is then privately embarrassed that she was not after all—embarrassed that she had had time to imagine her own personal crisis or even demise. The practice of emergency relief often involves risks and those risks inevitably engender imaginative scenarios, even when in principle it is part of one's professionalism to *not imagine, not think, just do*. Loss and grief. These may be witnessed and imagined in clinics and hospitals in the field every day, among patients so little known as to leave great spaces for guesswork and the imagination. Wounds. Certain kinds of wounds may confront the aid worker as evidence of a sadistic imagination.

Danger, loss and grief, wounds, and one's place on the scene of a disaster or in the world as a "humanitarian," are dynamically imagined, especially when they become relevant to one's own life, and in encounters and relationships with others. Sometimes they "imagine themselves in you," even against your will (pace Sartre).[15] As James Engell, following Kant, has suggested, some forms of imagination are discretionary and volitional, while others are unwilled; and often these coexist (Engell 1981:135–38; Kant 2008). How humanitarian needs and challenges are imagined is important. Often there are ways of making them *be*, and, then, of making them *not be*. Sometimes there is no such choice. Some problems aid agencies can fix and make *not be*, for example, while others are utterly unaffected by their volition. And the technologies of humanitarian advertising can similarly make things be and not be. Some disasters fade quickly for donor publics though long ongoing, while other newer problems are "made be." One powerful way of making be is "the logic of the one" (visualize one singular child, one singular benefactor): this can enter the imagination and leave one feeling *responsible* (see Bornstein 2003, 2012; Suski 2009; and chapters 2 and 3). This can happen to anyone—even aid workers. Is the responsibility "real" or "imagined"? What is the difference, exactly? Ethics can be thought of as an imaginative practice, and imagination as an ethical practice (Mittermaier 2011), and both of these can be—often have to be—improvisational practices (Cerwonka and Malkki 2007:164–79).

A great deal has of course been written about the imagination, and the real and the irreal; I will work here with only a few texts to clarify my uses of the term throughout this book. Cornelius Castoriadis makes a forceful argument for the importance of the theorization and understanding of the imagination. In "The Social Imaginary and the Institution" (1975), Castoriadis rightly argues that "representation, imagination, and imaginary have never been seen for themselves but always in relation to something else—to sensation, intellection, perception, or reality—*submitted to the normativity incorporated in the inherited ontology*, brought within the viewpoint of the true and the false, instrumentalized within a function, means judged according to their possible contribution to the accomplishment of the end that is truth or access to true being, the being of being (*ontos on*)" (1997:197, emphasis added).[16] I think his point is still important, for all the current, often market-driven, profit-focused valorization of "imagination," "innovation," and (especially) "creativity" today (Ricoeur 1994:119). In fact, it is newly and differently important now.[17] And yet the very old distrust or contempt for the imagination still also persists today. "In this way," continues Castoriadis, "there has not been the slightest concern with knowing what *making/doing* [*faire*] means, what the *being* of making/doing is and what it is that making/doing *makes be*, so obsessed have people been with these questions alone: What is it to do good or to do well, to do evil or to do badly. Making/doing has not been thought because no one has attempted to think of anything other than two particular moments of making/doing, the ethical moment and the technical moment." Castoriadis stops to observe how much of the social-historical is thought through the imposition of the "inherited logic-ontology" in the West (1997:197, 198, emphases added; cf. Bachelard 2005:xxvi).[18] He goes on to say that the things that are "irreducibly in excess or in deficit" of the inherited schemata become "scoria, illusion, contingency, chance—in short, unintelligible" (1997:198). They might be ignored as inessential to the real matter at hand: just noise and babble. Dross. Distraction. Or, as will emerge here, "the mere." The mere is not "political," nor relevant to "real" theoretical debates. It is that which is "appropriately" ignored. The concept of the mere is developed throughout the following chapters, and also concludes the book.

This mistrust of the imagination has ancient origins, and its force still has a surprising degree of caution, distancing, and even contempt around it now (see Kearney 1991; Crapanzano 2004; Bachelard 2005:xxvi).[19] Even as the imagination is thought the font of the next possible insight or invention, its wildness is not always instrumentally "useable" and it becomes vulnerable to pathologization, as Emily Martin (2009) has powerfully demonstrated (see also, e.g., Beckett 1966, Sass 1992, and Weller 2009). Nigel Thomas (n.d.:n.p.) writes about how, in ancient and medieval conceptions, the "imagination, although recognized as indispensable to cognition, was usually profoundly distrusted. Unless strictly disciplined by reason it would soon lead us into concupiscence and sin." This mistrust was compounded in European history by the iconophobia following the Reformation and its long afterlives (Belting 1994; Ricoeur 1994:119; Heinänen 2006).[20] But as Susan Sontag (like Thomas n.d.) has observed, "philosophers since Plato have tried to loosen our grip on images by evoking the standard of an image-free way of apprehending the real"—Plato's cave ever a warning (2007:80). And as Amira Mittermaier further suggests in *Dreams That Matter*, "the imagination was eyed with suspicion throughout the history of western philosophy because it might not merely transmit images but could also play with sense impressions, creating images of nonexistent things—a danger that could be circumvented only by reason's firm grip on the imagination" (2011:16; cf. Sartre [1940] 2004). The modern category of art emerged, in some sense, as a way not just to acknowledge the power of the imagination but also to contain its danger (Belting 1994). Harri Englund, in conversation with Castoriadis, makes a further interesting point: "No longer situated within the confines of 'a psychological or ego-logical horizon' (Castoriadis 1997:245), not to mention its reduction to the domain of the arts, the imagination assumes a profoundly social character, an inter-subjective sphere of experience and argument within which alternatives to dominant perspectives can attain collective purchase" (Englund 2011:15–16).[21] Gilles Deleuze (1997) develops parallel thoughts in *Essays Clinical and Critical*, noting that the most relevant distinction is not always that between the real and the imagined: "A real voyage, by itself, lacks the force necessary to be reflected in the imagination; the imaginary voyage, by itself, does not have the force, as Proust says, to be verified in the real. This is why the imaginary and the real must be, rather, like two juxtaposable or superimposable parts of a single trajectory, two faces that ceaselessly interchange with one another, a mobile mirror" (1997: 62–63).[22] Giving an example from Aboriginal Australia, Deleuze writes that there people link "nomadic itineraries" with "dream voyages" (1997:63). "At the limit, the imaginary is a virtual image that is interfused with the real object, and vice versa, thereby constituting a crystal of the unconscious" (1997:63). I would emphasize in response, with Englund, how often the imagination is intersubjective and profoundly social—and processual.

Doubts about the imagination became a prominent issue in my first fieldwork for *Purity and Exile* (1995). As I will describe in chapter 2, I did research in the mid-1980s with survivors of the 1972 genocide in Burundi who had been granted asylum in Tanzania. During the fieldwork with the Hutu refugees, I was warned by officials there not to "imagine things" as I listened to the refugees' accounts of their violent pasts, and their circumstances in exile. The refugees' (genocide survivors') accounts, often dismissed as grossly exaggerated—and, especially early on, as "hysterical"—were refused any solid reality or rationality.[23] Similarly, I, as researcher, was often regarded as gullible, too vulnerable to the refugees' "stories."[24] I was wasting my time and then letting my imagination run away with me. (Tragically, many of the grotesquely violent events and practices of which I was told at that time would then be repeated in well-documented detail in the 1994 Rwanda genocide.)

Now, what would it have looked like for the refugees to remember their experiences of the genocide and their flight in a "purely" non-imaginative way? What would it have looked like for them to produce a technical, dispassionate record of the "real" events, editing out what was so outlandish that it must be "irreal," or a nightmare? (cf. Mbembe 2001; De Boeck 2004; Ashforth 2005). But they themselves strove for painstaking technical accuracy and thoroughness. How could they accurately represent experiences that were as if from the most perverted and sadistic of horror films? *Why did they talk so much about this, wherever I went?*[25] But accurate records: this was what they were trying to deposit with me so that I might "inform the world" about them—they imagined that "the international community" would act to help them if only they had the correct information, the true historical record. I also expected accuracy and a (situated) thoroughness of myself (Haraway 2013). I could sense their sincerity, and my own; usually that just took us further into the relations and processes of imagination and memory. It was hard to take these accounts for real at times, so terrible were they. Their very power made them seem unreal. They made *me* feel unreal (see Mbembe 2001:145).[26]

My particular experiences in Tanzania are not surprising given that the imagination has been "equated with the unreal throughout much of Western history. This verdict became remarkably pronounced in the writings of Jean-Paul Sartre according to whom the imagination is 'an incantation destined to produce the object of one's thought, the thing one desires, in a manner that one can take possession of it'" (Mittermaier 2011:17). This is the (imaginary) unreal in the service of the safely real—no intrusive imaginings or involuntary thoughts here. Sartre's formulation is possible because the boundary he erects between the real and the imagined, at least here, is so solid (see Kearney 1991:54, 67).[27] "The act of imagination . . . is a magical act" (Sartre [1940] 2004:125). This conception is discussed by Elaine Scarry in *Dreaming by the Book*:

> Sartre identifies freedom as the imagination's great endowment to us: "[In the act of the imagination] there is always something of the imperious and the infantile, a refusal to take distance or difficulties into account. Thus, the very young child acts upon the world from his bed by orders and entreaties. The objects obey these orders of consciousness: they appear." Sartre returns to this attribute continually. We will the images into being: we will the images out of being. "Thus I can stop the existence of the unreal object at any moment, *I am not dragged along despite myself* to the specification of its qualities: it exists only while I know it and want it." We start it. We stop it. It *never takes us* "*by surprise.*" (2001:32–33, emphases added)

This conception seems curious to me; and it is profoundly inappropriate to the analysis of the social context of (and my work with) the Hutu refugees in Tanzania. There my imagination did "drag me along despite myself" and continually "took me by surprise." And even after all the research, I understood very little of what the refugees themselves—children, teenagers, men, women, and elders—had been dragged through. It was, in J. M. Coetzee's words, an "imaginative horror" (2001). This is important: the imaginary is "not false . . . nor illusory. *The imaginary is not a mode of unreality, but indeed a mode of actuality*," as Michel Foucault has written (1986:70, emphasis added; cf. Deleuze 1997:63; Mittermaier 2011:17–19). And it seems much more accurate to say, with Mittermaier: "Diverging from an objectivist mode of observation," an imagination "is not enclosed within an individual author-figure but instead creates a *dialogical in-between space* in which the visible and the invisible are intertwined" (2011:239, emphasis added; cf. Englund 2011:15–16).

Filip De Boeck (2004:12–13), describing conditions of life in modern Kinshasa, also writes about the imagination and experience in a way that directly helps to express the circumstances of the Hutu refugees in Tanzania at the time of my research with them. De Boeck's central question is: "[W]hat happens when people's material conditions of life become so incredibly hard that their very conceptions of what constitutes reality is affected[?]" He describes an "overproduction or an 'overheating' of meaning that gives expression to a disturbing unmooring of the social imagination" (2004:12; and see Achille Mbembe 2001:145). People, in all their complex interrelations with other people, face a kind of ontological "indiscernibleness" and uncertainty (2004:29).[28]

Yet the *volitional imagination* that Sartre described does have explanatory power in other contexts in this book, especially among donor publics motivated by a need to help alleviate human suffering in faraway catastrophes. In chapter 4, I will consider a 2007 Red Cross call to the public to knit Aid Bunnies to psychically assist children in conflict zones or natural disasters. Little did the Red Cross know that this project of making/doing would enchant thousands of eager knitters or that Aid Bunnies would eventually almost deluge its national logistics center. These bunnies were conjured by their makers. They were willed into being in just the way Sartre described. It is interesting that the bunny was always envisioned by the knitters in an intimate, exclusive relationship, not as one toy among many that groups of children could use. It was imagined, following the logic of the one, as the "special friend" and comforter of a single, special child in need of help and solace.

Kant's conception of the imagination was quite different, and useful in the present context. "When [Kant] says that the imagination is 'the faculty of representing in intuition an object that is not in itself present,' [h]e does not mean that it is the capacity for the mental imaging of absent objects. His view is rather that imagining involves two moments: immediate sensory awareness, or empirical intuition, and the taking or construing of that awareness as the awareness of something other, or something more, than what immediately appears" (Young 2009:142). Michael Young reiterates Kant's point thus: "it is not the capacity for mental imaging, but rather the capacity for construal or interpretation, that Kant characteristically has in mind as he develops his view of imagination" (2009:142, 155).[29]

What I find particularly helpful here is Kant's position that there are two general (usually coexistent) forms of imagination: the reproductive, combinatory, or re-creative imagination and the productive, or creative, imagination. (This is, of course, parallel to Castoriadis's formulation.) By reproductive imagination Kant means a function that is "empirical" and based on "association"; thus one may reproduce some combination of things one has encountered before (Young 2009:155; cf. Bachelard 2005:13). But this is what is of particular interest here: "while Kant holds that imagination and understanding are distinct faculties, he also believes that they may nonetheless come to be *intertwined* as we employ them" (Young 2009:155, emphasis added). Pauline von Bonsdorff writes along the same lines that reproductive imagination is an effort (only an effort) to make oneself as one with the position of the other (2009:29).[30]

As Mittermaier notes, Foucault has remarked on the consequences of such a blurring. "Shifting our attention from what the imagination *is* to what it *does*, Foucault describes an erasure of the sharp line between subject and object, between the absent and the present. The imagination makes me what I imagine. The 'like' is erased. Signifier and signified become one" (Mittermaier 2011:18; see also Foucault 1986).[31] The Finnish Red Cross very explicitly trains its outgoing teams to be professional and to manage the line between self and other. But as I show in chapter 2, despite solid professional experience and self-monitoring, this does not always work. Something unexpected gets to you. Often this something is an ill young child who crosses your path in a hospital or refugee camp. Through the daily intimacies of caring for the child, the aid worker might come to feel, "it's almost as if I were this child's parent." In a flash, she might suddenly imagine, just for a fraction of a second, "I *am* his mother." "I am *responsible!*" The "like" is erased. The aid worker starts imagining, even planning, possibilities of adoption, and envisioning the child's prospects for life in an arctic Finland wary of "foreigners." Then she imagines his future *here*—wherever here is—a refugee camp in East Africa perhaps. It may seem morally and ethically very wrong to sever the connection with that child when the mission is over. These kinds of cases, many of them, haunted the aid workers I have interviewed.[32] They have had to face painful and sometimes humiliating ethical and affective impasses—"limit experiences" of a kind. Anthropologists, as I write in chapter 2, often face comparable situations. These difficulties are a clear reminder that the imagination is not only a plaything: "*Einbildungskraft* is specifically a *power* [*voima*], not just a capacity or ability [*kyky*]. The difference is clear: the power can sweep you along, whereas a capacity is controlled."[33]

Alongside the re-creative, reproductive, or combinatory form of imagination is, of course, the productive, or creative, imagination. As Kant said, the two modes of imagination are not necessarily mutually exclusive. This is important. But for a very long time the creative—making/doing something quite new, being/doing newly, breaking molds, thinking completely otherwise—has been, and is still, considered "higher" in many contexts, and productive of more highly valued results than those of the reproductive imagination (as if *both* were not intersubjective social practices, as if both did not also depend on the imaginative work of others who have gone before). As I suggest in "Homemade Humanitarianism" (chapter 5), this is abundantly clear in the endless, predictable dismissals of the re-creative, "reproductive" imagination in gendered humanitarian handwork. Classified as the domestic arts, "handicrafts," "amateur crafts," or "hobbies," these are often assumed to be "merely" repetitive, "just copying" from predesigned models and patterns—and not even mimetic with any of the potential that that term opens up (see Taussig 1993; Frank 2000). They are nice "confectionaries" (Kester 2004:19, 33); they are "decorations" (Loos [1910] 2000; Kant 2006:108, 110–11)—mere *supplements* to "art" in Derrida's sense.

Challenging such dismissive attitudes, Grant Kester writes appreciatively about an aesthetic imagination that, in fact, looks once more like Kant's reproductive imagination (cf. Bourriaud 1998). Drawing the contrast with the old modern figure of the singular autonomous artist, Kester argues that a "dialogical aesthetic suggests a very different image of the artist, one defined in terms of openness, of *listening* . . . , and of a willingness to accept a position of dependence and *inter-subjective vulnerability* relative to the viewer or collaborator" (2004:110, emphasis added). This sounds very much like the process of ethnographic fieldwork. Kester continues: "It is in the nature of dialogical projects to be impure, to represent a practical negotiation (self-reflexive but nevertheless compromised) around issues of power, identity, and difference, even as they strive toward something more" (2004:123). Similar practical negotiations are necessary in the impure project that is anthropological fieldwork, and also in the imaginative work that I have suggested is so central to humanitarian action.

Perhaps the "productive" imagination is more present in the spheres I have been discussing than at first appears. For the term *re-creative* can also be translated as "to create again," which is related to artistic imitation or mimesis. "Mimetic imitation is not slavish copying, but the repetition of a thing differently, representation, that reaches for and at its best reaches some central features without necessarily looking the same, for example. . . . Looked at through art, the creative and the reproductive are perhaps not very far from one another, or even separate" (von Bonsdorff 2009:29–30; see also Taussig 1993). The numerous handwork projects I discuss in chapters 4 and 5, from the Aid Bunny to the Mother Teresa blankets, usually involved re-creation and not simple copying; things were made from resourcefully repurposed yarn, reclaimed fabric, found millinery in projects that were often some combination of individual and collective agency—and surprise. Instead of mechanical imitation there was a flow with a back-and-forth movement between the near automatic gesture of knitting and the aesthetic decision—and perhaps deliberative conversation and collaborative imagination.

Examined through ethnography, things look very much the same: the re-creative and the creative are both present in the dialogical, intersubjective social processes of interviews, the close listening, the seeing and envisioning, the making/doing with others, and other practices through which basic anthropological understanding emerges, both in the field and in the writing.[34] And, again, the parallel can be extended to emergency relief and aid work, as I learned from the Red Cross people I interviewed. I never heard an aid worker describe a mission as "more of the same old same old." Quite the contrary, international missions were occasions for personal and professional learning, and for pushing oneself. There was an anxious need to do things *really well*. This was not just a matter of doing what one was being paid to do. There was, I think, an expectation of putting one's "heart and soul" into one's work in the field. The professionalism required discipline, coordinated teamwork, following procedure, the management of affect, but, as with any mission, people also got entangled with risk, the necessity of improvisation and fast decision-making, and, continually, working with aid recipients faced with extreme circumstances. The imagination of the worlds (and the dangers) around them as they worked, ate, took breaks, washed, and slept, and the subtle changes to the self that were demanded in daily working with people (often in cultural contexts very different from their own) involved forms of both re-creative and creative imagination. These worlds in the field formed a certain kind of "dream space" that was, for many, good to inhabit and hard to relinquish when a mission came to an end (Tsing 2005).

So, to return to the beginning: Who are these people? Who are these aid workers? I will attempt to show through intersubjective, ethnographic engagement with them what I came to understand about their need to help, their need for "the world out there," their experiences of domestic attachments, the creative and re-creative processes and practices they became engaged in through their work in disaster zones of many kinds, and the transformations (willed and unwilled) of the relation of self to self that they experienced. Later in the book, I will also *make be*, in order to make meaningful, the worlds of loneliness and even abjection that the nonprofessional domestic humanitarians—old knitters and others—lived in. The forms of voluntarism and help that they offered to the needy involved creative and re-creative processes that were important to try to understand. They, too, needed a connection to the world "out there," elsewhere.

1. Professionals Abroad

Occupational Solidarity and International Desire as Humanitarian Motives

> In my case, international work and missions for the Red Cross have been the
> most significant events of my life, ones that have guided my later choices in . . .
> my life and career.
>
> —Liisa Riikonen, "'Kuran ja kuoleman keskelle sinne sinisten vuorten alle'"

A year or two after the Rwanda genocide, I saw a T-shirt with the shocking
text: "I'm in Rwanda because I'm a . . ." The three options were "Rogue,"
"Adventurer," and "Saint." The sentiment on this T-shirt was obviously sim-
plistic and more, but it encapsulated a set of current commonsense ideas
about the motivations underlying the work being done under the banner
of humanitarian intervention. What makes people do it? What pulls them
in? There is a great deal of guessing at and *attribution* of motive, the T-shirt
being but one instance of this. Sometimes more explicitly, sometimes less,
the humanitarians may be suspected of motives less or other than they ought
to be, of motives less than pure. What is it they're doing when they're "doing good"? Maybe they're in it for the glamour? Adventure? Glory? Money?
(see Redfield 2013). Maybe they aspire to be cool—cosmopolitans? Or maybe
they are holier-than-though world savers? Maybe they have Mother Teresa or
Jesus complexes? Are they playing God? What is it we're not seeing, or not
being told? When asked to make financial contributions to humanitarian
aid campaigns, people are now accustomed to suspect, sometimes rightly,
that their money is not going to its intended recipients and that their com-

passion is being sought on partially false pretenses. People suspect a trick of the heart, like a trick of the eye. As many have demonstrated, problems and harm are not hard to find in aid work, even in much state-of-the-art work done with the best of intentions and best practices.[1]

One of the key intentions of this book is to try to really *situate* one particular group of aid workers anthropologically, and to refuse the all-too-common move of simply assuming that the aid worker is an always already worldly, generically cosmopolitan, globally mobile figure operating from a position of relative strength and anonymous power vis-à-vis ("local," "helpless") aid recipients (Malkki 1992). What motivations did I myself attribute to the Finnish Red Cross workers and their logic of humanitarianism when I was initially beginning to interview them? That my own reasoning might not have been so far removed from that on the T-shirt is a sobering thought. The attribution of motive is one thing, but getting at the aid workers' own understandings of why they do their often difficult and dangerous work is a more involved process. Here the organizing themes at their most general are, on the one hand, interrelationships among internationalism, professionalism, and occupational solidarity, and on the other, the attraction and sense of possibility in work and life abroad. Under these broad headings is a more specific set of motivational, and intimately aspirational, themes that emerged in the ethnographic interviews. First there was the workers' own ethical and experiential obligation to help in humanitarian aid and emergency relief, and their engagement with a more collective, *national* obligation as a "citizen of the world" to help those who need it. People had a strong "home-grown" sense of international obligation and the importance of "internationalism," and more lately "global responsibility," as important cultural values and goals. (Internationalism and cosmopolitanism are not synonymous, of course [Malkki 1994].) Second, people aspired to and admired occupational solidarities and professional teamwork. Third, they expressed a desire, and a need, to travel and see the world in ways other than touristic, and to experience the excitement of "the international scene." The love of travel turned out to be a way of talking about the professional and personal challenges and rewards of international missions that made their work for the Red Cross so meaningful. Fourth, people expressed a desire to leave "home" (*koti*) and "homeland" (*kotimaa*) and to be "out in the world" (*olla maailmalla*), and *of* it, and to be transformed by it—but only "up to a point" (Mauss 1990; Tambiah 1984:340; see also chapter 4). Fifth, some, more than others, were motivated to seek the international as a site of sensual engagement and enhanced sociality, a more private sensual internationalism.[2] And finally, I examine here why people sometimes thought of their own national habitus as a burden or constraint—and as lacking in something—and how giving and helping, practices of generosity, came to seem like an alleviation of the helper's own neediness. (See also chapter 5 for an examination of these topics in another key.)

I will explore, in other words, a spectrum of motivations for Finnish aid work.[3] At one end, there is an ethical and political obligation to the international or global community, a duty to offer something of one's own abundance to those who need it, and the solidarity of internationalist professionalism; at the other is a "longing for the faraway" (kaukokaipuu), a neediness for the world and human contact, and an ever-present tension between solitude and conviviality, both prized (see chapter 5). This is not to suggest that people's motivations and aspirations could not be overlapping, or even mutually contradictory.

Part I: Professionalism, Solidarity, and Internationalism

As I sought to understand what drove the aid workers, two closely related forms of social solidarity came into view. The first was that of international obligation. Both the Finnish Red Cross and the aid workers it sent out conceptualized internationalism as a value to aspire to and help foster on missions. To be a good citizen it was desirable to be a good citizen of the world. The second form of solidarity was the translocal, transnational occupational solidarity of professionalism. The ethnographic evidence I have suggests that rather than seeing aid work in terms of an abstract (and fundamentally unilateral) calling, it may be more productive to think in terms of structural (even Durkheimian) forms of solidarity, and to attend to the significance of professional dispositions and forms of habitus (Bourdieu 2000; Mahmood 2005:136–40). For, in all the places in which the Red Cross medical teams work (usually under the umbrella of the ICRC and, less often, the IFRC), they have resident counterparts—that is, ideally, fellow professionals in other national-level Red Cross/Red Crescent societies, and their volunteers.[4] These locally based professionals work alongside the multinational expatriate teams, and they teach and are taught, often of necessity, in very improvisational ways.[5] (Julie Livingston has documented similar practices in Botswana in Improvising Medicine [2012]; see also Wendland [2010] and McKay [2012a, 2012b]). The internationalist, professional *ideal* (if not always the social reality) at work for the Finnish Red Cross is a Maussian exchange. Thus, an important part of situating the aid worker is also to challenge the "humanitarian"–"victim" or "aid recipient" binary, and to insist on the recognition of the presence of the professional resident aid worker and volunteer in whose own society the political and/or natural disaster is occurring.

"Professional, but Not 'Good'": Beyond Nurse Nightingale

My early questions to the Finnish Red Cross workers reflected my preconceptions and expectations—shaped to a startling degree, I was to realize, by the media coverage of violence, displacement, and humanitarian intervention in Africa. The first among these mass-mediated expectations was that I would discern a clear (and perhaps not very subtle) "humanitarian sensibility"—that is to say, an aspirationally selfless, generic calling to help a distant "suffering humanity" (cf. Boltanski 1993; Riikonen 1994:9–11; Haskell 1998:251–54; Fassin 2012). More to the point, I had expected that the Red Cross workers would readily identify themselves as humanitarians. This did not turn out to be the case in any straightforward manner. People came to international aid work through many different occupational routes and with a variety of dispositions (Bourdieu 2000), sensibilities, and personal histories.

As the 1994 genocide was happening in Rwanda, I tracked it daily in the media in California (Malkki 1996). The news cameras loved the expatriate (usually white) aid workers wearing T-shirts and identity tags or vests with their organizations' distinctive logos (MSF, ICRC, and the UN [United Nations], among many others). The cameras seemed especially partial to the women aid workers. That there were black professionals, Red Cross aid workers, and volunteers on the scene did not usually get picked up by the cameras. The journalists interviewed the white figures against a backdrop of vast masses of black African refugees and dusty, deforested camps that seemed to stretch as far as the eye could see. The framing of such scenes was very predictable. The aid workers' concerned faces (and inexplicably clean T-shirts) seemed to pop off the screen. The media clearly sought charismatic figures—maybe latter-day Nurse Nightingales and Doctor Schweitzers—among their ranks, just as they sought nameless victims (again, preferably, in the figuralities of innocent children, women, or women and children) among the refugees (Evans and Hall 2007:5). Selfless healers, selfless victims.

I did not realize for a while to what extent my own expectations had been shaped by that heroizing mass mediation of efficient, "saving" aid to help-less suffering until I actually began to do research with the Finnish Red Cross people who had worked in places like Burundi, Rwanda, Congo, Somalia, Chechnya, and Afghanistan, among other sites. I expected to hear the feminine machismo of the Mother Teresa-like figure with her indomitable humanitarian calling and life-long self-sacrifice (Prashad 1997). My expectations were matter-of-factly brushed aside.

One of my early approaches to the question of humanitarianism as "service to humanity" was to ask the Red Cross nurses and doctors in Helsinki what ideals or professional role models they might have. (A pretty silly question, I admit.) I offered as possible models famous, idealized "medical humanitarians." In retrospect, I realize that these models were not just ideal-typical models in Weber's sense; they were caricatures based on stereotypes. Eyebrows raised, my respondents refused this attribution. A former director of the international section of the Finnish Red Cross actually told me early on in the research that the very term *humanitarianism* was a troubled one. I should have paid more attention to her remark at the time. Instead, I persisted in looking for humanitarians.

One nurse, Lilja, reacted to my questions: "I don't believe anyone expects [any] sort of Mother Teresa of me—and least of all do I expect it of myself." She was quite emphatic: "In my opinion those are not values—for me personally. I don't aspire to anything like that. For me, it's important how I do my *work*, and how I get a contact to the people I'm helping. I don't see myself as a person who'd like to become the flagship of some system or organization." She smiled, "Because, personally, I don't see it as important—to be some extremely 'important' person. It's the *work*, what I *do*; that's what's most important to me" (cf. Riikonen 1994:31–33).

I asked a doctor, Leila, this time: "Is your work a calling or a job or . . . ?" She flashed me a smile: "Well, the Red Cross pays good salaries. So that already drops you from the pinnacles of self-sacrifice. Those [interested in self-sacrifice], they go to the MSF, where they pay minimum wages—people who have that kind of concern foremost." She added, "Those who have only the most cursory understanding of this [work], they say, 'Oh, I admire you so much for going there to do something good.'" Many others told me of similar exchanges. They found friends', acquaintances', relatives', and domestic colleagues' barbed humor about "doing good" or "going off to save the world again" to be hurtful and frustrating. Being able to talk with interested listeners about one's mission after the fact (aside from other Red Cross colleagues) was not among the rewards of this kind of work.[6] The doctor returned to the theme of self-sacrifice:

I remember when we were on a [10-week] training course in Copenhagen; there was a girl there who had come. . . . We were all doctors. . . . She had these sorts of ideas that she was going "to do good in India"—but she fell back to earth pretty quickly. She quit the course after two weeks. At the Red Cross course, there was no one who was so exaggeratedly that way [bent on self-sacrifice]. There [abroad], in practice, I haven't seen any sort of Nurse Nightingale thing among the nurses or doctors. But perhaps those people more often go [on international missions] through religious organizations? In my opinion, you don't need those sorts of people there. I think it should be people with a pretty solid grip [*jämäkkä ote*] who get sent there. . . . Of course, the two [models, of the calling and the solid professionalism,] don't necessarily preclude each other. If you have even the *slightest* grasp of the atmosphere and of people, that self-sacrifice business falls away pretty fast.[7]

Another doctor, Sanna, had similar views on self-sacrifice: "I would like this issue to be demystified. . . . It's about choices people make in their lives, to make them the best possible for themselves. Sometimes it is this kind of work, for some it is to make the most money, for some to have an average decent life. . . . We (in 'developed' countries at least, but also everywhere) have very many options to choose from!"[8] (cf. chapter 6). To underscore the point against self-sacrifice, she went on to discuss the extensive risk management training given to international delegates by the Finnish Red Cross.

An older war nurse, Kaarina, admitted (with an amused blush) that when she had first started out in international Red Cross work decades earlier, she had thought her mission to be to "heal the world" (*parantaa maailmaa*). She said: "You ask about seeking goodness? No, I don't think about that—that I am 'good.'" She laughed, "*Professional*, but not 'good'!" Emphasizing that Finns just work hard to prove that they're good professionals on the international scene, she went on to insist quite stridently upon certain generalizations about the interrelationship between work and Finnishness (*suomalaisuus*) (see Lehtonen, Löytty, and Ruuska 2004). In fact, these generalizations—as well as a marked cultural preoccupation with self-stereotyping—came up in some manner in all of the interviews I did.[9] Kaarina said, "Well: Finns generally have a very poor sense of self, so [we] always have a terrible need to prove that we're good [at what we do], that we work like crazy. So, many get a much bigger paycheck than we do, but we work like crazy [*hullun lailla*] to prove that we're good [at our jobs]. And that's Finnishness." She laughed, and went on: "I [saw] it already when I was au pairing [*piikomassa*] in the States; Finns were liked because they worked really hard . . . It's a pretty Nordic characteristic, although the Norwegians, Danes, and Swedes have a noticeably better sense of self [*itsetunto*]. We *need* to do it [work] to prove that we're good—and even then we don't really *believe* that we're good—and *that's* how Finnishness manifests itself!" This was a common way in which people understood their nationality to matter on international missions. In short, my search for "Humanitarians" was a relative failure. What I found among the workers instead was an embarrassed annoyance that people attributed any sort of heroism or halo to them (cf. Redfield 2013):[10] "Heroism. One of the biggest myths that's attached to work in crisis zones" (Hyvönen 2012:15).

Neither did the Finnish aid workers characterize themselves as being motivated by any sort of Christian calling. While both the ICRC's early history and the obvious symbolism of the cross might suggest at least a vaguely Christian contemporary orientation, aid workers categorically rejected the idea that it was anything other than a "secular" and pragmatic aid organization.[11] While Finland is formally a Lutheran country, most people view themselves as secular, and most aid workers, when asked, described themselves as "not religious." Religion was not a spontaneous topic in the interviews (see Asad 1993, 2003). Yet many had read surprisingly deeply into non-Lutheran cosmologies and philosophies—most notably different kinds of Islam and Buddhism—a will to knowledge, they said, inspired by their work abroad.[12] And despite their self-reported secularism (see chapter 6), the aid workers' very determination to serve all equally and without favor sometimes entailed deeply passionate commitments that *paralleled* certain sorts of Christian and Islamic commitment quite closely.

The disavowal of "religious" and "humanitarian" motives obviously does not mean that people didn't want to help those in need; they did, but they did not necessarily set out to "Do Good" or "Save Humanity." They did not say that their object was "humanity," although, significantly, "Humanity" is the most fundamental of the Seven Fundamental Principles of the ICRC, and of the International Red Cross and Red Crescent Movement (RCRCM) more generally. The seven principles—humanity, neutrality, impartiality, independence, voluntary service, unity, and universality—were not critically challenged head-on by the aid workers, but they were not usually a spontaneous topic of discussion in interviews, either. Yet, as many noted, their work was only possible when the key actors in tense political situations could be persuaded of the aid workers' strict adherence to the principles (often especially to neutrality and impartiality). As I show later, in one group interview where I asked the aid workers about the seven principles, "Humanity" (*ihmisyys*) was by consensus defined as humaneness (*inhimillisyys*).

All the Finnish aid workers I interviewed, and others I read about, had put themselves in harm's way on international missions. What made them do it?[13] They were all paid professionals. Even when their work got to be very difficult, as in the 1990s in Rwanda, Somalia, and Bosnia, in the aftermath of the 2004 tsunami, and in Darfur and Afghanistan, the one thing they held on to was their insistent professionalism and their willingness, or more accurately, *need*, to work hard. Again, they preferred to be called, when asked, not "humanitarians" but "aid workers" (*avustustyöntekijä*) or "emergency relief workers"; and they were of course also already trained "nurses," "doctors," and specialists in numerous other fields (ERUs [Emergency Response Units], electricians, mechanics, transport people, logisticians, administrators, and others who were often also on teams abroad depending on the needs at their destinations). A Red Cross administrator pointed out that the emphasis on professionalism might have been made even stronger in my interviews by the fact that "the workers really had had a very long road of training before they were ever offered a place on an international mission." First, they had of course the training of their own professions. Then, having applied to and passed the basic training course, the Red Cross further required many courses and workshops. This, she said, was a big part of why missions for the Finnish Red Cross felt more like "work" and less like "humanitarianism." Thus, these trajectories formed their occupational dispositions and personal aspirations. They were professionals abroad.

International Obligation

Forms of internationalism have long appealed to "the world" in different ways, and for different reasons. Socialist internationalism, of course, appealed not simply to a common humanity or an *inter*-national solidarity within a community of discrete, sovereign nation-states but also to *supra*- or *trans*-national ideals and political projects having to do with workers' solidarity, socioeconomic justice, and resistance to colonial, neocolonial, imperialist, and capitalist exploitation. It was a *universalism of supranational values*.[14] The postwar liberal internationalism exemplified by the United Nations, for example, is a different (if related) creature. Taking largely for granted the regime of territorially *sovereign nation-states*, it universalizes to a "world community" of nations (see Malkki 1994, 1997, 1998, 1999; Calhoun 2002; Tsing 2005; and chapter 3). In the post–World War II years, there were of course other universalist political projects also, among them mundialism, world federalism, and the Non-Aligned Movement (Romulo 1956; Wright 1956; Weiner 1968; Gupta 1992; Wittner 1995; Malkki 1998; Tsing 2005). But the latter's historic Bandung conference of 1955 was in some respects parallel to United Nations aspirations in that it expressed hopes for the success of anticolonial struggles worldwide, for world peace, and for *national sovereignty*. As Anna Tsing has noted, at "Bandung, the globe was a symbol of what might be possible: national sovereignty and world peace. This global dream space was made possible by other mid-twentieth century uses of the globe, for example in the United Nations" (Tsing 2005:84; see also Gupta 1992). The Cold War scuttled many of these projects of world-making as it did much else (Malkki 2002b). The Red Cross and Red Crescent Movement, like the ICRC, universalizes to an internationalist "world community" of sovereign nation-states within which individuals have both national and international obligations (one of the movement's fundamental principles is, of course, "universality").

One might say, with Durkheim, that such universalisms are "eminently social things" ([1912] 1995. As he wrote, "*the formation of an ideal is by no means an irreducible datum that eludes science. It rests on conditions that can be uncovered through observation. It is a natural product of social life*" ([1912] 1995:424, emphasis added). If Durkheim is right, then it is important to pay close attention to the specific forms of social life that sustain specific forms of universalization and world-making—in this case via international aid practices. Exploring different kinds of "situated universalism," as Harri Englund has put it (2005), or "engaged universalism," in Anna Tsing's terms (2005), is an *ethnographic*, and not only philosophical, task.

Like the United Nations, the Red Cross operates within the regime of sovereign nation-states.[15] This basically liberal internationalism is what came through in the interviews, too (see Malkki 1994). Arguing for shared social responsibility in the contemporary world, a nurse said that internationalism was "an extremely important thing because we live in a common, shared world and everyone's business is everyone's business. And everyone can influence how someone else in this world lives. . . . It's a common ball we all walk on." This view was taken for granted by everyone I interviewed.[16]

A younger nurse described her motivations for her Red Cross work thus:

Why do I do this work? I suppose it comes from wanting to help them. I think that somehow it's an obligation—an *international obligation to help*—whether it be war or a natural disaster—that a country that can't cope with it alone is assisted . . . We can't isolate ourselves on this globe—we're [inter]dependent . . . on the South, too. Fruit and food and whatever comes from the South, oil . . . I sometimes wonder what Africa would look like if it hadn't been robbed of its riches under colonialism. We have obligations to those peoples [*kansat*].

Here she was thinking of a *collective* obligation to the societies "robbed of their riches," and linked it with an obligation to "them" that she felt she should also acknowledge *personally*. She was responsible because she thought of herself as a Finn and a citizen of the world, but also because she assumed her membership in the "western world" and the wealthy Global North—in the society of those who robbed (and rob) but who also give aid.

A doctor had comparable views, but framed her sense of international obligation slightly differently. She said that Finns are "neutral" and in that sense "easy on international assignments—not too many burdens, political or otherwise." The fact that Finland is a small internationalist state (as well as geographically obscure) was a very positive aspect of her national situatedness. "We don't have burdens of colonialism on our conscience that we'd have to compensate for." Acknowledging that "neutrality" and "impartiality" to all were two central principles of the Red Cross and Red Crescent Movement, she nevertheless went on to say,

but somehow Third World people are getting a raw deal [*ovat alakynnessä*] and they should be supported, just like women are getting a raw deal and should be supported. With that kind of work, one can maybe balance things out a little bit. These western countries just continue this "development" of theirs and their high technologies, and they have to have more and more cars and comforts—without caring what happens there, *without even looking there!* In that sense, I have some ideological thinking here. I have a feeling that we've already gone to the end of development in many things, and already *over* some certain line. Now it's better to balance it all over there, on the other side. Whether that gets done well, that's another issue.

Thus, the internationalism of the Red Cross was one important motivation for people's work abroad. Another motivation particularly relevant here pre-dates the world wars, and has to do with occupational solidarities, *guild-like internationalist sensibilities* shared by professionals of various kinds (Krause 1996). This form of internationalism was, of course, there to be seen in the post-1945 world also. As Tsing (2005:84) wrote of the Bandung moment, "International cooperation among scientists formed a model for co-existence and respect" (see also Wittner 1995). These kinds of occupational solidarity, and respect, were much talked about and admired by the aid workers. They valued being a part of something much larger than themselves, larger than Finland. Across the board, they took great pleasure in recounting successful instances of international teamwork (and this despite their acknowledged shyness).[17] It was evident that their assignments abroad had, at their best, resulted in collegial loyalties and friendships with people from all over the world, as well as with other Finns. (A Red Cross administrator observed that this is similar to the kind of bonding that occurs among soldiers. In the same vein, many talked about "Red Cross veterans.") Their work and lives were often profoundly shaped, and changed, by these guild-like internationalist solidarities among fellow professionals. The solidarities were discussed more frequently than a generalized human solidarity with "suffering humanity" as categorical moral subject, for example.[18] As I suggest later, the aid workers tended to feel more attached to particular people—patients, colleagues, friends—than to any generalized "humanity."

As I show in chapter 2, Rwanda, Burundi, Congo, and other sites in Central and East Africa during and after the 1994 Rwanda genocide were among the most difficult assignments for the Red Cross professionals I interviewed (see chapter 2). Many harbored a sense of failure because the enormity of the crises so totally exceeded anything they or anyone could do. There were scenes of devastation everywhere as aid workers made their way to set up hospitals and refugee camps. One nurse, Minna, talked about how there were bodies everywhere. She told me a vivid story about professionalism and solidarity: "I had a Swiss colleague sitting next to me [in the car on the way from Rwanda to Goma] and every 10 meters she vomited into a bag." The nurse laughed softly. "And she held my hand so tightly that it was cramping and my wrist was bruised black and blue. She said she could not stay there—to which I said, 'Yes, you can; you *will* get used to it. And as a professional person, you *are* going to put yourself in order, and you *are* going to take care of this job.' [I told her], 'Let's see how this day goes, and if you then feel that you want to leave, then you leave.' And she stayed."

> LM: And she took care of things?
> Nurse, smiling proudly: She took care of it. All the way to the end.
> LM: What was "the end"?
> Nurse: I was there for a month. I was on [temporary] assignment from Somalia; I was sent there from Somalia. And [my Swiss colleague] was there for three months.

More generally, the Finnish workers recalled that the teams working in Rwanda had by many accounts been extraordinary in their solidarity and spirit. People had really supported each other through much that was extraordinarily demanding.

Mikko's Story

Another case, I will call it Mikko's story, is a powerful example of the dynamic interrelationships among a professionalism that can only be called steely, a commitment to work, a deep and abiding solidarity, and a loyal friendship. Mikko was doing challenging nonmedical aid work in precarious circumstances, mostly in Rwanda, from December 1993 onward. He was originally posted there to help set up camps for the refugees who had fled violence in Burundi and sought refuge in Rwanda. After the presidents of both Rwanda and Burundi were killed in a single well-planned plane crash, the Rwanda genocide began in April of 1994. Mikko worked with both Finnish and multinational groups of colleagues in planning and setting up camps and transporting refugees. The UNHCR (United Nations High Commissioner for Refugees) collaborated with the ICRC (International Committee of the Red Cross) in establishing the camps. Mikko met an extraordinary fellow professional who was working in Rwanda with the UNHCR. They had the chance to work together intensively, and to form an important friendship. The political situation became increasingly dangerous in Rwanda as well as Burundi. Sometime before Christmas of 1994, Mikko was told that if he was to leave for a break at all, it had to be on the transport plane that was about to take off for Nairobi because "the day after tomorrow" it might not be possible anymore. He was basically ordered to go on holiday. At the last minute he decided to get on the flight. His friend stayed behind to continue their work, and Mikko expected to be back in two weeks. While on the break in Finland, he received an ICRC situation report from Geneva informing him that his friend had been killed. Mikko knew instantly what had happened—he had been murdered—and was to learn more. His next decision was to get back to the work that he and his friend had been doing together. This is what I called "steely professionalism," but it also seemed like a desperate need to find solace in just pushing on, come what may. Two years after this had happened, Mikko was still grieving, and holding back tears as he spoke. We were at a sunny seaside café in Helsinki; the water and islands outside looked peaceful and ordinary. It was important to him that I understand that he had returned to the work he had been doing with his friend, and that his friend would have done the same in his place. He had asked himself endless questions: "What if I had not gone on holiday? Why didn't I stay? Would that have changed anything?" He said, "We took care of each other; we worked together." (Again I thought of the bonding that can happen between soldiers.) The Finnish Red Cross (FRC) tried to make it as easy as possible for him not to return to the mission. I asked him: "Couldn't you have left the mission, given it up?" He said, "I *could* have . . . ," laughing a bit, "but since I'm a Finn, dammit [*piru vie*], I don't give up. It was pretty tough." Continuing the work was his ethical and emotional compass. What Mikko's story shows about attitudes to work is culturally not uncommon in Finland (see Riikonen 2005:50). Working hard was a key element in professionalism, as people again and again made clear to me, and both were related to an understated, ambivalent, but deep national pride. Another element was calmness. Reading through my transcripts in this case and other interviews, I was struck that calmness was so universally assumed and expected. For all his grief, Mikko's description of the actual work he and his colleague had been doing was measured and calm (see Grönvall 2005; Lääperi 2007).

The ideals (if not always the practice) of international collaboration and good, professional teamwork were not confined to the Finns' work with expatriate colleagues. I had expected to hear accounts of technological know-how in the hands of expatriate experts flown into helpless, hapless Southern crisis zones. While there was some of that, the ideals of collaboration and exchange were more nuanced, and much more engaged, than I had expected. Often it was the case that the sites to which ICRC missions had been sent, Rwanda, for example, already had (or had had) a well-functioning national-level Red Cross. In an interview in *Sairaanhoitaja*, a nursing journal, the nurse Maritta Vuori said that one of the rewards of her international work was that "one sees how well people are cared for elsewhere, although in ways that differ [from care] in Finland" (Lääperi 2007).[19]

In a practice that the ICRC and the whole Red Cross and Red Crescent Movement term "institutional development" (*développement institutionel*), international teams are expected to support and strengthen national-level Red Cross societies during their missions. It is routine procedure for aid workers to seek their occupational counterparts in the host country, whenever possible—so a Finnish surgical nurse, for instance, would try to identify a resident counterpart with the same, or at least similar, training. Numerous occupational skills (not just medical) were also taught in these collaborations on both sides, resident and expatriate.

A very senior nurse talked about the kinds of things she had learned in the course of professional collaborations on missions:

> When you first get there, you need to have the patience to wait a little bit, maybe to wait for the whole first week—even if your head is full of ideas. You need to be patient enough to just be quiet [and mindful] and to chat with your counterpart for the first week—and not straightaway come in saying, "Okay, now this and this will be re-organized!" You have to *wait* to get into the situation a bit . . . so that you learn even a little about that community's needs—because of course I have my own needs that I bring there. And those aren't necessarily the right ones . . . because the people there are, after all, the experts on their own lives and circumstances. That has to be used productively because it's extremely important knowledge.

She said that a whole range of skills and ideas *not taught* in Finland anymore could be learned from one's Red Cross counterpart or another healthcare worker in the field abroad: "There are very *practical* things; from an African Community Health Worker you learn a million things about which you didn't have the foggiest idea. So, professionally, too, I have learned lots of different little tricks, and big things, and just things relating to my own work. In Finland, no one is even *capable* of teaching you such things." She said that the better the relationship that developed with her resident, national-level Red Cross counterpart, the better the work results. She added, "many times you have to learn that the things we bring from here, they don't even work in those systems! You have to be ready for the likelihood that s/he is much smarter or wiser, that counterpart of yours. And you have to accept it! If you don't do that, you might as well go home . . . What I personally experience as awfully important is that the community you're trying to help accepts you. That works very well through that counterpart" (cf. Wendland 2010; Livingston 2012; and McKay 2012a, 2012b).[20]

A part of the Red Cross teams' collaborative mission is also teaching residents of the areas where the missions have gone to take on some of the jobs of the international teams once they leave (equipment is also usually left on site). As one nurse, Kaarina, put it: "*Teaching* is awfully important, teaching of the [National Society] staff; that's, in a way, our gift to the country . . . And [as a nurse] you try to [identify] who can be trained as a nurse." She spent six months in Afghanistan, for example, trying to teach nursing to a group of refugee women. Her success was mixed, a fact she found very stressful.[21]

Professional practices never perfectly fit the institutional mandates and structures that produce them. They are negotiated in real time in the messy, often chaotic realities of specific circumstances usually only partially understood. Probably these professional practices are always, simultaneously, more *and* less than the abstract codifications of mandates. This is the case for the seven fundamental principles of the ICRC and IFRC, just as it is for physicians' and nurses' (and anthropologists') codes of ethics.

Writing about how diverse and even incompatible professional ethics can (and *should*) be, Émile Durkheim observed:

> As professors, we have duties which are not those of merchants. Those of the industrialist are quite different from those of the soldier, those of the soldier different from those of the priest, and so on . . . We might say in this connection that there are as many forms of morals as there are different callings, and since, in theory, each individual carries on only one calling, the result is that these different forms of morals apply to entirely different groups of individuals. These differences may even go so far as to present a clear contrast. Of these morals, not only is one kind distinct from the other, but between some kinds there is real opposition. The scientist has the duty of developing his critical sense, of submitting his judgment to no authority other than reason; he must school himself to have an open mind. The priest or the soldier, in some respects, have a wholly different duty. Passive obedience, within prescribed limits, may for them be obligatory. It is the doctor's duty on occasion to lie, or not to tell the truth he knows. A man of the other professions has a contrary duty. Here, then, we find within every society a plurality of morals that operate on parallel lines . . . *This moral particularism—if we may call it so—which has*

no place in individual morals . . . goes on to reach its climax in professional ethics, to decline with civic morals and to pass away once more with the morals that govern relations among men as human beings. (Durkheim [1957] 2005:5, emphasis added)

In the passage above, Durkheim thought of each of the different professional occupations—soldier, priest, merchant, scientist, physician—as a *calling*. I had expected to find humanitarians animated by a kind of calling. Yet what I found to be predominant was, again, something closer to the vocational or professional ethics on which Durkheim placed so much emphasis. People had become committed to international work with the Red Cross, and their intent was, as so many put it, "to help" (*auttaa*) (again, many talked in terms of an international obligation and a *need* to help [*tarve auttaa*]). But people were professionals before they were humanitarians (cf. Riikonen 2005:50–51). They worked on Red Cross missions to make a contribution as good doctors, nurses, and other professionals, and to do what they could in situations that frequently overwhelmed them. (But in doing so, they were also acting out of ethical and affective commitments that could be configured quite individually in another sense, as discussed in the next chapter; they often formed attachments to particular persons—colleagues, but also patients.)

One of the key reasons for the moral particularism of these Finnish aid workers was, as I mentioned earlier, that they already had advanced training in their own occupations before they ever applied for Red Cross training and missions. They were all specialized, but they shared what they variously described as an international obligation, a solidarity, a desire, and a need to be a part of something significant, something more challenging and greater than one's workaday context in Finland—and one's workaday self (Riikonen 2005:50).

At the same time, such occupational professionalism might not by itself supply sufficient motive, and a more generic "humanitarian attitude" (*humanitaarinen asenne*) was also sometimes acknowledged by some to have its place (Fassin 2012:2–12). In a conversation about humanitarian thinking and professionalism, a mid-level Red Cross manager said, "you . . . have to be a professional. On the other hand, with a professional stance alone, it honestly wouldn't be worth it and there wouldn't be enough motivation. [Therefore,] there has to be some humanitarian attitude in the background." (But she, like others I interviewed, did not conceptualize "the humanitarian attitude" as having to do with "being religious" or "spiritual.") I will have more to say on the relation between what Durkheim calls "particularistic" ethical commitments and universalistic ones in the conclusion to this chapter.

Part II: Attractions of the Abroad

Travel, Distinction, and the International

Everyone I interviewed talked at length about a deep love of travel. It was freely and unapologetically acknowledged to be one among several important motivations for seeking the training for international Red Cross work in the first place. As a surgical nurse put it: "I think that the group that goes there *wants* to work internationally. Probably this group finds its way [to the work] because it's interested in foreign countries and cultures, and in *working* there." She added, "It's a great wealth that I've gotten to work with *so many* different nationalities, whether trained or not." This love did not in any way preclude the desire—or the sense of personal and international obligation—to help. That was a given. "Of course there's a desire to help," said another nurse; "you've *chosen* this [helping] profession in the first place." Then she smiled dreamily, "But the beginning, it has been to seek experiences and adventures" (cf. Riikonen 2005:43–45). So unsurprising is travel as a motivation for international aid work that to point it out seems banal. But it turned out to be productive to examine it a bit more closely.

It was obvious from the start that travel on international missions meant something more, and other, than tourism or other common ways of getting around abroad (see Löfgren 1999). It was not the yearly "sun trip" (*aurinkomatka*) that Finns who can afford it seek in the dead of winter—if for nothing more than sunlight. People did, however, observe that most (if not all) of their missions took them south of Finland to warmer, sunnier climates. They also marveled at the physical beauty of many of the scenes of devastation they were sent to. Those who had worked in Rwanda were struck by awe that such nightmarish human cruelty and unfathomable suffering could be happening in such a magically beautiful landscape.

There was also an element of distinction-making in this travel. "Long ago already," said Leila, the doctor, "tourist trips" had begun to "taste like wood." She neatly distinguished herself from what she called "the meatball tourists" (*lihapullaturistit*). Many others' comments resembled hers: "Professionally [international work] is still experienced as a positive [high status] image in Finland . . . You're more international than those who've only gone to Spain or Mallorca or Athens" (common and somewhat "down-market" destinations for the sun trippers). "The international idea" was not just an institutional or professional ethos; it also shaped—often in unpredictably intimate ways—tastes, desires, affects, and needs.[22] And the idea of being abroad opened up attractive possibilities for the imagination. Sometimes it was about escaping one's Finnish self and *being otherwise* "out there in the world" (*siellä maailmalla*).

Leila was the only person who very bluntly explained that it was, for most aid workers, more international and prestigious when "you've been in rarer places in more difficult circumstances." There was, among most other aid workers I interviewed, a reluctant recognition that such a track record of work could be pleasing. Journalists, photographers, and anthropologists, among others, are of course familiar with this phenomenon—and they, like the aid workers, come to know that such a "track record" can also be psychically damaging.

Professional and Personal Challenges

Many were strongly motivated to return to international aid work again and again because of the professional growth it enabled, and demanded. One person pointed out that her work abroad made her a better nurse than she would have been, had she worked only in Finland. "I've said, as surely many of my colleagues have, that the work I do in Finland, many can do that. But the work that I do *out there*, that *can't* be done by everybody. Not everybody has systematically sought the training [that the Red Cross offers] or tried to develop through reading; and then the whole experiential world that you have [through this work], it's 'unique' [*ainutkertainen*]." Another person said, "I think that for quite a few doctors it is a certain kind of challenge to get to go elsewhere, [as opposed to staying] in some Finnish hospital circles. To learn new things—because it *does* train and teach us—and to get away from the quotidian" is valuable.

Both doctors and nurses, as mentioned before, described how satisfying it was to get to be more of a general practitioner on international missions. "You learn broad-based medical practice that is no longer taught in medical training or the workplace in Finland." This applied to surgery too; an administrator commented, "Especially for young surgeons, war surgery is an enormous learning experience." And when no ultrasound equipment was available, one doctor observed, the work of diagnosis had to be that much better. Also, being able to really follow up with one's patients was considered rewarding. The high level of medical specialization in Finland was in this context experienced as a barrier to the learning possibilities of a more general practice that needed flexibility and technical improvisation (Livingston 2012; McKay 2012b).

Leila discussed how aid work was sometimes associated with selflessness as self-sacrifice in the media and the broader society: "If you were to say that [aid work] is a challenge," she said, "that would sound cold to people because it would be understood as a challenge to your *career*. . . . Of course it's more of a *challenge to your personality*, and that's probably pretty difficult to explain to a general audience in a simple way. I think the person who would go there [abroad on a mission] to sacrifice herself would be *pathological*." She found her medical job in Finland unchallenging and unrewarding for a number of reasons, and therefore sought ever more specialized training whenever possible, principally so that she could work abroad more. She was not alone in being a highly trained medical professional who felt unchallenged by her domestic work, and experienced missions as a highly desirable habitus.

Kaisa, yet another nurse with multiple specializations, had already risen as high as was possible in her work at a Helsinki hospital. She had a great deal of responsibility and was regarded as a very successful professional, and yet she said: "My work here is often boring. . . . I work at the *same* hospital and I don't have the opportunity to *develop as a person*. When I've been somewhere else, there's more *energy* in me, a certain kind of *strength and self-confidence* [*voimaa ja itsevarmuutta*]." She explained that one gets to be "blind" to things that are so familiar and routine. "Abroad, when everything is so different, you get a lot of energy. . . . You have to take certain risks in life."[23] She drew a very sharp line between the domestic and the international, and between her domestic and her international selves. She went so far as to say that the difference between home and abroad was so radical that even difficult missions felt like a break, a "holiday," from the familiar routinized patterns of the everyday in Finland, or what most Finns call "mundane reality" (*arkitodellisuus*).

Her next comment was jarring. "Experiencing new things, seeing new things . . . It's just completely different from here. Then you're on *holiday* [*lomalla*]. Although you're *at work* [there], it's a vacation from this environment. And it's a new *challenge*. Of course it may be some really terrible situation, but it's *so totally a different, different thing*. . . . There you have to put your *whole personhood* on the line [*likoon*]." The experience of a social and sensual break with overfamiliar professional routines, with safe and boring quotidian social life in Finland—and perhaps especially with one's own *quotidian self*—was so powerful that it was possible for almost any mission to feel like a "holiday." It was very clear that by "holiday" she did not mean to imply a lack of humane engagement with the people she worked with and cared for, whether abroad or in Finland—and that she did not use "holiday" to mean not-work, laziness, or sight-seeing. She was not just "traveling abroad"; she was traveling in order to *work* abroad. The point was to work especially intensively, and to live up to the responsibility she had been assigned on the international scene. She was able to get at something important through *losing herself* in the work. I learned about this kind of pleasurable loss of self from many of those I interviewed (cf. chapter 5).

In another context a nurse talked quite intimately about how being "out there" had wrought self-transformation and how this, along with an obligation to help, drew her to more and more international missions:

> Of course it's *yourself* you learn most about there. I've never learned as much about myself as in a relationship or on a mission abroad. It's terrible when you realize how *naked* . . . how you have to undress your *self* and notice how you *really* are—"So, this is how I think!" Attitudes from *deep down* that you've learned as a child . . . [*It's mortifying.*] . . . Of course it's easy to criticize other people. "How could she do that in that way—or this way?!" ["How can she *think* like that?"] But then when you *really see yourself*—pretty depressing actually [*she laughs*]. . . . If you're able to change *a little bit*, if some little thing really sticks with you, then you dare to *say something* aloud. *You've* become someone who *defends*. . . . Let's say at a coffee table, there's talk about "*the* refugees" in general—or "*the* Somalis," or something like that. . . . You *can't* just listen without intervening. You're *just not able* [to listen to that] anymore. And then many experience you as . . . "Well! Here *she* is, all fancy because she's been in some refugee camp." How do you express your own opinions nicely, without hurting other people's feelings? In things like this, it's really difficult to keep your own feelings—so you don't . . . seethe.

Thus the professional challenge was also a deeply personal one, and could, in principle, lead to some degree of self-transformation. How permanent such self-transformation was or how it might change shape over time for all Red Cross aid workers, I do not know, of course. But thinking of my interviews together, and considering them longitudinally over many years, it seems to me that the changes to self were relatively transformative and surprisingly lasting in both psychic and social senses. This was readily accessible to observation, and common as a topic of conversation. Such conversations were often occasions for critical self-reflection, sometimes for looking back in surprise on a self sloughed off.[24]

The experience of intense personal and professional forms of engagement with "the world" becoming a single process was heady. It *was to lose oneself and yet be vitally alive.* In her study of Finnish Red Cross nurses, Liisa Riikonen, herself a nurse, found that people called that heady feeling "the burning" or "the burn" (*palo*) (2005:44, 47, 50–51); it was also what motivated them to go on missions in the first place. The burn was a form of intense and unpredictable creativity. Riikonen likened it to Csikszentmilhalyi's concept of the "flow" experience (Csikszentmilhalyi 1991; Riikonen 2005:50). Those I interviewed did not use these specific metaphors, but they certainly described experiences and states of being that resembled them.

"Long Dives into Something Different": Desire and Neediness in International Aid Work

It is not unique to Finland, of course, that travel has been sought as a chance to feel differently, to be differently embodied, differently gendered, differently classed, or just to be *otherwise*—but this experiential chance is not used in the same way by everyone. In this connection Leila, the doctor, and I were talking about how she would define a "good life." She said she had "a childish idea that there should be a nice amount of noise and color and happenings." Most of her missions had been to the Global South where she had sought, and usually found, these bright colors, ample sunshine, warmth, and different forms of kind and pleasurable sociality, or conviviality. She contrasted this to Finland as a lack, an emptiness, a coldness, a colorlessness— and a whiteness. She might have been describing Finland in winter, but I think she was referring to race as she did pro-immigrant work as part of her practice as a physician in Finland. As many scholars have shown, of course, white people tend to experience their whiteness as an unmarked culturelessness, as "nothing in particular" (see Ware 1992; Frankenberg 1993; Evans and Hall 2007; Roedigger 2007). The question of race did not emerge in the interviews; *nationality* was overwhelmingly the most important marker of the Finnish self (and often took form as a kind of species-thinking). This does not mean, naturally, that the Finnish aid workers were not classified as "whites" or "Europeans" by other people in their mission sites. As I was unable to accompany aid workers on missions, I could not observe how the dynamics of race played out in any given site. I assume that "white privilege" was the predominant dynamic.

Leila continued: "A good life is a very active life. You should always go toward the thing that interests you . . . so that you continually have the enthusiasm to really get inside things." She said it would be sad to become cynical. She also emphasized: "You do have to choose the kind of thing that you want to take care of well, a hundred percent well, as well as you know how. . . . It has to be intensive, whatever it is." She went on to specify that the pleasure one seeks should be "moral" and include "a desire to help others to have pleasure and satisfaction [mielihyvää] and well-being [hyvää oloa]." She said pleasure could be spiritual, but that for her it tended to be more sensual. "Of course, one seeks extremes all the time."

"Long dives into something different." That is what had always driven Leila to seek international work with the Red Cross. In many ways she was culturally unusual. "I have done [in my life] what is pleasurable. But I don't think that makes me more selfish than other people. A friend always tells me, 'Leila, you *devour* everything' . . . *life*." Leila laughed, and then held my gaze intently: "All that *beauty*—when I think how *important* beauty is to a human being, and then [to be] constrained by a [single] mold . . . ['the Finnish woman']." That is, I thought to myself, the last thing Leila wanted to be. She asked, "Have you read Anaïs Nin's books?" I said I hadn't. Leila didn't notice. Nin "had a heroine named Sabine who wanted to be *all* women. She wanted to transform herself and be different and in different shapes [hahmo]. I've thought that maybe I identify with her a little because I've had a bit of that kind of need, and somehow this traveling is an answer to that." Leila was atypical in that she so self-consciously sought such a thorough self-transformation through her travel and work abroad. Others wanted to shed, or get a reprieve from, certain *aspects* of themselves and of their "Finnishness," but did not want or expect to become wholly different people. Leila was also atypical in expressing her desire so boldly.

I asked Leila if she was looking for a "special effects reality," an intensified reality (tehostettu todellisuus). She said it was rather "a *search for theatricality.* There is some of that in me . . . , more than in an average person, and sometimes it feels like a kind of *childishness.* . . . It's a sense of drama that then approaches *aesthetics* and other things. That drama is real—how you *see* the extremes in those situations [on missions]." Later she added that she looked for "surrealistic experiences," but emphasized that these had to come from the everyday, the quotidian, and that they had to emerge from human relationships:

> I look for different ways of being a woman, but of course I don't look for just anything, [and certainly not a Maggie Thatcher] . . . I'm interested in those women in different cultures who in my opinion have an *interesting femininity*, and to *get it*. I don't want to go [on missions] as some kind of "*Finnish* woman" representing the "Finnish nationality"; rather I'd like to *absorb* those others because that makes a person more exciting. And for that reason I'm captivated by certain veils in Afghanistan and certain bangles in India. In other words, there are some different little details that the women there practice that make them in some way more feminine, more mysterious. In my opinion femininity is a very important matter. It enchants [*kiehtoo*] me, and I've always thought that it's a thing worth reaching for—and it's not just these external things of course—but through them you get to other dimensions of femininity. I do think that this is, for me, an important component that interests me in people. Of course men interest me too, but this is a thing I can take for *myself*, that I *learn* from those women, and I suppose my ideal [*ihanne*] is that I could be *all* those women . . . [A friend] always accused me of identifying with those people.[25]

(What did her friend mean by "those people?," I wondered.) Leila continued: "There's less to look at in men. [Women have] grace and sweetness."[26]

It would be quite possible, perhaps even warranted, to analyze Leila's desire and appreciation as a kind of sensual imperialism, a position that has usually assumed a relation of superiority to the difference of the Other. She was after all a very independent medical professional with the freedom of social and material resources at her disposal—thus in some cultural contexts structurally male. People are all too used to this appropriating, desirous gaze from western men, and perhaps there is something of that here (cf. Said 1979; Alloula 1986; Bhabha 1990; McClintock 1995; Grewal 1996; Dangarembga 2004; Fanon 2008; Pratt 2008; Mulvey 2009).

But what also came across in Leila's thinking was a sense of being trapped, possibly in the wrong body, and in the wrong nationality. Her counternational need left her feeling, if not inferior, not quite superior, either. Her desire and, as she put it, her love of beauty, came across as a kind of *neediness*. She said pensively: "Maybe I really was born in the wrong country." She made me really think about the fact that just because one was born in Finland did not automatically mean that one was born to be a Finn, or that one was a "born Finn." Then Leila told me about a friend, Jussi, a "bisexual diplomat with great friends in [the Mediterranean]. He became completely depressed when he was transferred back to Finland. I guess he was the kind of person who would not have endured it here. He was transferred to [the Middle East]. He was shot [and killed]. A triangle drama. Isn't it romantic? Better than a car accident in Kemijärvi. Jussi blossomed like a rose in [the Middle East]. His temperament just wasn't suited to Finland."[27] I felt in Leila's airy story about Jussi an undertow of something very sad.

In my interpretation, Leila saw herself and Jussi as having landed in Finland through some kind of cosmological mistake. For them, somewhere abroad, or "out there in the world" (tuolla maailmalla), was where they would both thrive. Travel promised to get them there—but not permanently. Of the people I interviewed, only Leila had seriously considered emigrating. She sought to keep open the possibility of even radical transformations of self and life, and hoped that the opportunities would not be closed off at some point. She remained undecided; there was after all a lot to lose in leaving Finland for good—a good job, a home, and the social safety nets of a welfare society being but some considerations.

So, what was it that so troubled her about life in Finland? She detested what she saw as its conventionality (sovinnaisuus), small-mindedness (pikkusieluisuus), and jealousy (kateus). She keenly felt Finland's "smallness." For her, as for many others I interviewed, there was "the outside world" (ulkomaailma), "the world out there" (maailma siellä), or even just "the world" (maailma), and then there was arctic Finland, the site of real reality, remoteness, and isolation. "Abroad" was simply a very meaningful site—a dream space (Tsing 2005)—as against the familiar habitus of mundane reality (arkinen todellisuus). In some sense, perhaps, abroad was simultaneously more vital and more important, and less real, than the mundanity of home and domestic "reality."

Along these lines, Kaarina, the war nurse, exclaimed one day, "Here we are, really at the ends of the earth [maailman äärillä], in some remote corner [jossain kolkassa], so if you didn't leave here you'd be pretty poor!" Another common expression is that Finland is so remote as to be "behind God's back" (Jumalan selän takana). The director Aki Kaurismäki's films set in Finland are ethnographically and experientially accurate for many people, including me; among them are Match Factory Girl, Shadows of Paradise, and The Man without a Past. Kaurismäki has a very fine eye for how the senses react to the silent minimalism of the environments he experiences in Finland.

The aid workers talked a great deal about what one might call sensory deprivation, and experienced it in two principal ways. First, Finland's northerly location on the globe makes it an extreme and demanding environment to live in; winter comes with fierce cold and an almost unbearably long darkness. It is a sensory and psychic challenge. (The summers are brief and magical.) The other form of deprivation was sourced to the formidable cultural expectations of social reserve and restraint, and constraint. In contrast, what people sought in their work abroad was conviviality and greater spontaneity. In the following, Kaarina poignantly described the rewards of her work in Afghanistan, and the deprivation she experienced on her return to Finland; I had asked her how she relaxed in the field.

> Reading and listening to music and getting together with friends [in Kandahar]. It was lovely to go to your own room after all the noise and work, and read a book or listen to music. And then on the other hand there are these friendship relationships that are born. . . . What you never get in Finland, what I think is relaxing—is that people *touch* each other. It had nothing to do with sexuality; but that someone could take you by the shoulders or . . . In Kabul in '92 when the war was really terrible and we weren't able to sleep well—but that people would touch [you] and ask, "How's it going today?" . . . And then when you come to Finland—it's pretty terrible.[28]

The Finnish Red Cross recently ran a domestic public awareness campaign encouraging people to "touch someone." The campaign poster had a large fingerprint on a plain white background. And below it was the single word *Kosketa* (touch).[29]

There was a sensual neediness, and a conviction that out in the world there was, in Leila's words, "a nice amount of color and noise and people." In Riikonen's study, a Red Cross nurse thoughtfully says, "More [often] I've experienced [on international missions] that we come from some poorer culture, because that is how it almost always is. If you think about the Near East, or the Far East, then . . . our culture is so insignificant. All this, our milieu, is so much more ascetic than the life of those other countries and [the source] from which they draw their life wisdom. So I at least think that the Finnish Red Cross nurses I've worked with have been really humble in accepting [those cultures]" (2005:139). Of course, they usually had a very partial understanding of the cultural contexts to which they were drawn. Rather than feeling a self-assured cultural superiority toward the people and societies they were sent to help, many found themselves accepting of and even needy for something valuable that, in their eyes, their own society lacked. They experienced their own insignificance. Nevertheless, despite all this widely expressed cultural claustrophobia and yearning, almost everyone I interviewed assumed the inescapable, ambivalent importance of "home" (in both a personal and a national sense). It also bears noting that the complex historico-political meanings and nuanced values associated with whiteness in a given social context might not have been fully within all aid workers' grasp, but it is safe to assume that their whiteness was, as a rule, a formidable privilege.

The Sociality of Home and Abroad

The calibration of social distance and proximity in the field, as Riikonen (2005:134–37) points out, was influenced by a number of factors, including the length and nature of particular missions; in short-term, acute crisis situations, the contacts might remain quite superficial and in that sense distant. She also mentions that if too-close friendships or other social relationships were formed (whether with patients or colleagues), they might interfere with Red Cross regulations about neutrality and impartiality, as well as with professional codes of ethics (2005:134). But there were also more intimate, affective calibrations of distance and proximity.

On missions abroad, the Finnish aid workers often experienced a strong tension between their need for solitude and their need for sociality. Every worker I interviewed stressed regular periods of solitude as a deep, if often frustrated, personal need on missions. This was not just a passing comment; it was really something people remembered about each mission. It was difficult (and sometimes impossible) to convince non-Finns on a multinational team, local Red Cross/Red Crescent colleagues, and other workers that one's need for solitude was not a sign of anger or alienation, or any kind of problem. People insisted on distinguishing solitude from loneliness (cf. chapter 5). They were bemused: "Some people really just don't know how to be alone." While most enjoyed the often intense conviviality of work, meals, and after-hours togetherness much of the time, they found it stressful to speak a language other than their own all the time—or simply to talk so much. Forced sociality and very close living quarters were often painful experiences.[30]

The interviews also gave ample evidence of a tension between shyness and self-restraint, on the one hand, and freer self-expression and sociality, on the other. It was remarkable to me to be told of deliberations by a group of Finnish aid workers in Afghanistan about whether they had "permission to cry" (lupa itkeä). Kaarina explained the situation, her hands folding and unfolding a napkin: "When an adult dies, you get used to it—that people die. But when a child dies: you never get used to that. In Kabul, we [on the Red Cross team] were talking about it, and we said that we *are* allowed to cry with the parents or the mother—that it's *not* wrong, that *these* feelings you *are* allowed to let out. A child's death, really no . . . you *never* get used to it." Why did they hesitate so? As medical professionals they had learned to keep their emotions in check—that is, to try to practice what Leif, a Red Cross doctor, called "emotional neutrality" (see chapter 6). They might also have worried about intruding on the grief of a parent. Yet clearly they felt a compelling need to comfort, and to express their own sadness and frustration.

What often held people back in these kinds of situations was häveliäisyys, an old-fashioned but still meaningful word that means modesty and shyness.[31] These sentiments are behind a very common beginning to a sentence, "No enhän mä nyt voi . . . ," "Well, I couldn't . . ." or "It's not for the likes of me to . . ." It has to be said that the people who ended up in international Red Cross work were those who had been able to *overcome* their shyness and self-constraint to a great extent. They *wanted* to experience difference from themselves and their own society, and to be challenged and taught by that difference. But they carried a great deal with them to missions.

And yet a distinguished old doctor observed: "It's just right under the surface [in Finland], the difficulty of accepting difference, and difference right away becomes a base on which inequality is constructed. And we're not *free* to accept difference." I agreed that there was ample proof of that within Finland—in the form of anti-immigrant and anti-Roma racism, for example—but added that a number of people had told me that they felt all around better abroad—that they in fact *craved* the difference from home. The doctor said, "Yes, when I've traveled internationally with groups of Finns, I've noticed that some kind of sensation of a straitjacket [pakkopaidan tunne] disappears and one is kind of *freer* . . . I've noticed *exactly* that, and this leads to the fact that when a Finnish delegation is working internationally, many on it booze too much [ryyppäävät liikaa]. There's some kind of jännitys [tension; excitement] that 'Here we are, in a new environment . . .' . . . There's this old *burden* somehow and the tension leads to excessive drinking."

Evidence to the contrary was also plentiful; the doctor had noticed that for many Finnish aid workers, being abroad on multinational teams with different cultural expectations about moderate alcohol use and sociality was a welcome break from the powerful social conventions of heavy drinking in Finland. The people I worked with often mentioned drinking in passing, and never sought to deny its prevalence, but it did not end up being a significant topic of discussion. People seemed to have a relatively relaxed attitude about it, and pointed out that many other nationalities did their share of drinking on international missions too.[32]

"My interpretation," the old doctor continued, "is that there's a certain tension between a *home dependency* [koti-, kotoriippuvuus] and the *free possibility of the outside world* [ulkomaailman vapaa mahdollisuus], [and] that you can't get rid of that tension somehow other than through liquor [viina]." I wanted a definition: "So, what is this burden that Finns carry?" He explained that it showed in things like the taciturn unwillingness to try new things involving any kind of sociality. He had often witnessed scenes at Red Cross training sessions in different parts of Finland where trainers had tried to introduce new ways of doing things, only to come up against an atmosphere of doubt and reluctance.[33] In one training session, in the far north of the country, new procedures for teamwork were being promoted to a resolutely silent audience—silent, that is, until a bear-like voice boomed from the back of the hall: "At these latitudes we don't do 'teamwork.'" The doctor concluded: "And that's just it, that the fear of teamwork is sort of a fear of *socialization* [sosialisoitumisen pelko]. . . . Yes, a certain lack of confidence [epävarmuus] leads people to prefer to be alone rather than working as part of a pack, if you can put it that way." This doctor's views on people not wanting to work on teams forms a point of contrast with most of my other interlocutors who spoke warmly about successful teamwork experiences—and were very upset by instances of poor teamwork, tense group dynamics, or mismanagement. These problems and sentiments also came up in my interviews with the psychologists who worked with Red Cross workers.

"Finns' lives are already burdened by an inborn self-discipline [itsekuri], a sense of inferiority, and a Lutheran work ethic," says a newspaper article about the absence of laughter in the Finnish novel. "Now it's even claimed that Finns don't know how to laugh happily—especially not Finnish prose writers." In the article, the writer Petri Tamminen is quoted as saying, "If the nation's strengths are a sense of responsibility, a sense of shame, and the hiding of feelings, well, that palette doesn't [leave a lot of room] for big, free, happy laughter" (Järvi 2007:C1). Of course the article was somewhat tongue-in-cheek (a characteristic tone when Finns speak of Finnishness). And this is just a single newspaper article, but it conveniently summarizes questions about Finnishness that came up continually in the course of this research. The "national character" (*kansan luonne*) was often referred to as, precisely, a "*burden,*" in the sense that the doctor above intended. It is not my purpose to argue here about whether there "really is" or "is not" a Finnish "national character" (the old anthropological "culture and personality" studies having done enough of that), but only to point out that people themselves *spoke* in those terms.[34] Everyone *assumed* the existence of a recognizable Finnishness (almost a "species-being"), and tended to characterize it in remarkably similar ways. While it was treated as a positive source of sensible thinking, honesty, hard work, grit (*sisu*), and certain very dry humor, it could also be a burden.[35] For some like Leila, it was quite heavy. But for most—whatever else it was—it was the compass and the site of safe return.

Conclusion

The motivation for humanitarian action is often thought to come, in the name of humanity, from a universalistic moral obligation to alleviate "distant suffering" (Haskell 1985; Boltanski 1993; see also the critiques by Fassin 2006, 2011; Barnett and Weiss 2008:19; Bornstein and Redfield 2010; Feldman and Ticktin 2010a, 2010b; among others). This chapter shows the need to help (*tarve auttaa*) emerging from a number of different sources, including the particularities of people's own subjectivities and subject positions, and their felt obligations to specific relationships defined by things like occupation, nationality, and an internationalist political imagination. Specifically, I found key sources of the aid workers' urge "to help" (*auttaa*) in two aspects of their locatedness. The first of these was the institutional and the social-structural, in other words, their membership in specific occupational and professional categories, and in the Red Cross as a national and international institution. Paradoxically, it was not principally out of an unqualified or universal "human" caring, but out of what Durkheim called a "moral particularism" that a humanitarian "calling" in fact became possible (a theme I return to in chapter 6). It was only out of a quite specific set of professional imperatives that an internationalist humanitarian imagination and practice were able to emerge in the form that they did (Malkki 1994, 1996).

The second source was a matter of geographical and cultural location: I want to help and *need* to help because I am from *here*. That is, I want to help as a specific ethical person, a Finn, a citizen of a rich country, a "citizen of the world," a member of the Global North—a person, consequently, with a very specific set of both obligations and desires vis-à-vis "the international" and "the world." I/we have international obligations and also a need for the world. It is out of being *someone, somewhere in particular*, that one ends up making greater ethical and imaginative connections. This is not a matter of saying, "We're all human" or "I act as a humanitarian: the particularities of my life are irrelevant." Nor is it so say, in a sacrificial spirit, "I am a humanitarian; my life does not matter." Actually existing ethical and political solidarities in this case did not emerge from setting aside the particularities of one's own location or its histories; quite the contrary, they came from intimately engaging with the responsibilities and vulnerabilities of that location (see Malkki 1998). Those vulnerabilities and needs were thoroughly "domestic" and at times almost embarrassingly personal. And they were constitutive of that relation to the imaginative figure, "the world out there," to which the aid workers aspired.

Finally, to look again at the Durkheimian tension between (or movement between) the general and the occupational, it might be productive to think of humanitarianism and professionalism, not (as Durkheim's terminology implies) as a relation between the universal and the particular but as two different modes of universalization—neither identical nor necessarily in contradiction. As Étienne Balibar suggests, "debates about the opposition of the universal and the particular, or *a fortiori* universalism and particularism, are far less interesting and determinant than debates opposing different conceptions of the universal, or different universalities" with their inevitable (if often disavowed) inclusions and exclusions (2007:2). For the Red Cross workers, different coexisting forms of universalism—driven not only by cosmopolitan loyalties to human personhood but equally by such things as professional ethics—came together to constitute not only a willingness, but often a need, to help.

2. Impossible Situations

Affective Impasses and Their Afterlives
in Humanitarian and Ethnographic Fieldwork

The dirty nurse, Experience.
—Alfred Tennyson, quoted in Susan Sontag, *Regarding the Pain of Others*

A nurse who worked for the Red Cross in the 1994 Rwanda genocide told me, "It's shocking. You know what's happening there, but you can't do anything. In other words, you hear the sounds of killing from behind the hill. And in the morning you go and see if anyone's alive. . . . You end up in these situations." The Red Cross medical and other aid workers I interviewed in Finland often faced what one person called "impossible situations" in their international aid work.[1] Such situations—affectively and ethically impossible somehow, impasses from which there is no obviously good way forward— can also arise in anthropological research and cast long shadows. Like anthropologists, aid workers are sometimes left feeling ambivalent, inadequate, and even impure about the work that they have done, despite their best efforts to fulfill the standards of their profession and their personal ethical commitments.[2]

These situations are yet another reminder that the conventional, widely popularized humanitarian position of moral high ground and mastery can actually be a fiction on many levels. Likewise, it may be true in some measure that people do this work because "it makes them feel good," but they also confront the common condition, in the aftermath of humanitarian work, of not feeling good at all. While even difficult aid missions may be personally very rewarding as a challenge met, they are often *also* experienced as psychically troubling, leaving feelings of guilt and regret in their wake. People may chase "a desire to be challenged but not undone" (Povinelli 2002:98).

No amount of good equipment or high-functioning teamwork was enough to quell the nagging sense among some of the people I worked with that theirs was in many ways a position of inadequacy and even, somehow, a dirty position, in the end. It is ironic that it was *experience*—the very experience they sought as professionals, and as human beings—that made them feel much less, not more, sure of the value of what they were doing. In a doctor's words: "The very accumulation of experience can cause a breakdown . . . So, in a way, the more professional you become, the more vulnerable you become. [There is m]uch variation in how people deal with it though."[3] Like these aid workers, anthropologists may also have a sense of affective and ethical insufficiency—of not having been or done enough—and a sense of guilt and dirtiness, in the aftermath of fieldwork. I certainly did.

In the first part of this chapter, I focus on the aid workers' accounts of their work in the field and its effects on them. After a brief introduction on the management of affect, I discuss impossible situations that come up in Red Cross work by using the accounts of three nurses as a general frame. These allow me to characterize recurrent themes in my research with them. In the second part of the chapter, I examine the impossible situations in my own early ethnographic research experience in Tanzania, and their personal and professional afterlives. In the third, I trace some of the connections between the Red Cross aid workers' fieldwork and mine by examining, through the specific cases, how affects may both produce and be formed by the impossible situation.

On the Management of Affect

Ordinary affects are the varied, surging capacities to affect and be affected that give everyday life the quality of a continual motion of relations, scenes, contingencies, and emergences.
—Kathleen Stewart, *Ordinary Affects*

The relations, scenes, and contingencies of the everyday that the aid workers experienced in their international fieldwork—in warzones, refugee camps, and other sites of humanitarian intervention—occurred in social contexts that were simultaneously ordinary and extraordinary.[4] On the one hand, there were routines in matters like medical procedure and the care of patients (and no matter the context, people still need help with chronic conditions, obstetrics and gynecology, and other things); on the other, there were jarring, often tragic, sometimes frightening, interruptions of those routines.[5] Analogously, their work produced both "ordinary affects" and what Hannah Appel, in engagement with Kathleen Stewart (2007), has called "extraordinary affects."[6] The ordinary and the extraordinary frequently seemed irreconcilable with each other, producing the kinds of impossible situations that the aid workers found hard to deal with in the moment and to get past in the aftermath. The irreconcilable and the impossible were, in effect, an inescapable part of their aid work (and, as I will show, my ethnographic work).

William Mazzarella has thoughtfully pointed out that it is productive to think about "the ritual and/or professional coordination of affect—what one might call 'affect management'—[as] a central principle of social life and institutional survival" (2009:298).[7] The need for affect management was well understood in the Red Cross. For the aid workers, maintaining a balance between humane professionalism and "affective neutrality," on the one hand, and less manageable and even institutionally dangerous affects, on the other, was simultaneously a regulating ideal and a constant struggle.[8]

Affect, in the sense used here, is not synonymous with emotion—if by emotion we mean recognizable, familiar, named states of mind like anger, fear, excitement, joy, et cetera. In this sense one can usefully think of affect as a less easily categorized, potentially more disruptive presence in a social world. Christina Schwenkel uses the term "to identify not individualized emotions and autonomous states of feeling, but the manifold passions that, Spinoza once argued, manifest intersubjectively and collectively through embodied actions and alliances" (2013:252).[9]

Acknowledging the usefulness of such a distinction, however, should not lead one into the romantic, "vitalist" position (sometimes taken by Brian Massumi [2002], for example) that affect is somehow immediate, or outside or beyond the social and the semiotic, a view effectively critiqued by Mazzarella (2009).[10] Taking his cue from Elias Canetti ([1960] 1984) and Émile Durkheim ([1912] 1995), among others, Mazzarella argues that affect is not "so much a radical site of otherness to be policed or preserved but rather a necessary moment of any institutional practice with aspirations to public efficacy. . . . In other words, mediation is the social condition of the fantasy of immediation, of a social essence (vital and/or cultural) that is autonomous of and prior to social processes of mediation" (2009:298, 303).

Aversion to "useless pity" and flashy emotions was not just an institutional expectation; it was also a base-line sensibility that the aid workers shared across the board, and this acted as a form of psychic protection (Le Carré 2003:10). It was also expected that, ideally, training and experience would protect people from two forms of excess: compassion fatigue and secondary traumatization, on the one hand, and indifference and emotional coldness, on the other. The psychologists who counseled the aid workers recognized the importance and difficulty of that balance.[11] Most of the psychologists' work takes place in Finland; they do not typically accompany aid workers on international missions. Psychologists in Geneva are also available to the aid workers. While I have interviewed psychologists on Finnish Red Cross reserve lists and make brief reference to those conversations here, it bears emphasizing that I have not done systematic research on psychological therapy; that would far exceed the scope of this book.

"[You have to] try to balance distance and proximity," said Leif, a doctor with long experience in the Red Cross. "That's the crucial nerve in all these situations. . . . You must allow yourself distance. A responsibility for the team leader is to create that distance. Otherwise, they [the aid workers] kill themselves with too much identification with patients." Talking about that elusive working balance, a psychologist emphasized that psychic flexibility and a readiness to improvise were crucial in stressful, unpredictable, and dangerous situations. She added that it was helpful and productive to have a variety of different temperaments and capabilities on a team in the field. "If a person is totally without feelings, s/he may not be able to recognize dangers [early enough] or to evaluate situations [astutely]. . . . This is some kind of urban legend or illusion—that the so-called sensible people [järkevät ihmiset] don't emote [eivät tunteile] and that is why they are sensible." In other words, good teams needed their canaries in the mines.

It was widely agreed that there were circumstances in which working methodically while suspending one's own emotional reactions was useful and necessary—a protective use of "affect management." A psychologist articulated what many mentioned: in catastrophes like the 1994 Rwanda genocide and its awful aftermath, the surgeon just "operates and operates and operates" without having to think about the individuality or political allegiance of the patient on the table. The pliant anonymity of the body facilitated disciplined adherence to procedure among the nurses too. In many ways, this is a sensible and ethically defensible reaction to the horror of a situation that is overwhelming in its scale, duration, and complexity. One response is to say, "We'll help as many people as we can." And, of course: "It will not be enough—in any way." A nurse said, "You can't stop to think, you just have to help"; she repeated it often: "You can't stop to think, not about the fact that you are in mortal danger, nor how little one person can do."[12]

But the suspension of affect, these professionals insisted, can go too far. Referring to a team working in the aftermath of a devastating natural disaster, a psychologist described how doctors, mostly men, but some women too, began to behave under great stress: "There was competition as to who could stay awake the longest . . . The doctors could be in a real *hurmiotila* [a trance or a state of ecstasy] in very intensive work situations. [One can] develop a *himo* [a lust, a craving] for these extreme conditions." Susan Sontag has written in *Regarding the Pain of Others* (2003) about the "perennial seductiveness of war." Clearly aid work can have a similarly seductive pull, and in that it resembles the work of journalists, photographers, soldiers, and even anthropologists.[13]

Some doctors in particular found it hard to accept any emotional help. The psychologists knew all too well that their presence in crisis situations was sometimes regarded as unnecessary and even "totally useless" (cf. Fassin and Rechtman 2009). "It's a kind of taboo: that helpers should be helped." It gets manifested in a "total denial: 'There's nothing wrong with us' . . . and in behaving like some *Ubermensch*. . . . I'll tell a surgeon, 'Look you've been awake and on duty for five days in these extreme conditions.' . . . That kind of total denial certainly isn't normal!" Five days without sleep, a psychologist explained, could result in hallucinations and even psychosis. This behavior was considered very problematic by the psychologists but was not spontaneously flagged by any of the doctors or nurses I interviewed.

A case anyone would consider ethically problematic emotional coldness, I was told, was that exemplified by an ambitious surgeon who reportedly went on an international Red Cross mission "solely" to get an intensive amount of war surgery under his belt as this would help him to advance in his specialized medical job in Finland. His conduct was regarded as unseemly careerism. At the other end were the times when it was impossible to suspend emotions.

Breaches in the management of affect were a frequent theme in the psychologists' work with the Red Cross people. These might happen in a range of situations, including things like teamwork going wrong on a mission (see chapter 1, note 30). But often, the psychologists explained, "it is when something *happens*, that's to say, when there is some sort of 'critical incident.'" Years after six members of their multinational Red Cross team were murdered in their beds in Novye Atagi, Chechnya, several aid workers still talked intently about this "critical incident" in interviews. The assassins had been a "group of masked men using weapons fitted with silencers" (Bierens de Haan 1997:1; Bugnion 1997). The Finnish personnel lost good friends and colleagues that night. "At other times," continued the psychologist, "the 'critical incidents' have been situations where one's life has been in danger, but nothing has actually happened. There has just been a *humiliation*." The psychologist had in mind situations where an aid worker might have lost a teammate, been taken hostage, or feared for her own life when threatened by gangs of armed men. Nonetheless my exchange with this psychologist was a bit puzzling. It seems to me that something *has* happened when a humiliation has occurred. And as Salli Saari, another psychologist in the Finnish Red Cross reserves (and a public figure), points out, "We don't just react to what really happened, but also to a mental image of what *could* have happened" (S. Saari 2000:33, emphasis added). *A problem of the imagination arises.* This was also a problem I encountered in my fieldwork, as I will show.

The aid workers carried, all of them, memories of events and relationships that had breached what Leif termed their "emotional neutrality."[14] In a conversation that became a touchstone in conceptualizing this chapter, Leif said, "Impartiality of course involves emotions just as does its opposite, partiality . . . It's all one—the emotional and the technical." There was no judgment or blame when he said, "Some people never return to the Red Cross [after their first mission]; the 'critical situations' are too much for them. For other kinds of persons, they rejoice in the inner growth that they experience in their Red Cross work."[15]

In a conversation about ethics and affect Leif thoughtfully said: "*Everyone* makes mistakes. How do you cope with mistakes? This . . . comes up in both formal and informal discussions [at Red Cross debriefings, reunions, and other occasions]. You need *courage* to admit mistakes; this is important. . . . About mistakes of omission and commission: you need to be forgiven. *It comes to that.* We're not good enough on that [in the Red Cross]." I asked him what the greatest psychic challenge for aid workers like him was. He didn't have to think about it: "The feeling of insufficiency. The feeling of insufficiency at different levels—technically knowing what is to be done, but not having the resources. This is one of the hardest things." Another doctor pointed out: "You can face impossible situations in Finland, too, while you're working. That's unavoidable—that you want to do something *more* than you can do. . . . And it's a very personal experience."

Many of the aid workers identified "technical insufficiency" as a painful and frustrating problem; shortages of blood and equipment were just two examples. Food and water provision on a massive scale were often also a very stressful problem for many specialists. One nurse, I was told, saw "lots of kids die of malnutrition" on one single mission; that is how she arrived at her personal "limit experience" (cf. Foucault 1991, 2000:241).[16] Leif was also talking about a deep, disturbing sense of affective and ethical insufficiency in situations where there was no "right balance" and no self-evidently "right way" forward—where there was an impasse.[17]

Heart Monologues

Sometimes these situations involved almost unbearable ethical choices that one was forced to make in the triage and care of patients. It was especially hard for the medical aid workers to deal with these situations when the patients were babies and children (see chapter 3). Some types of injury and treatment were also especially difficult. Burn wounds were among the worst because their care was unavoidably very painful. The difficulty was redoubled when compassion, and the purpose of procedures, was hard to communicate with looks and gestures across language barriers, even with the help of interpreters. "The significance of non-verbal communication through 'tone of voice, expressions, gestures, look, and touching,' [also] differed in meaning from one cultural context to another," as a nurse observed (Riikonen 1994:55). Many aid workers mentioned steep learning curves about such difference.

Nursing work in the field was full of difficult choices. Very often they involved not only the patient but the entire family. "The duty of the nurse was to help in the decision-making process. A difficult choice might be a limb amputation or another necessary [but] permanently debilitating operation. One of the kin, a father or husband [typically], decided whether a procedure was performed or not. To support his decision, he needed information and discussion, [a moment] where the role of the interpreter was significant" (Riikonen 1994:40–41). Sometimes parental deliberations were so lengthy that they were hard to watch; children's snakebites were time-sensitive situations often resulting in amputations. A week of negotiations might pass between the family and the medical staff before a decision could finally be made—but by that time a part of the child's leg or arm might already be gangrenous.[18]

The aid workers' memories of these situations spilled out in great "heart monologues" in a close interplay of ethics and affect (Malkki 2008). (The length, form, and intensity of these stories reminded me of the nature of the interviews I had done years earlier with Hutu refugees in Tanzania.) As various as their accounts were in substantive detail, they had in common a searching, self-critical stance—a mood of uncertainty and, sometimes, inadequacy. My interviews with them about extreme and impossible situations were typically many hours long, conceptually complex, very productive, and at times almost hypnotic. They were also emotionally draining. Here is a fragment of one woman's account (the first of three longer case stories).

Maija's Story

Maija, a multiply specialized nurse active in both domestic and international Red Cross work, was troubled by cases in which she had been powerless to help "save" people, especially children. She dwelt on a situation that had confronted her on her very first Red Cross mission, to Kosovo:

> It was quite difficult. I had such situations that—that—"how am I going to come through this?" There were such terribly irreconcilable . . . that—first of all, twins were born, to one lady, and they were both in really poor shape when they were born, and at the hospital, there was this children's intensive care unit. . . . So the twins were taken there. And at the same time, one other lady had just had a new child—it was her first child—and there were only two sets of resuscitation equipment [elvytys-laitteet]. There were only two ventilators [happikoneet]. And now a choice had to be made: which of these will be resuscitated, of these three? All of them had to be resuscitated. But there were not enough ventilators [happisekottimet] for everyone. What is going to be done here? . . . I didn't have to decide because the pediatrician—a local pediatrician—made the choice. Luckily. But in my own mind I was battling, "Why?! Why was it like this, that that one had to die?"

> LM: Did s/he die?
> Maija: S/he died! And we just monitored there, as it was dying [teki kuole-maa]. There was nothing to be done . . .

LM: How horrible! So one of the twins? [I had made my own impossible ethical calculations.]

M: One of the twins. Because two children were born to that lady. So she had to have one child left alive. And then, the other one was this other [woman's] first child, so it had to live . . . And since they were all—their condition was equally poor . . . So there come these terrible conflicts [ristiriita], that these kinds of choices have to be made.

While Maija was relieved that she had not had to make the doctor's critical decision, her part in the scene deeply troubled her. The situation had been impossible for everyone—patients, doctor, and nurse. They had been forced to face their own technical insufficiency, and to tolerate an intolerable outcome (Bierens de Haan 1997:4). They had been forced, in effect, to abandon one child's life to save two others'.

Horrible as the situation was, it was relatively brief. It did not involve a protracted process in which many different choices presented themselves along the way, each of which might change the course of subsequent choices yet to be made. It did not involve choices that snuck up on one, without ever even emerging as discrete choices. And it did not involve richly layered, dynamic social relationships between patients and medical workers unfolding over many weeks or months. The case to follow is temporally and socially more complex. But it is similar in the sense that it also involved a nurse's own searing guilt and grief over "abandoning" a child to her fate, about not "saving" her.

Elina's Story

Elina, another very experienced nurse, told me about her numerous international missions as well as her domestic projects on a white summer night in Finland. Her account of her work with refugees—extracted here from a much longer account—gives particularly clear form to the ethical and affective challenges that caring for children brought up for many aid workers. I will call it the story of "Mariama and the strays."[19]

"This little girl—I had a little girl who was even from a perfectly smart [fiksu] family that [consisted of two older brothers]." The boys spoke the language of the asylum country and English. They worked with the Red Cross as interpreters. "So I was walking around there, in the camp, and passed [the boys'] tent and I peeked inside—once I knew that they lived there—I don't know why I did that . . . [Elina blushed]. I found a small girl there—who was totally famished and rashy and she had no hair growing at all and she was—," Elina said, breathing in sharply, "in really very bad shape, and when I felt her, there was a terribly high fever." She could not at first believe that the child was the boys' little sister. "And I was like, 'To the hospital!' and I carried her there in my arms. And I was like, 'How can you have your little sister completely . . . at . . . death's door?'" The boys were very embarrassed, but refused to explain. The children's mother had died and their father was unaccounted for. They were in the care of an aged woman relative. Elina said that for some reason the old woman "did not like this little girl . . . [and thought] that the girl was 'possessed by evil spirits' [pahojen henkien riivaama] somehow.[20] And . . . well, no one else cared about her, either." Eventually she was nursed back to health and got nutritious food at the camp's feeding center and—Elina smiled—"she was in such good shape. . . . She was an eight-year-old, after all, so she managed all by herself, of course, and . . . she began to talk and smile and her hair started growing and she started to get better and she even had the energy to do some jobs there at home and everything, and everyone was terribly pleased. . . . And then one day she disappeared from the feeding center . . . and again I then"—Elina, worried, went once more to look into the tent—"and again she sat there, again feverish, sick, and enormous, infected incision wounds [viiltohaavat] on her arms. . . . Evil spirits had been driven from her and the gashes had been made on her so that the evil spirits could come out that way—somehow." Once again she was nursed back to health. Elina bought her some clothes, and found that people jokingly started calling her Mariama's—the girl's—mother, MaMariama.[21] Mariama was in good shape but, then, shortly before Elina was due to leave this mission, she disappeared once more. Elina, very uneasy now, said, "I thought to myself, 'Where is she?' and . . . then once I bumped into her there. . . . One of her eyes was blind. They said, the boys, that, 'Umm, yeah, she ran into some branch there in the forest.' But then I heard that that old granny was there again, in the home. And she had again chased out the riivaaja [evil spirit, demon, bibl. devil] and punctured her eye" (cf. Comaroff and Comaroff 1999; De Boeck 2004:157, 162).

Here Elina fell into a long, absent silence, then made a visible effort to refocus her attention. "Of course in these kinds of [situations], you always bruise—so, I too thought, 'Damn, if only I'd had some way of saving the girl from there!'"[22] Her smile was pained and I wanted to say something comforting, but she continued. "But these are the kinds of things that can awaken in an aid worker, a thing that . . . that . . . 'At least *one* child' . . . or something like that. . . . It's somehow just the same kind of thing as Save at least the Chil—, Save the Dogs dot org. So that working someplace like Kosovo, everyone [the expatriate aid workers] was all worked up about those stray dogs." Elina went on in a bitter singsong: "Because there were 'just *so many* of them' and 'isn't it *dreadful* how the Kosovars just *shoot* them?!' and . . . umm. . . . There was an awful tongue-wagging [about the dogs] and all the while the local residents were saying that, 'We have so many sorrows besides these stray dogs; we have to first get other things in order and then we can begin to take care of the dogs, too.' . . . Of course they were a sort of problem, the dogs, but still." Embarrassed, Elina explained:

> It is awakened really easily, something like this terrible need to save stray dogs or then to save some single child when you [really] *see* her—and I think that's quite okay. And I still feel very bad that the girl stayed there—that I didn't do my *utmost* so that I could have—that I didn't really seriously start searching out possibilities for how I could've brought her to Finland. . . . But *then* what? What would that child's life have been *then*? . . . There emerge these bad feelings in these strange things that can't be processed somehow—like, *"How should I have acted?"*[23]

Elina—a longtime "veteran" of Red Cross work and a warm-hearted, thoughtful person—did not profess any ethical or moral certainties in the course of her account. Her doubts readily slipped into self-blame as she contemplated the impossible situations in which she had played a part. She had had to watch the systematic deterioration of a child's quality of life, her systematic hurting, just as Maija had had to monitor another child's death. Elina belittled her own urge to adopt Mariama by likening it to expatriates' urges to adopt stray dogs in Kosovo.[24] In chapter 4, I show how humanitarian fundraising campaigns frequently invite people to imagine, make, give, or "adopt" dolls, "bunnies," "teddies," and other object-beings, using culturally widespread relations of analogy between children and animals. In chapter 3, I trace some of the historically situated affects and logics that frequently locate the child as a vital moral figure in conceptualizations of "suffering" and "humanity."

After telling me about Mariama and the strays, Elina went on to describe other fraught situations in her work in two wars. In one of them, in the early 1990s, she and her colleagues had gotten trapped but were eventually successfully evacuated by the Red Cross. After this "critical incident" she decided that she did not want to be posted to warzones anymore. "Somehow it was a rather terrifying experience. I mean that once you left there, you began to think about everything that *could* have happened. . . . Actually, you can't even *think* about that *there.* . . . It was a huge relief to get out of there."

Contrary to what one might assume, it was not the experiences in the refugee camp or even in the two warzones that were the most troubling experiences; it was what she encountered on her return to a Finland in deep recession in 1992. Her regular job had disappeared. "Then I realized that being there in the middle of the war and having a colleague die and another one sustain difficult burns in a mine explosion and all these things that happened, *sad* things; *that* was not the crisis . . . but rather that, that . . . that safe return that wasn't." She had surprised herself by being so undone by this problem at home. It was all too easy to belittle that, to make it a mere detail. Elina was ashamed to even mention it.

When I asked her colleague, Maija, whether she had received counseling after the difficult Kosovo mission, she said no: "These kinds of [problems] were pretty well taken care of *there* [in the field] with colleagues." But, like Elina, she had later used the opportunity to talk with a Red Cross psychologist, and also expressed some embarrassment that she had sought counseling in the wake of her work in Kosovo because, as she saw it, she had not been under "any *terrible* stress" there. An understated and quiet person, Maija was clearly not trying to assume a "battle-hardened" stance. So why had she not been under "terrible stress"? Was it because the Solomon's choice facing the pediatrician was a more difficult situation than hers? Was it because of the violence and dying going on around her? Was it because her own life had not been directly threatened? She, like many of her Red Cross colleagues, seemed to have in mind a tacit scale of calamity and distress; her situation was therefore—in comparison with the truly unfortunate—not the "terrible" one, and modesty prevented her from making much of her own difficult experiences. She was "the mere." I saw the operation of this same scalarity in most of the interviews I did.

Kaisa's Story

There were other scenes with a similarly troubled mood. On the outskirts of Helsinki, in one of a legion of modernist apartment buildings that rose after the wars, a consummate Red Cross professional sat balled up on her sofa with a bottle of wine. Kaisa was a dependably steady, feminist Red Cross reservist, a nurse like many I had interviewed. Very successful in her hospital job in Finland, and very skilled, she had experienced the cruelest of political conflicts and disasters abroad. She was the most impressive of Dirty Nurses, "a jewel in the crown of Finnish international aid work."[25] She had received her own diagnosis: breast cancer. She was overcome. Eventually she reached oblivion on the sofa. She told me about this as we sat in a busy Helsinki restaurant; I had trouble hearing her. It was embarrassing to her to talk about her cancer in a conversation about great violence and suffering. The problem was merely personal. For her (as for Maija and Elina), calamities like war and genocide (especially the Rwanda genocide) stood—at least for a time—as a moral yardstick for her own, personal disaster that failed, somehow, to measure up in comparison. One thing was "out of all proportion" to the other—and how could it have been otherwise?[26]

On Rwanda

Many of the people I interviewed for this study had been on Red Cross missions to Rwanda and Congo in 1994–95. Their accounts of those missions invariably included warm recollections of the amazing camaraderie on their teams there. They did think that they had done useful work there. But they also talked about struggles with profound feelings of insufficiency, and ethical and social uncertainty. Importantly, many discussed their own acute awareness of how little they knew about the sociopolitical complexities of the Great Lakes region. They emphasized that, although their understanding grew over the course of their work there, they initially knew very little about what was going on around them. There had not been time to prepare. For some, the decision about going to Rwanda had had to be made within forty-eight hours. People described their feverish efforts to get a sense of what was going on. "It's terrible when you don't even know the political situation there. . . . We didn't know anything about anything!" exclaimed one person who had been on an early team. "Or we knew that this horrible killing had started and that Hutu are killing Tutsi—with these knives, jungle knives, the killings had begun." Everyone had a sense of how faltering was their initial understanding of the social and historical contexts of the genocide, and of the hundreds of thousands of people around them—even with the Red Cross briefings when these were possible. This was, of course, the predicament that most, if not all, international aid organizations there shared. And this was true of almost any international mission: any more nuanced, profound understanding of the cultural and political contexts of emergency relief is constrained by the typically very "short time allowed for preparation, the limited contract," possible language barriers, very "rapid changes in situations, and difficult conditions" (Riikonen 2005:vi).

Missions during and right after the 1994 Rwanda genocide were among the most disturbing for those I worked with in Finland. They remembered having been overwhelmed and disoriented by the scale and brutality of the situation, in Rwanda and in Goma, Congo. They had felt unequal to it in every way, small and insignificant. Of Goma, one nurse said:

> 1.2 million people in that city. It was so full of people . . . that there was a claustrophobic feeling, like "What can we do here?!" There was nothing. And then you stood there on the rock with your little emergency kit—medications, bandages, and other little things—and there was no water so that people just fell—they fell dead on the ground, there around you . . . Just because there was no water. It felt then that "this cannot be possible." . . . But soon you began to think that, "Okay, I'll do what I can." When we went into the ICRC hospital, bodies had been stacked one on top of the other. Hundreds of dead people and since you didn't know who was alive and who dead, everyone had to be checked. And when we went to the [refugee] camp, when it was established, all the roadsides were full of dead people, wrapped in carpets—there.

The nurse's belittling, self-deprecating recollection—"And then you stood there on the rock with your little emergency kit"—was a sharp reminder of the impossible scale of the catastrophe.[27]

But it quickly became apparent that the situation was not just an undifferentiated chaos, not simply a "zone of exception" (cf. Agamben 2005; Fassin 2005). Procedures were put in place. But other kinds of patterns began to emerge; this in itself was chilling to people. One nurse remembered how many children there had been in relation to adults. "There were children everywhere." Tragically, that was a pattern. An oncology nurse, Annika, saw patterns in the types of trauma she treated, and was still troubled by this two years after the mission. "Pretty often feet had been hurt so that one couldn't walk, or then hands [had been cut off]. Children had been beaten with sticks and their femurs had snapped because, after all, they were still little so that it wasn't necessary to hit very hard. So foot [and leg] wounds were very numerous and faces had been slashed [with machetes]. I had a feeling that the goal was not to kill but to wound, so that in a way people were made helpless [toimintakyvytön]. I don't know if that was the case." Annika was vividly aware of having worked in horrifying conditions that she did not understand. Her mission in Rwanda had also been relatively brief. In some sense, the situation seems to have produced in her a need *not* to know, *not* to understand (cf. Garcia 2010a:179). As with the doctor who just "operated and operated and operated" without knowing his patient beyond his physical body, Annika's not-knowing was not a lack or absence but rather a certain kind of necessary affective strategy—a curbing of her memory and affective imagination. Our discussion about Rwanda (and Burundi) was brief and painful; I could see that she would not want to be interviewed further.

In a very long interview one evening, Kaisa, the nurse mentioned earlier, said: "I've sometimes thought about how people there [in Rwanda] experience death. Or it came up there. . . . We had an intensive care ward there and there was a *huge* number of patients." As Kaisa and a Dutch nurse made their evening rounds through the ward, they ran into a Rwandan nurse who was on night duty and simultaneously caring for her own sick child. She couldn't leave the child at home, and had put her in a small side area to rest. "We saw that the child was very sick. . . . It couldn't be examined. It was horrible, that situation. We had to take care of everyone—in other words those who had been in the war. But we saw that [she] was really phlegmatic." They gave her the attention they could. They continued their work. Later that evening, they again saw their Rwandan colleague: "She came and we saw that she was carrying the child and we guessed that she had died. Then she just said that—she had wrapped her in a blanket and ummm . . . I don't remember whether she was crying, but she was of course terribly sad and she said, 'Elle est morte' [She is dead]. I remember that . . . it was *so shocking*, and I couldn't just go and *ask*. . . . It was such a personal thing—and somehow I didn't know what I could say to her—neither of us knew.[28] We were probably a little shocked, too. We just tried, in some way, to express sympathy [myötätunto], or then maybe we didn't say anything—I don't remember that, either—but the nurse took the child somewhere, and came back and finished her work on that ward. That I remember. It was somehow unbelievable." She described other Rwandan colleagues and volunteers who had lost a child or family member and still returned to work. Referring to the nurse they had wanted to comfort, Kaisa said, "Then I thought about it: was it because their culture is different? Or was it because there was a war situation? . . . We probably acted quite differently too. But I don't believe that any Finnish woman—or a western woman—if her child dies, would go back to work.

Or then she was in such shock—or maybe it wasn't that either. I think it was somehow connected to that culture, to the way of reacting" (cf. Fassin and Rechtman 2009:186). I suggested that it could have been in part that keeping her job at the hospital was vital to her survival and possibly that of the rest of her family. Kaisa nodded, "Yes, it could have been that too." She was not at all confident about her own interpretations of the situation.

Empathy, embarrassment, and incomprehension—and a palpable awareness of that incomprehension—were all present in Kaisa's account. In a strange dream-like way it seemed that, as in Annika's case above, the not-knowing and not-understanding had protected her both affectively and socially. Perhaps not-knowing made possible at least an effort at "affective neutrality."[29] Thus, not-knowing may have enabled Kaisa as a professional to do the work she was trained for. It is also striking that—even in the face of her own lack of understanding of the Rwandan Red Cross nurse's emotions and decisions—she felt respect for her as a fellow professional, for returning to work on the ward. To feel *that* seems "out of proportion" and "out of order" in the face of the tragedy of the nurse's loss. But then again, to be so focused on *that* nurse is out of proportion to the cataclysmic scale of the genocide and the human tragedy everywhere. These situations produce scalar impossibilities (cf. Tsing 2005:57).

And what would a right balance between distance and proximity have looked like in Rwanda? What would the proper management of affect and the imagination have looked like? Affective neutrality? The interviews all documented feelings of insufficiency and doubt, and often embarrassment. People felt they had not done "enough" or felt what they ought to have felt. Yet many said that Rwanda had been a rewarding mission, as surprising as that might seem. They knew they had tried to do their work there as well as possible, and they had formed intense social relationships. The afterlives of these impossible situations were observable in all my interviews with them.

Ethnographic Fieldwork

> Yes, one has many thoughts, many. One has thoughts, thoughts, troubles during the night.
> —Rose-Felicité in Mishamo

The interviews with Red Cross workers in Finland enabled me to think more clearly about the extreme and impossible situations in my own early professional life. I now examine the fieldwork I did with Hutu refugees from Burundi, survivors of the 1972 genocide, who were given asylum in rural western Tanzania. I worked with them for one year in 1985–86, dividing my time between the Mishamo refugee camp in Rukwa Region and the spontaneously settling refugees in Kigoma Township on Lake Tanganyika. This work resulted, as I mentioned earlier, in the 1995 ethnographic monograph *Purity and Exile: Violence, Memory, and National Cosmology among Hutu Refugees in Tanzania.* Having completed that work, I moved away from researching genocide, violence, memory, and history, as well as from my regional focus on East and Central Africa. I cannot therefore claim any specialized knowledge of the excellent newer research on this region or set of topics.

Despite important friendships with people from both periods of fieldwork, I am also aware, of course, of significant differences between the aid workers and me, on the one hand, and between the refugees and me, on the other. I did not directly experience or witness the genocidal violence that the refugees had survived; neither did I participate in the often dangerous international missions that were "the field" for the Red Cross. Some of the first people in Rwanda were working there even as the killing began. I worked at a clear remove from physical violence and danger. My analytical focus in each case was on the ways in which people remembered and narratively formed their histories and experiences. In some respects, however, my social positioning as a Finnish ethnographer resembled that of the Finnish aid worker, and my field experience produced related forms of affect, and impasse.[30]

Early in my fieldwork with the Hutu refugees in Mishamo, I wrote a dramatic letter to a friend in the United States: "I have learned a dozen new ways to kill slowly. It would make you sick. It made me cry when I was still not used to it."[31] I see the edge of bravado and even melodrama in what I wrote then. But the letter is useful because it conveys something I came to understand better after fieldwork and while writing: some kinds of violence and representations of violence can involve a quite active learning process. Violence does not just teach ethical or cosmological lessons—life is inexpressibly precious—or reveal in a general way what magnitudes of cruelty and suffering can exist in the world. One's relationship to it can also involve a more technical kind of learning. It teaches specific new ways of seeing and doing things. For a long time after fieldwork, I had a quasi-specialist's reaction to hearing about forms of torture, violence, and terror. Often, as I was writing the dissertation, I found myself collecting and organizing evidence with an emotional flatness that I found (and still find) very troubling. Media reports failed to elicit in me decent, humane reactions like shock, indignation, or revulsion. In reading, post-fieldwork, about violent practices in, say, Pinochet's Chile or apartheid South Africa, I caught myself thinking: "That was unimaginative." "They could've done it this way." Technical knowledge preceded ethical humane emotion. The shock, when it came, was more about my own ghoulish reactions—or the ugly absence of emotion—than it was about what I had seen or read in the media. I watched myself in the process of becoming a "specialist."[32] It was as if I were Gregor Samsa in Franz Kafka's *Metamorphosis*: I imagined myself turning into an insect disgusting to those who saw it. Easy to kill. But I was also turning into an insect disgusting to myself because of my growing knowledge about cruelty and killing.[33]

The violence was everywhere in my field notes. I recorded discrete lists of techniques. Material of this kind was often related to me in the form of lists, and it was important to me to accurately record everything I could.[34]

Most were titled "methods of killing." Others were classified as "torture techniques," "dignified death (by bullet)," "methods of killing students" (cf. Christopher Taylor 2001:29–31), and others. It was important to me to accurately record everything I could.[35] There was a range of variation but also a good deal of redundancy in people's narratives about violence. Examining the notes in detail and considering ways of writing about them was a further process of specialization. Deciding what to include and what not to reveal was a continual ethical and affective uncertainty about the "need to know" and the ethical uses of evidence. I worked with the notes again in the aftermath of the 1994 Rwanda genocide. The specialist in me has been a hateful familiar for many years; it persists as a reminder of very human (and inhumane) capacities for learning—and of the great difficulty of unlearning and forgetting (cf. Deleuze [1962] 1983; Nietzsche 1966; Blanchot 1993; Garcia 2010a:20, 2010b).

About the imagination: If violence may be said to be pedagogical and to produce practical knowledge about how to hurt and kill people, violence (and narrative accounts of it) likewise produces a sense of "knowing" what it would be to be hurt. The violence produces the involuntary affective imagination of what it might be like to be the object of sadistic revulsion, to be made to witness another person's terror, or to be tormented to death (*pace* Sartre [1940] 2004). In the aftermath of this research, I have come to think that violence cultivates and vivifies imaginative capacities in specific ways, expanding and amplifying one's capacity to perceive with fewer filters what is possible in the world. Experientially, it produces points of imaginative communion.[36]

Hearing the accounts of violence for the first time in Tanzania was challenging—and different from the post-fieldwork writing and research processes of specialization I described above. In that first fieldwork, when I lived in Tanzania, I listened very intently, and was often disoriented and numbed by a feeling of unreality, especially in the camp. My mind alternated between seeing everything as somehow flat yet fantastical, unimportant because unreal, to almost being the sweating skin about to be split open by the blade of a sharpened knife. These points of involuntary communion had an agitating, distracting specificity to them. The shock is that one becomes able to imagine oneself both as the victim of violence and as its perpetrator, the object of sadism and the subject, the sadist. This is a terrible thing. It is something for which I have vaguely sought to make amends, out of motives that perhaps share something with those of the Red Cross workers.

Despite all this, however, my two field sites, Mishamo and Kigoma, were on the whole benign environments for me. I was generally very well received by a wide range of Hutu interlocutors and tolerated (and sometimes assisted) by the Tanzanian state officials who ran the camp. What, then, made them (and especially the camp) such extreme and impossible situations? I can only say that the excruciating detail in people's accounts of sadistic techniques of torture and killing was the ever-present experiential danger. It produced, in J. M. Coetzee's words, an "imaginative horror" (2001:65).[37]

The few expatriate aid workers left in the camp (after the handover of the camp from two aid agencies to the Tanzanian Ministry of Home Affairs) and the more numerous expatriates in Kigoma Township generally sought professional disengagement from the thoughts and views of the refugees. As they observed my activities and the company I kept, some warned me not to imagine things. In the words of one perennially confident aid worker: "You shouldn't believe everything you hear. Most of what people talk about these political things are just stories, not reality. Or maybe here and there are crumbs of reality." I often heard that "refugees exaggerate" and that "they always have their old stories" (cf. Malkki 1996). But my professional obligation was precisely to listen, not to ignore or dismiss. My aim was to take seriously what people said, and to see patterns and make connections. It was also, to the extent possible, to imaginatively enter their histories and circumstances.

Yet at the same time I myself worried about "just imagining things"—

imagining danger where there was nothing to worry about.[38] There were often intimations of something threatening without any particular threat, and this made me jumpy.[39] "Be careful," I was told by the refugees, of "spies," "informers," and "cowards." (In the very beginning of the fieldwork, the refugees had been concerned that I might be a spy for the government of Burundi.) I was cautioned, "Mr. ⸺ wants to meet you so we should go there, to his home. He can't be trusted; he's always like that, smiling, friendly, but don't trust him." I was hemmed in by all kinds of warnings. It remains unresolved in my mind whether the caution was necessary on all the fronts on which I, the refugees, and the camp administrators exercised it.

There were two factors that aggravated my worry about things being "merely" in my imagination. One was the isolation of the camp. At that time, communications were very limited: there was no post office and no telephone (let alone Internet) connection, and no regular through traffic of any kind. No buses or trains had routes in the area.[40] The second factor was my concern about not knowing, or not seeing, everything that was going on around me. Yet, at the same time, I developed a sense that a certain degree of not-knowing was actually what was keeping me safe, if indeed it was necessary to keep me safe from anything. The situation with the Red Cross aid workers was, of course, similar. Their frequently self-conscious not-knowing on missions was one precarious form of practicing affective and political neutrality, as I suggested above.

Overt social demonstrations of not-knowing became a useful practice in my fieldwork, too, even as not knowing *enough* was a chronic private worry. At the same time, there were demonstrations by the Tanzanian authorities about where the limits of my knowledge should lie. While I frequently imagined a vague threat, no one was cruel to me or purposely frightened me. Usually I was met with great kindness.

There was, however, one unexpected incident that did in fact involve an odd, gratuitous sadism that brought things to a kind of head. I was in Kigoma Township, toward the end of fieldwork, and looking for a home for my cat. I was worried about his future without me. Having followed several weeks of my fruitless efforts to find a home for him, one of the European aid workers in Kigoma said, "Why don't you just gas your cat in your oven?" It was embarrassing to start crying uncontrollably. That it should have been the cat that provoked such an eruption of sentiment, after everything, was humiliating and made me feel ridiculous.[41] It was a "mere" animal, of course. This is one among numerous instances where I have seen a parallel between my fieldwork and that of the Red Cross aid workers.[42] It reminds me, of course, of Elina's story of "Mariama and the strays" where she likened her impulse to adopt the little girl Mariama to expatriate aid workers' desires to adopt stray dogs in Kosovo. I did, in the end, find a good home for my cat.

Over the years, various emotions have come and gone, but what has endured has been something like guilt and, in the words of the Red Cross doctor above, feelings of insufficiency. When I told a Burundian friend that I needed to "help somehow," to do something "more than" writing, in the face of all the violence in the Great Lakes region, he said: "*Ecoute, tu n'es pas la Croix Rouge!*" (*Listen, you're not the Red Cross!*). Of course he was right. But, as I was to learn, the Red Cross people themselves were having similar thoughts.

The guilt assumed many forms over time. One was about my own psychic insufficiencies in doing the research, and in writing and teaching about it subsequently. I tried, for example, to steer students away from researching genocide and violence, not wanting them to be damaged by it, and not wanting to work on it through them. I felt guilty about progressing in my career "on the backs of the refugees." After tenure, I felt guilty about not being able to face more writing about violence. Expertise on genocide, violence, and mass displacement was the last thing I wanted, and I tried over many years to "de-specialize" myself.

In his powerful and sad book, *Eyewitness to a Genocide*, Michael Barnett has written: "genocide . . . rips a hole in what we believe is possible" (Barnett 2002:xii). That kind of violence, and even narratives about it, has a horrible capacity to open up the imagination. Everything in its wake is "out of all proportion." Again there is a scalar impossibility. Aid work and research seem like flecks of dust, at best. And there is no right balance between distance and proximity.

Conclusion

What is left is the impossible situation, the impasse. Elizabeth Povinelli has (in a different context) described the impasse as an "experiential nonpassage—rather than a dilemma or contradiction" (2002:14).[43] In the specific situations I have described here, aid work and ethnography produced impasses—rather than contradictions to be resolved or stable, secure subject positions (Englund 2011:87). Aid worker. Anthropologist. What happened made it difficult to claim either of these professional spaces, at least some of the time.

Experientially there was no place—or *no good place*—left to stand, or to move forward. Any emotion seemed irreconcilable with these extraordinary social situations. One experienced a perpetual "ought," a compulsion to have "feelings of morality" of a certain power and gravity, and a kind of inadequacy in the face of that (Povinelli 2002:108). I felt I ought to have felt differently. I ought to have felt outrage and grief, and not fallen apart. It was not enough, too much, not right.

These professional experiences produced extraordinary affects, but they also involved, somehow, *ordinary* affects—that was the scandal. The extraordinary and the ordinary were out of all proportion to each other, irreconcilable, yet occupied the same impossible space. They intruded into and distorted each other. It is this kind of impossible situation where psychic and ethical insufficiency is generated (Povinelli 2002:108). In a way there is a failure. You experience an "ought" and feel your own ordinariness.

One's strongest moral emotions can at such times seem embarrassingly banal and even contemptible. It was not just Elina who kept thinking about the little girl Mariama she left behind. Numerous aid workers told me about children to whom they had felt attachment in the field. It was sometimes implied that the children also felt attachment. The expatriates in Kosovo felt attached to stray dogs. And I was disproportionately sad when told, many months after I had left the field, that my cat had been killed by a pack of dogs in Tanzania. The sadness seemed silly at best and monstrous at worst. Was it evidence of an inability to feel attachment to people (other than children and animals) in the field? I know it was not. But is it possible to feel attached to "victims" in general? Is it possible to feel attached to "humanity" in general? We are now accustomed to think of humanitarianism as an asymmetrical relationship with the "suffering stranger" and we call it *compassion—not attachment*. (See, e.g., Haskell 1985; Boltanski 1993; Fassin 2005:368, 376; 2012:4–6; Bornstein and Redfield 2010; Wilson 2010:28; cf. Berlant 2004:9.) "Attachment" would seem to suggest something more ordinary, imaginatively intersubjective, and specific than "compassion" in its potential loftiness. Attachment may suggest a connection to need and neediness that compassion does not. And as Sharika Thiranagama writes, "the forces that make and unmake us are the sites of ceaselessly generative ambivalent attachments and investments" (2011:12).

Aid agencies are of course aware that people tend to feel imaginative attachment, and humane generosity, toward specific objects of their imagination (see Stoler 2004). The photographs of countless boys and girls, and sick and abandoned animals, that have long been used to capture hearts and minds, and to raise funds and awareness, attest to this (cf. Bornstein 2003, 2012). I explore this further in chapter 3; and in chapter 5 I describe a "desperate need for *attachment*" among the socially isolated in Finland.

The impossible situation makes people feel silly, ridiculous; in its scalar disproportion of suffering, it cuts people down to size.[44] But what is that size? The impossible may make some feel small—but others it may make larger than life, the latter laboring in the midst of extreme suffering and feeling a quixotic empowerment akin to missionary and/or revolutionary zeal. It may inspire some to outsized efforts at self-sacrifice (see chapter 6). Too big, too small, too much, too little: each may leave people (aid workers and anthropologists) feeling dirtied by the very experience they have sought.

This chapter has been about people setting out to do something ethical and useful, and being left feeling equivocal and even guilty, often for a long time. It is, centrally, about how people get stuck at the impasse and its afterlives (cf. Garcia 2010a). The literature on humanitarianism often seems to suggest that the medical and other aid workers who go to work at scenes of political violence or other disasters occupy a certain moral high ground—that theirs are missions of reason and rescue. There is of course evidence to support such a view, and I explored aid work in that more confident key in chapter 1; but focusing on that alone leaves some important dimensions of aid work out of view. To grasp the ambiguities and ambivalences in this sort of work (and the related ambiguities and ambivalences in any sort of politics associated with it), we need to pay closer attention to the unsatisfying and unsettling experiences that leave many of us feeling as much soiled as ennobled.

3. Figurations of the Human

Children, Humanity, and the
Infantilization of Peace

There is a special relationship between humanitarian logics and practices, on the one hand, and the figure of the child, on the other—a relationship that depends on imaginative, affective, and representational practices that are very widespread across the world—especially, but not only, in the Global North. They form what I call a transnational ritual sphere. Representations of children are, of course, a familiar part of humanitarian fund-raising (the big-eyed child, etc.). But I will argue that the imaginative, socially constitutive connection between humanitarian logics and figurations of the child is much deeper than this.

One aspect of this connection is revealed in the specific social and affective relationships that humanitarian aid workers themselves form with specific children in the course of their work. Attachments are formed, and with them, senses of ethical responsibility and need. It is, of course, very common that in these relationships ethics and affect are so entangled that the two can hardly be told apart.

The figure of the child was prominent in the "impossible situations" faced by the Red Cross professionals discussed in the previous chapter. For many of these aid workers, it was especially hard to deal with the inevitable suffering and dying of children in war zones, genocides, and refugee camps. One nurse faced her impasse, her limit, when she had to witness exceptionally high numbers of children dying from malnutrition in one refugee camp, while another was unable to forget the monitoring of one infant's death so that two others could live. Then there was eight-year-old Mariama, whose life prospects looked grim, and for whose likely fate a particular Finnish aid worker, Elina, still feels responsible. There were other nurses, too, among them Kaisa, who might confide in embarrassed tones, "Well, there was this little girl . . ." And Kaarina, the war nurse, reflected on children's deaths, which "you never get used to."

But children act here not only as recipients of aid and care encountered in the field. They are also central to widely circulating representations of "humanity" that are foundational to the whole affective and semiotic apparatus of concern and compassion for "the human" that underlies practices of humanitarian care. Here, my intent is to explore this deeper logic.

Unlike the previous chapters, this one is not based on ethnographic work with the Finnish Red Cross; it instead engages a broader variety of different sources and kinds of evidence. Its intent is both exploratory and programmatic; it seeks to identify deep, transnationally circulating imaginaries centering on children. It also raises questions about contemporary depoliticizing uses of children as moral subjects, and suggests how this both shapes and trivializes any talk about peace, making both peace and children "the mere."

As noted in the introduction and in chapter 5, "Homemade Humanitarianism," international humanitarianism is deeply domestic in two respects. On the one hand, it is domestic in the sense that aid workers' professional practices and desires for the international "out there in the world" (tuolla maailmalla) tend to originate in relation to specific cultural contexts, whether regional or national—in "home countries" that may be more or less "homey," more or less claustrophobic. The other sense of the domestic involves the traditionally heteronormative "domestic domain," and especially the "domestic arts" as practiced by nonprofessional givers of humanitarian help. In this second sense, the domestic is associated with both women and children, and things that they make and do (Castoriadis 1997)—such as a variety of handwork, including soft knitted objects like blankets and "baby animals." Sometimes aid organizations' publicity and fund-raising campaigns involve calls to knit creatures like "Aid Bunnies" and "Trauma Teddies" for children in crisis, as I will explain at more length in the next chapter. These are occasions that allow especially older knitters to feel otherwise than lonely and "useless" by positioning themselves not simply as vulnerable recipients of state aid but as givers of aid to imagined others in need (cf. Muehlebach 2011, 2012). As the following chapters will show, such would-be helpers discovered profound meaning in being able to do something as "silly" as to knit "mere" Aid Bunnies for the consolation of children in disaster zones.

What is it about children? What histories enable them to loom so large in the humanitarian imaginary? How is it that they have been in effective representational use from colonial times to the present? Here I consider these questions by examining the affective work done by the figure of the child in transnational ritual spheres, especially those involving issues of war and peace. I will suggest that this imaginative figurational work is ritual because it tends to follow widely meaningful conventions and to be classified—and to appear—as apolitical, even suprapolitical; yet the forms in question clearly have political effects. The child is often made to appear as the exemplary human, and as politically harmless and neutral—the most neutral of neutrals, hors combat—and is thus able to do a great deal of work in the affective imagination (Barthes 2005; Biehl 2005; Redfield 2010). Perhaps this is why the child is often such a potent ritual and political actor in war zones and genocides, and why we then find it so shocking when s/he takes up arms.

It should be underscored, perhaps, that while the figurations of the child and the human discussed here are putatively universal, they are in fact in many cases imagined by societies of the Global North, and are, in many ways, quite Christian.[1] Yet this putative universality is not simply a kind of error—it is, as I will suggest, a key part of the very real power that such representations have. Anna Tsing's thoughts on the universal are important here: "Universals are indeed local knowledge in the sense that they cannot be understood without the benefit of historically specific cultural assumptions. But to stop here makes dialogue impossible. Furthermore, it misses the point. To turn to universals is to identify knowledge that moves—mobile and mobilizing—across localities and cultures" (2005:7).

In examining specifically humanitarian and humanist modes of imagining world unity, one is looking at something a good deal more specific than just the transnational. At issue is a peculiarly self-conscious globalism, a set of cultural forms, structures of feeling (Williams 1985), and ritual practices that deliberately aim to be "global" by invoking a universal or global "human community" (Englund 2005, 2006; Tsing 2005), just as the Red Cross Red Crescent Movement does. These are forms that do not just somehow "end up" being international, transnational, or supranational in scope; they are moralizing visions conceived as globally encompassing from the start. These forms can, and do, include everything from Coca-Cola advertisements (as in "I'd like to buy the world a Coke") to famine relief, from school celebrations of "UN Day," "Peace Day," and "Earth Day" to UNICEF Christmas cards.

Such cultural forms of a globalizing humanism are indeed transnational (which, again, does not mean that they are universal), but they do not fully transcend the national, or escape its logic. To understand just how central the nation form (Balibar and Wallerstein 1992) remains to such supranational forms of moral imagination, we need to treat the question of the nation not only in the familiar forms of chauvinistic, exclusionary, or violent nationalism but also in the form of the liberal, tolerant, UNICEF and UNESCO kind of national imagination that envisions and celebrates the world as an ensemble of nations and presents itself as a form of antiracism (cf. Barthes [1957] 2013; Hall 1978; Gilroy 1991; Malkki 1994). These modes of imagining a world community involve special, observably standardized, representational uses of children—be they images of children themselves, images children have made, words they have written, or songs they have sung. These uses of children, in turn, produce other sets of effects that I will trace here.

My framing questions are as follows: Why are children's images everywhere in evidence in the widely traveling representational conventions of imagining international community, humanitarian concern, and human need? What do these images do? What do they depend upon for their efficacy? My analysis suggests that children very consistently appear in five interrelated registers: (1) as embodiments of a basic human goodness and innocence, (2) as sufferers, (3) as seers of truth, (4) as ambassadors of peace (and symbols of world harmony), and (5) as embodiments of the future. These registers depend on each other for their affective and ritual efficacy (Tambiah 1985; Butler 1997), and it is this efficacy that animates cultural practices like sponsoring children, enchanting the knitting of humanitarian "gifts," and privileging children as exemplars of "pure" human need.

Children as Embodiments of a Basic Human Goodness and Innocence

Children have long served western thought as *elementary forms of the human*— in some historical periods as embodiments of a basic human savagery and sinfulness (or even evil) and at other times of a basic human goodness and innocence. Scholarly histories by Peter Coveney (1957), Jo Boyden (1990), Carolyn Steedman (1995), Sharon Stephens (1995), Chris Jenks (1996), Allison James and Alan Prout (1997), Gill Valentine (1996), and many others have shown that children and childhood have long been recognized as historical, cultural, and political constructs, not as naturally (or developmentally) given. This work shows that before the seventeenth century in the West, children were often thought of as "inheritors of original sin" or as "savage" and uncivilized (Valentine 1996:583). In this Christian, western tradition, Calvin and Augustine are key figures. Augustine's *Confessions* is, of course, a classic meditation on the problems of sin and human evil: "no man is free from sin, not even a child who has lived only one day on earth" (quoted in Wall 2004:171). But as theologian John Wall (2004:170) argues, linking children with original sin does not necessarily mean that children carry greater sin than do adults: "The key benefit to viewing children as coming into the world with original sin . . . is that it acknowledges the profound humanity of their struggle to grow and develop in this world."

By the end of the seventeenth century (and especially from the mid-eighteenth century onward), scholarly writing, at least, tended to see an innate goodness in the child, and a distinction was made between goodness and innocence (see, e.g., Rosenblum 1988). The latter, as Valentine (1996:583) points out, "may only mean a neutral state—neither positively bad nor positively good." Locke, for instance, saw the child as a *tabula rasa*. Thus, "children are not animals to be civilized but vessels for the infusion of Reason. Children come into the world with enormous rational *potential*. They are each a *tabula rasa* or 'blank slate' upon which Reason may be written through enlightened education" (Wall 2004:163, emphasis in the original). By the second half of the eighteenth century, in the time of Rousseau and William Blake, there was, among many debates about the nature of children, a strong Romantic movement to link children with an original innocence (Higonnet 1998:9). Blake's "Songs of Innocence," for example, held up a pure, natural childhood against the corruptions of society (Blake [ca. 1826] 1992). The child embodied a "romantic protest against the 'experience' of society" (Coveney 1957:xii). Associated most strongly with Rousseau ([1762] 1978), and in contrast to the long Christian preoccupation with "original sin," the concept of the child's nature that informed the work of figures as diverse as Blake, Wordsworth, and Dickens was one of "original innocence." As Coveney (1957:6) has pointed out, "Rousseau's contribution was to give expression to the new sensibility, and to direct its interest toward childhood as the period of life when man most closely approximated to the 'state of nature.'" In other words, a child is not just a miniature adult, nor just an adult in the making. S/he is a being of another order, set apart by cultural prescriptions and proscriptions. Blake celebrated children's "oneness with nature," their capacity to transcend boundaries: "No barriers in the child's consciousness lie between himself and the ant; merely *a synthesizing compassion*" (Coveney 1957:21, emphasis added; cf. Rosenblum 1988:16). In this period in the West, "nature" was often understood in Christian terms, as the Christian God's "creation." If children were close to nature, it was because they were fresh, new images of their Creator. Theologian Friedrich Schleiermacher, for example, was of this opinion. In his later work, Schleiermacher "associates the child's special capability for 'pure reverence'—for 'the feeling of absolute dependence'—with its special closeness to what he calls the 'sacred sphere of nature.' As in Rousseau, nature is to be the guide for society and not the other way around. But unlike in Rousseau, nature in the form of the sacred gift of the child trumps even human reason as the true measure of human goodness" (Wall 2004:167–68; cf. Albert Schweitzer's [1950] credo of "reverence for life"). For Schleiermacher, as for many who have come after, the ideal corrective to the depredations of modern, western industrial societies was for adults to "become as little children" (DeVries 2001; also quoted in Wall 2004:168n23). Thus, children were elevated to the status of innocent sages, teachers as if despite themselves.

These histories of the construction of children as embodying a natural goodness and innocence have been examined by many scholars (see Valentine 1996). Here, I want simply to underscore the historical depth and continued vitality of the childhood-innocence-goodness links—and the separation between childhood and adulthood that has come to be so robustly naturalized since the late eighteenth century in the West (Rosenblum 1988:17). These links have great power and relevance in contemporary discourses of humanitarianism and liberal internationalism where childlike innocence is a way of making recipients of humanitarian assistance a tabula rasa, innocent of politics and history, innocent, in a way, about causes of war and enmity. Thus is their need for help neutralized. Pure need. (The humanitarian, as will become evident in the following chapter, is then left free to write her own script on the figure of the child.) Childlike innocence is also a mode of imagining archetypal "innocent victims." Valentine writes that the angel-devil tension and the ascendancy of the notion of innocence have to do with "a North American and European understanding of childhood which has been propagated in the rest of the world, for example, in the late 20th century through organizations such as the United Nations" (1996:58n1; see also Benjamin 1999a:101).[2] My work on internationalism and humanitarianism (1994, 1995a, 1995b, 2002a, 2002b) supports this argument, although I do think it is important to approach regional, historical, class, gender, and other differences in the shapes of childhoods empirically without attributing vectors of influence too early—and without assuming the *actual* universalization of that which is in fact only putatively universal. As Valentine points out, "The experience of childhood has never been universal; rather, what it means to be a particular age intersects with other [dimensions of subjectivity] so that experiences of poverty, [abuse], disability, ill health, being orphaned, taken into care, or having to look after a sick parent have all denied many children this idealized time of innocence and dependence" (Valentine 1996:587; cf. James and Prout 1997).

The social imagination of innocence has periodically been violently and horribly disrupted by highly publicized cases of children murdering and torturing other children, and recent years have seen an intensification of moral panics concerning childhood and danger. Sharon Stephens (1995) and others have written, for example, about the conceptualization of "children at risk" and "children as a risk." In the United Kingdom in 1993, Jamie Bulger, a two-year-old boy, died an almost unimaginably cruel death at the hands of two ten-year-old boys. There have been numerous similar contemporary cases since. Valentine argues that these cases ignited public processes of "othering" and demonizing children in the 1990s; she cites the *Guardian* as stating of the child of the 1990s: "There is a growing uncertainty about the parameters of childhood and a mounting terror of the anarchy and uncontrollability of unfettered youth" (1996:589). Similar trends continue.

In the transnational representational formations of internationalist humanitarianism, special attention has been devoted to child soldiers (Peters and Richards 1998, cited in Korbin 2003; Scheper-Hughes and Sargent 1998; Machel 2002; Boyden and de Berry 2005; Rosen 2005). The child soldier, or rebel fighter, is a figure that gravely troubles the image of the child as an innocent; and yet the international moral shock about the child soldier is perhaps as meaningful as it is precisely because of the generalized, universalizing expectation of children's innocence, the wishful expectation that children are beings *not yet* caught up in history or politics—perhaps *not yet* caught up in time (cf. Higonnet 1998:49). The attribution of innate and proper innocence to children suggests two things about innocence itself: first, that it is an allochronic (Fabian [1983] 2002), somehow timeless, state; and second, that innocence is a form of *not-knowing*, of not being "worldly." (In the previous chapter, of course, nurses and other aid workers sought psychic self-protection precisely in "not-knowing" and the "affective neutrality" that this promised to make possible.) All this makes the child soldier an abomination, and the "normal" soldier (who may be just a few years older) a taken-for-granted fact. The "normal" soldier can be decorated for valor, but decorating the child soldier thus strains the imagination. The trouble with child soldiers is that they cannot be set apart, made sacred, in allochronic time (by adults); and they can no longer be (for adults) innocent in the other sense of a blameless not-knowing. They cannot be imagined as transcendent figures.[3] They are profane, a category mistake that disturbs the poetics of "our common humanity."

Children fighting in Palestine also trouble the morally laden binary of child versus adult. Not surprisingly, they are often categorized in the mainstream, western press as "youths" as opposed to "children." Likewise, when children are referred to as "teens" or "teenagers," their moral authority as innocents is attenuated or even denied. The temporal progression built into the category of "children" is also a developmentalist moral progression: it is easiest to attribute to children a pure, innocent presociality when they are youngest.[4] "As they grow older, gain knowledge and worldly understanding, develop 'vehement passions' [Philip Fisher 2002] of their own, and form connections beyond family boundaries, they become more 'tainted' and less worthy of special treatment as children." (Witness the debates in the United States about the legal age at which children should be prosecuted as adults for crimes of violence.)[5] U.S. immigration politics can also be examined through this temporal/moral lens.

Children as Sufferers

Images of children as sufferers are everywhere in humanitarian appeals in print and digital media. The international Red Cross is no stranger to the "hard sell" of using the child as a spur and enticement to the humanitarian imagination of the potential donor. As Erica Burman puts it, "the individual starving child functions as the general idiom for hunger, and hunger comes to operate as the quintessential index of need. It is important to consider what is elided by this set of equivalences" (Burman 1994:241; see also Fassin 2012:21–23). Hunger promises to be a form of suffering that can often be "fixed," at least for a time.

In these appeals we see—or are urgently, benevolently, invited to see—small bundles of humanity, young bodies that could belong to "any of us" (cf. Agamben 1998). This, of course, is what sometimes flashed in Red Cross aid workers' minds as they cared for unaccompanied children in the field: I could be his mother! I am responsible! They were, many of them, as I wrote in chapter 2, haunted by the children they had left behind when their missions ended. Attachments were broken. They had worked with actual, specific children, but they had all, of course, also seen humanitarian posters with children in need. The posters did not seem to lose their power to evoke compassion even then.

In a certain way, the images of these small figures are charismatic in their suffering in spite of the fact that they exhibit a profound absence of historical, cultural, biographical specificity (cf. Burman 1994:239; Suski 2009). There is usually also a gaping absence where the child's parents, siblings, friends, and other caregivers stand—although in some situations children really are alone, having been separated from their families or those they know. Even while they are photographic documents of actual, living children, these are pictures of *human children*, not photographs of specific *persons* or *people* with specific histories, however short. It is all too easy to strip children of their personhood and to fill them with a pure humanity and an unspoiled nature instead. In the process, we (adults) place them outside the complications of history, beyond the lines drawn by political violence. They are the innocent representatives of a common humanity, able to appeal— across the boundaries of race, culture, and nation—to an underlying, essential humanity many of us (at certain times) believe we all share.

In a horribly titled but thoughtful article, "Fresh Maimed Babies: The Uses of Innocence," McKenzie Wark (1995) examines the affective, moral, and political uses of children as sufferers and ideal, innocent victims. He begins in a rather shell-shocked way:

> The most innocent-looking media images are sometimes the most sinister. Take Somalia, where United Nations forces found themselves buried up to their baby-blue bonnets in cynical *realpolitik*. . . . How did it all start? With pictures of starving children. Poor innocents with frail limbs and big, brown eyes and flies crawling up their nostrils. They stared at us out of smudgy newsprint or pixelated images from satellite newsfeeds, but always with a resolution hard enough to make my heart leap into my mouth. Who wouldn't want to help them, these blameless victims—as soon as possible, no questions asked? When I see these images, it is I who becomes childlike. I want someone to make it all better. The child

occupies such a sacred place in our structures of feeling that one cannot help but feel—something. (36)

Wark traces the anatomy of a "conscience industry of global proportions" (1995:40) and finds that children occupy a key place in it. In this capacity they are more powerful than adults; they are attributed an affective authority that adult refugees and other victims can generally never hope to possess. The Red Cross nurses' reactions to the children they treated in the field attest to this. Wark takes the reader to Bosnia: "Being certified refugees, they were for the most part adults who had done something to make themselves refugees. . . . Like old toys, they were rejected in favor of the new season's hit doll. Bosnian babies had an added feature—innocence. It makes them a most satisfying gift for yourself when you feel the itch to feel good in an ingenuous, 'We Are the World' sort of a way. Dollar for dollar, pound for pound, adult refugees are nowhere near the value. There's always the suspicion that they may be adulterated by impurities—such as politics" (1995:40).

The point is that children as sufferers are charismatic figures with an affective authority of cosmological proportions, an authority that seems to stand the test of time. The visual appeals also educate children in peaceful, wealthy societies in the Global North and perhaps elsewhere. This is visible, for instance, in children's books. Eleanor Coerr's *Sadako and the Thousand Paper Cranes* (1977) is one of many in its genre. It is the story of how a young girl, Sadako Sasaki, died of leukemia because she had been irradiated by the bomb the American forces dropped on the city of Hiroshima when she was only two years old. The little book is Sadako's story; it mentions nothing about the American forces, or the politics of the decision to drop the atomic bombs that destroyed Hiroshima and Nagasaki. Leaving the book's tragic contents out, I concentrate on its outer skin. The back cover indicates that the book was written by an American author for the benefit of American children: "Eleanor Coerr lived in Japan years ago and heard about Sadako and the paper cranes. . . . The author decided to find out as much as she could about the brave young girl's life and recreate it for American children." Why? It seems that she wanted to communicate the message that war is bad, and, especially, bad for children. This is a generic, intentionally uncontroversial and humanist pacifism (within a more general but unspoken context of U.S. militarism) that relies on the figure of the child as an innocent and pan-human sufferer. It does not address any specific war, any specific bombs, any specific or historically situated political stakes or ideological programs.[6]

What happens to the moral authority of such suffering? How can authority (of any kind) exist there if nobody has to take it seriously? Does a U.S. president read such a book and decide that nuclear disarmament is the only possible course of action? Is the moral claim of such representations not so bland and uncontroversial as to be in the end utterly unthreatening and unnoticeable to the actual makers of war? This is the problem with the affective, moral authority of children as sufferers: they stand upon an "ethereal pedestal" (Wall 2004:170) that dissipates altogether when practically necessary. Their authority is of a transnational ritual nature alone, carefully kept apart from the realm of "real-world" political history. That does not mean that this ritualized moral authority does nothing; rousing people to send money to starving or sick children is not nothing. But in the final analysis, it is very limited in the position it occupies in the thick of history and politics. Even while this authority is understood to address "the world," it is remarkably unworldly. Even the most urgent humanitarian appeals (currently on behalf of people in Somalia, Sudan, Syria, Mali, and other regions) are hobbled by the highly conventionalized and ritually circumscribed nature of the affective authority of children as sufferers. In large measure, this disabling rests on (and is naturalized by) the western opposition of affect and reason (see Stoler 2004).

The moralized, sentimentalized figure of children as sufferers works in much the same manner as do those of suffering animals. Both do affective cultural work as expressive moral subjects (but not as rational, knowing subjects [cf. Coetzee 2001]). Both are "good to think" as innocent victims. Animals and children are so often made more human than anyone. This idea, of anthropomorphized animals as "exemplary humans," is discussed at some length in the following chapter. Sadako belongs to the same ritual world (and historical moment) as do the "faithful elephants" of Tokyo's Ueno Zoo. In 1951, after the Second World War, Yukio Tsuchiya wrote a children's book about three elephants, John, Tonky, and Wanly, and about how they had to be starved to death by their heartbroken keepers. "During the last stage of World War II, Tokyo was often attacked from the air. At the city zoo, the keepers, with tears in their eyes, had to kill many of the animals for fear that they would run amuck in the city if the zoo were bombed directly. Faithful Elephants describes how three elephants died in the Ueno Zoo in Tokyo at that time" (Tsuchiya [1951] 1988:n.p.). The elephants were blameless, faithful, giving, and innocent. To read how they died is heartbreaking. The rain of anticipated bombs is once again nameless, and the estimated 100,000 Tokyo citizens who died in one night of firebombing unremarked (Coleman 2005). This, too, is a children's book. It is part of their sentimental education.

Children as Seers of Truth

Children are also hailed in these humanitarian representations and the broader transnational ritual sphere as seers of truth, small humans with the capacity of seeing through "barriers" of culture, nationality, race, class, and religion. Whereas in some contexts (anthropology and critical human rights discourses, for example) cultural differences are thought to deserve our highest regard and protection, in other arenas they become *obstacles* to the articulation of a common, universal humanity. This was very clearly stated in the opening address of the former UN Secretary General Boutros Boutros-Ghali at the June 1993 World Conference on Human Rights in Vienna:

> Human rights, viewed at the universal level, bring us face-to-face with the most challenging dialectical conflict ever: between "identity" and "otherness," between the "myself" and "others." They teach us in a direct, straightforward manner that we are at the same time identical and different. Thus the human rights that we proclaim and seek to safeguard can be brought about only if we transcend ourselves, only if we make a conscious effort to find our common essence *beyond our apparent divisions, our temporary differences, our ideological and cultural barriers.* In sum, what I mean to say, with all solemnity, is that the human rights we are about to discuss here at Vienna are not the lowest common denominator among all nations, but rather what I should like to describe as the "*irreducible human element,*" in other words, the quintessential values through which we affirm together that we are *a single human community.* (Boutros-Ghali 1993, emphases added)[7]

This ritual address could have been written by the Red Cross Red Crescent Movement, and, indeed, it practically was:

> When we bring together and compare different moral systems and dispose of the non-essentials, that is to say their special peculiarities, we find in the crucible a pure metal, the *universal heritage of mankind.* . . . There is no unmitigable collision between the "different worlds" which we have placed in contrast. All doctrines can lead to the great law of the Red Cross, but each one by its own pathway, in accordance with the convictions and

characters of the various peoples. The Red Cross serves to unite, and not to divide. It is thus for the Red Cross to proclaim norms which have universal validity, because they are fully in accordance with human nature. (Pictet 1979:4, emphasis added; cf. Barthes [1957] 2013)

This passage is quoted in full in chapter 5, but it so closely approximates the United Nations statement that is was necessary to set these side by side. In both, cultural difference is a barrier and obstacle, never a relationship to be celebrated and studied. Children have long been constituted as visionaries of such a common humanity, as beings empowered to *see through* what we like to gloss simply as the "folly" of war. Anne Frank was such a being. Zlata Filipovic became another. Many years ago, there was a sudden spate of television and print coverage of the latest literary fad in Paris: *Le journal de Zlata Filipovic*—the diary of a young girl who began writing and drawing about the war in the former Yugoslavia when she was eleven years old (Filipovic 1994). Her book has since been translated into many languages. The dust jacket of the English-language edition introduces the diary as follows: "In a voice both innocent and wise, touchingly reminiscent of Anne Frank's, Zlata Filipovic's diary has awoken the conscience of the world" (Filipovic 1994). One of today's preeminent virtuous child figures is Malala Yousafzai.[8] Born in Pakistan in 1997, she became an education and women's rights activist while still a schoolgirl. The Taliban attempted to assassinate her while she was on her way home from school (October 9, 2012). She was gravely wounded but recovered in the United Kingdom, and "carried on her message." The UN Secretary General Ban Ki-moon named November 10 Malala Day. She has become yet another kind of world conscience on an ethereal pedestal— worshipped by some and ignored by annoyed others. She received the Nobel Peace Prize in 2014.

The pervasive social imagination of children as keepers of universal truths is evident in the many contemporary picture books that have been published on war and peace and children's art. *I Dream of Peace: Images of War by Children of Former Yugoslavia*, for example, is a collection of drawings and writings gathered by UNICEF from schools and refugee camps as part of a "psychosocial assistance program for war-traumatized children" (United Nations Children's Fund 1994: dust jacket). The preface to this book was written by Maurice Sendak, author of classic children's books in the United States:

The children know. They have always known. But we choose to think otherwise; it hurts to know the children know. The children see. If we obfuscate, they will not see. Thus we conspire to keep them from knowing and seeing. And if we insist, then the children, to please us, will make believe they do not know, they do not see. Children make that sacrifice for our sake—to keep us pacified. They are remarkably patient, loving, and all-forgiving. It is a sad comedy: the children knowing and pretending they don't know to protect us from knowing they know.

In the former Yugoslavia, there is no time left for such genteel dissembling. We have betrayed the children; we are killing them. The pictures they paint and their words tell us so. In these pictures and words, the children shout out their terrible fear and grief; they rebuke us and plead with us to spare them. And in that awful shouting they reveal the health, vitality, natural grace, and artistry of childhood. Who better than children to sum up, without artifice or sentimentality, the monumental stupidity of war!

Despite our betrayal, these fierce images do not speak of blame, only of sick despair and desperation that blossoms, eerily, into radiant hope. They are ready to forgive us. They always are. Nemanja, eleven years old, cries out: "I do not want to grow old while still just a child." And Sandra, ten, sends this message: "Don't ever hurt the children. They're not guilty of anything." And the children in a fifth-grade class ask: "Like Anne Frank fifty years ago, we wait for peace. She didn't live to see it. Will we?" Will they? (United Nations Children's Fund 1994:5)

In his book on the uses of child art in modernism, *The Innocent Eye: Children's Art and the Modern Artist*, art historian Jonathan Fineberg (1997:xx) writes: "Although there is an ancient tradition of *the child as an unknowing seer*, it was the [R]omantics who allied the naiveté of the child with genius . . . Thus the nineteenth century inherited a double legacy about the child's 'innocent eye'; it was innocent enough of convention to see through the emperor's new clothes, so to speak, and at the same time the child was gifted with a privileged view into the mysteries of the divine plan." This formulation is still recognizable in humanitarian representational regimes and in other globally circulating systems of signification.[9]

The linking of children and truth is neither simple nor innocent. As Sharon Stephens has pointed out, children may be conceptualized as seers of truth in relation to "emotional truths," but they are

NOT seen as credible witnesses in courts of law, for example, in relation to child abuse cases. While they are capable of grasping emotional truths, beyond and beneath the artificialities of culture, they are not seen as cognitively able to distinguish between fact and fantasy, between "what really happened" and what some adult or another child may have suggested happened. . . . Consider the heated legal debates, for [example], about children as witnesses in court. On the one hand, they're seen as vessels of unmediated truth, bearing witness to the artificialities and duplicities of adults. On the other hand, they're seen as irrational, fanciful, unable to tell reality from imagination. In both cases, children are denied existence as complex social beings who know the world and represent themselves through language and culturally mediated understandings.[10]

The very virtues and special powers attributed to children in the representational conventions under consideration circumscribe and trivialize children's authority. This all-too-easy trivialization marks them as *"mere" children*, babes in the woods. Theirs is a "universal" but non-specific, generally powerless, form of truth. The ritualized figure of children as unknowing seers divides "truth" into two mutually exclusive kinds: universal, transcendent, timeless, affective, moral, incontestable truth, on the one hand, and factual, temporal, historical, political, ambiguous, contestable, specific, rational truth, on the other. Children have allochronic, transcendent "wisdom" as a birthright; adults have historical, factual "knowledge." It is remarkable that this imagined divide survives as robustly as it has done in key ritual transnational spheres.

Children as Ambassadors of Peace

It would be impossible to list all the books, music, and other cultural artifacts that link children with peace, particularly in the Global North.[11] To pick one example from a multitude, Joan Walsh Anglund's diminutive picture book for children, Peace Is a Circle of Love (1993), is dedicated "for the children of the world, our teachers of peace." In this genre, children are positioned as teachers of adults, as the pure human beings who innocently speak truths about world peace. Musical versions of the same message abound. One example is a compact disc, World Peace: The Children's Dream! A Multicultural Musical for the Whole Family! (Melody 1997; see also Pinder 1995). Another is the musical director's score Peace Child: A Musical Fantasy about Children Bringing Peace to the World (Peace Child Foundation 1987). It is surely the case that children may have much to teach adults, and I obviously do not want to suggest that children are not honest, imaginative, insightful, and generous—they are, remarkably often, just as are adults. It is more interesting to ask: What do these books on peace do, affectively and socially? How are their intended audiences constituted? The cultural conventions and materials connecting children and peace (like children and animals, children and nature, and children and the environment) are located in a sphere of selectively transnational production usually quite disconnected from the transnational arenas of "real" politics, "real" business, and "real" history—that is to say, "practical reason." Yet politicians and businessmen, too, might buy books and music on peace for their children, as part of their children's moral and sentimental education, just as they might buy books about "baby animals" to teach them *compassion*. After all, one does not want to raise a child without compassion, a child who is cruel to animals. It is as if the figure of "peace" were ritually sealed off in certain cultural and temporal sites—like the time set apart as "early childhood" and transnational ritual spheres like the United Nations, the Red Cross and Red Crescent, and their international ceremonial discourses (see, e.g., Vittachi 1993).

This opens up a host of questions about what "peace" might mean, and how, when, and where the concept is in use. It is conspicuously *not* an anthropological category, perhaps for good reasons. Describing the status quo in 1966, José Luis Arangurén wrote: "Order means peace and, from our point of view, international peace—peace in the minimal sense of no war, coexistence . . . Can war perhaps be prevented through expounding and defending the abstract principle of peace? It is to be doubted . . . The manifestoes of intellectuals who are given to making appeals to the collective conscience, and so forth, serve as 'tranquillizers' to their signatories, give a luster to that object of beauty which is their '*bonne conscience*'" (1966:591). All too obviously, the figure of children can also act as such a tranquillizer. That is, children as moral subjects are used in international ceremonial discourses as *ritual fetishes of peace*, as the diminutive consciences of the "world community." Of course, many such appeals for peace and justice arise from very real and urgent concerns.[12] Nevertheless, these appeals and images of children as teachers and ambassadors of peace are also used in less urgent ways— precisely as a *tranquillizing convention*. Sometimes it even seems that calls for world peace, or peace of any kind, are doomed to be infantilized and that once they leave their ritually ascribed realm of "early childhood," elementary school, or "UN Days," they find no place in the adult world of "real" politics, "real" history. They become *mere caricatures*, as in the 1960s, when calls for peace were dismissed as utopian pipe dreams of strung-out flower children.

One example of this tranquillizing dynamic, at its most cynical, is former president George W. Bush's post–September 11 campaign to have each American child send a dollar to an Afghan child, care of "America's Fund for Afghan Children."

President Bush thanked America's youngest citizens for helping to ease the burdens of their counterparts in Afghanistan, where the United States continues to bomb. "Winter arrives early in Afghanistan and it's cold and the children need clothes, food and medicine. Thanks to American children, fewer of them will be cold there," he said. President Bush said that by contributing to the fund, American children could join the war against terrorism. *"There's evil in this world, and we can overcome evil,"* he said, later reassuring the young crowd that the U.S. government is "doing everything it can to make you safe." . . . Penny King-Vaughan, a Boys and Girls Club leader from Norfolk, Va., said the event has given her an opportunity to teach club members about the predicament of Afghan children. *"They didn't understand why we were sending money to [a country the United States was bombing],"* she said. "We had to make them understand it's a small group of people *hurting us*, not a whole country. It is not children hurting us." (Kriner 2001:2, brackets in the original, emphasis added)

This is, of course, coldly calculated political posturing, akin to politicians kissing babies. As a political maneuver, however, "America's Fund for Afghan Children" is effective precisely because it appears to be above politics, transcendent; it is the signifying power of children that enables the chilling maneuver.

Remembering her own childhood in the former Soviet Union, in what is now Kazakhstan, Zhanara Nauruzbayeva wrote:

It was general custom all across the Soviet schools to have *urok mira* (peace lesson) on the first day of school on September 1st. I distinctly remember my first day of the first grade in 1985. Our teacher . . . introduced herself and said that our first lesson would be the lesson of peace . . . I recall clearly the conversation about Samantha Smith, a little girl from America who wrote letters to Ronald Reagan and Mikhail Gorbachev asking them to stop the arms race. Her example found a lot of inspiration and sparked a girl in the Soviet Union, Katya Lycheva, to follow her example. Katya also wrote letters to the leaders of the two countries begging them to pursue peaceful means and stop destruction. There was a poster in our classroom that had a picture of the smiling Samantha Smith. . . . Also, I remember that all throughout our drawing/arts classes, we used to draw pictures featuring the globe, the dove of peace, and bombs with the words NATO or USA on them crossed out with red. From my recollection, these items were pretty ubiquitous in all of the drawings of my classmates. Most of my pictures were various renderings of these same elements. I remember that I got quite skillful in drawing the olive branch in the beak of the dove, [and] the meridians and parallels on the globe. Thus, not only are the children used/represented as ambassadors of peace in the media, but this image is also instilled in children ourselves, thus creating circles of reproduction.[13]

In most of its elements, this imaginative grammar—conjugating peace through children, doves, and the image of the globe—could be a description of many elementary schools in many parts of the world. Absent the bombs identified as "NATO" or "USA," the images are familiar. And Nauruzbayeva is right: while children's drawings, letters, and poems about peace and hope may be consumed by adults (at least some adults) as *spontaneous* truths from innocent minds as yet untainted by politics or calculation, the genre is actually meticulously taught, learned, and conventionalized.[14]

In the small creases of these highly managed, ceremonial, and sentimental appeals in glossy publications are different, dissonant messages from children.[15] The large coffee-table book *Dear World: "How I'd Put the World Right"*—*By the Children of over 50 Nations* (Exley and Exley 1985)[16] is filled with children's drawings and writings that conform very precisely to this formula of children as innocent teachers and ambassadors of world peace: "If we all loved each other we would not fight. We would hold hands. We would share. Ramdaye Singh, 5, Trinidad" (13). Yet, every now and then, other sorts of messages come through: "All women must think theirselves the value of a pearl, in the sight of men. Jannett Pusey, 16, Jamaica" (108). "The 'World Powers' store the end of the world. John C. Khumalo, 16, Botswana" (105). In another elementary school, children were invited to make a wish in celebration of Martin Luther King Jr. Day; there was only one outlier: "I wish there was no Three St[r]ikes Law."

Contemporary uses of children as ambassadors of world peace reveal something of the hollowed-out political meanings that "world peace" tends to have now. Whereas in the immediate aftermath of the Second World War the necessity of "world peace" was urgently and earnestly debated by formidable adults like Albert Einstein and Eleanor Roosevelt, during the Cold War and still now, world peace is a trivialized utopia, rhetorically deployed (rarely) by all sides in appropriate ritual contexts. Many of these ritualized contexts are strongly pedagogical in intent, but this is paradoxical, as Laurie Kain Hart has pointed out: "Logically, these peace messages and pedagogies for children are coals to Newcastle. If children are, by their very nature, naked humanity, peace, and goodwill, why 'teach' them about it? This 'teaching' is clearly not pedagogy to form the adult because we don't expect the kids to grow into 220 lb. men who cuddle baby animals. Rather, it's a form of 'appropriate activity' for children, a kind of confinement in what is meant to be their nature."[17]

Peace in the sense of world peace has thus undergone an infantilization by being identified with childhood. It has been made "mere." This is comparable to the frequent trivializing dismissals of international conventions, the International Criminal Court, and the Universal Declaration of Human Rights. For example, the former U.S. ambassador to the United Nations, Jeanne Kirkpatrick, dismissed the category of Economic, Social, and Cultural Rights in the Universal Declaration as "a letter to Santa Claus" (quoted in Chomsky 1999:21).[18]

Children as Embodiments of the Future

"Children are our future" is a hackneyed cliché, of course. Popular songs, saccharin sayings, and innumerable sites in public culture in the West proclaim this equation, which also travels transnationally, if unevenly.[19] It is also made by way of a fiduciary logic.[20] That is, to help, heal, protect, or educate children *now* is to "invest in the future." The United Nations Children's Fund (UNICEF) encourages us to think of "investing" in girls as an investment in women (Kurz and Prather 1995). The journal *Corrections Today* carries the article "America's Future: The Necessity of Investing in Children" (Breed 1990), while *Issues in Science and Technology* describes healthy children as an investment in the future (Omenn 1988). And as Wall (2004:165) remarks, "One of the most influential books on childhood in recent years is the Nobel Prize–winning economist Gary Becker's 1981 *Treatise on the Family*. Here, Becker applies 'rational choice' economic theory to child rearing to show that everything parents and society do for children is really a subtle and complex calculation of market self-interest. . . . That is, parental 'investment' of time, money, and resources should be calculated in view of its anticipated short- and long-term emotional, familial, and financial payoff." Not all fiduciary calculations pertaining to children are as shockingly cold and individualistic as Becker's, of course.

While the equation of children with the future of humanity appears universal, and undoubtedly travels a wide transnational route, that does not mean that historically and culturally specific assumptions are not embedded in it. One example of this cultural specificity is that children-are-our-future depends for its efficacy on specific chronotopes. If children are about new beginnings and about futures as yet unspoilt and unmarked, it is possibly because time is rendered in a linear, Christian way. Each new dot in the line is an opportunity for self-improvement, and for the improvement of others, for bettering "the world" (cf. Weber [1930] 2000). The equation also depends upon an implicitly declaratory, moralizing universalism; this is one constitutive dimension of the transnational ritual sphere being traced here. It is everywhere in evidence in the discursive and other social practices of international organizations and nongovernmental organizations whose mandate is "children," and who work under the banner of an unmarked modernist universalism.

And yet, alongside the ritual sphere, in other cultural contexts, other understandings of the figure of the child exist. As Veena Das has demonstrated, for example, children in India are neither blank slates nor naked bundles of pure humanity; they are persons with histories, and there is "no assumption that the child embodies innocence" (Das 1989:263). "In Indian society the child is not regarded as a tabula rasa on which society inscribes whatever it wishes. Rather, the child is believed to bring with him memories of his previous birth as well as preconception memories—the *samskaras* he may have formed in the mother's womb. . . . The child . . . is seen as coming into the world with a memory and an understanding of languages that elude the adult" (Das 1989:264, 265; see also Gupta 2001). In the Indian context, then, as in many others, the equation "children are our future" may look impoverished or even like a cosmological mistake (see, e.g., Amadi 1991; Okri 1993, 1996; Reynolds 1996; Gottlieb 2004). It is important, nevertheless, to recognize that the equation carries weight in many contexts; it underwrites many humanitarian projects around the world, as Erica Bornstein (2003:67–95) has shown in her ethnographic research on child sponsorship and Christian evangelism in contemporary Zimbabwe. There, the phenomenon of western sponsors sending money and gifts to Zimbabwean children whom they have "adopted" often creates tensions in actually existing, impoverished families and communities. While the faraway western sponsors might think of "their" children along "the logic of the one," actually existing Zimbabwean parents and others struggle to understand why one specific child and not another (and not the child's wider social network) is singled out for aid and attention. The western/Northern lessons of Christian charity and duty to the future sometimes seem out of place and difficult to decipher there. As Bornstein points out, "the discourse that fuels a good deal of global humanitarian aid is neither neutral nor secular; it is often Christian" (2003:170). Much of what has been examined here is indeed part of a long Christian tradition of thinking about children. That tradition, with all of its structures of feeling and moral economies, is implicit in many (although by no means all) contemporary humanitarian practices and expectations.

One figure that tends to get smuggled into the "children are the future" equation is the family. In his article "Children of the Future," Marshall Berman notes: "'the family' equals the future; to not have kids is to 'get out as early as you can' from life" (1993:222). In many contexts, it is not just any kind of future that requires tending in the present; it is the future of *humanity*, a *universalized* future that depends on symbolic and political generational reproduction. Humanity and universality are, of course, two of the seven fundamental principles of the Red Cross and Red Crescent Movement. These will be taken up especially in chapter 6.

The mechanism of reproduction is often imagined in these discursive contexts as very orderly. It is not about liminality or dangerous transformations or eruptions of the unexpected (though, of course, in other sites of futuristic cultural production, the things to come can be profoundly unnerving). Perhaps reacting to the conservatism of the "children are the future" equation, the Sex Pistols, the once groundbreaking punk band, said: "We are the future / there is no future" (Berman 1993:221). In a similar vein, the band Serial Killer put out a T-shirt with the words "Children Are The Future." The words were printed on a photograph of a "pretty little white girl" pointing a gun; she wore a stern expression and a red crocheted hat. Behind her stood a grown white man with a black cap, sunglasses, and a beard. Is this really to be "our future," then? Wall concludes his article on children by affirming that "children should be viewed as the hope of the world" (Wall 2004:182). Hayden White (1998) has suggested that children are often thought of as a kind of "principle of hope" that gets set against the logic of "History" and "Reality." Ernst Bloch (1986), of course, famously defined utopia as "the principle of hope."

If we accept that the liberal internationalist and humanitarian representational regimes traced here often depend on a "domestication of hope," and a domestication of the imagination, we need to study how that domestication occurs, and with what consequences (see chapter 6). One of the effects of the symbolic and ritual practices in which children augur "our future" is depoliticization, not only of children and childhood but of the projects in which figures of children are deployed in this idealizing way in various transnational spheres (e.g., the United Nations, Save the Children, World Vision, Peace Child, Médecins sans Frontières, the international Red Cross/Red Crescent). This is evident in the framing of humanitarian crises in Central Africa, for example. There, in the aftermath of genocide and in the midst of continuing war, aid organizations and visiting dignitaries have held, in their photo opportunities, in their arms the figure of the child as the principle of hope in Ernst Bloch's sense. The child is the principle of hope on which many futuristic utopias depend, and also a universalizing (but not universal) standard of a certain basic purity, and pure suffering. These compelling and charismatic figures of children are often understood to have important functions, not only in fund-raising but also, often naïvely, in "civilizing" and "humanizing" parties to political conflict. In the aftermath of great violence and loss of trust, children easily come to embody the possibility of other, better futures, and of "peace" (as elusive a concept as that is, analytically). Peace and innocence thus come to be coupled in enticing (but also *deeply disempowering*) ways. Such discursive and representational practices involve a certain "domestication of hope" and a domestication of children as the *subjects* of history, subversion, and imagination. They are relegated to the realm of the mere.

Conclusion

> A critique is not a matter of saying that things are not right as they are. It is a matter of pointing out on what kinds of assumptions, what kinds of familiar, unchallenged, unconsidered modes of thought the practices that we accept rest. . . . Practicing criticism is a matter of making such facile gestures difficult.
> —Michel Foucault (1988)

I have tried here to identify the (often facile) moralizing and affective uses of children as embodiments of a basic human goodness/innocence, as sufferers, as seers of truth, as ambassadors of peace, as embodiments of the future, and, indeed, as elementary forms of an ideal humanity (a humanity idealized in a historically particular manner). I have tried to examine these moralizing representational practices critically. But one might well ask, and I have been asked: Are these moving, hopeful visions not, after all, better than their opposites: racism and xenophobia, war and violence? Are they not forms of antiracism and pacifism? Is humanitarianism not better than the cold cost-benefit rationalities of market capitalism and U.S. imperialism? Do they not therefore deserve a more tender and respectful regard, especially in these political times? A critical respect is what I have tried to give them here. It is easier to develop a critical analysis of racisms than of antiracisms and easier to analyze the prosecution of war than the making of peace (in all of its regional and historical specificities, and bitter compromises). But both practices of criticism are important. It is in the spirit of Foucault's remarks about criticism that I make some concluding thoughts and questions here.

The work of Stuart Hall (1978), Paul Gilroy (1991, 2000), and others shows that just as racisms are historically situated cultural systems, so, too, are antiracisms. If the "anatomy of racism" (D. T. Goldberg 1990) is complex and important to analyze, so, too, is the anatomy of antiracisms. Antiracisms take many forms—for example, socialist antiracism, or Christian antiracism as it came to be exemplified in the antislavery campaign. As I mentioned earlier, they may also take the form of liberal tolerance: "We are all different, and we should value those differences." Liberal tolerance may likewise assert the exact opposite: "we are all the same" after all—"humanity," "the global family," the "Family of Man" (a trope that Barthes brilliantly analyzed in [1957] 2013). Liberal humanist tolerance, then, easily switches from classifying and cherishing cultural difference to the ritual elevation of an ultimate, underlying essence of sameness. We see this in the speeches of both Jean Pictet (1979) of the ICRC and Boutros-Ghali (1993), secretary-general of the United Nations. It is in this dual mode, as I have suggested, that the figure of children is often set in representational motion: children know innocent, timeless, ultimate, cosmological truths about our human sameness and our fundamental (if often obscured) human goodness. They see beyond the "barriers" and "obstacles" of cultural, religious, national, racial, and other differences. Here, children are asked to stand up and be counted as generically human moral subjects, and to address "the world." They are placed on an ethereal pedestal (Wall 2004) in the transnational ritual sphere, and this is of course especially evident in the broad field of humanitarian practice and its audiences. Often, specific children (usually big-eyed, prepubescent girls) stand there alone, uncertain, shy, as they are made (at least visually) representatives of all children and of the (deeply sentimentalized) moral conscience of the world.

Anne Frank, Zlata Filipovic, Irma Hadzimuratovic, Sadako Sasaki, Samantha Smith, Katya Lycheva, Kim Phuc (the famously photographed young Vietnamese girl whose body was burned by American napalm), and Malala Yousufzai have all stood there and touched the hearts of millions—perhaps momentarily. The trouble is that, from this pedestal, it is nearly impossible for actual children to act in the world as effective political, historical subjects. They are set apart by adults in an infantile utopian dimension that is freely celebrated and almost as freely ignored. They are called upon to speak for mankind and ritually miniaturized into silence. They are made the mere. All this could be otherwise.

Are there sites, then, where children are not so without agency, not thus sealed off and made sacred? Perhaps they are Outside over There, as Maurice Sendak (1981) has suggested. Following him there, I am reminded of all the other children's tales and stories where adults are only vaguely, ineffectually, irrelevantly present, or then quite killed off by the storyteller. In these stories, children are the real, knowing subjects. They are often separated from their parents as in The Famous Five books by Enid Blyton, or their remaining parent is a permissive, gregarious sea captain who is usually away, as in the Pippi Longstocking books by Astrid Lindgren. The heroes and heroines are remarkably often orphans (or specifically motherless) like Cinderella, Snow White, Bambi, Little Orphan Annie, Little Foot, and scores of others. It is true that children's stories often naturalize the largely western, modernist, middle-class idea that childhood is somehow essentially different from adulthood. As Stephens has remarked, "Many children's stories and songs—as well as works by romantically inclined child researchers—represent childhood as 'another country.'"[21] But it is equally striking that children in many of these stories engage in some very grown-up sorts of agency. Forming political solidarities? Killing adults? Killing enemies? Violence and death are key themes in the literature that many children actually read. Hansel and Gretel push an old woman into a burning oven. Jack the Giant Killer is a child soldier. So is Mulan. The Harry Potter books are full of killing.

In the humanist antiracism that informs mainstream humanitarian practices and sensibilities (Haskell 1985), there is little space for children who know "too much" or for children who hate particular presidents, political regimes, or, indeed, anyone. Children are not supposed to hate. They are not supposed to take up arms (not unwillingly and even less willingly). They are not supposed to hurt or kill, or to be hurt or killed. Yet most actual children are worldly in ways that do not fit the transnational ritual sphere that I have analyzed here. Stephens has reflected that "more and more children these days are being seen as deviations from the norm of the 'ideal child' living 'an ideal childhood.' But at what point does the accumulation of deviations begin to constitute a crisis for modern, widely circulating definitions of children and childhood? At what point must new definitions and new paradigms be developed?"[22]

Actual living, and dying, children do not displace the ritual children who inhabit the transnational ritual sphere. The latter have an efficacy of their own. And, importantly, many actual children around the world are subject to the pedagogies of ritual childhood in their schools on occasions like Peace Day, as Zhanara Nauruzbayeva recounted. These pedagogies aimed at children run through books, film, music, and other sources. Actual children and their idealized counterparts are subject to similar forces of depoliticization and dehistoricization. In questioning the depoliticization and dehistoricization of children, I do not intend to deny that children are both subjects and objects. They are objects of love and protection, desire and nostalgia, cruelty and violence—whether by adults or other children. As numerous scholars have done before me (e.g., Ivy 1995; Stephens 1995; James and Prout 1997; James 2004, among many others), I am suggesting that there is room for rethinking children as *subjects*—as *persons* and not just as elementary forms of "our shared humanity," a tranquilizing convention. By suggesting that children be permitted to be *persons* and to step off the "ethereal pedestal" (Wall 2004), I am not arguing that children as subjects should then be treated exactly like adult subjects, let alone that their proper destiny is as maximizing, autonomous, bounded individuals making rational choices. Like adults, children live in *relationships* with other people (adults and children). This simple fact of relationality is often missing from the sphere I have tried to make visible here. *Children* is a relational term; it is rendered meaningful by its opposition to the unmarked category *adults*. If we take the former seriously as an object of study, the latter is made productively stranger, too.

If we doubt the spaces opened up to children by liberal humanism, what are the alternatives? How can we think better about children and politics, and children as political beings? This is a very thorny question, as Hannah Arendt was to realize (see also James and Prout 1997:xiii). A bitter controversy was provoked by her essay "Reflections on Little Rock," in which she "resoundingly thumped the school desegregationists [in the United States] for putting children on the front line of a political battle" (Elshtain 1994:4). Jean Bethke Elshtain's essay "Political Children" is a thoughtful account of this controversy. She explains Arendt's reasons for her deeply unpopular stance: "Arendt's own memories . . . were of German young people engrafted into the Nazi state through massive mobilization efforts that had as their explicit aim eviscerating independent parental authority and private life" (Elshtain 1994:8). Arendt perceptively states that we should not insist on "separating children from the adult community as though they were not living in the same world and as though childhood were an autonomous human state, capable of living by its own laws" (Arendt, quoted in Elshtain 1994:7). Nevertheless, Elshtain argues (paraphrasing Arendt) that childhood should be protected by shielding it from public, political life. "Childhood is not a political condition from which children must be (misguidedly) liberated. It is a necessary form or container for human being in its most fragile state, a time of concealment and preparation. We abandon and betray children if we deprive them of this protection" (Elshtain 1994:7, paraphrasing Arendt). Elshtain goes on to consider children's roles (or, as some would argue, the political uses of children) in other contexts such as the more recent antiabortion protests. Her conclusion, and mine, is to recognize that "children are never *spared* politics. Every child must take his or her bearings in a particular time and place. . . . Childhood does not exist, and has never existed, in a *cordon sanitaire*" (Elshtain 1994:13; see also Coles 1986).

Those who care about the conditions of the poor or of children "out there" abroad should also care more about the specific regional and historical circumstances that create those conditions. People may want to help and to give, and yet not want to get involved in *knowing* about the political complexities of, say, violence and suffering in Congo or Syria. It is easier to just give money to the apparently unaccompanied, shy little child, "the special one," as aid organizations are aware. It is important to note, too, that there is a wide range of variation among the organizations that make representational use of children. Some organizations are more inclined than others to contextualize suffering within a sustained political and economic analysis. Two different organizations that deploy the same representational devices for fund-raising might have very different organizational and political strategies. These issues open up a series of answerable questions.

Key among these would be to examine empirically what these representations actually mean to people, and this I attempt to do to some extent in chapters 4 and 5. It might be, for instance, that what may appear to be a universalistic call to bare humanity may be heard by some people as a call to Christians. Others, like most of the Finns, might be hailed as "internationalists," "Scandinavians," members of "rich countries" of the Global North. Thus, it would be important to consider the specific contexts in which people receive these representations (see Feldman and Ticktin 2010a, 2010b; Ticktin 2011; Bornstein 2012). It is important, too, to consider the givers of aid—like the recipients—as political subjects, as I seek to do in this book.

Another terrain of questioning is opened up by tracing affect and sentiment in the humanitarian and humanistic uses of children, as I do in the following two chapters. In "Affective States" (2004), Ann Stoler marshals historical and ethnographic evidence to show how the naturalized division of reason and affect, and the privileging of the former, has hobbled analyses of colonial rule. Her insights are enabling for theorizing the "affect management" currently done by representational and imaginative figurations of children (Mazzarella 2009). Citing Janis Jenkins (1991), Stoler observes that "states [aspire to] do more than control emotional discourse, they attempt to 'culturally standardize the organization of feeling' and produce as well as harness emotional discourse within it" (2004:9; see also Berlant 2004:11). She suggests further that "such a focus opens another possible premise: that the role of the state is not only as Antonio Gramsci defined it, in the business of 'educating consent.' More basically, such consent is made possible, not through some abstract process of 'internalization,' but by shaping appropriate and reasoned affect, by directing affective judgments, by severing some affective bonds and establishing others, by adjudicating what constitutes moral sentiments—in short, by educating the proper distribution of sentiments and desires" (Stoler 2004:9; see also Berlant 2004; Mazzarella 2009). These are, of course, historically and culturally specific practices (Stoler 2004:10; Haskell 1998). As Alasdair MacIntyre writes, "Virtues are dispositions not only to act in particular ways, but also to *feel* in particular ways. To act virtuously is not to act against inclination; it is to act from inclination formed by the cultivation of virtues. Moral education is an '*éducation sentimentale*'" (MacIntyre 1984:149, quoted in Stoler 2004:11; see also Mahmood 2005:27–28).

The historical shaping of "international opinion" against such practices as torture and for human rights, women's rights, and children's rights has much to do with the shaping and circulation of affect, and with the ritual transnational spheres I have examined here. In what follows, I trace the effects of the figure of the child in "educating the distribution of sentiments."

Finally, there are researchable questions about the concept of peace. Making peace and keeping the peace is at least as complicated as making war. Linking children with peace in the ritualized and sentimentalized manner described here trivializes both children and peace, makes them both the mere. But what would it mean to examine forms of peace ethnographically? Just as racism is not a timeless, decontextualizable evil and antiracism a timeless, decontextualizable good, war and peace are not moral absolutes; they are, obviously, historically, culturally specific practices and processes. Both can be ambiguous, and ethically/affectively fraught political configurations. The questions for these times might be: Why is peace so readily infantilized (and thus depoliticized)? Why does it seem to flourish as a fuzzy and sentimental concept that has so little bearing on actual politics as practiced? What is the historical relationship between the infantilization of peace and the pacification or domestication of the category of children? Attention to the representational uses of children in the constitution of a depoliticized "humanity" may help us to imagine new ways of thinking about both children and peace in the midst of politics and history.

4. Bear Humanity

Children, Animals, and Other Power Objects of the Humanitarian Imagination

It has always amazed me how people substitute slushy emotions for such great words like friendship, compassion. You might feel soft and mushy about a little doggie.

—Bessie Head, A Woman Alone

I animate Murray into giving me what I need, even as I know that he is an assembly of cotton and stitches.

—Tracy Gleason, "Murray"

This chapter seeks to chart and analyze an enormous, expanding constellation of phenomena—objects, practices, moral economies, forms of social imagination, techniques of enchantment, and spurs to affect—that are commonly belittled, considered trivial, amusing, "childish," even "ridiculous," and that are nevertheless pervasive in and around humanitarian and "helping" practices.[1] These things dwell in the realm of "the mere." They include toys and toy-like objects like Trauma Teddies, Teddies for Tragedies, Aid Bunnies, Huggie Puppies, UNICEF dolls, Forward Bears, Shwe-Shwe Poppis, Kenana Critters, and a legion of others, and they live on the edges of contemporary humanitarian aid. Despite their pervasiveness, they are often considered "inessential" and unserious (albeit not so for their makers; as I demonstrate in the following chapter), and they are sometimes even a logistical hindrance to the work of emergency relief and aid. What all these objects have in common is that they are morally "soft" and "pure." They evoke the infantile, the powerless/harmless, and the vulnerable: innocent children and blameless (especially baby) animals. In their neoteny, they become "neutral" and neutralized (see chapters 3 and 6).[2] They are a part of the aesthetics of humanitarianism that operate in the thick of what are often complex ethics and fraught politics. That they are handmade and homemade, primarily by women and girls, genders their neutrality and perhaps facilitates their ability to cross charged lines of war and violence (if they do not end up in a ditch). They are like optimistic, cheerful, diplomatic emissaries of the distant care and compassion of invisible strangers (see Thrift 2004; Turkle 2007). (How they are perceived by their intended recipients must remain an open question here, of course.)

They are the mere to the "real" of humanitarian aid. But then humanitarian aid itself is often dismissed as the mere to "real" politics, or "real" social transformation. Humanitarian aid is "nice," perhaps even "noble," but it is not considered "world-changing." These now familiar dismissals are—whether thought warranted or not in particular cases—parallel to, and clarified by, quite another: "serious" modernist and contemporary artists, cultural critics, and philosophers have long tended to disparage the "merely" decorative and ornamental, along with "handicrafts" and the "domestic arts," the cosmetic and the beautiful (Jean Comaroff and John Comaroff 1992; Frank 2000; Scarry 2001; chapter 5). I discuss misogyny and the decorative in the next chapter. My more overarching aim here is to demonstrate what such forms of the mere—as the domestic, the child, and the animal—might have to do with the cosmological and cosmopolitical, and to reflect on what they do, and do not do, in different contexts of humanitarian practice, and affective imagination. In order to do so, I will offer a great deal of ethnographic detail on things and beings that many readers may consider unimportant—and perhaps uninteresting because culturally familiar. But as Malinowski long ago showed in *Coral Gardens and Their Magic*, reading in detail can be illuminating. It is in this spirit that generations of anthropologists have learned more about yam gardens than they ever thought possible ([1935] 1978).

Trauma Teddies

Trauma Teddies have long been used by the Australian and British Red Crosses, and their use has since spread to other countries and contexts (Newby n.d.) (see fig. 4.1). The initial Australian fund-raising event was launched in 1997,

FIGURE 4.1 Trauma Teddies knitted for the Australian Red Cross by Katy Griffis. Photograph courtesy of Katy Griffis.

and received such a positive public response that the knitted bears are still being made by volunteers there and around the world, and are now in use in many hospitals, police cars, fire trucks, and ambulances.[3]

The tactile and visual attributes of the Trauma Teddies are as follows: they are usually knitted with bright, cheerful colors of soft yarn, and their faces are meant to be smiling and friendly. Their bodies are pleasingly plump. Their size, approximately 25 x 35 cm, makes them easy for a young child to hold. Based on available photographs of them on the web, they appear to be quite androgynous—or at least quite lightly gendered. But much more importantly than that, they are teddies, childlike and even baby-like with all the affective and moral power of neoteny (Gould 1979, 1980; Sturken 2007). What are they not? They are not adult bears. They are not predators, nor are they threatening, sexual, old, sick, or dirty. They are not naturalistic simulacra of specific bears or species of bear. They are, in highly conventionalized ways, *teddy* bears, *abstract* bears (Haraway 1990). They are not animals tout court—or at all, really. Their primary place is in other categories; they are "baby animals," "toys," "therapy toys," "trauma toys" (*traumalelu*) and often *animated* as "friends" and "buddies."[4]

These knitting projects, and others like them, depend on the imaginative, ethical, gendering principle of voluntarism in particular, usually domestic, contexts. The principle of voluntarism here is marked apart from remunerated or waged labor. It is also kept strictly apart from mass production and commodification. The Trauma Teddies—like the other humanitarian "object-beings" (Povinelli 2002) that I will discuss here—cannot be bought or sold. They have to be handmade. And categorically they are gifts (Mauss 1990; Tambiah 1984; Derrida 1994; Laidlaw 2000; Sturken 2007; Bornstein 2012). Like the "home front" socks once knitted for soldiers, the teddies are a "gift of time" and care. It would, of course, be much more economical in terms of both time and money to just buy factory-made teddy bears (or socks, for that matter) and send them on their way. And it would be even more practical to send bare money. But clearly, voluntary, unpaid, sensual labor is here a core part of the imaginative "making/doing" of the gift (Castoriadis 1997). More is demanded of the gift than of the commodity, and the giver actively seeks to feel a connection to the figure of the needy or suffering child, and, through her, to a common humanity and to "the world out there" (see chapter 5).[5] Her need to help is intimately related to what might be called an enchanted connectivity (cf. Gell 1988; Mitchell 2001). Objects are in this way "able to catalyze self-creation" (Turkle 2007:9). Teddy bears appear in a wide range of humanitarian sites. The Trauma Teddy has been a part of Red Cross aid shipments to survivors of earthquakes and to the 2004 "tsunami orphans." Trauma Teddies were also sent to New York in the aftermath of the attacks of September 11, 2001. But of course, even mass-produced, factory-made teddy bears do a great deal of affective and symbolic work, and not only among children. As Elizabeth Cameron (1996) has noted, ready-made teddy bears are often placed (along with cards, flowers, candles, and other mementos) at sites of disaster and tragedy like the wreckage of the Twin Towers, the more recent Boston bombings, and, one might add, the places affected by Malaysia Airlines Flight 17 shot down over eastern Ukraine (see also Sturken 2007). They also appear at sites of fatal traffic accidents and gang murders, and in hospitals.

After the tragic 2012 school shootings at Sandy Hook Elementary School in Newtown, Connecticut, the town was deluged with gifts from all over the country, and even from around the world—cards, letters, children's art, and countless stuffed animals, among them teddy bears. "The town decided to keep it all, either in its original form, as an archived photo or as recycled material that officials are calling 'sacred soil.' . . . Nothing was thrown into a landfill." Among the gifts were thirty boxes of handmade objects. These were placed in municipal storage and would be made available for a "future art installation" in Newtown. About "400 cubic yards' worth of letters, votive candles, wreaths, and teddy bears left in makeshift shrines all over Newtown" were transported to a "trash-to-energy plant," where the public works director promised that everything would be "treated with the utmost respect. The machines were cleaned, and plant operators made sure nothing from Newtown was mixed with anything else. The process of cremating the items was also filmed to ensure nothing was taken as a souvenir." The incinerated ashes were given in a box to Yolie Moreno, the Newtown resident overseeing the ordering and archiving process. Moreno said: "We did a blessing on it. The respect and reverence for it was phenomenal. It was like a cremation, a transformation of all this love" (Eaton-Robb 2013). This extraordinary process in Newtown, of what an anthropologist would recognize as a kind of "making sacred" and "marking apart" (Turner 1970; Tambiah 1984; Douglas 2002) unfolded according to affective and ethical logics that are culturally very legible in the United States, and elsewhere.

There is a robust history of Northern knitters sending their soft gifts to "the needy" of the Global South. But these form an uneven kula ring. There is also a lively phenomenon of toys and other crafts being made in poor countries in the South and sent to the North. These southern object-beings are still within the realm of humanitarian concern, but are available *for sale* to tourists and other travelers to the South, and to retailers in the North. In other words, while the Northern Trauma Teddies, Aid Bunnies, and their ilk are kept strictly apart from the mundane, "vulgarized" spheres of commodification (Tambiah 1984:336)—somewhat like the "priceless child" written about by Viviana Zelizer (1994)—the object-beings handmade in the impoverished South are priced and involve a moral and ethical transaction mediated by money, but always money for "a good cause," like HIV/AIDS prevention or community development. The examples are numerous. Shwe-Shwe Poppis (Shwe-Shwe dolls; see figs. 4.2 and 4.3) are sewn in Soweto in South Africa to "benefit children." Reportedly modeled on young children's own drawings, they were at one time available at chain retail stores like Anthropologie in the United States and boutiques like Pulu in Helsinki, where they cost thirty-three euros (Jaakkola 2009).

Likewise, South African sewn and elaborately embroidered Forward Bears often tell of the tragic history of HIV/AIDS there.[6] These object-beings truly have a charismatic presence (Pietz 1985, 1987, 1988; MacGaffey and Harris 1993; Belting 1994; Meskell 2005) (see fig. 4.4).

FIGURE 4.2. Shwe-shwe dolls from Soweto, South Africa. Author's collection; photograph by Christine R. Choi.

FIGURE 4.3. Shwe-shwe doll "Faith" from Soweto, South Africa.
Author's collection; photograph by Christine R. Choi.

FIGURE 4.4. Forward Bear, South Africa. Kind gift of Jean Comaroff; photograph by Christine R. Choi.

Another southern toy found in a gift shop is an "earthily" rough-knitted giraffe on whose label is written: "Homespun wool hand knitted by rural women in Kenya." The giraffes were meant to promote "women's development" and "entrepreneurship." There exists, in other words, an uneven transnational *circulation* of handmade object-beings that, to different degrees in different contexts, can capture the affective and moral imagination (Povinelli 2002:102; cf. Gell 1998; Latour 2005).

The Aid Bunny Phenomenon

I initially came to think about these issues not in relation to teddy bears but to woolen "bunnies" knitted by the thousands in Finland. The extreme national popularity of a Finnish Red Cross 2006–7 publicity and aid campaign around these so-called Aid Bunnies (sing., *apupupu*) led to questions. Why do people make/do such things? What do they consider that they are doing when they are making Aid Bunnies? What are the affective and imaginative effects of these forms of "re/creative" practice? (see Castoriadis 1997; Kant 2008; and introduction). This section is a close ethnography of the Aid Bunny phenomenon. The detail enabled by consideration of a single case will, I hope, amplify and extend understanding of the broader class of objects at issue (cf. Meskell 2005).[7] Accordingly, the chapter will then turn to a more general theoretical analysis of how these objects, or, more accurately, "object-beings"—like Trauma Teddies, Aid Bunnies, and Shwe-Shwe Poppis—are related and what these kinds of practices (so easily dismissed as trivial and a "waste" of time) are about, and how they might matter in more curious ways than is at first apparent (Povinelli 2002:102; Butler 1993).

In the autumn of 2006, the Finnish Red Cross and the venerable publishing house of Otava jointly issued a call to the general public to knit a special kind of therapeutic object, the Aid Bunny (see fig. 4.5). This nationwide campaign was launched to draw attention to the specific predicaments of children in political conflicts and other disasters around the world. Its purpose was to remind people that children's experiences and challenges in these contexts often differ significantly from those of adults, and to their great detriment (see Stephens 1996; Malkki and Martin 2003).

The Aid Bunny was designed by Anu Harkki, a writer and prolific young knitter and designer. In the May 2008 issue of *Gloria*, an upscale fashion magazine, Harkki was also referred to as a "visualist" and a "TV announcer" (*TV-juontaja*). She was featured there as one of Finland's ten best-dressed

FIGURE 4.5. Aid Bunnies, Finnish Red Cross, Finland. *Avun Maailma* (cover image).

women (Talvitie 2008). These personal details are of sociological interest to the extent that they challenge well-worn stereotypes about knitters as "little old ladies," "biddies," and "grannies." These affectionately derogatory objectifications are not as harmless as they may appear, as I suggest in the following chapter. They are also quite inaccurate because knitting, in particular, has become very much a fashion again among younger people (even if in an unevenly transnational fashion). This fashion is also part of the widespread contemporary ethics and aesthetics of simplicity, recycling, repurposing, and DIY (do-it-yourself) movements (Levine and Heimerl 2008); trends in social art; and many different environmentalisms (see, e.g., Bourriaud 1998; Kester 2004, 2011; Kwon 2004; Coyne and Knutzen 2008; Jackson 2011; N. Thompson 2012).

Harkki's pattern and precise instructions for the Aid Bunny were published on the Red Cross website, in her own knitting book for young people, *Puikoissa!* (2006), and in numerous knitting magazines and other more general-readership publications around the country (e.g., *Moda* and *Kotiliesi*). News of the Aid Bunny also spread like wildfire on the Internet and it was adopted as a project in many schools' arts and crafts classes, day care centers, old age homes, and other institutions. The great majority of the knitters were women and girls, of all ages. Hundreds of bloggers wrote about and posted photographs of bunnies they had knitted. Here is the original Red Cross call:

The Aid Bunny

The Aid Bunny has a very special vocation in life [*elämäntehtävä*]. It was born to console and thus also to help!

Aid bunnies generally travel to children who have had to experience difficult things. Aid bunnies appear in the midst of tears, but hopefully bring smiles and joy with them.

Aid Bunnies have "cousins" around the world. For example, the Australian Trauma Teddy does the same work as our Aid Bunny.

Finnish [A]id Bunnies will find their own new friends with the help of the Finnish Red Cross [FRC]. The FRC delivers Aid Bunnies to children damaged by profound shock, both in Finland and abroad. They are a part of the Red Cross's programmatic whole [*ohjelmakokonaisuus*] for psychic support. In this way, the bunnies might be helping victims of an accident in Finland and children suffering from drought, earthquakes or exile in Asia, Africa, or South America. The Red Cross sends aid to tens of different countries annually. Aid bunnies are added to aid shipments when it is known that children needing psychic support are present [at the destinations]. Aid Bunnies born in Finland can be mailed to the Finnish Red Cross Logistics Centre at [address]. ("Apupupu," www.redcross.fi)[8]

The Finnish Red Cross requested that the completed bunnies be posted to Kalkku, the main logistics center of the FRC in the city of Tampere. Kalkku is a monumental three-story space blasted and carved into granite bedrock. Its original use as a munitions factory accounts for the unusual shapes of its interior corridors and other structural details. It is extraordinarily well camouflaged, with ordinary woodland growing on top of it. At one time, it also served as a Nokia rubber boot factory. It is an unlikely place for the Red Cross.

The Red Cross staff in Kalkku packed the public's contributions into standard-sized, sturdy cardboard boxes and labeled each: "APUPUPUJA 60 KPL" (aid bunnies, 60 count). The boxes were sent out along with aid shipments when appropriate. Impressive walls of these boxes towered above my head on my visit to the cavernous underground spaces of the logistics center where everything else, too, was efficiently packed, shelved, labeled, and inventoried in a perpetual state of readiness.

Nobody, least of all the Red Cross, seemed to have anticipated the extraordinary nationwide popularity of the yearlong Aid Bunny campaign. It took on robust lives of its own in numerous social fields. The target set in the original FRC call had been 10,000 bunnies. By the time the campaign was called to a halt in December 2007, approximately 25,000 bunnies had been received at Kalkku, and there was every indication that more would have been forthcoming. One "old lady" (*vanha rouva*) had, I was told, knitted 130 Aid Bunnies to mark the 130th anniversary of the Finnish Red Cross. Knitters expressed regret and frustration at the ending of the campaign, on blogs and in other ways. Here I will first report on conversations about the bunnies with Finnish Red Cross staff. I will then give a brief account of the thoughts and motivations of the thousands of knitters enchanted and mobilized by the campaign.

In a group discussion with Red Cross staff, one man said: "Since it's a lot of work [to make these bunnies], [the donors] want to know, 'So, where's this one going?'" Another added that it is understandable to feel that way "since the bunnies are made by hand all by oneself; it's a very personal way of participating." A young woman countered, "We always tell them that we can't individualize anybody. We can't determine whether it will go to a certain country or a certain group. How they get distributed depends on the need there [abroad]." The bunny is felt to be a part of its maker; like an aide-mémoire, it is an aid to the imagination enabling its maker to imagine a world to which s/he is connected. Sherry Turkle's writing about "evocative objects" is apt here: "Objects become part of our inner life: . . . we use them to extend the reach of our sympathies by bringing the world within" (2007:307; cf. Kopytoff 1986).

Talking about volunteering and handicrafts, one young Red Cross staffer explained earnestly: "This is a really good model because it's a concrete way of doing something, and since it is targeted at kids on top of that, it appeals even more. . . . It's great that the schools are [involved] in [these craft projects], too. . . . The Red Cross becomes better known and more generally attitudes [may change for the better] and then, later, your purse strings will open more easily if you know more and can imagine [where the aid goes]." Then one intensely quiet man spoke up: "We've got 11,000 Aid Bunnies here. We're drowning in them. . . . The countries that request aid from us . . . well, they're not familiar with Aid Bunnies. They don't request bunnies." The group of us dissolved in laughter. The conversation continued. Sari said: "You know, the bunnies also involve marketing issues. . . . It feels silly to market aid bunnies." Jaakko grinned: "[There you are, saying], 'And we even have these bunnies for you'!" Emma reflected: "Offhand one could suppose that parents would think that their child needs proper shoes—so, umm, at that point that Aid Bunny could even be irritating somehow." Jaakko made a scale with his arms to indicate a choice: "The bunny or the shoes . . ." Sari concluded firmly: "After the Bam earthquake, [so many people] donated balls and everything . . . and how much time it took to sort out these [toys] when we were really busy with real things and essential supplies!! Balls and bunnies must come after these."

Some shipments of Aid Bunnies have been held up or never delivered. This was the case with a shipment to Lebanon. As of late summer in 2007, the bunnies were still on standby in Jordan. One person quipped, "Maybe they'll get through somehow—maybe as stowaways." The bunnies had been turned away at the border because they had failed to conform to international toy safety standards; they were handmade and the knitting wool lacked synthetic fire retardant.[9]

The Knitters

Intended as therapy toys for children, the Aid Bunnies accomplished a great deal of other affective and cultural work as well, in the process likely affecting the lives of the bunny-givers more than those of the bunny-recipients. The knitters' thoughts, experiences, and imaginative uses of the bunnies were to some extent accessible to study: in addition to conversations in yarn shops and other venues, I took to knitting and crocheting on trains, and in public places when waiting for something or someone. Sometimes, women (of all ages) asked what I was making. This presented an opportunity to talk about the research—knitting and humanitarianism, in particular—and to inquire about people's own artisanal or other creative projects, as well as their possible involvement with the Red Cross or other humanitarian or activist work. It was surprising to realize how many people I spoke with engaged in some form of creative "making/doing" and how many were also involved in some kind of volunteer and/or activist work—and, most of all, how many had heard of the Aid Bunny campaign.

One of the effects of the Aid Bunny campaign was that dense narrative and visual threads appeared on the web as knitters posted elaborate photographic inventories of their work and comments about them. The discussions ranged from technical matters (appropriate wool types, stitches, needle sizes, the challenges of embroidering nice expressions on the bunnies' faces, and so on) to information-sharing about "knit-alongs" (talkoot) and other events, and also to a playful, often saccharin, anthropomorphism that developed narratives about the "mission" of this or that Aid Bunny. Some blogs took the form of diaries while others were conversations. I studied these ever-changing threads closely.

Another related effect of the campaign was that it enabled particular forms of sociality among the knitters; online activity was a virtual, anonymous, and thus highly manageable form of sociality. One might think of the knitter-bloggers as a "community in anonymity" along the lines of Benedict Anderson's newspaper readers (1991). But the Aid Bunny campaign also generated some degree of face-to-face sociality. Some knitters got together socially, whether for knit-alongs, knitting circles, or other events advertised online, in the print media, or by word of mouth, and frequently wrote about them on the web afterward. The format of these events appeared to be such that, again, people were very much in control of their own time and levels of engagement, and, second, that they often met strangers there. I did not see significant evidence on the web of neighbors and relatives attending together. Spatial proximity and kin relations did not appear to be the relevant forms of community; it was the Aid Bunny project as a vehicle for "helping" that brought people together. It bears emphasizing, as I do in the following chapter, that people wanted to keep tight control of the amounts of time and sociality that they gave—and that many older knitters participated because they felt themselves profoundly needy of sociality and conviviality.

Despite the fact that the Aid Bunny was launched as a Finnish Red Cross campaign, the socialities it engendered were not organized by the Red Cross administration; the multifarious activities seemed to take form spontaneously. And the Aid Bunny project was clearly not the first "knitting for charity" project for many people, but it was one of the most popular. Following one *apupupu* knit-along, someone wrote a note of appreciation: "While on a blog tour, I noticed the news about the upcoming Aid Bunny knit-along[;] I decided to participate in the event. My basket full of yarn [in one hand] and a bag of cotton wool [for stuffing] in the other, I made my way toward Myötämäki. During the evening, the bunny progressed nicely and it was only wanting one more hand. This morning I completed my 'first-born.' . . . It was really nice to meet other eager knitters and good-doers [*hyväntekijöitä*]."[10] Another person wrote: "I'm going to participate in the knitting of the Red Cross's Aid Bunnies, too. For once you get to feel good without great expense, and there's no schedule, either."[11]

The temporal "figurality" (Evans and Hall 2007:5) of the Aid Bunny in the process of making enabled the knitters to imagine a relationship with the very human (indeed, ultrahuman) need of the child in crisis. It was clear from a number of blogs that many knitters had formed, first, an image of the child being comforted by the Aid Bunny they were making, and, second, the thought that "this could be my own child" (cf. chapter 2). Very often, however, the bloggers' imaginations were most vividly captured by the process of *animating* the product of their work, the bunny—giving it a name, a disposition, a calling, a biography, and more (cf. Tambiah 1985:335–47; Appadurai 1986; Kopytoff 1986; Gell 1998; Povinelli 2002; Latour 2005).

The Aid Bunnies as Cultural Artifacts

The Red Cross's original call encouraged knitters to make their aid bunnies "courageously individual," but the very precise instructions given as to the materials to be used, the size and shape of the bunnies, and the minimum number of colors to be used (four), et cetera, had the effect of giving them a rather uniform, standardized look. They all "wore" trousers, a long-sleeved sweater, and a scarf (firmly attached to the back of the bunny's neck). That is, their lower bodies consisted of trousers and "bunny-colored" feet, while their upper bodies were mostly long-sleeved sweaters, with "bunny-colored" hands, head, and ears. The "bunny color" I saw was most often creamy white, suggesting rabbits with their white winter coats, but also perhaps speaking to some connection between the colors of the bunnies and those of their makers. There were little physical variations in the bunnies: some had whiskers while others did not; some had longer ears than others; some had eyes set further apart than others, and then there were the slightly over- or under-stuffed ones. Patterned or multicolored trousers and sweaters told of skill, perhaps even competitive prowess—or perhaps, simply, a desire to give pleasure to a child. But these variations seemed only to confirm or emphasize the overall uniformity and sameness of the bunnies. They were, in fact, anonymous (like their makers and, indeed, the child recipients). Their gender unmarked and generally unspecified, these warmly dressed bunnies also shared, to my mind, something with their makers. At the least, they were dressed for cold climates. Further, they told of soft spots—even pleasurable silliness—in otherwise relatively reserved (often even dour) personae.

One blogger wrote: "Aid Bunny 006 steps up to service, ready to do battle against coldness and indifference. Its secret weapons are a happy mind and a proper hug."[12] On December 19, 2006, just before midnight, the same blogger, "Maartsi," posted a new message announcing the completion of her seventh bunny, "007 and a license to hug." Maartsi anticipated that it would be a bit sad to see all these bunnies leaving for the Red Cross.[13] The theme of service appeared often, as in the following: "Aid bunny Pekka ready to step up to service as a hug buddy [halikaveri], [or] sleep buddy [unikaveri]."[14]

Now comes an imagined interview with a "Mr. Aid Bunny," written by its maker, "Hannaliini," in August 2006:

Hannaliini: Excuse me, who are you?
Pupu [Bunny]: I am Mr. Aid Bunny, but in the future I will also come to recognize all the names by which my future owner calls me.

H: An Aid Bunny? What does one do?

P: [It] brings joy and solace to one who needs it. [It] is a friend.

H: To whom?

P: To whomever a Red Cross mission delivers me.

H: From where have these Aid Bunnies appeared in the world, now, all of a sudden?

P: As you have surely noted in reviewing knitting blogs, there are a lot of us (on some blogs, by the way, there have been some truly charming bunny maidens!). And all the time there are more, hopefully lots more so that everyone needing one can be found one.

H: If I've understood correctly, you are only at the beginning of your work. What will the first challenge in your career be?

P: To travel in a postal packet to Tampere, to the FRC's logistics center, whence I will be delivered where I am needed. Traveling is an important part of an Aid Bunny's work at the beginning of its career. But that is not a problem as we Aid Bunnies do not suffer from claustrophobia or fear of flying.

H: How long does a mission last?

P: A lifetime. This is a calling [kutsumustyö] for which one is born and which one lives.

H: Good luck for the challenges of the future, and thanks for the interview!

P: Thank you, and greetings to all of Finland's Aid Bunnies! Till Tampere![15]

The knitters' sometimes baffling scripts for their Aid Bunnies' social and moral biographies could be elaborate. The bunnies were "born" to a calling as servants and "buddies" to suffering children around the world. The idea of a lifelong calling is interesting because it mirrors the popular, romanticized image of what a Red Cross aid worker might feel and do (Kopytoff 1986). And yet, as the nurses, doctors, and other personnel I interviewed said (chapters 1, 2, and 6), *professionalism* was what they strove for—and definitely not a self-sacrificing calling to "humanity." And it should be mentioned that the professional aid worker did not necessarily know anything at all about the Aid Bunny phenomenon.

The bunnies "talked" a great deal: "Heipsan [hi]. We are Sisu [Grit] and Apila [Clover]. Saara is our cousin. Saara is going to go out into the world with the FRC. But instead of the FRC's container, we get to be in Santa's backpack. It's apparently exciting there! First we're wrapped in fancy papers, then we get to go on a sleigh ride, and finally a nice Santa-uncle gives us in our wrapping to little children. We're waiting eagerly."[16] On the same blog site, but on August 20, 2006, the knitter posts a photograph of a new bunny and writes: "Saara Paula Ristiina's first portrait. Age, 10 minutes. . . . The strategic dimensions: weight 72g, height 34cm. A bit mini, but girls are always a bit smaller =)."

Another photograph on a different site has this greeting: "Hi, I'm Apu-pupu Anselmi. I finally saw daylight today on August 28, 2006. My maker has been slow for no good reason; supposedly making a scarf from some gift yarn and cleaning house and juice-making were more important . . . With bunny greetings and wanderlust, Anselmi."[17] "Butterfly Maiden" (Perhoneito) introduces her bunny: "Next week, it is heading toward new adventures, but here it is posing for the media."[18] "As bunnies tend to do, these are going to multiply wildly," blogs yet another knitter.[19]

Much of the foregoing can perhaps be understood as a pleasurable, largely private and anonymous pastime, a self-conscious silliness and as evidence of adults at play. Fantasy and other kinds of play and toys are—like childhood itself—made simultaneously a trait, an impulse, a need, a right of children.[20] A child who does not know how to play raises diagnostic red flags. A child who has been wounded psychically and/or bodily may receive play therapy in which toys, music, and drawing are vitally important. That is the state of things in those parts of the contemporary world and segments of society in which children have stopped working, as Zelizer (1994) points out in Pricing the Priceless Child (see also Ariès 1962; Steedman 1995; Stephens 1995). The foregoing evidence of adults playing while "helping"—easy to ridicule, no doubt—belongs in the realm of the mere. This case holds a perhaps uncomfortable mirror up to much other activity around the world that is done in the name of "aid"—and in the name of children.

"Doing Something" (But Never Enough)

Just giving a financial donation clearly does not produce all the social, affective, and ethical effects that giving time, skills, and imagination can. It does not allow for self-making in the same way. The Finnish Red Cross itself says: "Financial assistance is an easy and convenient way of helping, but there are also other ways and means of participating [osallistua]. Instead of money, one can give, for instance, time, say, by knitting . . . aid bunnies for use by the Red Cross" (emphasis added).[21] The term osallistua can be translated as participating or taking part in something, but it can also connote making oneself a part of something. Yet there was always ambivalence about how valuable "mere" knitting could be, accompanied by the comforting rationalization that one was "at least doing *something*," however small, trivial, or humble. As the sentiment is widely expressed in English, one was at least "making a difference."

One English-speaking blogger expressed the ambivalence thus:

> Knitting and crocheting . . . [are] an act without prejudice or bias, and there is something within the knitter or crocheter that longs to warm others in hard times. Even if the artisan brings her own bias to the craft, *ultimately* only good can come of it. *You can't knit a bomb or a gun*, but you can knit some socks for a soldier who hasn't seen his family in a year and let him know that somebody cares about him, *even a total stranger*. You can knit a hat for an Afghani child who's lost her entire family, and show her that somebody does care about her welfare. The point of this article isn't [to] get all hippied out, but to remind you [that,] *even if you can't change the world*, offering a token of comfort to somebody you've never met to remind them that there are good things in the world cannot be a bad thing, regardless of who you are and your personal beliefs. If you're going to be knitting or crocheting anyway, why not put something for a charity next on your "to do" list. It can be as small as a toque, or as large as an afghan. *It can be for animals or people.* There's a charity out there for everybody[;] you alone are not going to start a revolution, but if enough people do it, it just might. (Gilliam 2007:1, emphases added)

This individual, U.S.-based appeal to kindhearted artisans is a rich and curious cultural document that expresses some of the key concerns I saw in the blogs and chats of the Finnish knitters. A certain ambivalence and even defensive embarrassment were palpable, just as in the passage above. To summarize these widely shared sentiments, people were all too conscious of the fact that knitting, crocheting, "handicrafts," and other (usually gendered) work of the hand tend to be *always already* "less than." "Handicrafts" and "crafts" are *less than* "fine art" or *less than* "fine craft" and design (see chapter 5). Knitted gifts—whether under the banner of aid or charity—are *less than* "real" humanitarian assistance in the form of medicine and doctors, food and water, shelter, and other "basic needs." Finally, these cuddly, homemade "tokens" of care and sentiment are ambivalent objects even for their makers because, as Gilliam (2007:1) wrote, they are not going to "start a revolution." They will not effect real political change, structural and radical change, in the world. This, as mentioned earlier, is also a criticism commonly leveled at humanitarian organizations like the Red Cross: they patch things up, thus maintaining the status quo, and attempt to "steer clear" of politics while nevertheless working in politically very fraught conflict zones, contexts where neutrality itself is a precarious political tactic (see Redfield 2010; chapter 6). This kind of robust realism was sometimes affirmed, sometimes denied, but it always somehow hovered over the activity of making more "mere" bunnies. The aesthetics and politics of the mere—the ostensibly apolitical, harmless, neutral—parallel the way that ideas of "world peace" or even just "peace" are literally domesticated by being associated with childhood (and thus, naïveté and impracticality)—what I called "the infantilization of peace" in the preceding chapter.

But while the knitting of bunnies did not "start a revolution," it did produce certain effects. Among these, the *affective imagination of connection*, of relationship to the imagined child in need of help and comforting, was prominent. It was important to people to be able to envision this as intimate, handmade, person-to-person help (*ihmiseltä ihmiselle*). One knitter imagined the relationship between her particular bunny and a child; she thought the bunny was especially nice to make because she "knew" that it would become "really dear and important to a child." The personhood of the Aid Bunny enabled an affective, ethical link with the imagined child in need "somewhere out there" in the world (*siellä jossain maailmalla*). (This of course assumed the likability and cultural decipherability of the bunnies among children in unknown contexts.)

The enchantment in imagining distance and proximity, anonymity and intimacy, through the travels of the bunnies was powerful for these knitters. Perhaps the distance and anonymity allowed for some degree of *enchantment of the self*. There were many photographs on the Internet of groups of Aid Bunnies with captions such as: "Tornio's Aid Bunnies ready, on their way out into the world! [*Tornion Apupuput valmiina lähdössä maailmalle!*]." Tornio is the name of a city and province in Finland's Lapland. To knit an Aid Bunny in the frozen North and to try to envision its destination—in, say, Mozambique or Mali—is an evocative form of making virtual and enchanted (even fantastical) connectivities among persons and object-beings, and adults and children (and, sometimes, children and children).

The Red Cross—along with other humanitarian organizations—has had to become increasingly sensitive to donors' desires to know where their handmade gifts would travel. In its December 2007 thank-you message to the public, the organization gave a general accounting of the destinations of the bunnies: "Aid Bunnies have thus far been sent along with aid shipments to Nepal, Mongolia, China, Palestine, Morocco, Tunisia, Ukraine, Byelorus, and Tadzhikistan. The next shipment will take place on Wednesday, December 19, when 3660 aid bunnies will leave for Tadzhikistan." Many people want to be able to see, or at least *visualize*, not only the regional destination of their gift but also the form of need alleviated, and even the individual young recipient. But again, this remains a frustrated, and extravagant, desire given the institutional, logistical costs and time investment that would go into arranging such reciprocity. Institutions like the Red Cross therefore have to perform delicate metaphorical translations and metonymical substitutions in the interplay between the particular and the general, the unique and the generic, the singular and the universal, the intimate and the other, the near and the distant. In these increasingly sophisticated humanitarian and pastoral technologies of power, the sensory and the affective are both key to the social imagination of need and neediness—and of the self in the world.

How is one to analyze this kind of material? One might begin by noting that these practices have antecedents in a rich western history of making things on the "home front" for the benefit of one's troops on the battlefront. The very term *home front* of course indicates the ambivalence and instability of the category of "civilians" who now, more often than not, are pawns, targets, and even participants in contemporary conflicts. Through knitting socks and sweaters, civilians in many wars have fashioned imaginative, affective links to their children, partners, friends, siblings, and parents on the front (cf. Lutz 2001).[22] These expressions and practices of domesticity are perhaps too easily dismissed as trivialities, just like certain gendered practices of quilting, embroidery, crocheting, and sewing clothes.

The Aid Bunnies are also *creatures*—and creatures of a particular kind. But of what *kind*? Is the bunny a "toy," a "stuffed animal," "an animal," "a baby animal," "a baby," "a child," "a companion," "a friend," "a therapy object," a potential "commodity," a "marketing idea" to be copied, or something else? Is it lovable, comforting, valuable, laughable, embarrassing—or "just stupid"? Is it animate?

Clearly, the answers depend on who is doing the classifying and why. Clearly, too, the meaning and status of the object-being is likely to vary among those who encounter it. I have not had the opportunity of talking with children who have received Aid Bunnies, but psychologists who have worked on international missions find Aid Bunnies and other toys valuable in play therapy (cf. Winnicott [1971] 2005; Paley 2004). The FRC membership magazine, *Avun Maailma*, quotes Kirsi Palonen, a member of the Red Cross's psychologists' reserve team: "Drawing, telling stories to plush toys and many games are children's natural ways of [processing or unpacking] [*purkaa*] shocking experiences. In this work [of therapy], the plush toy is an important tool" (*Avun Maailma*, March 2006, 46).

The critic in me immediately thinks about the historical and cultural specificities of toys, and stuffed animals in particular, but the evidence for the efficacy of stuffed toys and play in therapeutic work, even cross-culturally, is convincing according to Red Cross–affiliated psychologists I have interviewed. Again, the object-beings of homemade humanitarianism are not just any old "plush toys." Again and again, we are dealing with animals—especially baby animals. We are confronted, repeatedly, with a powerful triangulation of animality, childness, and humanity (see chapter 3). This humanity is, upon inspection, not so bare at all, *pace* Giorgio Agamben (1998). The children and animals do not just constitute some minimal sort of humanity; they are, in their imagined goodness, innocence and presumed universality, exemplary humans.

The Aid Bunnies, Trauma Teddies, and other denizens of these (always unevenly transcultural) force fields of imagination and enchantment reveal complex practices and processes of anthropomorphism, and animism. These, in turn, vitally depend on neoteny—on the "cuteness" of baby-ness (cf. Allison 2004). Human babies, "baby animals," dolls, and stuffed animals are all *culturally and morally animate* in a particular way here (cf. Coveney 1957; Gell 1998:121; Genosko 2005).

Toy stuffed animals, of course, have a less than cuddly genealogy. Their ancestors were living animals killed and stuffed and preserved through taxidermy—sometimes in the name of science and, at other times, as trophies—famously by Ernest Hemingway and Teddy Roosevelt (Haraway 1990, 2008). But what started as a way of objectifying animality and animating objects has over time become a way of personifying humanity. Bunnies are not just animals, nor just "rabbits"; they are "baby animals" (Ritvo 1985). As babies, they are already humanized, and as neotenous "cute" animals, they are *almost more-than-human*—just as human children as moral subjects often seem *more than* human adults.

Of course, these figures are not just a detail of humanitarian cosmopolitics; they travel more widely. Baby animals people the pages of children's books. They are teachers of morality, just as the figure of the child is often thought to be, as I argued in the preceding chapter. Injunctions to "be kind to animals" and trips to the zoo are important lessons in this specific historically middle-class moral pedagogy. As Harriet Ritvo (1985) has written, animals have long been used to teach children about their own humanity and moral personhood. Here, humanness and humaneness converge.

Bear Humanity

Aid Bunnies, Trauma Teddies, Huggy-Puppies, "Universal Child" ragdolls, abandoned animals, baby animals, and images of children-who-need-your-help-so-call-today are among the cultural figures that provoke and cultivate the humanitarian imagination. Human-animal, nature-culture forms of relationship are so "good to think" (Lévi-Strauss 1966) that they form cosmological constellations all over the world. In these constellations, soft toys, children, and animals all seem to stand for each other somehow, and are part of the infantilization of lofty cosmopolitical goals and ideals like "world peace" and even "saving the planet." Irony here acts as a check on idealism. The only persons who can legitimately take all this in earnest, we are shown, are children. Practices, pedagogies, and forms of materiality and visuality associated with "children's culture" (usually an unmarked middle-class, western children's culture) are thus really quite central to humanitarian aid, philanthropy, and charity.

The Aid Bunnies and their kind are truly cultural objects in which many forces and meanings converge. They are at once gifts, toys, therapy objects, and "handicrafts." They are nonpolitical and noncommodified. They are animals, but also quite human, in a specifically infantile way. They can be therianthropic, shape-shifting from human to animal. There is much in classic anthropological theory that can help in the analysis of these powerful object-beings. I will very briefly discuss a small fraction of these theories, ones that seem most compelling here and that work together synergistically.

One can begin by thinking about the Aid Bunnies as "power objects" (MacGaffey and Harris 1993). European missionaries famously encountered such power objects in Africa, misrecognized them as "heathen fetishes," and set about on campaigns against them. Many the iconoclasts destroyed and some they took away to museums—sometimes under the classification of "primitive art" and, at other times, curious artifacts and proofs of savagery. Others ended up in places like the Natural History Museum of Los Angeles.[23]

FIGURE 4.6. Kongo Nkisi, Central Africa. Courtesy of the Iris & B. Gerald Cantor Center for Visual Arts at Stanford University; anonymous gift.

The Congolese power objects, for example *minkisi* and *minkonde*, analyzed by Wyatt MacGaffey and Michael Harris (1993), William Pietz (1985, 1987, 1988), and others, stood among these.

MacGaffey and Harris (1993) show what kinds of cosmological work these power objects (their term) have done, and still do, and in the process they develop a compelling analysis of the "*ritual personhood of objects.*" Aid Bunnies do not have the awe-inspiring spectrum of powers of *minkisi*, powers that can hurt as well as heal, but I suggest that they do have ritual and social personhood, and powers of their own (cf. Pietz 1985, 1987, 1988; Kopytoff 1986).

In a thoughtful re-engagement with Max Weber and Marcel Mauss, a now-classic analysis by the late Stanley J. Tambiah pushes further the analytical and imaginative possibilities of the concepts of charisma and the gift. He does so in the context of research in Thailand in *The Buddhist Saints of the Forest and the Cult of Amulets* (1984). The Greek term *charisma*, he notes, is rendered as "gift" in the King James Bible (1984:321). But Weber's famous analysis of charisma ignored the connection of charisma with objects, or what Tambiah terms "*the objectification of charisma in talismans, amulets, charms, regalia, palladia, and so forth*—a phenomenon as old as religion, indeed as old as all forms of leadership" (1984:335, emphasis added). In the Thai context, he notes, "people attribute virtues and energies to persons because of their ascetic conduct; [and] these persons are seen as capable of transmitting their charisma to persons directly or, more usually lastingly, through amulets they have charged and activated. The charisma is concretized and *sedimented* in objects; these objects are repositories of power" (1984:335, emphasis added). This is relevant to the effort to understand the Aid Bunnies, I suggest, even if we are not accustomed to associating "mere" toys with such "real" objects of political theory as charisma.

Returning to Mauss, Tambiah argued, "Hau, or reciprocity, has multiple meanings. It can figure in the humiliation of rank, as in the agonistic prestations of Kwakiutl potlatch, or it can establish the solidarity of the exchanges, as in the kula ring. *This is so because when people exchange 'things' they are exchanging social relationships, therefore exchanging themselves up to a point*" (Tambiah 1984:340, emphasis added).

The knitters of the Aid Bunnies were motivated by a desire to help, to give *of themselves*—of their time, skills, materials, and imagination—good egalitarians, but taking multiple structural inequalities between themselves and the imagined recipients for granted. But the knitters were not just motivated by unidirectional charity—charity that usually involves "humiliations of rank" and the de facto accentuation of social distance (Bornstein 2013, 2012). If I have understood correctly, many of the knitters were motivated by an imagined "solidarity of the exchanges" in Tambiah's sense above. It is important, too, that the knitters were "exchanging themselves *up to a point*." Where one might want to knit Aid Bunnies for people in need "out there," one might not want "the needy" or the "foreign" to come knocking at one's door.

But if we can speak of "the *hau* of the Aid Bunny," are we not thereby obliged to reconsider the question of reciprocity (Mauss 1990)? In this chapter, I have dealt with a class of objects—such as Aid Bunnies and Trauma Teddies—that were insistently styled as *gifts*. But as I have briefly noted, a flow of other sorts of dolls, teddies, and object-beings form a countercircuit from South to North, from impoverished regions of the world to wealthy ones, also in the name of aid, "helping," and humanity.

As if inspired by the *hau* of the Aid Bunny, the Shwe-Shwe Poppi makes its way back North, completing the circle of reciprocity, and balancing, in a necessarily imperfect way, the decidedly imbalanced trade in humanitarian power objects. But there was another reciprocity in the apparently "pure" gifts (Laidlaw 2000) of the Aid Bunnies and Trauma Teddies, too. Their Finnish makers got in return for their gifts not only forms of sensual and aesthetic pleasure from the processes involved in hand-making but also vehicles for imagining a strong connectedness to the "world out there," and to an imagined child in need. The knitters satisfied—at least in some measure—their need to help. Just how acute a need that was, for some of them, is examined in the following chapter.

Conclusion

If we can take seriously the idea of the Aid Bunnies as power objects, then the question to ask of them (as with *minkisi*) is not "Is their magic real?" Rather, the question is: "*What do people do with this object?*" "*What effects does it enable and produce?*" as Foucault once asked of the imagination (Foucault [1954] 1986:70, emphasis added; see also the introduction).[24]

In chapter 5, I discuss humanitarianism as a counter to what Hannah Arendt once described as "thoughtlessness"—thoughtlessness understood precisely as a *failure of the imagination* (Arendt 2006). Susan Sontag has used the same term in *Regarding the Pain of Others* (2003:8). If there is anything to this, then perhaps we might think of Aid Bunnies and Trauma Teddies first of all as power objects for warding off thoughtlessness.

Those who wish to enhance their faculty of memory practice specific exercises for strengthening it. Perhaps we might see the humanitarian practices I have described here as comparable exercises, for the enhancement not of memory but of the faculty of empathetic imagination. Such exercises are perhaps not world-shaking in their importance. They certainly will not "start a revolution." They only, "merely," create little obstacles to those failures of the imagination that we know as thoughtlessness and cruelty.

5. Homemade Humanitarianism
Knitting and Loneliness

Loneliness and the experience of feeling abandoned are the most horrifying kind of poverty.

— Mother Teresa, quoted in Juho Saari, "Yksinäisenä yhteisössä"

The Sense of Giving and Helping

If the good gift is expected to spring from selfless generosity, and thus a form of *selflessness*, then it is surprising and even jarring for the secretary general of the Finnish Red Cross, Kristiina Kumpula, to look at the world around her and remark that giving can be a form of entertainment and a pleasurable pastime (Björkman 2010:14; cf. Tammisto and Lahtinen 1994; Stebbins and Graham 2004).[1] Is this not an implicit criticism? No, it is based on observation. And it is not a problem according to Kumpula. Helping is not necessarily or only a calling, paid work, or a professional practice—and giving is often not just a singular act. Both helping and giving are very popular forms of associational life, and social life more generally, and often they take the form of voluntarism (see Poikolainen 1997; J. Wilson 2000; Rajaniemi 2007; Kumpula 2008; Mykrä 2010; Laasanen 2011; Muehlebach 2012). Estimates vary, but Kumpula states: "Over a third of all Finns uses thousands of hours annually in volunteer activity" (2008:46). A 2010 study indicates that over 30 percent of Finns offer their time to voluntary activity

(Mykrä 2010:7; see also Pessi and Saari 2011; Bornstein 2012; Muehlebach 2011, 2012).[2]

"'Of course volunteer work is a value choice [arvoratkaisu] for many. People want to be involved in building something greater than themselves,' she says. . . . 'Volunteer work should never replace the welfare society, it is always only its complement,' Kumpula stresses; [nevertheless,] 'Helping brings happiness' [Auttaminen tuo onnea]" (Björkman 2010:14, emphasis added; see also Kumpula 2008). And as a slogan in the Red Cross's monthly membership magazine, Avun Maailma, promises, "auttaminen auttaa": helping helps (Avun Maailma, 2010, cover). One way that "helping helps" is that, beyond entertainment, helping can enable forms of sociality and conviviality that may, in turn, offer some degree of protection against loneliness, social isolation, and asocial time (cf. Muehlebach 2011). Sending one's gifts of aid "out into the world" (tuonne maailmalle), connecting the familiar with the unknown, the self and the imagined other, offers also a kind of company to people who, as will become clear, are badly in need of it. And voluntarism is, of course, one of the seven fundamental principles of the International Red Cross and Red Crescent Movement.[3] The relation between the domestic and the international is both an imaginative and an ethical one.

The domestic and the international are related here in quite a specific way. Kumpula sees a clear link between the Red Cross's domestic projects and its international work of emergency relief and aid: "Finns are . . . active in international aid largely because we have such a diversity of national activity" (Björkman 2010:14). Domestic involvement can extend into a commitment to the international, to suffering and need "out in the world" (maailmalla). In this way, Finns' practices in domestic programs can create aids to the imagination, of a connection to something greater than themselves. But what I will suggest here is that the urge to help faraway others has domestic roots in a different sense too, for it is quite specific characteristics of the home society that both create a deep need to help and allow us to question anew whom, exactly, we should regard as the needy.[4]

A scene of helping as pastime might look like this: On a brisk September afternoon a group of friends huddle together on a busy shopping street, each holding a red plastic Hunger Day collection box. As they reach their boxes toward passersby, wearing their requisite Red Cross aprons, they are engaged in guessing who looks like they will donate and who does not. Every few minutes they appear to see something funny. They look happy and a little self-conscious.

A scene of helping might also look like this: An older woman in a bland, medium-sized town braves the icy pricks of the November wind on her face to get to the yarn shop before it closes. She is looking forward to knitting in front of the television. She will work on a baby jacket to give to a humanitarian project she has read about. She lingers, a little too long, to exchange a few words with the shopkeeper.

In the course of this project, I spent a good deal of time in yarn shops, both as an anthropologist and a customer. I heard and often participated in conversations there, noticing that in these settings customers talked with each other relatively freely—more so than they might in a grocery store or other settings, at any rate. I saw how they enjoyed touching and weighing the yarns in their hands and discreetly smelling them, playing with color and texture combinations, and taking time over their selections. People took pleasure, as I did, in just being there and breathing in the scent of wool. In a good yarn shop there are things to see and touch, and to smell (cf. Tammisto and Lahtinen 1994; Sonneveld 2007). The walls of yarn even make a pleasing acoustic environment. These are safe places of comfort and pleasure. When I told the shopkeepers and customers about my research interest in humanitarianism and handwork, they seemed engaged. I generally got interested comments, and everyone knew what I was referring to when I talked about the "humanitarian handicraft campaigns" discussed in the previous chapter. One woman happened to be a handwork (käsityö) teacher at a Helsinki high school and—while showing me a crocheting technique—told me about all the humanitarian projects she had been involved in teaching and doing, from the Red Cross Aid Bunnies to UNICEF's Anna and Toivo dolls to the Mother Teresa blankets. She hesitated, however, to follow up our conversation with an interview later. It seemed to me, sadly, that she was worried about being made to seem silly by the anthropologist. I was reminded yet again of the commonness of belittling when it comes to "handicrafts" and "craftsy people"—which, I imagine, might have been one cause of her worry (see Adamson 2007, 2010; Alfoldy 2007a:xv–xvi; Lippard 2010; and below).[5]

On a slow afternoon in one Helsinki yarn shop, the owner observed that, while the age range of knitters and other yarn artisans was wide—the popularity of knitting being once more clearly on the rise—there was a category of people for whom knitting held special importance. She said that for old people, "knitting in order to help others" (neulominen avuksi muille) was a very important part of their lives. She then began to say, "Often I am the first living person [elollinen ihminen] who has spoken to the elder [vanhus]—" I jumped in, anticipating her next words: "—all day." She corrected me: "Well—or for *many* days."

A study of "old age and vulnerability" in Finland examines the many factors that may cause such isolation, among them the weakening of the senses. People may become hesitant to go out in public, with the result that "in a week there may be many days when no one talks to one, asks questions, or comments on one's thoughts. The aged person cannot avoid the experience that her life doesn't interest anybody" (Sarvimäki, Heimonen, and Mäki-Petäjä-Leinonen 2010:110).[6] A person's falling away from time, becoming unmoored—time becoming truly *asocial* time—is a frightening prospect (see DeLillo 2002).

The owner of a small-town shop in the southwest of Finland told me about a woman in her eighties, a regular, who always said that knitting for others "kept her alive, quite literally."[7] Like her colleagues in other shops, she wanted to emphasize that for her aged customers, knitting *to help others* was what was particularly meaningful. Knitting for kin was not mentioned in this connection. Perhaps this was because there are only so many knitted things that friends and family can use. It is also possible that relations with relatives may be ambivalent, strained, or nonexistent, and that at an advanced age one has lost many friends and kin alike. For many, there was also enchantment in addressing a gift of warmth and comfort, and of the *self*, to an unknown, distant other in need—a "distant sufferer." This was a major theme in the Internet exchanges I described in chapter 4.

The imagined others in need, I learned from the shopkeepers, were usually—but not necessarily—thought to be "out in the world" (*maailmalla*), "there" (*siellä*). Over the years, they had all sold a lot of yarn for humanitarian projects. People's projects had varied, but the greatest quantities of wool by far, I was told, had been bought for Mother Teresa blankets (discussed below), and these have ended up in Finland as well as abroad.

The owner of one of the Helsinki shops corroborated what I had already heard: "It is hard for Finns to think that our own people should be helped, too . . . And yet, there are actually food queues in Espoo!"[8] Some knitters "do also make socks and scarves for people who have fallen between the cracks and for drunkards" (sing., *pultsari*); she blushed at her own use of the derogatory *pultsari*, but shrugged apologetically: "Well, that's just how it is" (*No niin se vaan on*). (I thought of the overlap between the vulnerabilities of old age and those of becoming alcoholized.) The figure of the needy shifted shape as she thought about her various different customers and their knitting projects, and their intended beneficiaries.

That a yarn shop should be the first place in which an old person has had direct human contact with another living person in days is not unusual for Finland (or for much of northerly Europe, I imagine). In a society that prides itself on self-reliance, grit (sisu), and a fierce love of privacy and solitude, and where furthermore people do not readily engage in "useless chatter" (e.g., turha pulina, höpötys, paapatus), especially not with strangers, it is possible to be very alone, and very silent.[9] In urban and semi-urban areas where apartment living is the norm, and where people do not generally interact much with their neighbors, loneliness can become compounded. Sometimes such solitude is welcome, of course, as I explained in chapter 1. But often it is not.[10]

In this chapter, I will follow some of the thematic directions that came from my work in the yarn shops. First, I will briefly address loneliness and its sometimes desolate results in Finland, a key context for the forms of giving and associational life that I will be concerned with here. Second, I will examine one of the many social assistance projects run by the Red Cross domestically within Finland, the Friendship Service (Ystäväpalvelu), which addresses loneliness and other kinds of need. I will also make very schematic suggestions about the significance of voluntarism in this context. Finally, I will give an interpretation of how work of the hand like knitting, crocheting, and sewing becomes a way of thickening one's connectedness to a larger, living society, and how this makes giving and helping, for some people, not just an entertaining pleasure or casual choice but a response to a sharper kind of need—managing time as a way of keeping dead time at bay. The social connections forged in this way may be fragile and temporary, but they are, for many, a vitally meaningful "care of the self" (Foucault 1986).[11]

Loneliness, Silence, and Social Isolation

In order, then, to understand a key motivation for internationalist helping (kansainvälinen apu) in Finland, it is necessary to consider the domestic social issue of solitude and loneliness as one element in larger formations.[12] While people (whether young or old) do often enjoy voluntary solitude as I suggested in chapter 1, loneliness remains an oppressive and painful condition for many, as is well documented in the literature (see, e.g., Kauranen 1993; Hytönen 2002; Jokinen 2005; Tiikkainen 2006; Saari 2009; Sarvimäki, Heimonen, and Mäki-Petäjä-Leivonen 2010; Heiskanen and Saaristo 2011; Uotila 2011). Social isolation (*eristäytyminen*), alienation (*vieraantuminen*), marginalization (*syrjääntyminen*), and falling between the cracks (*väliinputoaminen*) are routinely discussed and debated in Finland as serious social problems, as endemic as depression, alcoholism, and suicide. Truly asocial time, where sociality and conviviality are missing to an extreme degree, is a specter but also a real possibility. Finland is not of course unique in having these problems (see Muehlebach 2011, 2012); what may be more unusual is their prevalence and particular social resonance—and perhaps also a greater public willingness to take them up as subjects of debate and discussion than might be the case in other societies (cf. Apo 1998). These are of course problems for both men and women who are aged, and there is some gender differentiation in their experiences. (This is of course true for younger people as well.) But in this chapter—as in much of the rest of the book—it is women who constitute the majority of my informants.

In their study "Elders' Loneliness," Viktoria Ahonen and Hanna Bukis (2008) write that the daily living of loneliness in old age is common and has been identified as one of the most acute challenges of gerontology. Loneliness has been demonstrated to lead to increased mortality, suicide risk, the growing use of health services, the weakening of memory, and institutional care. Often, unsurprisingly, loneliness is covered up by symptoms of depression (Kangas and Keski-Heroja 2000; Ahonen and Bukis 2008). Alcohol is a form of self-medication for many, regardless of age, gender, or class, as many studies have long shown (e.g., Ahlström 2007; Aalto and Holopainen 2008; Laitalainen, Helakorpi, and Uutela 2008; Ahlström and Mäkelä 2009; Mäkelä, Mustonen, and Huhtanen 2009; Viljanen 2010). There has been an increase in alcohol use by the oldest age cohorts, and men and women in these cohorts are increasingly drinking similar amounts (Mäkelä, Mustonen, and Huhtanen 2009:282, 284–86). There is much that is bleak here, and much space for what Foucault (1991), among others, has called the "limit experience" (see chapters 2, 6, and the conclusion).

In different measures, aspects of these life circumstances could be examined in relation to what Lauren Berlant (following Bataille 2000, Foucault 1991, and others) has called "slow death": "Slow death prospers not in traumatic events, as discrete time-framed phenomena like military encounters and genocides can appear to do, but in temporally labile environments whose qualities and whose contours in time and space are often identified with the presentness of ordinariness itself, that domain of living on in which everyday activity; memory, needs, and desires; and diverse temporalities and horizons of the taken-for-granted are brought into proximity and lived through" (Berlant 2011:100, see also 285n67; cf. Kauranen 1993). Finding the term *crisis ordinariness* useful in this connection, she continues, "Often when scholars and activists apprehend the phenomenon of slow death in long-term conditions of privation, they choose to misrepresent the duration and scale of the situation by calling a crisis that which is a fact of life and has been a defining fact of life for a given population that lives that crisis in ordinary time" (Berlant 2011:101).[13] And here is perhaps the clearest statement of the problem: "*slow death . . . is neither a state of exception nor the opposite, mere banality, but a domain where an upsetting scene of living is revealed to be interwoven with ordinary life*" (Berlant 2011:102, emphasis added). Crisis ordinariness seems to me an accurate description of the lives that many old and isolated Finns find themselves in (Kangas and Keski-Heroja 2000:2). Andrea Mue-hlebach (2011:69) compellingly discusses the horrifying sense of "*absolute non-usefulness*" that often accompanies no longer working in Italy; this is a key dimension of what I am describing here.

Ahonen and Bukis found, perhaps unsurprisingly, that the strongest feelings of loneliness came "in the evenings, at night, on weekends, and on holidays." People told the researchers that getting outdoors, and visiting stores and markets, as well as all kinds of social interaction, were very valued, while, at home, listening to the radio and watching television eased the feelings of loneliness (2008:n.p.; see also Nihtilä and Martikainen 2004). Silence, and not being able to talk to anyone, was oppressive—a kind of *atemporal selflessness, a loss of self.*[14]

In the course of researching this chapter, I came across numerous people on the Internet reflecting on how long they had been silent and how it felt. Since Finnish does not have gender-specific pronouns, it was in many cases impossible to know how the writers were gendered. How old they were also usually remained unclear. A conversation about solitude, loneliness, and not speaking appeared on "Suomi24, Finland's largest web society." The August 30, 2009, comment that started this particular conversation asked: "Should I be getting worried about myself since I calculated today that I've gone exactly a month without speaking to anyone?" S/he explained:

> I haven't met anyone but the shop cashier. I don't go to work and I don't have any hobbies where I'd meet people. Haven't even gotten to the bar. I'm wondering whether your vocal chords will shrivel up if you go long

enough without using them? For some reason this loneliness doesn't bother me much, though, and that [in itself] is a little scary. It'd be sensible to go and seek out some company since I'm not at all anti-social by temperament. But I'm tired of people, and of the social relationships of my past life that involved intoxicants [päihteet], I don't [want to go] back there. If I died, I'd probably become one of those mummified bodies that are found after ten years by accident. No one would miss me since I don't have any kind of social network that I meet regularly and that would know to miss me. There are probably others in the same situation or?[15]

Several replies were left on the same day. One person wrote reassuringly that probably the only thing that would shrivel up would be one's vocabulary, and s/he offered a few words of comfort:

A month without talking to anyone is not a long time, it's not worth worrying about that. Of course our culture has shaped us such that we see bogeys where we shouldn't—we are also very social animals. In Eastern religions there's a custom of going into a so-called retreat—to think alone. The idea is to spend from a month to even a decade in solitude pondering the meaning of life, etc. So it's not worth being afraid even if you are social by temperament. And if you do want to talk with someone, take one for the road [ota pohjat] and go to a bar to babble [kapakkaan höpöttämään]. That'll sort it out.[16]

On the same day, under the subject line "A short time," someone wrote simply: "I've been two years without speaking."[17] Several people agreed that there does not tend to be much public sociality that does not also involve alcohol use. On September 5, 2009, another person added to the conversation, "I've sometimes been in the same situation. Somehow I began to enjoy the loneliness. First I suffered and then I sank into some wondrous philosophical loneliness, but after that began despair. In my opinion it's worth getting to a place where you see some people and where you *have* to say something, so you retain some sort of sense [taju]. Rare [is the person] who is truly a hermit [erakko]. Of course there are those too. I wish you well because I've gone through the same phase."[18] Someone else said on September 6, 2009: "It would be good to find a golden middle way. Everyone needs his/her own peace [oma rauha] sometimes. But total hermitage [erakkous] suits only very rare, strong souls."[19] A September 7, 2009, comment read: "Fine expression, that, 'strong soul.' You said a lot in a few words."[20]

In her Internet article "Alone in the Middle of Everything 18.12.2008," Kaisa Halonen writes, "Loneliness is the human being's lot, but an unreasonable amount of it has befallen some. Finland in December is a dark country inhabited by a people ill with loneliness. Little school-aged children have to manage at home alone without their parents for hours, 10 percent of high school students have not a single friend, and a quarter of those over sixty-five feel themselves to be lonely" (Halonen 2008:1–2; see also Kangas and Keski-Heroja 2000).

A 2011 article in the Finnish Red Cross membership magazine, *Avun maailma*, is titled "Yksinäisten asialla" (In the cause of the lonely) and centers on an extensive interview with Juho Saari, a professor of sociology and the author of the book *Yksinäisten yhteiskunta* (The society of the lonely) (Saari 2009). As I did in my own web search above, journalist Kimmo Holopainen (who interviewed Saari) easily found supporting evidence: his simple search word, *yksinäisyys* (loneliness), produced 187 blogs at the time. He opened the article with the following sampling of entries:

I've already gotten used to being alone. I have been alone my whole life. [*Koko pienen ikäni olen ollut yksin*; the expression here suggests that the writer is a chronically lonely young person.] Sometimes you think of a good story that you'd like to tell someone, but then you notice there's no one to tell. It hurts.

I tear up when I look at people with their friends. They talk and laugh. That's how it is, I suppose, friendship. It's hard to know anymore when you've lived alone for so long.

Sometimes I wonder how long I would lie at home dead before someone missed me.

Saari says, "Loneliness doesn't smell or taste of anything. In that sense it differs from other more traditional social problems like poverty or illness that are visible to fellow humans [*kanssaihmiset*; Germ. *Mitmenschen*]" (Holopainen 2011:36). The extent of the problem has become more visible as Internet use has become more widespread; Saari estimates that 5–20 percent of Finns experience different degrees of loneliness, and claims that this is not actually an extremely high percentage as compared to other countries (Holopainen 2011:36; see also J. Saari 2009). This does not, of course, reveal how specific aspects of people's societies may affect how loneliness is experienced or valued; that Finland is a highly Internet-connected society, for example, is relevant to people's experiences and expressions of loneliness (see Saari 2009:141–202). Finnish Red Cross Secretary General Kumpula has observed that one fast-spreading kind of volunteer activity happens in the virtual world, for example, in the form of peer support activity (2008:45).

"When an elder [vanhus] goes to a doctor for anxiety and distress [ahdis-tuneisuus], the diagnosis is never loneliness. When a middle-aged [person] seeks out a hobby group, the reason is never [given as] a desire to be with other people, but, rather, for example, an interest in choir singing. When an estimated ten percent of school-aged children stand alone in the schoolyard during class breaks, they are not classified as lonely, Saari says" (Holopainen 2011:36).

Profound chronic loneliness is significantly linked with specific categories of people: the old, the young, the unemployed, those living alone, and single parents, among others.[21] Living alone has become much more widespread in recent decades, and it is estimated that 40 percent of all households are run by people living alone (Jokinen 2005:9). The number of people over sixty-five living alone has also been steadily rising since the Second World War (Nihtilä and Martikainen 2004:135). One study points to "the contemporary lifestyle where responsibility for people is bounded by the edges of the nuclear family"; it adds, "Nowadays with the emphasis on independent coping and society's role in meeting people's needs for help, a person doesn't have to feel the same kind of responsibility for answering for the needs of their fellow beings as when communal sociality was more pronounced" (Kangas and Keski-Heroja 2000:30). While there is a diversity of reasons for people living by themselves, there is a close relationship between loneliness and living alone (Jokinen 2005:10). There is a widely (but by no means universally) shared sense that "loneliness has become Finns' new national illness" (Jokinen 2005:9; see also Forsblom 1998; Uotila, Lumme-Sandt, and Saaren-heimo 2010:112). These are "zones of social abandonment," zones where the abandonment is all too easily made to seem "unproblematic and acceptable" (Biehl 2005:20).

The popular Common Responsibility organization (www.yhteisvastuu .fi), active in Finland in many kinds of aid work since 1950, also highlighted loneliness in 2011.[22] Its 2011 theme was helping "young people suffering from loneliness."[23] It had an estimated forty thousand volunteers canvassing around Finland (Härkönen 1999a, 1999b:113). Researchers Juho Saari and Krista Lagus, with the cooperation of the Finnish Red Cross, ran an affiliated research project that solicited accounts of loneliness from Finns of all ages. The aim of the project was to collect information about people's experiences of loneliness through questionnaires, and to develop methods of helping. The stories submitted to the project "describe[d] in detail the abuse of medications and intoxicants [päihde] meant to deaden feeling so bad." "Empty free time is used in shopping because the shopkeeper is kind." People "submit to sexual intercourse only so that at least someone would be close." "The last option is suicide, which is planned in detail in the writings. It is described how and when it will be done, and people worry that no one will come to take away the mummified body, and they wonder if anyone will come to the funeral. People expect to carry out these plans after their parents have died because they don't want to cause them suffering."[24]

"You can say," Saari remarks, "that the reduction of loneliness is one core task in all associational life. This has not been recorded anywhere—nor should it be—but it is in the background a vital reason for many people to participate," to be a part of something greater than oneself (Holopainen 2011:39). Saari himself was a member of a Red Cross first aid team for ten years. I will return to Red Cross volunteering as a practice of connection and sociality.

Loneliness and Mummification

Hylätyksi tulemisen tunne on kaikkein vaarallisin.
The sensation of having been abandoned is the most dangerous.
—Anja Kauranen, quoted in Hille Puusaari, "Kuolemaan on hyvä saatella"

It is not for nothing that the bloggers and questionnaire respondents above worried about the circumstances of their own deaths. For people classified as "elderly," deaths can go unnoticed for quite a while. It frequently happens that people living alone—often elders—are only found weeks after they have died; this does not become news. In more extreme cases, however, the deceased are only discovered after months or even years, by which time the bodies have reached a state commonly described as mummified. It is estimated by police that such "mummified" bodies are discovered at the rate of one per year (Björkman 2010:11). These exceptional, if recurring, cases provide a vivid dramatization of extreme isolation (see Campobasso et al. 2009), and are clearly capable of seizing the imaginations of people (like those quoted above) who are thinking about their own social isolation. It is somehow threatening to realize, introspectively, that these "ex-persons" have been "terminally excluded from what counts as reality" (Biehl 2005:52; DeLillo 2002).

There are several reasons for long delays in the discovery of bodies. One of them lies in the social and built environments that are highly typical (and remarkably uniform) for urban and smaller semi-urban areas, as mentioned earlier (see also Jokinen and Saaristo 2006:160). Apartment living is very common and rather anonymous, and there is often little contact with neighbors (Kairema 2000:19–20). The dwellings are typically well insulated and have solid concrete walls. Neither sound nor scent readily pass from one apartment to another. Mail is dropped into a narrow, low slot in a solid wood front door and falls onto the floor of a foyer in the apartment. In this form of apartment living, then, there are no personal mailboxes outside the front door that could overflow, thus becoming warning signs. Many, if not most, people have all their routine financial transactions automated. Debits and credits appear on schedule. The convergence of all these factors facilitates solitude and privacy. Yet the fact remains that those not found have apparently been so socially isolated that their disappearance has not been noticed by anyone—neither friends, neighbors, nor family.

In January 2010, a window renovation project on an apartment building was undertaken in greater Helsinki. Workers on a scaffold outside saw the mummified body of a woman inside one of the apartments. Detective Chief Inspector Juha Rautaheimo said in a statement that the woman, born in 1930, was thought to have died in May 2007. No crime was suspected in the case (Yle News 2010). She had never had children nor been married. The police were trying to track down other relatives. Rautaheimo said, "We annually find tens of deceased who have been dead for a few months; that's a big city phenomenon, but those deceased years ago [*vuosia sitten menehtyneitä*] are found only about once a year" (Yle News 2010).

An infamous case—one with which other similar cases are still compared—involves a man who lay dead in his apartment for over six years before he was discovered. It looked like he had lain down onto his bed for a nap, with the window ajar. Detective Chief Inspector Kari Tolvanen characterized the death on television as "a sad kind of record." The deceased became popularly known as the "Mummy of Maunula." He was born in Helsinki in 1938, and lived alone at the time of his death. He had been an only child. Over the years, he had had many different jobs and homes. He had committed numerous property crimes and had been in prison (a heavy sentence by today's standards in Finland). He was briefly married and had two children, but was estranged from them. At the end of the 1980s, he rented an apartment in Maunula, a suburb of Helsinki. At that time he also began receiving a disability pension because of a cardiac infarction. His pension and payments were routed via social services so that credits and debits occurred automatically in his bank account. This was one of many reasons that he was not missed. His mummified body was found when janitorial services had to go in to install a new smoke alarm; they had made numerous previous attempts to reach the apartment occupant by written notice and by ringing the doorbell. Based on the unopened mail in the foyer and other evidence, it was possible to confirm the day of death as February 15, 1994. His identity has been withheld.[25] This man's fate provoked discussion and soul-searching in Finland.

Most of those discovered in a mummified state have been aged people, of both sexes, and they leave sad evidence of loneliness and social isolation.[26] Sometimes the evidence also reveals a chilling indifference. On February 4, 2010, the evening newspaper *Ilta-sanomat* reported that an eighty-year-old woman had been discovered eight months after her death.[27] A close male relative had begun to wonder why the old woman did not answer her phone, but only many months later did he go to actually check on her in person. That is when he discovered her body. He was described as her "next of kin." A psychologist I interviewed said that in her work she had come across clients whose parents had died in this way. "People who have been on bad terms with a parent may come to therapy because the parent has been dead there [in her own home] for two months" before being discovered.

These extreme cases grip the imagination. The questions ask themselves: How could this happen? Where were the children, other family, friends, and neighbors? How does it come to pass that in a relatively wealthy and well-ordered society, a welfare society with significant social resources and a social safety net, this could happen? As Finns ask themselves these questions, they are reminded of just how alone it is possible to be. There has been public discussion, the psychologist said, about whether Finland has become a "hard country" (*kova maa*).

The Friendship Service

The international work of the Finnish Red Cross is the organization's most visible work and it generates the most media attention; it is also what inspires much of the giving by the Finnish public. My own research with the Red Cross aid workers, of course, also focused on the international aid and emergency relief. When I began this research, I did not really think about the domestic side of the organization's work.[28] It is only in the later stages of the project that I began to form a basic understanding of the significance of the interconnections between its international and domestic operations. It became apparent that the international and the domestic were partially co-constitutive, and that domesticity itself (in the full range of that word's meaning) was surprisingly central to Finnish internationalism. I had not expected this.

The Finnish Red Cross domestic services form a long list: the blood service (veripalvelu), first aid training (ensiapukoulutus), first aid team operations (ensiapuryhmätoiminta), the rescue service (pelastuspalvelu), volunteer rescue service (vapaaehtoinen pelastuspalvelu), first aid teams for psychic support (henkisen tuen ensihuoltoryhmät), drug and alcohol work (päihdetyö), HIV and other health education (HIV-valistus tai muu terveyskasvatus), youth work (nuorisotyö), safe houses for young people (nuorten turvatalot), emergency houses and safe houses (ensi-ja turvakodit), crime victim emergency service (rikosuhripäivystys), homecare support (omaishoitajien tuki), immigrant support (maahanmuuttajatuki), antiracism work (rasismin vastainen työ), Operation Hunger Day (Operaatio Nälkäpäivä), a flea market system (Kontti-ketju), the Friendship Service (Ystäväpalvelu), and others (Tanskanen 2009; see also Markkanen 2009 and Roponen 2010).[29] In addition to regular domestic employees, approximately forty-five thousand trained volunteers work in these programs across the country (El Said and Patja 2011:25; cf. Aalto-Setälä n.d.). (The projects listed here include one-off events, annual campaigns, regular services, and permanent programs.) It should also be emphasized that the state has a relatively wide range of social services for retirees.[30]

Here I will focus on the longstanding Red Cross Friendship Service, a popular (if often deeply ambivalent) form of "stranger sociality" (Povinelli 2006). This is a service (originally modeled on a Norwegian program) that seeks to provide "volunteer friends" for people who are old and lonely, or in need of other kinds of support (Tammisto and Lahtinen 1994). The majority of the friends tend to be middle-aged women, but there is evidence of young people also joining the program. Some people have been active in it for several decades, while others have participated only at some phases in their lives. I will consider this service in the more general context of endemic loneliness and social isolation in Finland before moving on (in the following section) to suggest how the domestic work of knitting (and other handwork) facilitates people's social and imaginative practices of connecting with living others and with the wider world of need and help. Lest there be any doubt about the social and affective need for such a friendship service, consider the title of one study, *Antakaa minulle ihminen!* (Give me a human being!) (Tammisto and Lahtinen 1994).

A middle-aged volunteer friend, interviewed in 1998, said: "Old people are lonely and endlessly considerate. They call us when they don't want to bother their daughter or son, even if they live right next door. It's sad, we walk past each other and don't dare to talk. It's easier to ask for help from a total stranger than from a close relative [*omainen*]" (Tilus 1998:8).

For over "fifty years the Finnish Red Cross has connected friends for example [with] institutions or [with] the old and handicapped who are at home. The goal of our activity is to support another person, to offer revitalization, as well as to alleviate loneliness."[31] The Friendship Service supports numerous different activities in all its districts nationwide. One can serve as a friend to an aged person or an immigrant (Hursti 2002), as a support for a person in the process of mental health rehabilitation (*mielenterveyskuntoutuja*), as a prison visitor, as a friend to a handicapped person or a young person, as part of a circle of volunteer friends, as a support in the revitalization of aged people, as a volunteer in a hospital or an old age home, and as a trainer of other volunteers (Punainen Risti n.d.). Not all volunteers are by any means young; a study titled "The Aged in Associational and Volunteer Activity" found that very significant numbers of people between fifty-five and seventy-four served as volunteers in a number of capacities, among them volunteer friends and support persons (Rajaniemi 2007:3). Also, in the course of her life, a person might well change status from being the giver of volunteer friendship to becoming its recipient (Rajaniemi 2007:4). Volunteers could work individually or in groups. According to an October 2011 estimate by the Red Cross, nine thousand people were involved in the Friendship Service; others have put the figure at ten thousand (Vähäsarja 2009; Hursti 2002:101). Yki Hytönen, writing for the Finnish Red Cross, observes that what all the social categories needing help share is loneliness (2002:179).

Valentine's Day (known as Friend's Day in Finland) is one occasion when "the Red Cross campaigns [in order] to recruit new young adults to be voluntary friends. The 2011 campaign slogan was 'Ole hyvä. Ole ystävä.' It played on multiple meanings; most literally it meant, 'Be good. Be a friend.' It can also be rendered as 'Please. Be a friend' and 'You're welcome. Be a friend.'"[32] As the campaign literature further explained, "On February 14 Friend's Day is celebrated, but more and more [people] have no one to send a friend's day card to. Loneliness has increased in all age groups, but Red Cross volunteers especially see the loneliness of the young and the aged."[33] One of the numerous activities of Friendship Day is to make coordinated group visits to old age institutions. A 2010 newspaper ran a story under the title "Young Friends Occupy Old Age Homes."[34]

A study conducted by Maria El Said and Sanna Patja in the Department of Media Studies at the University of Jyväskylä is one interesting window into this service as well as into the broader social context in which it is practiced.[35] The study first sets out widely accepted principles of volunteer work: it is to be, first, voluntary, and also unsalaried and otherwise unpaid, confidential, nonprofessional, egalitarian, and a shared joy or pleasure for the parties involved (El Said and Patja 2011:11). It is important, they note, that volunteering be personally rewarding, for example in helping the volunteers to "build their own identity, and to get experiences of participating and making a difference"; it may also be motivated by the volunteer's personal desire or longing for more social contact (El Said and Patja 2011:12, 13; see also Ruohonen 2003). In this sense, it is a practice of working on the self (Foucault 1986; Allahyari 2000), not wholly unlike the practices of the more aged and lonely I will discuss below.

The Red Cross training for the Friendship Service includes a review of the principles of volunteering and also of the seven fundamental principles of the Red Cross, a descriptive account of the kinds of scenarios volunteers typically encounter, and guidelines in calibrating social distance and intimacy in the relationships that form; it is recommended that they not share personal contact information such as surnames, addresses, or telephone numbers (El Said and Patja 2011:46). It was of course up to individual volunteers how they made these decisions.

A majority of the people whom the volunteers served were old people, whether living alone in their own homes or in care facilities. Aid workers going into zones of armed conflict may be admired for their courage; a volunteer going into elder care—an aid worker of another sort—may also need a certain sort of courage. In both types of work, people are obliged to confront their own mortality close up. Both also involve calibrations of intimacy and stranger sociality. Both demand a great deal from one's ethical and affective imagination, and one's professionalism.

Most of El Said and Patja's interviewees had been in a volunteer friendship on average between one and three years; one relationship had lasted ten years at the time of their study (2011:58). Kangas and Keski-Heroja report in their study that friendship relationships had lasted an impressive average of eleven years, and that people had experience in the service anywhere from three to twenty-two years—and that sometimes the unemployed and the retired found something significant to do by serving as friends (2000:6–7, 28).

The balancing of distance and proximity (in what was of course an asymmetrical relationship) was frequently an issue despite the guidelines, and this was poignantly reflected in the ambivalent compound term by which the intended beneficiaries of the service were referred to: "client-friend" (*asiakasystävä*); none of the "volunteer friends" had invited their "client-friends" to their own homes and on the few occasions that a client-friend had gotten a volunteer's phone number, this was mostly regretted as a mistake (El Said and Patja 2011:59, 73; cf. Hursti 2002). Kangas and Keski-Heroja report that the terms in general use were friend (*ystävä*) and counter-friend (*vastaystävä*) (2000:6). The client-friends seemed often to be wishing for more contact and intimacy than the volunteer friends found themselves able to give. Many spent a few hours a week on this service (Kangas and Keski-Heroja 2000:33). Their gift of time and companionship was not boundless or selfless, nor should it have been, if by selflessness we mean self-sacrifice, or self-denial. Presumably the client-friends would not have asked for that either.

There were, likewise, some friend relationships that were more demanding than others due to certain complicating factors: advanced dementia, depression and other psychological problems, and alcoholism were among these (Kangas and Keski-Heroja 2000:48, 54).

The problem of what could be expected of the volunteer friend was also insightfully brought up in a study of Red Cross volunteer friends' work with immigrants to Finland (Hursti 2002:61–63). The basic guidelines regarding the volunteers' right to privacy (and control of their schedules) were the same as in the volunteers' work with the aged. But this sometimes created misunderstandings and ambivalence between the two parties as to the meaning and expectations of friendship. One immigrant expressed confusion to the researcher about what "Finnish friendship" actually meant: "The friend is a little unclear to me. In our culture a friend means more than here. I don't understand this, because all my Finnish friends here, I don't know their address. I've learned that if someone comes to [my place], I go to theirs. But it's not like that here. I don't really know who you are" (Hursti 2002:61). On the other end of the friendship relationship, several volunteer friends said they sometimes found themselves exhausted in their relationships with their immigrant friends, especially in negotiating the intensity of the need for contact and the amount of time entailed (Hursti 2002:61; cf. Kangas and Keski-Heroja 2000; Rastas 2007). But one volunteer cheerfully explained: "It hasn't been heavy for me because I have not let it get heavy. If it starts feeling like this is too much, then you have to put a break on it. So it shouldn't take over your whole life, so that you feel it to be a duty, so there should be a balance" (Hursti 2002:63). These relationships varied widely, of course, some becoming very close. But it should be emphasized that the immigrants' neediness (or dependency) in their relationships with Red Cross friends and other Finnish contacts should be understood in a social context of widespread anti-immigrant and racist sentiment, and even violence (Rastas 2007). It also took a lot of thought and energy to usefully help these "client-friends" to navigate Finnish society at different levels. The immigrants stood out as "different" and "foreign," and very vulnerable in their situational social visibility (a problem that came up in my interviews, and is addressed by the Red Cross and numerous scholars). The aged Finns, on the other hand, found themselves vulnerable because they suffered from the opposite problem: *situational social invisibility*. Their invisibility stemmed from the thinness of their social relationships. Being left very alone with the self, there was a potential experiential diminishment of personhood (cf. Biehl 2005; Mauss 1985).

Typical one-on-one outings with the aged client-friend might be visits to relatively neutral public places like shops, cafés, museums, art galleries, and anywhere outdoors to get fresh air; other more collective outings might be sewing and craft circles in which people (numerous volunteer friends and their client-friends together) chatted and made handwork like Mother Teresa blankets and Aid Bunnies, hats and socks, mittens and scarves to benefit Red Cross aid programs (El Said and Patja 2011:59, 88, 107). A finding that surprised the researchers was that it was especially the shared handwork evenings, and the pieces made to directly benefit the Red Cross's work, that seemed to them to produce a wider sense of connectedness to the organization and its goals; this was certainly the case for the volunteers (El Said and Patja 2011:107, 118). While theirs was a study of the volunteers and not the aged client-friends, evidence from the yarn shops would suggest that this particular kind of handwork, made in aid of others (*neulominen avuksi muille*), might have been meaningful to the aged for the same kinds of reasons. And in addition to working on a piece in the group settings, people could continue working on it at home, or start a new one—a welcome domestic activity when alone at home.

Both volunteer friends and client-friends, then, imagined a connection to a wider world and a greater purpose through the work of their hands. The handwork was imagined as a "concrete benefit *somewhere far away in the world*"; in the words of a volunteer friend making Aid Bunnies: "and to think that a child *somewhere on the globe* gets one of these in his/her arms" (El Said and Patja 2011:108, emphasis added; see also chapter 4). It is striking how often the benefit was imagined to be "far away in the world (*kaukana maailmalla*)," "somewhere on the globe (*jossain päin maapalloa*)." The faraway world enabled the people gathered around the table—like the women in the yarn shops—to see themselves as a source of something *useful* and *generous*, and as a link in a longer chain. I think that in giving of themselves, they were confirming to themselves that they *were*—and, also, that *they were as they thought themselves to be*. If finding yourself old, too alone, and generally invisible is a kind of out-of-body experience, then these practices ("merely" knitting, "merely" crocheting) could possibly help you to feel yourself as a positive presence in the world, to embody yourself differently. Perhaps they might affect in some subtle way the person you see in the bathroom mirror.[36] You are not an ex-person.

The majority of the volunteers here had become Red Cross members after they had started in the Friendship Service; they tended to experience the service as part of a membership in a larger community of helping. One volunteer was quoted as saying that s/he even felt like a member of the larger "international activity [of the Red Cross] in a certain way, aiding and gathering funds for those disaster areas, so yes in that way it's of course motivating to be a part of it" (El Said and Patja 2011:104).[37] Others I have interviewed felt the same. The handwork was a means by which to be connected to the "worldwide helping" (*maailmanlaajuinen apu*) that the Finnish Red Cross represents. Through handwork, "the volunteers participate concretely in a chain of help and the realization of the goals of the organization," and in this way belong to "a greater community of helpers" (El Said and Patja 2011:111). This imagined "chain of help"—compelling for the younger volunteers but also for the older "client-friends," who might at other points in the chain of helping be themselves volunteers—is one vivid instantiation of the domesticity of the international.

The co-constitution of the domestic and the international was clear in the material considered in this chapter—ethnographic observation, interviews, web discussions, theses, or other documentary sources—and had a decidedly Durkheimian cast. In their domestic, cultural practices people here had sought to become a part of "*something greater than themselves.*" The volunteers just quoted wanted to become Red Cross members so that they might belong to "*a greater community of helpers.*" The sociologist Juho Saari, cited earlier, made the compelling point that the "reduction of loneliness . . . is a vital reason for many people to participate," to be a part of *something greater than themselves* (Holopainen 2011:39). And the secretary general of the Finnish Red Cross of course explained the popularity of volunteer work like this: "People want to be involved in building *something greater than themselves*" (Björkman 2010:14). Durkheim ([1912] 1995) defined society as that which preexists any individual person and carries on after that person's life, and suggested that it is in this sense immortal. Knitting and loneliness turn out to be cosmological issues. Trying to be part of something greater than oneself is also a temporal practice. Managing time in social isolation is, as I suggested, a practice of working on the self. Time-work is a care of the self meant to keep at bay the danger of atemporal, asocial selflessness. You don't want to be, in Don DeLillo's words, "Like a man anonymous to himself" (2002:95).

All the projects and campaigns mentioned here could be dismissed as more or less contrived and artificial forms of sociality—institutionally designed and implemented, domesticated kinds of "stranger sociality," as if by definition a pale and bloodless version of denser, more intimate, spontaneous face-to-face forms of sociality. One could point out that the Red Cross "voluntary friends" were not, after all, "real" friends. The lonely old women who knit: in placing their trust in *voluntary* services, were they not perhaps allowing themselves dependence on something quite tenuous and temporary after all?[38]

In *The Empire of Love*, Elizabeth Povinelli makes a powerful critique of easy oppositions between "real" sociality based on kinship and the deep recognition of friendship, on the one hand, and a somehow less real stranger sociality, on the other. "I examine," she explains, "how discourses of individual freedom and social constraint—what I refer to as *autological* and *genealogical* imaginaries—animate and enflesh love, sociality, and bodies; how they operate as strategic maneuvers of power whose purpose—or result—is to distribute life, goods, and values across social space and how they contribute to the hardiness of liberalism as a normative horizon" (Povinelli 2006:3–4, emphasis in the original). The autological (individual freedom) and the genealogical (social constraint) are positioned in liberal humanism as each other's opposites, but this is misleading. "Autological and genealogical discourses are not in this view different in kind even though they are used to differentiate kinds of people, societies, and civilizational orders. They both make a liberal humanist claim that what makes us most human is our capacity to base our most intimate relations, our most robust governmental institutions, and our economic relations on mutual and free recognition of the worth and value of another person, rather than basing these connections on, for example, social status or the bare facts of the body" (Povinelli 2006: 5–6). In this dominant view, autonomous individuality and familial intimacy/constraint exhaust the social field, even as either one, in the extreme, is understood as pathological.[39] What alternative can be conceptualized beyond this? Povinelli writes about "immanent dependencies": "Thinking of the social relations within and among the people I know as immanent dependencies allows me to dislodge certain commonsense views of the social matrix of indigenous and queer people in which the dependencies of indigenous persons are so saturated by determination that the immanent is only a sign of the breakdown of the indigenous order and in which the dependencies of queer persons are so annulled by portraits of stranger sociality that dependency itself is hard to imagine" (Povinelli 2006:6).

My account of people's experiences of loneliness and the Friendship Service contains many examples of stranger sociality and also immanent dependency. It supports Povinelli's claim that there are forms of dependency and intimacy that we lose track of too easily if we try to reduce them to a family-intimacy-versus-individual-autonomy binary scheme. One could argue, of course, that "voluntary friends" and casual acquaintances in yarn shops are neither "real" friends, nor "real" family, but just lame stand-ins for them. But one has to entertain the all-too-real possibility that the relationships that spring from the Friendship Service, or the casual connections of knitting groups, did not necessarily displace "real" friends, family, or face-to-face sociality. In a context where social networks are small and family relations often strained or distant, we must consider the possibility that there was (at least in some cases) nothing particular there to displace (Kangas and Keski-Heroja 2000; cf. Butler 2004). The voluntary friends from the Friendship Service, like the fleeting stranger socialities of the yarn shop, might be understood neither as faux friendships nor as compensations for an inexplicably absent family but instead as fragile forms of real intimacy in the midst of a wider environment of abject loneliness and need. Neediness is all around here, and generosity too. But they co-constitute each other in ways that are much less socially stable, and much less predictable in their effects, than is sometimes assumed in social research on topics like development and humanitarianism. As I discussed in chapter 1, when aid workers I interviewed came home from international missions, what they often missed most were the sociality and conviviality of the mission sites and societies they had just left behind. One nurse valued the fact that in many parts of the world, family was always around you, and that *you did not have to be alone* at any stage of life.[40] Another nurse, also mentioned earlier, felt a very specific kind of neediness upon her return to Finland from missions. She experienced as painful the deprivation of easy sociality and friendly sensuous contact when she returned from international missions; people do not touch each other in Finland as spontaneously as in the other societies in which she had worked (see chapter 1). When we talked about this, she was recalling her life in Afghanistan. She was depressed and lonely, and annoyed, in her neediness. In this predicament, shared by most of my informants, the imagination of connectedness with the lively world "out there" became very important—just as with "the old women who knit." Again, while (volitional) solitude was valued, loneliness and social disconnection were not.

Such observations appear to underlie a remarkable recent project in Germany that brings together many of the themes treated here (while also showing perhaps that they are not unique to Finland). "Adopted" began as an imaginative art project by Gudrun Widlock, based in Berlin. One day she was eyeing a leaflet from a charitable organization that had "pairs of love-hungry eyes" on it. Widlock, feeling down, happened to place a photograph of herself next to it, and began to wonder if "lonely, melancholy city dwellers like herself" could not be linked to warm and caring families in the "Third World." It occurred to her that she could arrange an adoption service where "Africa Adopts" lonely European adults. Widlock explained: "Many people wish for company but at the same time want to stay unattached and uncommitted. Which is why I help them find a new, symbolic family in countries where this kind of family life still exists." This venture grew far beyond her initial art project and she eventually began actually arranging such links between lonely, unattached European applicants and families in Africa and elsewhere. The project did not involve "materialistic" exchange, only "pure emotional exchange" (Brown 2003). The story does not tell how this looked from the point of view of the "families in Africa" who were thus called upon to adopt lonely strangers from the wealthy North.

Mother Teresa Blankets: On the Useful and the Useless

After 1945, . . . amateurism was seen as a great problem for the crafts, and professionals sought to distance themselves from association with hobbyism whenever possible. In a prospectus written for the omnibus craft exhibition *Objects: USA* in 1968, curator Lee Nordness wrote: "the term crafts confusedly connotes in many people's minds *something done as an avocation, something done as a therapy, something done by the aged*. Actually, what is being created by the top artisans in the United States should be associated with such names as Benvenuto Cellini, Fabergé, and Paul Revere."

—Lee Nordness, quoted in Glenn Adamson, *Thinking through Craft*, emphasis added

Crafts (and, worse, handicrafts) have been trivialized and devalued in many quarters and for a very long time, as I suggested in chapter 4, and as has been widely discussed (see, e.g., Loos [1910] 2000; Taussig 1993:44; Frank 2000; Kelley 2003:23; Heinänen 2006; Kant 2006:183; Adamson 2007:5; Risatti 2007; Koskennurmi-Sivonen, Raunio, and Luutonen 2009; Adamson 2010; Auther 2010; Lippard 2010; but see Kjörup 2010; Ingold 2013). As early as 1751, Denis Diderot, in his *Encyclopédie* essay, "Art," was frustrated by the fact that "very often little is known of the origin of mechanical arts and not much more of their history. This is the natural outcome of the contempt felt in all ages and by all nations, whether scholarly or warlike, for those who engage in them" (Alfoldy 2007a:xv–xvi; see also Adamson 2010:4–5). Many artisans since then have felt the sting of that contempt, and still do (and perhaps not only in the wealthy Global North). The makers of things who are especially condescended to today are women and amateurs, and, worse still, "hobbyists" (Parker and Pollock 1981; Parker [1984] 2010; Heikkinen 1997:2; Mindry 1999; Adamson 2007:139–63; Hung and Magliaro 2007: preface; Auther 2010:21). Women knitting, crocheting, sewing, quilting, embroidering, and doing other work of the hand are *the mere* to art's aura—and to "high craft," as well (Auther 2010:93–162; Risatti 2007; and chapter 4). Add *age* to the handmade objects and they might one day be transformed from "kitsch," "frippery," and "all that *stuff*" to "heirlooms," "antiques," or even "heritage."[41] Add *age to the women* who make them, however, and they become grannies, biddies, little old ladies, crones, and so forth, and the contempt begins to show its teeth.[42] It is easy to see the connections between the devaluation of the domestic arts and the devaluation of women—and the two are brought together in the misogynist belittling that commonly converges on old women who knit, crochet, and ornament (Loos [1910] 2000; Tammisto and Lahtinen 1994; Kelley 2003:32; Heinänen 2006). Such labels are often used playfully and even affectionately but can be trivializing and ultimately demeaning in their effect. In the thicket of such labels, a woman might be forgiven for losing track of her own personhood, and dignity. Writer Johanna Korhonen remarks: "A writer turned eighty, needed everyday help, and turned to us other people, to society. From the responses she got, she suddenly understood that she no longer was the person she had thought she was. *She was a mere elder, an ex-person, a being without qualities*" (J. Korhonen 2012:C1; cf. Musil 1996a, 1996b; Biehl 2005).

These problems are ambivalently, even painfully, engaged in a quilt by the late Los Angeles artist Mike Kelley, who was at one point interested in using "hobbyist craft" for thinking about the "uncanny aura of the craft item"; Glenn Adamson says of the piece, "Both in its title and its materials, *More Love Hours Than Can Ever Be Repaid*—a collection of found stuffed animals sewn onto a found handmade quilt—evokes the wretched excess and pathos of domestic craft activity" (2007:159, 161, 199n89; cf. Stals 1997). "As the work's title implies," Adamson adds, "the plenitude of craft labor expended on these worthless objects, which Kelley found 'abandoned' in thrift stores, makes sense only within an asymmetrical emotional economy of gift-giving" (2007:161; cf. Mauss 1990; Laidlaw 2000; Bornstein 2012). Kelley himself said, "Here's a structure that's loaded with pathos . . . *You want to kick it*" (quoted in Adamson 2007: 160, emphasis added). "For me, craft is a species of kitsch, and the expenditures of effort and skill that are lavished on craft objects reap only pity" (Adamson 2007:160). Kelley's work speaks volumes on the resentment and guilt, revulsion and love, ambivalence and affection that often inflect gendered intergenerational kin relationships, and their material accretions.

Mike Kelley's revulsion against *the mere ornament*, mere hobbyist decoration, has a long pedigree, of course. Already in 1910 in his influential essay "Ornament and Crime," the architect and "modernist" Adolf Loos wrote (in unabashedly elitist and evolutionist terms) about "the ornament disease" and decried the "tortured, strained, and morbid quality of modern ornaments" (Frank 2000:290, 293). Both Kelley and Loos, writing in very different historical contexts and with different purposes, give insight into "asymmetrical emotional [economies] of gift-giving" that are likewise vital in thinking about the domesticities involved in international aid (see also Schwenkel 2012).

The people I write about here—those who handmade Mother Teresa blankets and other humanitarian handwork projects in aid of others—did not think generally of themselves as artisans (käsityöläinen), let alone as artists (taiteilija); they might well, if asked to put a name to it, modestly term themselves mere hobbyists (harrastelija vaan) (see Heinänen 2006; Pöllänen 2006; Kjörup 2010). The skill level typically required in these projects made them relatively widely accessible, and many of them involved predesigned models or directions—they were mostly not "free" creations from the clear blue of one's own imagination (see Engell 1981:130–36; Rundell 1994a, 1994b; Castoriadis 1997; Kant 2006:109, 110–11, 183; Kant 2008; and chapter 1). But it would be an anthropological mistake on many levels to make a dismissive aesthetic judgment here and not look more closely (see Frank 2000; Lippard 2010). It is relevant to know, at the minimum, that handwork (käsityö) is taught in all Finnish schools—and has been since the nineteenth century, typically by very well-trained teachers, and that there is, therefore, a relatively good knowledge of handwork skills in the general population (see Koskennurmi-Sivonen, Raunio, and Luutonen 2009; see also Kjörup 2010). The skill sets among those seeking human company through handwork can actually be quite various and well developed. It is not relevant for present purposes to produce hierarchies of skill; my point is simply that the "hobbyists" could generally be assumed to know what they were doing, and to be in a strong position from which to learn new techniques. Other things, however, were more important: it is pleasing and empowering to know how to do something well, to be able to show/teach others how to do it, and to be able to do it to help others; equally importantly, the very processuality, temporality, and embodiment of handwork can be intensely rewarding in and of themselves, and may involve what Frankenhaeuser (1999) has called a "pleasureable stress" and even, perhaps, what Csikszentmihalyi has called a "flow" experience (1991; see also Pöllänen 2006:74).[43] In a Red Cross sewing club, participants mentioned therapy but also emphasized the opportunity for self-expression (Kotila 2012:21). In her ethnography of northern Karelian women's handwork, Kaija Heikkinen concluded simply, "For them handwork is joy, rest, intellectual stimulation, creative practice and meditation" (1997:90).[44] Invoking John Ruskin's and William Morris's philosophies (see Frank 2000), Heinänen also writes: "specifically craftsman-like work produces the joy of work and the aesthetic experience—and not just high art representing freedom and beauty, as philosophers like Kant have [thought]" (2006:143, 11; see also Frank 2000:14–18; Adamson 2007:139–63; Kant 2008; Kjörup 2010).

The people in the Mother Teresa circles, and in the many other groups like them, would most likely have agreed with this. But they might also have seen Mike Kelley's point. The title of his piece, "More Love Hours Than Can Ever Be Repaid," led me to reconsider why the often lonely customers of the yarn shops I visited so frequently "knitted " in aid of others"—specifically in aid of unknown others (and *not* family).

On a website for older people (seniori.netti.fi), I found a lively conversation about the Mother Teresa blankets.[45] On March 26, 2010, one person wrote: "I've started to knit in the Mother Teresa circle [*piiri*] patches for blankets that are going to Calcutta . . . So if you're lonely and you don't have enough to do, why not make patches for the Mother Teresa blankets as your pastime?" She got a quick response: "I *have* always thought that 'then' in retirement I would knit my old wool into patches." There ensued a discussion about using up yarn left over from other projects. "In our Teresa club [under parish auspices] we've probably knitted almost all of the waste and repurposed yarn in this town into blankets." Old socks, mittens, scarves, hats, sweaters, and other woolens in good condition, whether from thrift shops or one's own closet, can be unraveled and the yarn knitted anew. "In part you have to buy new yarn, but the principle is that new yarn isn't used." (This was, of course, like the green logic of the Aid Bunny in chapter 4.) There was also a plea, "Do you have old wool yarns? Donate them!"[46] Still on the same day, someone wrote: "I have many, many plastic bags cluttering up my limited storage space. When I was working I didn't have the energy to [do much more than] take out my yarns and look at them. Now it's nice to start the blankets; I can't watch TV without some knitting in my hands . . . Somewhere I saw instructions for making little babies' jackets [*nuttu*] for India. I lost the paper. Then I've seen an article about knitting socks for Russia's child prisoners. *There is a lot to do.*"[47]

Mother Teresa blankets have been made in Finland for some thirty years, and coordinating their collection and distribution has been variously organized by volunteers in numerous different groups (some of them church groups) and organizations, among them Vaaka ry and the Finnish Red Cross. The basic idea is that you knit patches of 18 cm x 18 cm from yarn that is at least 50 percent wool. An adult's blanket needs 9 x 7 patches for a total of sixty-three patches. A child's blanket takes thirty patches. You can join the patches together yourself to make a finished blanket, and donate that. But some organizations accept unjoined patches that can be sent singly or in unjoined batches, as well as loose yarn for others to knit. The volunteers will then lay out all the different patches that people have donated, consider how they might look best together or what pleasing patterns they might make, and join them together to make complete blankets. Should it be your express wish, your blanket can even be sent to India through the Missionaries of Charity (Rakkauden lähetyssisaret); otherwise they are sent wherever a need is identified.

Vaaka ry, one of the organizations actively involved in this Mother Teresa project, gave an exact accounting of the numbers of blankets knitted by Finns and of their recipients.[48] Destinations in the first decade of the twenty-first century included: a children's hospital in a Chernobyl-affected area in Gomel, Byelo-Russia; an orphanage in Russian Karelia; an abandoned children's ward in a hospital in Pristina, Kosovo; a camp for Palestinian refugees in Lebanon; Estonian under-aged mothers and their children via the Eesti-Caritas organization, and many more. In 2010 (as of a November Vaaka ry tally), 256 children's blankets and 75 adults' blankets had been delivered to various destinations. These blankets had a total of 7,700 patches. They were sent mostly to different regions in Russia. By the end of the year 2009, Vaaka ry—with the collaboration of several different organizations—had delivered 3,000 blankets (totaling 76,000 patches) to dozens of different destinations around the world.[49] The 2009 list included destinations in Russia, but many others besides. I noted in particular that domestic sites included old-age homes, family centers, mother-and-child homes and safe houses (ensi-and turvakoti), alcohol and drug rehabilitation centers, a reception home for twelve- to seventeen-year-olds who cannot live at home, daycare centers, the Tampere city care home for disabled war veterans (Tampereen veljeskoti), and others. The Lutheran church also uses them in its social work (seurakunnan diakoniatyö). In April 2009, an exceptionally large shipment of 502 blankets of different sizes was delivered to Kalkku, the central logistics center of the Finnish Red Cross. The blankets were then baled there into standard-sized units for delivery to disaster areas in Asia, Africa, and/or Europe, as part of other aid shipments. Even Finnish peacekeepers have on occasion found themselves delivering Mother Teresa blankets to recipients like the Women's Affairs Department of Samangan Province in Afghanistan.

Although many of these blankets were likely knitted by women who, in their loneliness, were needy, they were also a fairly extravagant gift. Woolen yarn can be expensive, and the weight of a complete blanket makes shipping costs high. I did not see worry about these issues among the knitters, but one unidentified blogger estimated a blanket's cost (if knitted from new wool) to be at least 70 euros, and asked, somewhat cynically: "Why won't [3 euro] blankets from Jysk [discount store] do? . . . Why won't store-bought products do? . . . Why should I send hand-knitted design-blankets [somewhere] when I don't have one myself? But it would be unethical, the IKEA blanket made in a developing country, I suppose?"[50]

But the extravagance of the gift was not, I think, in the money. The gift of time is more interesting, and complicated. Without a significant expenditure of time the blankets would not have been made. Knitting the blanket (perhaps over some weeks) was a pleasurable pastime, a way to structure and give a rhythm to one's private, domestic time—a sensual way of embodying time. It was an important gift to oneself—and *of* oneself—and an alleviation of claustrophobic solitude for many. For the lonely the slowness of the process was possibly a part of its appeal. You can leave the blanket in progress when you go to sleep at night and know that it will be there, needing your attention in the morning. In some sense at least, I think that this is about trying to be in and of social time. This is one life-affirming alternative to more desolate visions of time and self (DeLillo 2002, 2010). These practices of generosity are "caring for oneself" (Muehlebach 2011:70).

These Mother Teresa blankets, made with such thought and care, and so much time and wool, were quite valuable gifts, then—and sometimes deeply personal ones. They, many of them, were gifts of the self, formed out of neediness. It is startling, therefore, to visualize the systematic baling of the blankets into standard-sized units (as the Red Cross logistics center in Tampere does, for example). Of course, the compressed bales minimize the need for storage space; in this form the blankets are packed against the elements, and their bulk transport is efficient. They become impersonal units, quantities measurable by means other than "love hours." All the time and work they took to make are compressed in the baling, as are the affects involved. There is a potlatch-like quality to this operation. It is quite possible that at their destinations these bales unfolded beautifully into "useful," handmade gifts of time and care, and that they were comforting to their recipients, but it is also possible that they just got in the way of aid operations, or were in other ways "useless."

Knitting as Sociality, Knitting as Therapy

Knitting enables an ethical and imaginative connection to be made between oneself and an unknown other in need, and with a wider world in need. It is a pleasing "structure of thinking" (Adamson 2007:6)—and of "feeling" (Williams 1985). The connection is also sensual. Wool especially is a compelling metaphor for warmth—and not simply a metaphor: its social warmth is linked to its sensual, physical warmth.[51] In the discipline of anthropology, among other social and historical sciences, of course, knitting—like linking, weaving, connecting, sewing, and fabricating—has been a key metaphor for the social from the very beginning. The social thread, the fabric of society, and the close-knit community are among the most used tropes of social theory. Yet the women from the yarn shops were doing something more complicated than producing a functional/ist "social fabric," something more ambivalent and precarious than a close-knit community. There were also sets of practices there like escaping the self—and of caring for the self in its state of abandonment. And the care of the self was made more meaningful and "important" because it helped "the truly needy." In this sense, the care of the self was related to ethical practice—another means of claiming personhood, an *ethical subjectivity* (Feldman 2008:96–97).

As I have already suggested, knitting (knowing how) was sometimes a spur to becoming a member of craft circles and other groups—to find forms of volunteering and *associational* activity that might otherwise have seemed beyond reach. Many might not want to put themselves forward or draw attention to themselves, and might therefore end up not joining things. Again, as mentioned previously, many people in Finland all too readily demure, "No, enhän minä nyt voi . . ." and "No, eihän meikäläinen nyt sentään . . ." ("Well, I couldn't . . ." or "Well, not for the likes of me . . .").

People who did join shared of themselves (and thus came to belong) in the knitting as a social process, and they found themselves convivially together, working to contribute to something larger than themselves (Uotila 2011:68). They found themselves sensually engaged also; the fact of handmaking alone was a sensual thinking/making process—as well as a sort of "making/doing" (Castoriadis 1997:197; chapter 1).

The blankets were a soft instantiation of multiple intersecting processes. The knitting needed a reason to happen; the Aid Bunny and the Mother Teresa blanket were two such reasons. It needed yarn and trips to the yarn shop. It needed the courage to attempt to make human connection and various socialities, even if temporary and precarious (see Butler 2004). It was a practice of alleviating loneliness, purposelessness, and *uselessness* (Uotila 2011:10; Muehlebach 2011, 2012). It was a method, perhaps, of not feeling oneself so much a bother (*vaiva*) or burden (*taakka*) on others, a worry all too familiar among the people I have talked with and others I have read about (Kairema 2000:25–26; El Said and Patja 2011).[52] It was a giving of one's skill, of time, and of oneself *in aid of* others, and linking it with others' skills and giving. It was a way of imagining oneself as *a member of the lively world*, and of something greater than oneself. One could think of this simultaneously generous and self-interested practice as a *self-humanizing practice*—again, a care of the self. This is not about the romantic notion that craftwork in and of itself is necessarily humanizing. This is more about having the *dignity of giving* and sharing useful *"knowledge about making things"* (Press 2007:265; see also Ruismäki and Ruokonen 2011a, 2011b).

The fact of hand-making is important here. The hands and the sense of touch are important. As mentioned earlier, it is an embodying pleasure for the knitter (and, it may be hoped, for the recipient). The "therapeutic" effect of wool and work of the hand has been much written about, in Finland and elsewhere. This is too large and complex a field to engage here in any depth. Just to point to possible areas for further anthropological research, then, I will refer to a very few interesting insights from others' work. Sinikka Pöllänen of the Savonlinna Teacher Training Institute (Savonlinnan opettajankoulutuslaitos) established in 2007 a lively online discussion forum on "art as a field for holistic life-figuration" (*taide kokonaisvaltaisen elämänhahmotuksen alueena*) (Pöllänen 2007a).

The discussion was used as part of teaching handwork-science (*käsityötiede*) students a course segment on "handwork and wellbeing" (*käsityö ja hyvinvointi*) (see also Ruismäki and Ruohonen 2011a, 2011b). Pöllänen explains how and why handwork can act as a form of therapy, as "a context that makes change possible," in many different ways; in this process, "the focus is on the handwork, the action and the feelings, the experiences, and the languages, and not on [one's] difference, handicap, illness, pain, feeling of worthlessness, or any other matter experienced as a difficulty" (2007a). She also discusses the specific value of handwork in working with old people in poor shape. She sees some of its advantages as sensual comfort, escapism, the therapeutic interrelating of body and self, and as a medium for mourning, among others (2007a).

In the sense that involvement in the pleasurable intensity and "flow" of handwork enabled a *temporary escape from the self* for the aged knitters, it resembles the meanings attached to international relief and aid work by the Red Cross nurses, doctors, and other professionals whom I examine in chapters 1, 2, and 6 (Csikszenmihalyi 1991; Riikonen 2005; see also Pöllänen 2006). Many of these medical professionals similarly sought in the flow and intensity of their work abroad a temporary escape from the self. This intensity, when experienced as professionalism, could also be a form of psychic protection as I suggested in chapter 2. In this sense, both kinds of practices could be thought of as *techniques of selflessness*—not the celebrated (and troubled) selflessness of "altruism" or self-sacrifice but rather the partial and precarious selflessness of escapism and the openness to stranger sociality (Butler 2004; Povinelli 2006).

In the online forum initiated by Pöllänen (2007a), a person writes thoughtfully: "Issues relating to elders' handwork are likely to become timely as the number of elders rises, and active elders might even demand activity in the [institutional] environment where they have ended up, for example because of an illness . . . Doing handwork, they might forget [for a spell] that they are in a care facility [hoitokoti], as for some elders this may feel like a very heavy thing."[53] "Erkoskel" writes: "For anyone who does handwork, [its] therapeutic and wellbeing-enhancing effect is utterly obvious."[54] The mere title of another study, "Knitting is like aspirin to me!," is to the point (Nissinen 2004). "Ira" affirms the therapeutic power of handwork and tells a story: "My father has often told me about a man (I don't know if he's still alive) who has developed into one of the best lace-makers in the country through a terrible tragedy. He had a very beautiful teenage daughter who died as a victim of brutal violence. For the father it was impossible to get past his great sorrow, and as if by chance he began to make lace. Through this handwork hobby, he was able to process his loss, but continued lace-making for decades. Who knows how much 'legend' there is in this story, but I myself can really understand it as true."[55] What is the mere, trivial, fine, painstaking activity of lace-making—or mere handwork in any form—to the loss the man suffered? There is a scalar impossibility: the mere of the lace to the enormity of the loss. Yet it was the father himself who made the link.

Conclusion: A Line Drawn in Water

The secretary general of the Finnish Red Cross, Kristiina Kumpula, observes: "The difference between the helper and the helped is a line drawn in water. An accident, fire, foreclosure, illness, loneliness, and the danger of marginalization can threaten anyone. The helper may become the helped and the helped the helper" (Hietaniemi 2007:14–15). Sometimes these differences collapse (Nousiainen 2005).[56]

Giving is often styled as emanating from an abundance ("We who have so much . . ." or "We should remember those less fortunate"), but in the contexts I have described, *giving emerges out of stark need*. As Kumpula said, in a quite anthropological way, there is often no clear line between giving and receiving. Need is everywhere, and it takes many different (sometimes radically different) forms, just like violence and loss. The social significance and scale of volunteering and associational life in Finland speaks to this. Domestic neediness is one source of international generosity. In this sense, all of the "giving" practices examined in this book form a map of vulnerabilities.

Is a person stricken by frightening loneliness—and perhaps numerous other problems—in any position to offer compassion? In such circumstances are you not yourself the proper object of compassion or intervention? Can you really (really) make yourself useful? Are you strong enough or even *worthy* of offering your help to others? *Seeing the urge to help as proceeding simply from compassion assumes that compassion is yours to give, that you are working from a position of relative strength.*[57] But many of the older knitters and other makers here were giving less out of strength than out of a kind of fragility and "crisis ordinariness." Here, as in other contexts I have explored in this book, the ethical generosity of "givers" and "helpers" overlay an intent *need for attachment*, and for living in social time.

6. A Zealous Humanism and Its Limits

Sacrifice and the Hazards of Neutrality

"Of Men and Gods": Humanity and Sacrifice

I requested and was kindly given two interviews with a Red Cross staffer whom I will call Sanna. The focus of the interviews was to be the principle of neutrality. Before we met, she mentioned in an e-mail a French film she liked that could be of relevance to our conversation: *Of Men and Gods*.[1] It had won the Grand Prix in Cannes in 2010. Based on a true story, the film was simply and beautifully directed by Xavier Beauvois (2010). It was set in the Atlas Mountains of northern Algeria during the civil war of the 1990s. A crumbling but inviting monastery stood near a village, Tibhirine. The film suggests that the Benedictine Cistercian monks had warm relations with their Muslim neighbors. Both groups cultivated the land and sold their goods at market, and the monks ran a small medical clinic open to everyone impartially. No sign of conversion efforts was visible; rather the monks simply took pains to be of service to the villagers, in other words, "to serve humanity" and "to do good works" according to their creed. Algeria's ten-year civil war had begun when the army rejected the election results of 1992 and seized power. There was a marked rise in political tensions in the region. Despite clashes between the government troops and the Islamists, the monks decided to remain in their abbey and with the residents of the region (Björkbacka 2011).

In the film, the Islamists, having initially attacked government targets, begin to attack civilians, including massacring an apparently random group of Croatian construction workers in broad daylight. The monks happen to be driving by and witness the scene of the freshly murdered bodies. They are waved on. After what may have been a moment of shamed hesitation, they do so in silence. The next day, the monks give medical treatment to a wounded guerilla. Local residents blame them for helping the "terrorists."

As the situation becomes progressively tense and dangerous, the monks face ethical dilemmas: One says, "Dying for my faith should *not* be one of my choices." Another asks, "Why be martyrs?" Abbot Christian responds: "We'd be martyrs of love. Love endures everything. We are brothers to everyone." In the meantime, all the monks, like the villagers, wait for more trouble. According to one account of the film's real-world, historical context, "in 1997 alone, twelve bloodbaths happened in twelve different Algerian villages. The Algerian army [was] blamed for not doing enough to prevent the mass murders." The violence came day by day closer to the monastery, which tried to carry on its "industrious practices of devotion" (Björkbacka 2011). The monks had declined armed protection. On a Christmas night, a gun-wielding group of guerillas crashes into the monastery. They demand to take away medication and Luc, the monk who is a doctor. Abbot Christian, very tense, says steadily, "This is a house of peace," and refuses to negotiate within the walls of the monastery as long as there are weapons present. An eye-to-eye standoff between Christian and the guerilla leader ensues. The negotiations move outside. Christian quotes thoughts from the Koran, and the guerilla leader's eyes change expression slightly. The doctor treats a wounded fighter, and the guerillas leave. There is a suggestion that the monastery is now under the protection of these particular guerillas. The conflicts come ever closer to the village and monastery, and eventually the leader of the guerillas with whom Christian negotiated at Christmas is killed, leaving the monastery even more vulnerable. The police chief of the village, "irritably preparing to wash his hands of the imminent bloodbath, tells Christian, 'I blame French colonization for not letting Algeria grow up'" (Bradshaw 2010). This is one of the very few direct references in the film to the brutal history of the French colonization in Algeria. This politics—as well as the ten-year Algerian civil war—are in fact left quite obscure in comparison to the painful *ethical* issues and human dilemmas considered in the film. Politics is always present as the danger to be kept at bay.

Throughout the film, the monks deliberate about whether to leave or to stay. Their reasons remain varied; twice they take votes. The abbot is steadfast in his personal decision to stay: "The good shepherd does not abandon his flock." His flock: Does this refer to his brothers, or the villagers, or both? Does he include the guerillas? Is he the good shepherd? How exactly does he imagine and experience his own status there?

For his fellows it is not so clear-cut, and it makes their personal deliberations surprisingly lonely. One brother wants to leave, saying he didn't become a monk to commit group suicide. Another says, "Let's leave for good." Someone else says, "*partir c'est fuite*" (to leave is to run away). "I came here to *live*, not to have my throat cut," says another. An old monk says he will stay because he has nowhere else to go (that may have been the case for a number of the monks). A brother suggests seeking out a safer place for a mission, "perhaps somewhere in Africa." Another concludes: "To leave is to die, I am staying [*Partir c'est mourir, je reste*]." "Some feel that their work there is not completed. Others wonder: Is going cowardice? Is staying arrogance? Is martyrdom their destiny? What higher purpose will their martyrdom serve?" (Bradshaw 2010). Their second and final vote is unanimous: they will stay in the monastery. Finally, the winter evening arrives when a militia group comes for the monks. Seven of them are led away in single file in the gentle silence of a snowfall. The men finally disappear from view. The expected gun shots are never heard. In historical reality, the monks were killed in 1996; it remains unclear by which party.

One cannot help but see the parallels, great and small, between the work of the Cistercian monks and that of the ICRC.[2] Most obviously, both are militantly apolitical.[3] The political immunity (and neutrality) of the ICRC is written into international law (Haug n.d.:463). (This is one aspect of its claim to universality.) The monks also expected immunity in their place of worship—Christian's words were: "This is a house of peace." A prohibition on weapons and a refusal of military or police protection are also shared principles. Very importantly, "the International Red Cross and Red Crescent ethos is one of *selfless* voluntary service" (ICRC 1996:12, emphasis added). The Cistercians' daily lives were also ordered by their form of selflessness. Service to "humanity" was foundational for both institutions.[4]

Although the ICRC is "accommodating" of all religions, and not exclusive to any one (its symbols are thus not only the cross but also the crescent, and more lately the red diamond), "its idea of *humanity* is also rooted in religious doctrines" (of many faiths) (Haug n.d.:463, emphasis added). The "good works" of the Benedictines, especially medical care, are freely and impartially offered, according to the film, without regard to political, religious, or other affiliation. Impartiality and voluntary service are, of course, another two of the fundamental principles of the Red Cross and Red Crescent Movement. In a thoughtful review of the film, Peter Bradshaw intimates that both the Christian monks and the Muslim fighters might have been "secretly infatuated with the idea of . . . martyrdom" (2010).

The setting of my interview with Sanna, the modernist headquarters of the Finnish Red Cross in Helsinki, could not have been more different from the scenes in Algeria that still stayed with me. But I was left wondering if some of the extreme (even extremist) selflessness of the Christians and Muslims there might not hold a subtle fascination for Sanna, who herself had in her own long professional career been on the most hazardous of the Red Cross missions I learned about over the course of this research. Some of the teams on those missions had had to make decisions about whether to stay or leave, too. Rwanda had been a very difficult experience for many, including her (see chapter 2). Sometimes the medical teams there received orders to evacuate to safer ground because of nearby bombardment—meanwhile they had patients in mid-surgery. The team members had had to deliberate. Do they leave the patients? Do they stay? Is a doctor's or nurse's life more important than others' because if s/he lives, s/he will be able to help more people? In one case I was told about, consensus was hard to reach; finally, the medical team evacuated, with their anaesthetized patients in tow.

Sanna was, in her words, decidedly "not religious," but the kind of extreme courage some of her missions had required of her made me think about the life-and-death choices the monks had deliberated, and about their relevance for her.[5] How often had Sanna had to imagine such choices? What had she had to take into account? She had mostly not been alone, but was a member of a professional team trained to assess risk and secure exit options, as well as having the support of resident members of the national Red Cross or Red Crescent societies. Nevertheless, the challenges to courage had been all too real for her. All my other Finnish interlocutors refused the idea of self-sacrifice, Leila most forcefully perhaps. Asked directly, Sanna did so too.

In *Cool Passion*, a genealogy of the zealous commitment to abstraction, Thomas Blom Hansen turns to Bataille's interpretation of sacrifice to draw the outlines of "modern conviction as a global grammar of interiority"

(2009:20). For Bataille, Hansen writes, "sacrifice is premised upon the division of the world into two realms—an ordinary and intelligible world of things, utility and necessity, that is fully mastered by humans; and, a world of intimacy, a realm that reveals 'the invisible brilliance of life that is not a thing' (47), a realm we may call 'the sacred' in its broadest sense." Hansen asks: "Can we not plausibly see the person of conviction as someone who willingly attempts to cross that line into another dimension, where life is more risky, more intense, more lived to the full and where the self is united with the world through a metaphysics of purpose?" (2009:27). In my interpretation, Sanna was such a person of conviction.[6]

Martyrdom was not culturally sensible in the Finnish context (see chapter 1). But then martyrdom is not part of the Cistercian creed either, argues A. O. Scott (2011). He writes that in *Of Men and Gods* Abbot Christian and his brothers were inspired by "an almost *fanatical humanism*, strict adherence to an idea of *compassion* that leads Luc to treat a wounded Jihadist and Christian to pray for the soul of a murderer and to pre-emptively forgive his own likely assassin" (Scott 2011, emphases added). This is yet another point at which the monks' discipline began overtly to resemble the ICRC's strict adherence to principles. Scott suggests that Beauvois, the director, is "clearly fascinated by the *radicalism* of the monks, an expression of *religious zeal* whose *extremism* lies in its insistence on preserving peace and dignity in all circumstances" (Scott 2011, emphases added).

Of Men and Gods is, then, as one commentator writes, a "humanist film" in which "*the men are more important than the gods*" (emphasis added).[7] The International Red Cross and Red Crescent Movement is also a humanist movement, and there is a case to be made that at its core is a similarly *radical* and *zealous* humanism (see Pictet 1979). I use the term *zealous* advisedly, both as a strategic interruption of the way that terms like *radicalism, zeal, extremism,* and *fanaticism* are so freely thrown around in anti-Islam rhetoric today, and also to signify the way that a certain extreme and absolute commitment lies at the heart of the ICRC's own, *explicitly secular vows*.[8]

The Red Cross has seven "Fundamental Principles," but only one of these is called "the essential principle" and that is humanity. All the other principles, including neutrality, flow from this.

The principle of Humanity

The International Red Cross and Red Crescent Movement, born of a desire to bring assistance without discrimination to the wounded on the battlefield, endeavours, in its international and national capacity, to prevent and alleviate human suffering wherever it may be found. Its purpose is to protect life and health and to ensure respect for the human being. It promotes mutual understanding, friendship, cooperation and lasting peace amongst all peoples.

In our first interview, Sanna began with a rapid inventory of wrenching yet typical ethical dilemmas in aid work in what she recognized as a world of often matter-of-fact cruelty and banalized inhumaneness. She conjured up a map of a world that freely accepts unacceptable arrangements in questions of life and death—and in some cases even calls it all "culture." "What is here that is *fair? How are we equal* in this world—that less than a dollar is too expensive [for a measles vaccine] and then hundreds of thousands is not too expensive—for [treating] one person" whose prognosis is poor (cf. Fassin 2010b)?[9]

Sanna made me think about such globally circulating, taken-for-granted conventions of stark inequality and naturalized cruelty through the lens of her Red Cross colleagues' personal limits in extreme situations (cf. chapter 2). They often have to decide whether their work is worth getting injured for, or even dying. And then, assuming that they continue to go on new missions, they make jarring moves "between . . . two realities," the mission and "home." "And . . . it's a challenge. You, *you*, have to learn to live with it. . . . Ethics doesn't have one real answer, ever. . . . That's why I recommended that film, *Of Men and Gods*—because everyone is [making] their decision" on a personal level. "They are *allowed* to do that, and I think it was a very wise film. In the end everyone has to take their own decision on their own behalf. And . . . that's about ethics, how far it goes, and—we [too, in the Red Cross] have to decide about our *own* ethics." Sanna moved on to sacrifice. "What are we willing—because sometimes it can be a matter of choice, not always, but sometimes it's a matter of choice—*what are we willing to sacrifice for our own ethics?* And that was a dilemma in the movie . . . for each of them, the monks, to decide how much they [were] willing and ready to sacrifice." Although almost everyone among my interlocutors explicitly *rejected* the very idea of sacrifice as a descriptor for what they were doing, Sanna's account underlines that there arise unforeseen social situations where the question of sacrifice is never really absent. Sacrifice here goes beyond "religion" narrowly understood—it entails a very particular imagining of the relation of self to self.

Sanna said that, their futures being necessarily unpredictable, all the Red Cross workers should think about these issues more deeply and personally prior to going on missions. Perhaps she was right: while many of my other interlocutors did talk about necessary preparations before leaving on missions in a very practical spirit, no one told me of having stopped to reflect on ultimate limits. This does not mean, of course, that such meditation did not happen. Taking leave of friends, partners, and family, and, in some cases, one's young children, must surely have brought up these private thoughts. And many of the workers had indeed come up against such "ultimate limits."

"I mean," Sanna continued, "at least for the people who are working in very dangerous situations and missions for humanitarian work which could be [very] worthwhile, probably you don't really know your final decision until you are facing it, [when] you have to take the final decision." She leaned forward, "It's easy to say here [in Helsinki] that 'I would do that' and 'I would never do that' . . . but when you're facing a decision, you will reconsider. Because of the trade-off—and because it's real." She added intently, "When you are faced with a critical situation . . . it's easier when you have thought about that [in advance]—that that situation might come . . . Should I stay or should I go: where is the limit?" As I show in chapter 2, the Red Cross people I interviewed had come up against numerous impasses, and limit experiences in the course of their work. (And these had long imaginative and experiential consequences in their lives.)

Sanna described several missions where security was bad (Afghanistan, Liberia, and Uganda, for example), but added that "there was not, I would say, this kind of breakpoint like in Rwanda." She thought that *Of Men and Gods* was "very good for that." She acknowledged that most people she knew who had seen the film thought it was "dead boring." The monks' dilemmas seemed very distant from the lives of most people. "But it's an issue that many people need to think about . . . And this is very particular to humanitarian work, that you need to think about it."

I had not specifically sought out discussions about facing ultimate limits in my other Red Cross interviews, nor, indeed, had I sought it here. But I did not have many interviews in which people did not discuss specific difficult cases of illness or injury they had tried to treat and deaths they had tried to prevent. These, too, involved ultimate questions, and—as incredibly frustrating as it was—the outcomes were often out of their hands. That was partly what made the missions so psychically demanding. Sometimes it was a single incident or particular patient that became a kind of limit for them (see chapter 2). For many, it was what the ICRC terms a "critical incident," where the life of the aid worker has been in danger. For others, as Sanna noted, it was a more gradual accumulation of hard cases that eventually required attention to one's psychic state.

Sanna, on the basis of her long history with the Red Cross, saw parallels between the ultimate choices between life and death for the monks of Tibhirine and those for the Red Cross aid workers. For the monks, the sacrifice of their lives involved a very difficult moral struggle.[10] One assumes, however, that they ultimately sacrificed themselves on behalf of humanity, and because it was meaningful in the eyes of their God. Sanna, it was clear, did decidedly think (in her "godless" way) that aid workers, too, should prepare themselves better for such ethical, and cosmological, limits.

The monks were members of a worldwide brotherhood, an imagined *world community* of Christian Benedictine monks whose universalist mandate, which they experienced as divinely inspired, was compassion and service to "humanity." The Red Cross is also imagined as a universal ethical and moral community—indeed, a *"world community"* (see Haug 1993; cf. Malkki 1998; Tsing 2005; and Devji 2008). Its core mandate rests on the principle of humanity in the face of suffering that is also regarded as of transcendent value and importance. Lest one think these parallels overdrawn, here is an excerpt from Jean Pictet's influential ICRC *Commentary on the Fundamental Principles of the Red Cross:* "The doctrine of the Red Cross is permanent. It is the expression of long-term wisdom, indifferent to the ebb and flow of popular opinions and ideologies of the moment. It outlived those who created it and this lasting character is perhaps a sign of its superiority over everything that happens here on earth" (Pictet 1979:4). My jaw dropped and my mind turned to Durkheim's famous characterization of the divine. The passage goes on to say that to be universal, the doctrine "must be expressed in words which are understood by everyone" (Pictet 1979:4). The fundamental principles have been translated into the languages spoken in all the member states of the movement worldwide—but of course Pictet meant more than that, appealing to a common humanity understood in his cosmological terms. "While people differ, human nature everywhere is the same—and *there is nothing more widespread than human suffering to which all men are equally vulnerable and sensitive"* (Pictet 1979:4, emphasis added; cf. Barthes [1957] 2013). So humanity encompasses human nature in one great transcendent sameness. (This is the kind of language used in the charters of many aid organizations, churches, and other social institutions.) The ICRC commentary goes on to state:

> However, even though we recognize today the unity of human feelings, we no longer believe that there is only one valid civilization, worthy of the name. On the contrary, we now acknowledge the pluralism of cultures and the need to become acquainted with them and study them deeply. In doing so we realize that humanitarian principles belong to all peoples and take root under all favorable conditions. When we bring together and compare different moral systems and dispose of the non-essentials, that is to say their special peculiarities, we find in the crucible a pure metal, *the universal heritage of mankind* . . . There is no unmitigable collision between the "different worlds" which we have placed in contrast. All doctrines can lead to the great law of the Red Cross, but each one by its own pathway, in accordance with the convictions and characters of the various peoples. The Red Cross serves to unite, and not to divide. *It is thus for the Red Cross to proclaim norms which have universal validity, because they are fully in accordance with human nature.* (Pictet 1979:4, emphasis added; cf. Barthes [1957] 2013)

These extraordinary, and in their own way, quite plainly religious texts notwithstanding, Sanna, like so many others I interviewed, said: "You work for this organization because it's not attached to religion. This is a good organization for us because it's not based on religion." (All but one of my interlocutors had said the same, and even the lone outlier was "not a practicing Christian.") But the Red Cross claim to secularity is enabled by the prior institutional operation of appropriating and fusing of all different cosmologies and philosophies around the world into a single universal, *zealous humanism*, understood as immutable and transcendent.[11]

Yet the interrelationship between an abstract commitment to humanity, on the one hand, and a practical ethics, on the other, was by no means straightforward. Indeed, observing the fundamental principles of humanity and universality could be seen as good and even noble in some contexts and as unconscionable and unethical in other, co-present circumstances. "Sometimes," said Sanna, "you *may* end up in . . . [a situation where] your decision based on humanity is a difficult choice. And then the personality [of the aid worker]—*who* sees it and *how*—comes up." Sanna gave prison work as an example of the difficulty of the practice of humanity. Visiting political detainees is important human rights work for the Red Cross.[12] "I think prison work is pretty difficult." Extraordinary pressures are placed on ICRC prison visitors ("protection delegates"), especially when security is bad, as it was in Rwanda. Sanna explained, "We came [into the prisons] regularly because we also distributed the food and hygiene and water and everything." Their ICRC clients were not common-law prisoners, she explained, but rather "prisoners detained as high-security prisoners" and "political prisoners who [had been] detained in a context of conflict." They were there because they were accused of genocide. The ICRC was there to ensure that these prisoners were treated humanely in accordance with international humanitarian law. Uncompromising universalism and humanity here demanded that one serve and protect even the accused perpetrators of genocidal violence. For some, such a practice might raise the question of the extent to which it was justified or even possible to be simply neutral and humanitarian in such cases. What is the limit? What would that look like? Is there a limit?

The issue of neutrality and its difficulty emerged as an important theme in the research—both in the sense of political or operational neutrality (which I discuss in the next section) and in terms of emotional or psychic neutrality (an issue I take up in this chapter's final section).

Political and Operational Neutrality

Neutrality manifests itself above all in relation to politics, national and international, and Red Cross institutions must beware of politics as they would of poison, for it threatens their very lives.
—Jean Pictet, ICRC

Dante once said that the hottest places in hell are reserved for those who in a period of moral crisis maintain their neutrality.
—John F. Kennedy

Indeed we have not in Finland conceived the object of neutrality as international seclusion. On the contrary, neutrality is in fact the means by which we feel we can best maintain contact with the rest of the world, the means by which we will keep up, deepen and develop our contacts with everyone. . . . When all is said and done, neutrality is by no means the easiest foreign policy. . . . Neutrality cannot be pursued passively. . . . Neutrality presupposes a constant endeavour to maintain the balance alertly and energetically, however threatening the storm clouds look. But neutrality is not and must not be an end in itself. Its purpose, like that of all foreign policy, is to further the country's interests. It is a means, not an end.
—Urho Kekkonen, 1965

In a contemporary transnational sense, "neutrality" (neutraalius) would seem to come easily to Finns.[13] It has long been a key part of Finland's foreign policy and international image (from the depths of the Cold War to today's international peacekeeping).[14] This helps to explain the heavy representation of Finns on ICRC missions in politically difficult conflicts elsewhere around the world, especially in Africa and the Middle East.[15] But to oppose neutrality to the "poison" of politics (in Jean Pictet's terms) would not make sense vis-à-vis Finland's commitment to neutrality, which was precisely a kind of politics. For most of its modern history, neutrality has been a strategic defense issue of great significance (Meinander 1999, 2006; Palosaari 2011). This policy was long a Cold War arrangement. Keijo Korhonen has characterized the arrangement as follows: "Neutrality-politics was a way for us to keep [a certain distance from] the large Eastern neighbor. We wanted to be marked as a neutral Nordic country so that we would not [drift into being] a vague half-satellite, half-Baltic country" (K. Korhonen 1999, quoted in Kallenautio 2005:286, emphasis added). It had to do with national unity and defense, and international standing (see Hertog and Kruizinga 2011). The end of the Cold War and the formation of the European Union in 1995 brought to an end a decades-old policy of political neutrality and the dissolution of the "Pact of Friendship and Mutual Assistance" (Ystävyys- ja Avunantosopimus [YYA]) that Finland had had as part of its postwar arrangement with the Soviet Union. Today many people feel quite differently about the country they live in, and regard Finnish neutrality as something of a Cold War relic. A colleague told me: "Every now and then someone still says in public that 'Finland is a neutral country' [Suomi on puolueeton maa]."[16] This "old neutrality" (puolueettomuus) is still important to some, and especially to older generations (cf. Jakobson 1968; Maude 1976).

But today, officially, Finland is in fact no longer a neutral country but rather "non-aligned" ("militarily non-aligned") and "independent" in terms of defense (cf. Natarajan 1955; Romulo 1956; Wright 1956; Gupta 1992; Tsing 2005). It is not a North Atlantic Treaty Organization (NATO) member, although the possibility of that membership is publically much debated (Rahkonen 2004, 2006; Tierala 2006).[17]

Nevertheless, the ICRC, the United Nations, and many other international bodies still operate with the old de facto understanding that "neutral Finland" is to all intents and purposes a disinterested "small state" and therefore easy to send on international missions in various capacities (see Pajunen 1982:164; cf. Viktorin 2008). No one even knows where it is, as many Red

Cross workers remarked, so no one has any particular animosity toward it. And Finnish leaders still seek to position Finland in well-worn ways. Now as in the past it has always striven to be a "good international citizen," or "citizen of the world," and oriented to an imagined "out-there-ness" (Viktorin 2008:131; cf. chapter 1). (A case is sometimes made that "Finnish security can be increased by actions that take place geographically far from its borders" [Rahkonen 2006:214].)

But this dominant understanding of Finland's neutrality and place in the world leaves important historical facts off-frame. "The idea that Finland is innocent in relation to colonialism is largely built on the fact that Finns never established any colonies for themselves. . . . Finland was [itself] part of the Swedish realm until 1809, and after that, [the] Grand Duchy of Finland in the Russian Empire before becoming an independent state in 1917" (Rastas 2012:102–3). This does not mean that Finland did not reap the economic benefits of colonialism, or send out missionaries; the exceptionalist narrative of "Finland as 'neutral' and 'harmless'" is an interested simplification, as Rastas correctly argues (2012:103).

Then, too, Finland's *generosity* in terms of humanitarian aid and "development cooperation" with countries in the Global South is not matched with equal *hospitality* to non-Finns at home. Refugees, immigrants, and minorities from around the world (and especially their children) might be "Finns" both culturally and in terms of citizenship—but they are still often the object of xenophobic slurs and attacks. In marked contrast to my own informants' subjectivities, subject positions, and political convictions, Rastas convincingly documents an aspect of "Finnish exceptionalism" in which nonwhite "foreigners" in Finland, perennially vulnerable, are regarded with "moral superiority" (Rastas 2012). Interestingly, my own interlocutors (all white) seemed often to have an inferiority complex on missions abroad and spoke of having "to prove themselves" on the international scene. As I mentioned in chapter 1, many were so preoccupied with their Finnish poor sense of self that they may not really have realized how very "white" a location they occupied on most of their missions abroad.[18]

The older understanding of Finnish neutrality (*puolueettomuus*) informed how I was brought up. Living as a child in East Africa in the late 1960s, I simply "knew" that good citizenship and conduct in the eyes of others was an essential element of being Finnish, in the everyday practice of neutrality and inoffensiveness, in "representing" my country well. Internationalism, the United Nations, neutrality, diplomacy, and development work in the newly independent African countries formed a hopeful, dynamic whole that was supposed to explain why we were there (in Sudan, and then in Ethiopia and Kenya). All these were ways of connecting Finland to "the world out there" or "being in [and of] the world" (Aaltola 2003:249).

Like Cold War Finland, the ICRC professes a neutrality that has elements of both principle and strategy (cf. Weiner 1968). One of the key areas of work for the ICRC in this historical moment lies in the Middle East, and specifically Afghanistan. "The ICRC is very much enmeshed in the Islamic World"; it is therefore logical that the "ICRC wants to establish that IHL [international humanitarian law] does not contradict the tenets of Shari'a" (Rieffer-Flanagan 2009:911, 912). Indeed, the ICRC has also held numerous conferences (in Qom, Kabul, Islamabad, Aden, and Dar es Salaam) on the compatibility and overlap between Islamic law and IHL (see, importantly, Devji 2008).[19] The purpose of these efforts is to show that there are different paths to humanitarian protection (see, e.g., Devji 2008; Bellal, Giacca, and Casey-Maslen 2011; Donini 2011; Geiss and Siegrist 2011; Munir 2011; Pejic 2011; Sarwary 2011; and Tabassum 2011). "As [ICRC's Andreas] Wigger [has] noted, 'Islam has a very rich tradition for ensuring dignity and respect for victims of conflicts.'"[20] Establishing relations of mutual respect and collaboration here are necessary if humanitarian work is to proceed at all. As for Finland, so for the ICRC, neutrality is not just an abstract principle but also a necessary means to an end (cf. Redfield 2010:53).

As I mentioned, Sanna developed a close parallel between the work of the Benedictine monks in Algeria and that of the Red Cross in Afghanistan. The following statement well reflects the ICRC's official position on its decades-long presence in Afghanistan (it started there in 1987). (The USSR had invaded in 1979; U.S. interest in Afghanistan, Afghan refugees, and NGOs in Pakistan also grew at that time. See, e.g., Baitenman 1990:63, 75.)

> The Red Cross and Red Crescent have *only one cause*—that of people who are *suffering* today or will be suffering tomorrow—and only one means of defending it: *persuasion*. The Red Cross and Red Crescent leaders must be willing to talk even to corrupt officials who are responsible for violations of human rights and of international humanitarian law. They cannot pass judgment on them publicly, but must speak to them on behalf of those to whom speech is denied, and who have nowhere else to turn . . . They often do so at considerable risk to their own personal safety and their words may fall on deaf ears, but if *this policy of refraining from public denunciation*

makes it possible to alleviate the suffering of just one man, woman or child, that is ample recompense. (ICRC 1996:8, emphasis added)[21]

As the passage above indicates, the ICRC freely admits that it is "not always an easy task to apply the principle of neutrality, not least because everyone has personal convictions" (ICRC 1996:8). The organization does not expect "fully programmed" members, and realizes that its people have multiple allegiances and constraints (see Pandolfi 2010:234). It also recognizes how hard, and dangerous, it may become for national-level Red Societies to maneuver around the issue of neutrality; they are, of course, auxiliary to their governments (cf. Hammond 2008:175). (And the signatory state has formally accepted the seven Red Cross and Red Crescent principles, among them neutrality.) "Neutrality is not a well-loved principle. There are those who express indignation at the neutrality of the Red Cross and Red Crescent, in the mistaken belief that neutrality betokens lack of commitment and courage" (ICRC 1996:7; see also Hansen 2009; Redfield 2010:55).

In his lecture course on "The Neutral" at the Collège de France (1977–78), Roland Barthes mentions the attribution of apathy to neutrality, as one of its many negative connotations; he also says: "Subject in the Neutral: said to flee one's responsibilities, to flee conflict, in a word, most defamatory: to flee . . . The Neutral: affinity for the muffled. Applied to a person: contemptuous notion: mixture of dullness, of hypocrisy, of the taste for narrow convenience" (2005:70). According to Johann-Gottlieb Fichte (1845:218–19, quoted in Barthes 2005:69): "In this fake being, limp, distended, multiple . . . The men in question hold nothing for true and nothing for false, they love nothing, they hate nothing." Maurice Blanchot (1993:311) explains: "The neutral does not seduce, does not attract." Referring specifically to political neutrality, Barthes says: "Pure expression of the anti-Neutral: obligation to choose, no matter what side: the Neutral is more enemy than the enemy: it's the beast to kill, to exclude; tyranny of the paradigm in all its purity" (Barthes 2005:183).

To counter the widespread disdain and suspicion of neutrality, the ICRC points (as former President Kekkonen did for Finland) to the important ends that neutrality can secure. Thus, the movement considers consciousness-raising about the fundamental principles and worldwide "institution building" (*développement institutionelle*) to be essential practices on all missions around the world. Institution building refers to development, teaching, and support for the national Red Cross and Red Crescent societies that can be key players in the exercise of tactical neutrality. Their presence on the scene of conflicts strongly underscores the fact that strategies of neutrality are always delicately relational, situational, and provisional. ICRC practitioners are acutely aware of this. It is important that "the strategic construction of *administrative* neutrality is in fact a political choice with significant implications for political conflict" (Huber 2007:5). Administrative procedure may (or may not) help to neutralize politics.[22] The fabrication of Weberian "professional neutrality" embedded on the local scene may help augment the strategic efficacy and authority of neutrality (see chapter 1). It is not the intent that outside teams undermine or compromise the position of national Red Crosses or Red Crescents in their own societies. The ICRC would not have lasted in Afghanistan without the close cooperation between them and the national and local Red Crescent societies. Both bodies understand that (convincing) claims to fairness and consistency allow bureaucracies to appear "above politics."

"When tension mounts and passions are aroused, every member of the Red Cross or Red Crescent is called upon to exercise great self-control and to refrain from expressing his opinions in the discharge of his duties. Volunteers are not asked to 'be' neutral—everyone is entitled to an opinion—but to *behave neutrally*. That is an important distinction" (ICRC 1996:8, emphasis added; cf. Redfield 2010:63). Here, again, military codes of conduct are comparable. (See also Muhammad Munir [2011] for Islamic *jus in bello*.) Neutrality becomes a temporally circumscribed *tactic* that demands performative efficacy and affect management (Mazzarella 2009).

In many conflicts, the ICRC recognizes, "Anyone trying to work on both sides to help non-combatants is considered at best naïve and at worst a traitor. . . . Not taking a stand is a hostile act in itself" (ICRC 1996:9). This is an accusation that has often been leveled against the ICRC, probably by all of the proliferating parties to the seemingly unending thirty-year conflict in Afghanistan. And there are histories of ICRC neutrality, of course, that will not go away. The greatest moral, ethical, and political blot on the ICRC's record is its "neutral" conduct during the rise of Nazism in Hitler's Germany (Slim 2001:144; Terry 2002; Rieffer-Flanagan 2009:899). This terrible history is by now well documented, by the ICRC itself and others.[23]

When is neutrality unconscionable in current conflicts? Ethically, this is unforgiving terrain. It was absolutely clear to Sanna that "the ICRC is doing a very difficult mission in Afghanistan," and equally clear that "it's a very important mission to be [there]." She said the ICRC members "were the first ones to have direct contact with the Taliban." And "it was difficult to reach them because no one had reached [out to] them before to negotiate." She described the initial contacts: "[We said:] 'Let's talk, let's have a dialogue about these [health care] issues, [about] how we can work here.'" The organization had a great deal of difficulty in making a convincing case that it was not a party to the conflict, nor, at various junctures, subcontracted by the United Nations, the European Union, or any other body. It was a struggle to win anything approaching trust from the Taliban. More recent counterinsurgency tactics deployed by the United States or "coalition forces" in a strategy to win hearts and minds have obviously complicated Red Cross work. A recent, problematic example of the instrumentalization of humanitarian aid are FETs (Female Engagement Teams), which are used in "an attempt to reframe the U.S. military intervention in Afghanistan as a humanitarian, even progressive, mission" (McBride and Wibben 2010:200). Mariella Pandolfi writes that the ever more entwined relationship between war and humanitarianism has become very "troubling . . . in the past two decades with the emergence of a grey zone among conflicts, humanitarian aid, development, and security" (Pandolfi 2010:227). This has made ICRC work more dangerous than it was ever before.

The ICRC—and presumably other aid agencies such as Médecins Sans Frontières (MSF)—has been under great pressure from the forces fighting against the Taliban. Sanna recalled earlier times: "Of course, during that time it was *not accepted*; it was considered a thing *not to do* . . . Everyone thought it was a *criminal act* to reach [out to] the Taliban to negotiate." The ICRC has been roundly criticized all along for giving medical care "to everyone, regardless of political affiliations. It has often been accused of 'harbouring terrorists.'" The ICRC works with whoever is in power. Sanna reiterated that this was "considered almost a *criminal* thing [in the mid-2000s], to be negotiating with the Taliban." But she also pointed out that the ICRC "have made *very hard choices* there, they have stayed over time, the governments have come and gone, come and gone, and the people in power have come and gone, but the ICRC has stayed, which has given it credibility and . . . an image of neutrality . . . even now with the Karzai government and . . . [the] Taliban and Al-Qaeda conflict." The ICRC has worked hard to make this status convincing, and remains mindful of how little it would take for it, and all the work behind it, to evaporate in an instant.

Little by little, over the years, according to Sanna, the ICRC has made itself a "permanent" part of the social and political landscape in Afghanistan. In 2006–7, "the ICRC was able to expand activities in the South." It was always discreet. It started up first aid programs. "So, first the training for [Afghan] volunteers who were working in Taliban-held areas. They are people who may not be Taliban themselves—we don't ask—but they are at least accepted by [the] Taliban." They are allowed to be present and to give medical care there. "So we started to train them in first aid, in casualty care—very discreetly, but still." Sanna laughed and added: "This was an interesting start."

But many medical delegates had understandably found that what they were doing involved them in extremely difficult ethical dilemmas: "So, why, [when] they are doing [such] bad things—terrible things to people, [using] these suicide bombs, . . . IEDs [improvised explosive devices] and all kinds of things that happen over there. Why do we, why do we, work in these areas when the people there, the locals, are so terrible? And there's your personal dilemma, then. And some people felt very strongly about that." One can only imagine the intensity of the ethical debates and struggles.[24]

But there was great need for more medical care throughout the country. "The people there, the women and children, and the papas and mamas, were in the area and needed help. [Then] of course, when they get that help [from the ICRC], they probably think that, 'well, maybe the Taliban are not so bad'—and everyone was suffering and, and, and . . ." She fell into a long silence; I felt like I was waiting for her on the outside.

Finally she continued: "And of course the Taliban were not always so friendly and nice toward the ICRC even. I mean they killed, they murdered a delegate in 2003. That was done by the Taliban." The Taliban have also made threats and other attacks against the ICRC. The ICRC delegate murdered in 2003 was water engineer Ricardo Munguia; he was "deliberately killed" in March 2003 "as he travelled from Kandahar to Tirin Kot [and] this shocked the ICRC to its core" (Terry 2011:175). Up to that point, the ICRC had been more or less able to assume immunity from attack. (In fact, the ICRC's head of delegation in Afghanistan at the time, Reto Stocker, said in a 2010 interview that as of 2003, "the country became significantly more dangerous for humanitarian personnel, a development that culminated in the murder of [Munguia]. That marked the end of humanitarian access as we knew it, and the beginning of a full-fledged insurgency" [ICRC 2010].) The ICRC had an unambiguous record of neutrality and was widely considered to have done good and useful work. It was shocking to find out that "neither the man who ordered the killing nor the man who carried it out was a stranger to the

ICRC's work: *they each wore an ICRC prosthesis on one leg*. Yet this did not stop them killing Ricardo as a symbol of the imperialist West which they considered was waging a war on Islam" (Terry 2011:175, emphasis added).

At this point, I return to the moral logic of "the one" that I have mentioned previously. The opening ICRC document said, "if this policy of refraining from public denunciation makes it possible to alleviate the suffering of just one man, woman or child, that is ample recompense" (ICRC 1996:8, emphasis added). Perhaps the surgeons and nurses operating on the two men thought in this way, too—perhaps they were helping two single human beings in danger of losing their lives, and that was the most important thing in that moment. The problem was that the patients were not merely "human beings," not merely "sufferers," and not merely "victims"; they were also militants and fighters with their own ethical and political convictions—and depending on when they had come of age, and what they had already been through, they were warriors against a "West" they understood to be engaged in a "War on Islam" (see Terry 2011:186). They were not only human in the substratal, foundational sense that the humanitarian imagination and sentiment would make universal: human = human. Suddenly, the logic of "saving" human beings can appear as quite a naïve position where the one who is to be saved may use his saved life precisely to kill you (Redfield and Bornstein 2010). Such realities seem to confound the shared belief and ethical understanding in the precious "substratum" of a shared humanity in the ICRC's terms. This is the essential principle, the cornerstone of the Red Cross and Red Crescent Movement. How can it be so formidable in one ethical context and so seemingly naïve in another?

It has been claimed that "the *sentimental method of humanization* [often] creates a subject in the thrall of victimhood, restricted to a state of innocence, passivity, and political impotence" (Festa 2010:14; see also Malkki 1996; Ticktin 2011; and chapter 3). But this may grant the humanitarian framing more power than it actually has. Those for whom the help is intended are not necessarily thinking in terms of a concept like "shared humanity," nor do they set aside their political agency in favor of some "deeper" relation of human to human.

In this context one must return to Sanna's insistent question: What does the terrain of limits look like? What did she really mean by a limit of humanity? A limit can mean many things. Was there a limit for the killers? Was it the first time they took a human life? Was this work in Afghanistan an ethical and affective limit, an impasse, for some of the other Red Cross and Red Crescent workers? Did their principles of neutrality and humanity make their position impossible? (see Redfield 2010:53). Sanna's account makes clear the relevance of the film *Of Men and Gods*. According to her, no ICRC personnel left the field following the murder of Ricardo Munguia. And the ICRC as an organization did not leave, although it did curtail its work significantly. Among other key projects, it "continued to visit suspected Taliban and other fighters [detained] around the country, advocating humane treatment for them in accordance with international law" just as had been done in its prison visits to suspected *génocidaires* in Rwanda (Terry 2011:177). This extremely disciplined practice of political neutrality and safeguarding of the Geneva Conventions must have seemed perverse and incomprehensible to many kinds of actors on the ground.

Was this commitment to humanity really just a pragmatic "urge to help" (as my informants maintained)? Or was it something more like a zealous adherence to an ultimate principle? A zealous humanism? An extremist humanism? And what are the limits of what can or should be sacrificed in the name of such a principle? Here I think of the Benedictine monks: like the ICRC, they worked to alleviate human suffering and to serve humanity. When their own ultimate dilemmas came, they very understandably thought about their own mortalities and their limits. In the end, we are asked to assume, they sacrificed themselves out of love for humanity. But we are also allowed to doubt.

The principles of humanity and neutrality in Sanna's account were tough and unyielding: "It's not our business to decide whether their position is right or wrong." She was, after all, the veteran ICRC worker. Then she made the question of dilemmas and ultimate choices even more extreme. Among the Finnish soldiers deployed in Afghanistan under UN command with the International Security Assistance Force (ISAF), "there might even be friends or acquaintances [*tuttuja*] fighting against the Taliban, and they might even get killed, and there you are giving medical care to people in Taliban-held areas [who might well be the ones who did the killing]. And there's this *dilemma*: why do we work in this area where the power-holders are so awful [*kamala*]??"

She did not accept this as a limit. Rather, she underscored yet again: "I think this is very interesting work and *good* work and *absolutely* the kind of place where the Red Cross needs to be working—even with all the risks." She said it was a good thing to be able to discuss these dilemmas openly, to debate right and wrong, and to observe the pathways opened up and closed off by one's taking sides. She talked about an "emotional dilemma" where one might think, "Why do I bother with them?" (*Mitä mä näistä?*). But, she said, "in the same way that the delegates are human beings, so are they." This is not the "soft" humanist universalism of the sentimental "We Are the World" invocation of shared humanity, or the imaginative play of the Aid Bunny and Trauma Teddy described in chapter 4, but it is the logical conclusion of taking such an essential humanity as an absolute principle. It underlines the hard stakes involved in actually taking humanist universalism to its limit. Sanna's bottom line was an uncompromising "humanity." There was something steely—even extreme—in her commitment to this ideal.

Affective Neutrality and Suffering

> Professionals are not supposed to feel desire or disgust for their clients, and they
> presumably begin to learn "affective neutrality" in professional schools.
> —Allen C. Smith III and Sherryl Kleinman

The ICRC recognizes that emergency relief work (in distinction to a wide variety of other less intensive aid work) continually raises ethical, political, and affective challenges demanding prompt responses.[25] It recognizes, too, that this work has both intended and unintended consequences for many parties, including the aid workers and their psyches. In all emergencies, observing the principle of neutrality is nevertheless expected and operationally relied upon. Most of the time, the ICRC conceptualizes neutrality as a *code of conduct*, but in a 1996 document on the Fundamental Principles, the ICRC also says: "*neutrality is a state of mind*" (ICRC 1996:8, emphasis added). The Red Cross people I asked about this agreed that neutrality is usually used to refer to a code of conduct, but they also accepted this other definition—reminiscent of the painstaking work on the state of mind that the Cistercian monks daily undertook.

In a series of conversations with Leif, the doctor I have mentioned before, it came up that for him there was not just one neutrality (as laid out in the ICRC code of conduct), but several different possible forms. I wanted to confirm: "So you *would* say that there are different forms of neutrality?" He answered (in English): "It's *essential* to think in this way. Up in the air, it's one thing. Coming down, you see different neutralities. You're Finnish, you're Red Cross . . . even if your nationality isn't foremost in your work in the Red Cross. Conflicts among different neutralities occur. How do you cope with that? [This can cause] emotional problems. The easy way out is to prioritize one neutrality [over others]. On missions, ICRC neutrality takes precedence." What Leif said next again reminded me of the Cistercian brothers and religious orders in general, as well as military creeds: "It's essential to build up this inner person who starts living impartiality and neutrality, not just believing in the principles . . . There is emotional neutrality. Mature Red Cross workers have emotional neutrality."

Another person at the Helsinki headquarters expressed the institutional expectation of commitment to the principles in this way: "The fundamental principles have to be embedded in our personal principles also; you cannot really perform your duties if you just read them as rules [stuck] to the wall of your office!" She was "a mature Red Cross worker."

Neutrality—like humanity (Laqueur 1989, 2009; Feldman and Ticktin 2010a:4)—has often been thought about in terms of sentiment and disposition in other domains as well. In psychoanalysis, of course, it has been central since Freud first introduced it (G. Thompson 1996; A. Goldberg 2007). In the 1950s, Talcott Parsons referred to "affective neutrality" as an important element in medical practice (Parsons 1951; see also Smith and Kleinman 1989).[26] The danger of such neutrality is of course that it can be carried too far; as Redfield (2010) notes, neutrality (and ICRC neutrality in specific) has variously been taken for a lack of feeling, indifference, disinterest, passiveness, selfishness, a desire to stand apart, and affective abstinence. Yet my ethnographic evidence suggests that affective neutrality was lived by field workers as a continual aspirational practice of self-discipline. Those with the longest Red Cross careers could rely on it more automatically perhaps than newer workers, but it is worth reiterating that all Red Cross medical workers joined the organization already being medical professionals familiar with affective neutrality. The same was largely true of the other occupations on missions as well.

There was a concern, on missions, to have close and humane practices of care with patients, but without that becoming such identification with any one patient, her suffering, or her life circumstances that it would become professionally disabling. I found that this concern was raised especially in the work of nurses since they typically spent more time with patients than did doctors. Nurses talked about their relations with patients a great deal, and the issue of excessive closeness with some—especially children (see Truog 2012:584; and chapter 2).

The Red Cross aid workers' insistence on professionalism in extreme situations was a means of exercising affective neutrality.[27] Sometimes, particularly in the accounts from Rwanda, it seemed to me that holding on to their professionalism was the only option people had left (see chapters 1 and 2). It was a method of keeping things together, and maintaining a measure of *distance* between themselves and patients, themselves and the dangerous situations they were working in, and themselves and their own thoughts and imaginations. "Affect management" (Mazzarella 2009) was crucial in these situations.

A doctor—saying that affective neutrality was useful—pointed out, "Breaches of international humanitarian law have to be taken up [by ICRC workers] without exception with all parties to a conflict; these situations can become very stressful—and *especially* so for local and national-level Red Cross or Red Crescent personnel" who are socially embedded in their home societies and yet expected to behave neutrally. Thus, while the national Red Cross could technically cover a given problematic situation, it is sometimes easier when an expatriate is substituted; that may defuse tensions and make more room for negotiation for everyone. One can try, for example, to neutralize a politically and affectively charged problem by making it into a technical one. Any organization has to take account of the "potential vagrancy of emotions and the threat they pose to self-possession" (Festa 2010:7).

In a long and curious interview, Eeva, a psychologist, expressed often quite contradictory, if powerful, views on affective neutrality. At first she flatly challenged the very possibility of affective neutrality in relief work. She thought that affective neutrality in crises and war situations was practically impossible; at times she also seemed to disapprove of it. "Neutrality as a psychological term is a pretty impossible thing. I mean I understand that in conflict situations and crises, some sort of term has to be found for it . . . But if you think about being a *human being* [*ihminen*], in relation to another human being, as a helper . . . That one would be *capable* of this kind of neutrality, can it really *be*—I mean in this kind of psychological sense? Just our being *human beings* makes it impossible."

Yet she then accepted that a surgeon's effort at such neutrality could be a crucial form of psychic protection (*psyykkinen suoja*), as could the distantiation between herself and her patients; it preserved her ability to keep working effectively. "It's possible that to be capable of *doing* those things and *being* in conflict situations . . . you have to distance yourself from it because if you really begin to think about what's happening around you, why you're there, or why you go and patch up some people in this war situation, it becomes *impossible, ethically and morally, in the middle of [people's] suffering*" (emphasis added). Saying to yourself that you're allowed to be affectively neutral may make it "easier to live with yourself," and "to be there."

To be able to "live with yourself" (*voida elää itsensä kanssa*) seems at first an odd formulation; the relief teams were there to *help*, after all. Yet from my interviews with this psychologist and other Red Cross people, I got the sense that this ethical and affective predicament was not unfamiliar. The workers might feel bad about themselves for a number of reasons. What does it mean to "care" or to "help" in a war or genocide? Are they "feeling enough"? What are their true motives for being in the middle of this or that disaster? Why did they *really* accept this mission and not some other? They might ask themselves whether this fieldwork is more important than their medical work in a hospital back in Finland. They might feel heavy guilt about not "doing enough"—but what would "enough" be in a crisis of overwhelming scale, for example Rwanda? Again, in such situations they face a scalar impossibility (cf. Tsing 2005). There were simply too many people to treat. Yet there are always particulars: how could you allow someone—*that* person with *those* kids—to die? You feel your own smallness and are called upon to witness unspeakable things on an impossible scale. And there are ethically difficult decisions to make, one after another. The aid workers come up against many such extreme limits that, in Sanna's terms, "test their humanity." Here it is hard to even consider the possibility of affective neutrality. Yet an aspiration to that was assumed by the aid workers when they insisted on their professionalism.

Later Eeva turned to the less seemly side of affective neutrality—never very far, either, on aid missions, she argued. While she saw good reasons for medical personnel's relative distantiation from patients' fear and suffering, some surgeons in her opinion were emotionless "cutters"/"operators" (*leikkaaja*) who had lost all track of the living persons breathing under their hands. She told me about a specific case: "So, [in that case] even though the *intent* [was] good, and this person [on the operating table] [did] get well," there was an automatism in the surgeon's conduct that revolted her. Eeva looked straight into my eyes and said: "Crudely put, it [was] *meat cutting* [*lihan leikkaaminen*]." Was she using this directness to close off any possibility of imaginative distantiation of any kind? I found myself holding my breath. Or was she creating an even greater distance—enacting, as it were, the hovering Martian view of an unsituated, emotionally void observer? There is a woman cutting another woman's flesh. There is a man sawing off another man's leg.

I understood her to be criticizing not all surgeons but some surgeons' "god-trick" of being somehow *above* everything, and not experientially encountering the quality of another's suffering at all. Affective neutrality here meant a grave failure of the imagination. Some surgeons failed to see patients truly as fellow persons (*kanssaihmiset*; Germ. *Mitmenschen*). But adjust perspective slightly, and one might instead see skilled physicians who exhibited admirable calm in an acute emergency.

Maintaining the "superhuman" affective neutrality that some missions seem to demand can exact its toll later on. Eeva found that after these intense missions, some workers "crashed" upon returning to Finland. Some of them engaged in various kinds of self-destructive behavior, for example, drinking, gambling, and other addictions. Others managed their psychic situations by going on mission after mission without significant breaks; in Eeva's estimation some of these aid workers were psychically "in bad shape." But I also have very convincing reports of, and meetings with, aid workers who thrived on frequent missions.[28] They felt very alive and open. These were times of intense personal growth for them, as Leif explained earlier (chapter 1). Several administrators made the same observation. There was wide variation, in other words.

Eeva foregrounded nurses' field experiences at many points in the interview. At one point she discussed differences in people's affective *hexa*. "Not everyone is capable of going into situations where there are people in acute crisis; [not everyone] can bear [*sietää*] others' very powerful and unbearable feelings." This skill and strength—of bearing unbearable feelings—are part of the professionalism of a psychologist. But Eeva also attributed it to the medical aid workers', especially the nurses', professionalism. Strange, then, that she had initially discounted such professional neutrality as impossible and inhuman.

"I had an advisor," Eeva recalled about her studies, "who said that you have to have one foot in your *own* life and the other in the patient's. Then you are present as your own self. That you have one foot strongly in your own self is, in my opinion, a professionalism to be aspired to . . . You're able to be there as a human being in a way without *drowning* in your helping—you're there as your own *self*." This is, of course, the purpose in trying to maintain some kind of affective (and imaginative) neutrality: to avoid drowning. (Eeva's own duties on a particular mission we discussed had been extremely hard; they had almost forced her on disability leave.)

Being an ethical human being and being yourself while trying to retain some affective neutrality was, she said, an unsteady balancing act. "If a [patient] experiences that 'That one doesn't care,' that 'S/he has no emotional contact to this situation'—or [the patient thinks:] 'You can't live this with me at all' [myötäelää], the [patient] doesn't get helped . . . But if the [aid worker] is there, and you see that she bears it with you and doesn't drown in it," it helps a lot. This requires being there sincerely, as yourself, while also being a professional.

We discussed psychologists' presence on missions in general, and interesting issues came up. On the one hand, Eeva made a compelling argument for psychologists' ability to help people like UN peacekeepers on longer missions to deal with processing fear, for example. (Unsurprisingly, having to cross a minefield every day to get to and from work caused fear in many peacekeepers.) But, on the other hand, she also considered it understandable that "psychologists don't [routinely] go on international relief missions because the aid workers' ability to help would be adversely affected. If they had to start processing things too deeply there on the spot, their work would suffer." She acknowledged that the Finnish Red Cross tries to follow up on psychic issues after the fact, in Finland, but added that it could do a better job of it. Her last comment especially suggests that while affective neutrality is expected as the professional hexus, it is vulnerable in the breach—and also in long aftermaths in Finland that are too often lonely.

In sum, ideally, affective neutrality is neither indifference nor an unwillingness to act or engage, nor a lack of affect. It is perhaps usefully thought of as an aspirational practice that is strengthened through professional experience in extreme situations. In the end, what I heard from Leif, Eeva, and others suggests that it is protective of both aid workers and their patients, and reassuring to both in different ways. It makes possible the effort to bear the unbearable. It makes possible a (temporally delimited) imaginative self-discipline that can end up being very humane.

None of the people I came to know were in any way heartless or cold, or lacking in imagination. Nobody was unwilling to think very honestly about the complex implications and effects of their work; in fact, they welcomed it—just as they welcomed the chance to just talk at length about their missions. They were not unwilling, either, to acknowledge that their emotions and senses were deeply implicated in their work in the field. This did not mean that they did not exercise affective neutrality—a kind of "affect management"—in their professional work (Mazzarella 2009).

There is a commonplace popular view that "the humanitarian" is one who "feels." He feels compassion, and is powerful. When asked about it, people shrank away from this figure as a false reflection of themselves. They overwhelmingly countered that their preferred term was *aid worker*. What they all shared, they shared with many other Finns: "a need to help" and a need to be "a part of something larger" than themselves (see chapter 5). Their professionalism enabled them to get there.

Neutrality in Other Worlds

In J. M. Coetzee's book *Elizabeth Costello*, a character of the same name has made a long bus journey and been let off at a station in a dream-like scene. There are people at tables on a public square and a lodge house. She has come there to pass through a gate, the gate. Before she can do so, she is told by a man at the lodge house to write a statement of belief. Incredulous, she counters, "What if I do not believe? What if I am not a believer?" (2003:194). The man who asked for the statement answers: "We all believe. We are not cattle. For each of us there is something we believe. Write it down, what you believe. Put it in the statement" (2003:194). She needs to pass through the gate, but she can't write what they ask. Finally she produces a statement, to be read by an odd jury of characters. She writes: "'I am a writer, a trader in fictions . . . I maintain beliefs only provisionally: fixed beliefs would stand in my way. I change beliefs as I change my habitation or my clothes, according to my needs. On these grounds—professional, vocational—I request exemption from a rule of which I now hear for the first time, namely that every petitioner at the gate should hold to one or more beliefs'" (2003:195). Her petition is rejected. She writes many more drafts, makes many more arguments, and gets nowhere. She tries again: "'I am a writer, and what I write is what I hear. I am a secretary of the invisible, one of the many secretaries over the ages. That is my calling: dictation secretary. It is not for me to interrogate, to judge what is given me. I merely write down the words and then test them, test their soundness, to make sure I have heard right . . . Before I can pass on I am required to state my beliefs,' she reads. 'I reply: a good secretary should have no beliefs. It is inappropriate to the function. A secretary should merely be in readiness, waiting for the call'" (2003:199–200).

Affective neutrality in the field, in emergency relief and aid work, requires a *methodological distancing* that is reminiscent of kinds of writing. It is also reminiscent of aspects of ethnographic fieldwork. As an anthropologist you participate in your interlocutors' lives (if that is what your intellectual project needs and if they do not object) and you record things. You take field notes.

On many occasions you *aspire* to be the neutral dictation secretary. You have your own opinions and politics, but you try to set them aside (to some degree appropriate to the context)—not forever, but provisionally, lest they get in the way of the more urgent, practical task of understanding. As your understanding and imagination grow, you try not to drown.

What I want to explain (it is my professional injunction as an anthropologist to explain) is how people imagine, think about, feel, make/do something. Suppose I am an anthropologist in a very large, dusty refugee camp in East Africa. In one family, a perfect, healthy baby is born. On the following night, it dies. It has died for no apparent reason at all, and the grieving parents and those around them begin the process of finding out who could have caused such a tragedy. A diviner is called in. The guilty party is identified in the person of an old woman.

As an anthropologist, I am not interested in arguing with those who teach me about witchcraft, but in learning to understand how they think about this issue. I have to hold on to the possibility that there is a point of view from which all this makes perfect sense. This is a familiar kind of *methodological* relativism—a kind of neutrality that may seem very strange to non-anthropologists but that is a long-established part of anthropology's methodological repertory, and of its professional sensibility. In principle, in my trained professional capacity, I take the ideas of others as seriously as I take my own. I have to suspend my own certainties (if any) for a time, and remain open to being surprised. I take dictation. This does not mean discarding my own ideas about why the baby died. And it does not absolve me, perhaps, of trying to intervene to stop the people whom the diviner told to drive the old woman out of the camp. It does entail a kind of provisional, improvisational, unstable neutrality, but one that inevitably runs up against its limits. Here, too—as in chapter 2—the impossibilities of aid work in the field find an uncanny parallel in ethnography.

Conclusion: Humanity, Animality, and Limits

In this chapter I have examined, through a variety of different scenarios and traditions, two of the seven interlinked fundamental principles of the International Red Cross and Red Crescent Movement: humanity and neutrality. It is the essential principle of a common, universal humanity and the unconditional obligation to alleviate universal suffering that I will explore yet further here. The language of the fundamental principles seems out of time, in some way still trapped in the nineteenth century. Yet, as Feldman and Ticktin (2010a:1), among many other contemporary scholars of humanitarianism, point out: "Surveying the contemporary political scene one finds humanity mobilized in a remarkable array of circumstances. . . . A claim to speak on behalf of humanity stakes out a powerful position" now (see, e.g., Englund 2005, 2010; R. A. Wilson and Brown 2008; R. A. Wilson 2010, among others).

Throughout the book, humanity has been accompanied (and interrupted) by children, stuffed animals, living animals, dolls, toys, and other non- or part-human power-objects. I have documented how people feel such imaginative empathy with nonhuman or part-human beings and object-beings as to want to create, play, mimic, protect, and even adopt them. The game of animation—making animal? making live?—has, for example, caused women and girls all over Finland to knit Aid Bunnies for children in need out there in the world. Another person may pick up off the ground a Save the Children postcard with a portrait of a needy child. Adopt me! The one. Randomness is a disturbing but inescapable element of much humanitarian aid. "From love of man one occasionally embraces someone at random (because one cannot embrace all): but one must not tell him this" (Nietzsche 1966:92; see also Bornstein 2012).

All too easily, engagements with a humanity understood in such generic terms can turn into political disempowerment, as Hannah Arendt and others have shown. On the idea of specifically human rights, Arendt famously wrote:

> Even worse was that all societies formed for the protection of the Rights of Man, all attempts to arrive at a new bill of human rights were sponsored by marginal figures—by a few international jurists without political experience or professional philanthropists supported by uncertain sentiments or professional idealists. The groups they formed, the declarations they issued, showed an uncanny similarity in language and composition to that of the societies for the prevention of cruelty to animals. No statesman, no political figure of any importance could possibly take them seriously. ([1951] 1973:292, emphasis added)

Severed from the real protections that could be guaranteed by a state, "human rights" could only be a sentimental ideal (cf. Rancière 2011:72). Karl Marx and Friedrich Engels, of course, similarly lumped together "philanthropists, humanitarians, improvers of the condition of the working class, organizers of charity, members of societ[ies] for the prevention of cruelty to animals," and so on, in their thoughts on "Conservative, or Bourgeois

Socialism" in the *Communist Manifesto* (cf. Laqueur 2009).[29] In this context at least, Arendt, Marx, and Engels all saw sentimental humanitarianism, like affective reactions to cruelty to animals, as politically insignificant, in the realm of the mere. Similar dynamics operate today, of course.

Indeed, the relegation of the "barely" human who stands outside of politics to the realm of animality can become catastrophic, as Arendt and others have so insightfully shown for Jews, Roma, gays, and stateless people in the Nazi era. In the Rwanda genocide, too (and the less known Burundi genocides before that), people were systematically dehumanized by being likened to animals. Dehumanization, and the making of people into animals, we surely know by now, can serve as a rationale for discarding and killing people on an industrial scale (Arendt [1951] 1973). The danger of dehumanization in that sense can never be discounted. Arendt famously warned, too, how dangerous and disempowering it was to be "merely" human (Arendt [1951] 1973; see also Agamben 1998; Biehl 2005).

Among the critics of a universal, do-gooding humanitarianism, none has been as biting as Nietzsche. Humanity was often linked to animality in his work. His animus was against the thick equivalences among the (merely ordinary) human, the herd mentality, and the domesticated animal—like the sheep (the Christian flock). In his eyes, a leveling humanism of this sort was an unhealthy and unattractive triumph of the weak. It led people to follow reactively instead of thinking actively for themselves and creating societies where *creating* was the point of life.

Just as he hated "selflessness," "altruism," and "pity," Nietzsche would have hated the Cistercian monks, the humanitarian aid workers, and the "needy masses" awaiting help (cf. Rancière 2004, cited in Englund 2011:74–75). Refusing to collaborate in any compassionate gaze, he might well have thought of them as sheep. And he would have broken out in nervous hives upon sight of the sentimentalizing, well-intentioned, imaginative humanism of the Aid Bunnies, Trauma Teddies, and Mother Teresa blankets. His misogyny against the lonely old women who knit would have been ruthless: "Old: a dragon denizen" (Nietzsche 1966:166). He would have hated their weakness—a weakness so profound, as I wrote in chapter 5, that some of the women themselves wondered if they were even *worthy* of helping others, let alone participating in humanitarianism. They were needy. "What is pity? It is this tolerance for states of life close to zero" (Deleuze [1962] 1983:149).

Nietzsche wrote against the socialists and anarchists of his time, "brotherhood enthusiasts," who wanted a "Free Society," and saw their aspirations as being toward an "*autonomous herd*" (1966:116, emphasis in the original). And here is the crux: "But *they are also at one in the religion of pity, in feeling with all who feel, live, and suffer (down to the animal, up to 'God'—the excess of a 'pity with God' belongs in a democratic age). They are at one, the lot of them, in the cry and the impatience of pity, in their deadly hatred of suffering generally, in their almost feminine inability to remain spectators, to let someone suffer*" (Nietzsche 1966:116–17, emphasis added).

This is among Nietzsche's most important and powerful legacies, this critique of humanism. Yet it was also overwhelmingly misogynistic—and this is key for me in this project—and displayed a revulsion specifically against *the domestic*. For Nietzsche, there was little reason to refrain from dismissing the domestic as sentimental, silly, pitiful, reactive, uncreative—as the mere (1966:166; cf. Castoriadis 1997; Kant 2008; and the introduction).[30]

Yet the animal, like the child, need not be figured (as it is for all of these theorists) as the less-than. "Charismatic megafauna" like elephants and whales, as Amanda Moore (2008) has thoughtfully shown, can elevate and even *sanctify*. When it comes to sentiment and the imagination, many people today seem to have no trouble whatever in identifying with, wanting to care for and live with, or be taken over by beings other than human, almost human, or beings in whom animal and human is blurred. Sometimes—in terms of the moral imagination, too—the line between human and animal is almost lifted (Haraway 2008; A. L. Moore 2008; see also Latour 2004; Kirksey and Helmreich 2010; Kosek 2010; and cf. Laqueur 2009:47). Animality confirms and *vivifies for the imagination* the humanity of people in many ways, in many parts of the world. Animals, like children, as I suggested earlier, are often exemplary humans (see chapter 3). In many traditions of storytelling and many social imaginaries around the world (Lévi-Strauss 1971), all this is perfectly obvious: people are animals and animals are people and both are moral subjects.

I return once more to Elizabeth Costello; she is now in a very different context, at a small North American liberal arts college giving an invited lecture series on "The Lives of Animals." She works hard to win over her audience to the idea that animals should not be industrially raised, killed, and eaten by us, that they share a vital aliveness with us: "The heart is the seat of a faculty, *sympathy, that allows us to share at times the being of another. . . . There are no bounds to the sympathetic imagination. . . . If I can think my way into the existence of a being who has never existed* [a character in a novel], then I can think my way into the existence of a bat or a chimpanzee or an oyster, any being with whom I share the substrate of life"—and "the sensation of being alive to the world" together (Coetzee 2001:34–35; Gutmann 1999:5, first emphasis in the original; cf. Haraway 2008, 2013).

At a dinner after one of her lectures, an unfortunate guest happens to ask her how she became a vegetarian. Elizabeth Costello faces the polite, liberal-tolerant dinner party in a confrontational, almost desperate way, with Plutarch as her support: "You ask me why I refuse to eat flesh. I, for my part, am astonished that you can put in your mouth the corpse of a dead animal, astonished that you do not find it nasty to chew hacked flesh and swallow the juices of death-wounds" (Coetzee 2001:38).[31]

At the last of her lectures, someone from the audience challenges her, saying condescendingly that community with animals is merely a wish and, as such, "just a prelapsarian wistfulness" (Coetzee 2001:65). Elizabeth Costello answers: "Anyone who says that life matters less to animals than it does to us has not held in his hand an animal fighting for its life. The whole of the being of the animal is thrown into that fight, without reserve"; she concedes only that "the fight lacks a dimension of intellectual or imaginative horror" that is distinctly human (Coetzee 2001:65).

"*There are no bounds to the sympathetic imagination.*" This is always a potential affective and operational problem in humanitarian aid work, as I have tried to show throughout in different contexts—in contexts where the humanity/ animality line often blurs or even dissipates (Asad 2003:155–60). It may be that aid workers do everything in their power to save a life only to fail. Sometimes making sure that one person survives feels like "nothing" in a great sea of suffering. But, curiously, seeing a puppy kicked or a child hit can elicit very strong reactions. The challenge to the aid workers can also be much crueler, as I mentioned earlier: their sympathetic imaginations alive, they are called upon to treat perpetrators of horrible acts because they are sworn to help humanity and alleviate suffering impartially. At what ethical and psychic cost does the professional do her job? She shares something with the puppy and the child, and she knows she shares humanity (a common human substrate) with the killers. Doesn't she want to stop being an aid worker, to stop accepting humanity as any kind of guiding principle or ethical demand? I return to Sanna's tough questions: "*Are there limits to humanity?*" "*When is humanity finished?*" Is it in fact reasonable—even possible—to live with "no bounds to the sympathetic imagination"? And if not, where do the limits lie?

In practice, the principles of neutrality and humanity depend on one another, and, as the ICRC well knows, the hard question of limits is crucial in the practice of both. Both emerge as hard-edged, uncompromising values in the examples in this chapter.[32] The principles of humanity and neutrality are reinforced in many ways by another key ICRC principle, universality. This principle makes the others even more absolute. But rather than generating universal agreement, such absolute, world-embracing credos generate only further layers of dispute and contestation. Indeed, universals today are precisely what people fight over (Tsing 2005). Suspicions and contestations over universality abound. Étienne Balibar remarks that these "are a good sign of the fact that every speaker (and every discourse) of the universal is located *within*, not *outside*, the field of discourses and ideologies that he/she/it wants to map" (2007:3; cf. Tsing 2005). The "extensive universalism" of a concept like humanity would seem to remove *all* limits—but there is an endlessness to the contestations here, too, because "the contradiction is already included in the definition of the universal itself"; Balibar adds that "certain forms of universality at least derive their institutional strength not from that fact that the institutions in which they are embodied are absolute themselves, but *rather from the fact that they are the site of endless contestations* on the basis of their own principles, or discourse" (2007:4, emphasis added).

To return to the beginning finally, a tragic limit was forced into the lives of the Benedictine Cistercian monks in Algeria. There was no sudden, violent disruption of their monastic neutrality. They had had warnings. They watched as the space of the monastery gradually lost its immunity from the political struggles raging around it. The monks had a long time to reflect on their decisions individually, and to deliberate together. A key part of their creed was "service to humanity" and "love for humanity." At what point did practical considerations such as physical safety impose a limit on their creed? This too the monks debated among themselves. In the end, they chose a radical, or zealous, humanism and an absolute adherence to their faith, even as they knew the likely outcome.

I have written here of zealous humanism for several reasons. I wanted to highlight the sacrosanct, nonnegotiable status of humanity in the ICRC movement; this is unlikely to change in the foreseeable future. It is a demanding and perhaps even impossibly hard principle to face. It demands a great deal in terms of affect and the imagination. Importantly, the word *zealous* also conjures up contemporary connections with political and spiritual forms of radicalism, fundamentalism, extremism, and absolutism that are not ordinarily associated with humanism or humanitarianism but, currently, and wrongly, with Islam as a whole, undifferentiated religion. One is never well served by reducing complex systems of thought and action to a kind of irrational passion (as the language of "fanaticism," etc., so often does in the case of Islam [see Devji 2008]). But I want to insist that there *was* a zealousness to the principle of humanity as used by Sanna and others I interviewed, and that this (as she seemed to recognize) does resemble the zealousness of the Benedictine Cistercian credo of service to humanity in significant ways. One might think of cool-headed professionalism as proceeding from a calm and dispassionate "rationality" (see, however, chapter 1). But when it, like the service of the Benedictine monks, is pursued without limits, without regard to extremely dangerous circumstances and ethically fraught consequences, "professional commitment" is revealed to have its own sort of zealousness.

It is easy to think of zealotry as a cause of conflict and violence, and humanitarian care as its rational and neutral opposite. But, in fact, an unblinking, absolute commitment to neutrality (as to universality) involves its own kind of zealotry. A human is a human. There is a kind of absolutism to this when it is unsparingly applied to the personal decisions people make under conditions of grave danger. The Taliban in Afghanistan kill countless people and sometimes ICRC personnel have not been an exception. The aid workers know this as they continue working, treating young fighters so that they can return to the "battlefield." This entails a very real vulnerability to harm and, yes, perhaps sacrifice after all. And inevitably, such zealous commitment encounters limits. Like the monks, the aid workers realized this, and reflected on it. There was no simple resolution, just a continuing discussion. This encountering of, and reflecting on, limits is an inescapable element of modern humanitarian practice. It can mean dwelling in the domain of the impossible.

Conclusion. The Power of the Mere

Humanitarianism as Domestic Art and
Imaginative Politics

As Roland Barthes (1957 [2013]) long ago pointed out in his classic essay on "The Great Family of Man" exhibition, there are dangers in trying to connect the world via a universal human subject—"Humanity"—that is, in privileging a form of international or global solidarity (and being) that abstracts away from specific sociopolitical circumstances and regional histories, and from different forms of subjectivity.[1] The "ritualized and institutionalized evocation of a common humanity" easily yields to an idealized "higher harmony of the World Spirit" (Nairn 1977:430; Malkki 1994:41). Classic humanitarianism such as what underlies the ICRC and the whole Red Cross and Red Crescent Movement is mandated to be apolitical and to be guided first and foremost by the alleviation of the need and suffering of human beings. Compassion and responsibility are based, in principle, on a universally shared, basic humanity. As I have shown in earlier work (1994, 1995a, 1995b, 1996, 1998), such humanitarian approaches to, for example, "refugees," as ahistorical subjects—merely "human," merely "victims"—depoliticizes and hinders our understanding of their actual circumstances, yielding the perverse result of a humanitarianism that dehumanizes (and sometimes actively harms) its objects by reducing actors in a complex and meaningful historical process into nakedly human objects of compassion, zoë, or in Agamben's terms, "bare life" (see Arendt [1951] 1973; Nietzsche 1966; Foucault 1978; Malkki 1996; Agamben 1998; Biehl 2005; Englund 2005; Rancière 2011:62–75). As I wrote at the outset of this book, my earlier fieldwork was devoted to understanding the world through the points of view of particular groups of refugees in their historicity, political specificity, and difference. I came to this current project, then, ready to see a dangerous kind of antipolitics in invocations of an unsituated "Humanity" such as those found in the guiding principles of the ICRC.

Are the ICRC and the worldwide Red Cross and Red Crescent Movement in fact depoliticized and depoliticizing in this way, then? There is much that would support such a view. The movement's mandate (with elements of its nineteenth-century language still in evidence) is explicitly apolitical (cf. IFRC 2011). Being or acting in a specifically "political" way, according to the official tenets of the movement, endangers the mission of accessing and aiding those in need, as well as the aid workers themselves. And yet, as I came to understand in the course of this research, there is more to it than this. The negotiations that the ICRC undertakes with states and other stakeholders in order to be able to carry out its work are actually intensely political even when framed as neutrally technical—one reason they are closely guarded from the general public and the media (making the organization difficult to research). The duties enshrined in the fundamental principles of the ICRC and the entire Red Cross and Red Crescent Movement—humanity, impartiality, neutrality, independence, voluntary service, unity, universality—certainly seem to be a clear example of a deeply ahistorical, decontextualized conception of "the human" and the humanitarian obligation to help. The fundamental principles are continually reviewed in Red Cross basic training and its many subsequent courses.

But one of the first things I discovered in studying the Finnish Red Cross was that most of my interlocutors in fact engaged with others on international missions not as powerful, self-sacrificing humanitarians and not via helping/saving an abstractly suffering "Humanity" but first of all as professionals from a small, "neutral" Nordic country. They worked with and developed professional solidarities with other multinational aid workers and with the resident counterparts of the national and regional Red Cross and Red Crescent societies of the affected countries, and often together negotiated with a host of government officials and others. These involved delicate political strategies. It was in tandem with the resident colleagues and their volunteers (if the local Red Cross/Red Crescent society was still standing) that the multinational teams engaged with people as patients (cf. Wendland 2010; Livingston 2012). Here, a Durkheimian notion of *professional solidarity* worked against the empty humanism rightly critiqued by Barthes and others (cf. Durkheim [1957] 2005; Malkki 1994; and chapters 1 and 6). Again, a central part of professional practice by the multinational ICRC (and IFRC) teams is, in conjunction with medical care, "institution building" (*développement institutionel*)—teaching, and being taught, and trying to strengthen the capacity and sociopolitical standing of the local Red Cross or Red Crescent society. This often entailed not a "personal relation" to anonymous masses of "barely" human sufferers but a much more specific and inter-subjective set of engagements with particular persons and institutions. Thus, while the aid workers had all been exhaustively trained in the seven fundamental principles and international humanitarian law, and while they might generally agree with and value them when asked, their everyday practices were guided by a more complex, subtle, dynamic set of professional dispositions, imaginative practices and processes, and unforeseen attachments—as well as private "details" that would, in the light of day, be relegated to the realm of the mere.

Another thing that emerged was that the Finnish doctors, nurses, and other specialists I interviewed often had personal, quite idiosyncratic reasons for accepting a mission. As described in chapter 1, all of them admitted to a love of travel. Many spoke compellingly about the sensual, sensorial attraction of new places and people—and desirable forms of sociality and warmth. One person talked movingly about how she missed the casual, friendly, bodily contact she had with teammates and patients on missions but not in Finland. She was often left feeling alienated and needy; no wonder that she was abroad on assignment so much of the time. Her preferred habitus was elsewhere.[2] There was a neediness more generally underlying many people's love of travel—and an imaginative/intellectual excitement in being involved in something different from and somehow larger (even "greater") than their usual working and personal lives in Finland.[3]

I also learned that to begin to understand the Red Cross practices I saw and the accounts I was given, I had to understand the imagination and its powerful inter-relationality with affect, ethics, and politics. Here it was important not to belittle or ignore any of these dimensions. In chapter 2 especially, I showed how this belittling might come from the aid workers themselves and from the ethnographer—and at what cost. In another context (chapter 4), I warned against allowing a Barthes-style critique, as potent as it is, to lead one to be dismissive of the mere Aid Bunny, for instance. The temptation, of course, is to see such imaginative practices as handwork as mere bourgeois sentimentality built on just the sort of false universalism and humanism that Barthes rightly decried ("What child wouldn't like to play with . . . ?"). But we should not be too quick to suppose that we know what such practices do, or that *we know that they do nothing*. Many who grow up in societies like Finland, where international responsibilities are enacted from childhood via such "mere" imaginative practices (in schools but also in homes), develop a strong sense of responsibility for, and solidarity with, "disadvantaged others in faraway places"—a kind of imaginative and affective formation that has often enough had political consequences that even the fiercest critics would be able to recognize as "real" (including a foreign policy based on ideals of solidarity and "development cooperation," aid to anti-imperialist movements like SWAPO, the Sandinistas, etc.). Also, very often, those who knitted these objects and object-beings did so not out of a diffuse loyalty to a bare life or an abstract humanity, but out of a *deeply situated* romance with the world as a visualizable globe with which one can, in small ways, claim very personal kinds of membership (Tsing 2005). The way in which the knitters imagined the recipients of these object-beings was quite lively and idiosyncratic, in spite of the fact that conceptions of "the needy" were usually quite abstract, often particularized only in the figure of the child.

One of the most difficult challenges in analyzing practices of this kind has been to avoid the urge to dismiss, to trivialize—to see them as somehow less than "real." A very effective nurse (Kaisa) once surprised me greatly with her account of how in her hospital work at home in Finland as well as in some refugee camps and other mission sites abroad, she tried, where possible, to "straighten up a little," to change the water in the flowers by the patient's bed, to ask if the pillows needed plumping, to make sure the patient's possessions were where the patient wanted them, "to take care of the aesthetic side of things." She said, "I sort of think this is a feminine [*naisellinen*] thing. [A woman] can *see*."[4] Kaisa was a member of an early ICRC team in Rwanda. Her mission to Rwanda had been quite long, and had begun when the massacres were still going on. I asked if "even there"—after the first period of emergency was over—she had made these little gestures of care and comfort. Now abashed, she said yes. I had not meant to criticize her, but I deeply embarrassed her: Was it not utterly ridiculous and worse to think about flowers and pillows in the middle of a genocide?[5]

What is the proper status of such details in that context of scalar impossibility? Would prayer have made a more proper or symmetrical correspondence with genocide than flowers? Would thinking about the gods have been more important and proper than thinking about the pillows? Why look for a "proper" symmetry? Does it offend the order of things in the world that the calamitous and tragic be brought into such close contact with the ornamental, the decorative, the "confectionary"—*the cosmological with the cosmetic* (Kester 2004:33)?[6] The realm of the mere contaminates the "really real" of humanitarian intervention; but, then again, humanitarianism itself is the mere to what is commonly (and often reductively) understood as the political.

The inadequacies and embarrassments of "the mere" always stood, of course, against the horrifying accounts of acute emergencies and "real suffering" from international missions I was given by the Finnish Red Cross workers. What was "real" here? Was it the look on the aid worker's face? Was it the horror or the homemade gifts? Did "real" simply mean important and geopolitical? Settling on the worst horror as the most real and the most political had a kind of logic, but it meant in practice the decision *not* to see a world of other connections and practices—most generally those among the imaginative, the affective, and the political in a wider view. A poster of a child's scruffy teddy bear crushed in the mud by a tank's treads is an image both powerful and clichéd: could its power be well analyzed without an understanding of the mutually productive relations among affect, politics, and the imagination?

In some sense, humanitarian aid work—and Red Cross aid work in particular, because of its uncompromising stance on political neutrality, public silence, and quiet diplomacy—is especially vulnerable to trivialization as the mere; as I have mentioned, it is expected to be "ethical" but not "political."[7] The Red Cross and Red Crescent Movement seeks to alleviate suffering and to "save" people's lives in such a view, but it does not contribute to "real" "structural" change, just as it does not, as a rule, publically condemn human rights abuses (Guantánamo Bay being a recent exception). It is very effective at doing what it is mandated to do but powerless to take direct action against most *causes* of political and social injustice. It "merely" relieves suffering, as is required in its central principle of "humanity." Politically it seeks to be "neutral" (cf. IFRC 2011; see chapter 6 on "zealous humanism"). But by what logic do we presume situated, tactical (and tactful) neutralities to be somehow not "real," not "political"—somehow "mere"?[8]

In chapter 3, "Figurations of the Human," I described how concepts like world peace, global social justice, and non-alignment (Romulo 1956; Wright 1956; Gupta 1992; Tsing 2005) could be transformed from serious political goals in one era, the 1940s to 1960s, to trivialized and infantilized ones in another—to the point (as mentioned earlier) that a former U.S. ambassador to the United Nations, Jean Kirkpatrick, could dismiss the category of "economic, social, and cultural rights" in the Universal Declaration of Human Rights as "a letter to Santa Claus" (Englund 2006:47; see also chapter 3). In parallel fashion, the Geneva Conventions, international humanitarian law, the International Criminal Court (ICC), the United Nations, the global Red Cross and Red Crescent Movement (RCRCM), and other international and nongovernmental organizations are often brushed aside as *mere decorum* to "real" power politics and corporate interests. "Idealistic" projects of world peace that once engaged statesmen and social movements alike in this way become childish—simultaneously valorized and dismissed.

Regardless of the actions of actual children, the figure of the child is elevated beyond politics; she is the most civilian of civilians (Stephens 1995; Barthes 2005). In her sentimentalized innocence, she stands for world peace, and the social imagination of world peace is thereby consigned to the realm of the mere. There is a political cost to this diminishment. It disregards children as the political actors that they de facto are (Stephens 1995). It also helps to ignore how affect, sentiment, and the imagination work politically through uses of children, and among children. As I suggest in chapter 3, "attention to the representational uses of children in the constitution of a depoliticized 'humanity' may help us to imagine new ways of thinking about both children *and* peace in the midst of politics and history."

Alongside the sentimentalized neutrality and presumed peaceability of humanitarians and children sits another kind of mere: the abjectly needy old women I classified as "lonely knitters" in chapter 5. They are obscenely easily diminished to the apolitical mere—the useless, "hobbyist," "amateur" makers of unnecessary "ornaments," "decorations," and so on (Loos [1910] 2000; cf. Coomaraswamy [1946] 2007:71–83)—mere supplements (Derrida 1998). Some might say that they are making toys for children and blankets for comfort, instead of doing something "real." Yet why is it, I have asked, that we cannot see the forging (through gifts) of imaginative links—even these unilateral ones—between people perhaps thousands of miles away as something "real"? Why are we so quick to disparage or despise these acts of care that simultaneously ease the often abject neediness of their socially isolated *makers* (and give them *pleasure*), and, in the case of the blankets, provide warmth to people who may need it? Why do we suppose that nothing has "really" happened when something has passed between two imaginations?

Why has the imagination to be "a mode of unreality" instead of "a mode of actuality" (Foucault [1954] 1986:70)?

In these same contexts, of domestic neediness, I wrote about the alleviation of loneliness through the "friendship services" run by the Red Cross (and other organizations). This service, in very abbreviated form, consisted of volunteers of all ages visiting and acting as "friends" to a variety of people including new immigrants, but mostly the old and socially isolated (see Muehlebach 2012). As I wrote, friends from the Friendship Service were sometimes derided as mere stand-ins for "the real thing." The problem was, of course, that often there was no "real" there to supplant. "What is the real and what the unreal (or mere)?" may not be the most useful question to ask here (cf. Castoriadis 1997). The imaginative possibilities of "stranger sociality" are more interesting, and more important to try to understand, than we have perhaps allowed (Povinelli 2006).

In "Bear Humanity" (chapter 4), the gifts/object-beings themselves became animate in various imaginative (often silly) ways. I suggested why it might make sense to give center stage—even momentarily—to the Aid Bunnies and Trauma Teddies, to the realm of the mere par excellence. Who could take this seriously as aid—let alone as politics? I hope I was nevertheless able to demonstrate the interconnections. The animated Aid Bunnies, Trauma Teddies, babies and children, and baby animals were, in many significant ways, "exemplary humans"—more human, more exemplary, than the human adult. In this humanitarian logic, woman is more human than man because she is taken for more vulnerable, more innocent, more mere. And she is an essential element in the compound figure of mother-and-child. Her "innocent baby" is the most human of all. We fail to see a great deal if we refuse to take these often hackneyed things for the power objects that they are—potent, as I have suggested, like the Congolese minkisi, that could be said to do "nothing" only by the most unimaginative and unanthropological of observers.

In all of these instances, one must recognize that a certain kind of power resides in objects and practices repeatedly and habitually dismissed as "the mere." And insofar as every power implies a kind of politics, I here insist on the importance and potency of what I term *imaginative politics*. Just as an analysis of central African politics would not be satisfactory without acknowledging and understanding the power of the *minkisi* and other power objects, so, too, will it be necessary to cultivate a more expansive and less dismissive notion of the political if we are to understand a wider range of motives and powers currently engaged in humanitarian practice.

If one key theme of this book has been the effects of imaginative acts conventionally situated in the realm of domesticity (knitting, caring, comforting), a second has concerned the "domesticity" of aid in a national sense. In important ways, the practices of aiding "distant others" that I have analyzed here are as domestic as they are foreign—as much about "the home" (the home society and its specific characteristics, the career and personal circumstances of the professional, the emotional needs of the would-be giver) as they are about any foreign elsewheres.

When we (in the academy but also in the aid world, the media, and policy circles) talk about humanitarian intervention, we tend to imagine it as always already global (it being understood that the world capital of need is Africa). Aid is supranational and global in reach, and highly mobile. Impressive sums of money and supplies are at stake in the whole project of aid looked at from afar. A dizzying array of organizations sends seemingly inexhaustible numbers of aid workers and volunteers (and things) more quickly and easily than ever to a multiplicity of destinations (unfortunately, often at cross-purposes, duplicating what is already there, and competing among one another). They enter and exit sites of humanitarian emergency in ways that may make little sense to aid recipients. From a distance, it is as if there were a generic aid worker, culturally anonymous somehow—the very embodiment of the global, the cosmopolitan, the worldly, "the aid world."

And yet these apparently "global" and "cosmopolitan" figures and projects *must always begin somewhere in particular*. Logistically and administratively there is a great deal of necessary standardization, routinization, and, in a technical sense, universalization that goes into everything associated with emergency relief, and medical professionalism in general. But it does matter that it is the Finnish Red Cross that happens to be sending people out in any given emergency. It matters that the people think of themselves so self-consciously as Finns. International aid work is a *domestic* art in this way, but not in this way alone. As I have tried to show here, much imaginative, affective, cultural, political, and historical specificity goes (often unannounced) into international aid work in the person of the aid worker.

Anna Tsing's *Friction* has provided an evocative, historically informed set of images for thinking about all this. She writes:

The universal bridge to a global dream space still beckons to us. The bridge might take us out of our imagined isolation into a space of unity and transcendence: the whole world . . . The bridge of universal truths promises to take us there. Yet we walk across that bridge, and we find ourselves, not everywhere, but somewhere in particular. Even if our bridge aims toward the most lofty universal truths—the insights of science, the freedom of individual rights, the possibility of wealth for all—we find ourselves hemmed in by the specificity of rules and practices, with their petty prejudices, unreasonable hierarchies, and cruel exclusions. We must make do, enmeshing our desires in the compromise of practical action. (2005:85)

Tsing's arresting vision captures the way that universal ideals always do their work only by engaging with particularities; such "frictions" are not the sites where universalisms slip or fail but rather where they find traction, and thereby make something happen. The story I have told in this book suggests that such encounters with the particular are not only (as the bridge metaphor suggests) a point that lies "across the bridge," the destination; there is friction from the very beginning, before the crossing ever begins. We walk across the bridge and find ourselves somewhere in particular, but we also *leave* from somewhere very particular, where friction is always already consequential. The friction of our domesticities and alienations, socialities and abandonments, our neediness and our need to help, are already powerfully present. The friction is among other things an awkwardness, a self-consciousness, a melancholy, and sometimes a dizzying fearlessness—if not a will to self-destruction. For those I worked with, the world at the other end of the bridge *was* always somewhere in particular, with many practical frustrations, technical difficulties, bureaucratic paperwork, and significant dangers, most definitely so, but even in the midst of terrible circumstances, it was also an elsewhereness, a promise of being-in-the-world-differently—a dream space.

Throughout this book I have sought to demonstrate, from a series of different angles, that the trivialization and consignment of whole classes of objects, practices, people, and logics into the realm of the mere is only made possible by a reductive understanding of politics. Recognizing the power of such objects, practices, people, and logics—a power that derives from acts of imaginative communion no less than from funding and institutions—might allow us to better appreciate their possibilities and potentials. Neither saintly self-sacrifice nor sentimental distraction subject to a contemptuous dismissal, humanitarian practice might finally be recognized as merely real.

Notes

Introduction. Need, Imagination, and the Care of the Self

1. I have altered details in this scene to ensure anonymity.

2. See Englund's (2006:8) insightful discussion of this.

3. See, e.g., Terry (2002); Bornstein (2001, 2003, 2012); Duffield (2001); Redfield (2006, 2010, 2013); Ticktin (2006a, 2006b, 2011); Feldman (2007); Calhoun (2008, 2010); Forsythe (2009); Benthall (2010); Bornstein and Redfield (2010); de Waal (2010); Fassin (2010a, 2010b, 2012); McFalls (2010); Ophir (2010); Pandolfi (2010); Pupavac (2010); Donini (2011), among many others. Several texts also give good reviews of the most current literature. Among them are Barnett and Weiss (2008); Bornstein and Redfield (2010); Fassin and Pandolfi (2010); and Feldman and Ticktin (2010a). This is a very partial list of an important body of work.

4. Sometimes these "obstacles" arose from cultural differences that were difficult and lengthy to negotiate with patients, their kin, and others. Sometimes local suppliers and government officials were the "obstacles." My interviewees usually commented on their professional frustrations with a surprising degree of self-reflection and humor. They had a keen insight into the extent to which they themselves had their own very set ways of doing things, their "very Finnish" expectations.

5. For none of my interlocutors did this appear to be a "religious" need. They were, on the whole, by their own reckoning, staunch secularists. They were very used to having to answer the question: "Isn't this a Christian organization? You have a cross on your cars." They spent a good deal of time trying to convince people that their mission was "strictly medical" and "humanitarian," "not religious," but they could not of course control other interpretations of the intended official meaning of the symbol, or the uses to which it was put (see Asad 1993, 2003; and chapter 6). The Swiss historical foundation of

the international Red Cross was deeply Christian, of course. This has been extensively studied (see Hutchinson 1996; Moorehead 1998; and Forsythe 2005).

6. In my second research site, in Tanzania, Kigoma Township, there were more aid workers representing two international organizations dealing with refugees, the UNHCR (United Nations High Commissioner for Refugees) and the Tanganyika Christian Refugee Service (TCRS), a local arm of the Lutheran World Federation, but their presence was minimal compared to that of the organizations and aid workers in Rwanda and Congo.

7. Chapters 1 and 2 contain very partial accounts of their work in Rwanda.

8. *Pace* Badiou (2001), the "good-Man, the white-Man" is often a woman.

9. Anna Tsing has written insightfully about scale-making: "scale is not just a neutral frame for viewing the world; scale must be brought into being: proposed, practiced, and evaded, as well as taken for granted. Scales are claimed and contested in cultural and political projects" (2005:58). The Red Cross and other aid organizations are likely quite aware of the significance of projecting scales of need to the donor public. This includes time scales, of course.

10. Well-tended plants on windowsills seemed as ubiquitous as knitting. Potted plants were also a medium for momentary socialities.

11. See Grant Kester's economical and interesting account of Adrian Piper's views (Kester 2004:78, 210n61); see also Piper (1991:741–42, 744).

12. Foucault sought "that point of life which lies as close as possible to the impossibility of living, which lies at the limit or the extreme" (1991:30–31).

13. In some ways, a comparison with the experiences of soldiers would not be far-fetched.

14. There is a wealth of volunteer, training, and work possibilities on the Finnish Red Cross website—from first aid and emergency response to work on behalf of new immigrants and refugees, antiracist work, friendship services, and prison visits, to name just a few (see chapter 5). They address need in Finland. In a group interview, participants with both national and international experience spoke of their Red Cross work, waxing poetic about it—by their own laughing yet emotional admission. They agreed among themselves that the Red Cross was a profound and meaningful part of their lives. Many had worked for the organization for decades. Listening to the interview tapes, I got a sense that many would have been adrift and very alone without the Red Cross. In working for the Red Cross, they were taking measures against their own neediness—that is, loneliness and social disconnection.

15. Jean-Paul Sartre was peculiarly insistent that the imagination is volitional. Aid work, like political violence, challenges this view. Sartre's conception has been roundly criticized by Richard Kearney (1991:92–95) and others. See also Gaston Bachelard (2005).

16. Charles Taylor's *Modern Social Imaginaries* is a prominent example of the tendencies that Castoriadis critiques. Informed by a liberal, functionalist holism, Taylor tends to hypostatize the imaginary as a matter of a "whole society," and to associate it with "images, stories, and legends" (2004:23). Sneath, Holbraad, and Pedersen (2009:5–6,

8) point out that many anthropologists, like social theorist Taylor, treat the imagination holistically as if it were "a culture," and "instrumentally" in the way that Castoriadis criticized. They lean on Immanuel Kant's work in order to argue that "the imagination is pervasive in all human apprehension" and should be understood processually (Sneath, Holbraad, and Pedersen 2009:6; cf. Moore 1978).

17. Newer texts on the imagination do not necessarily agree with each other. Cf. Englund (2011:15–16); Tsing (2005); Sneath, Holbraad, and Pedersen (2009); and Bottici and Challand (2011a). The latter suggest: "In contrast to the 'imaginary' as an adjective, which fundamentally means 'fictitious, unreal,' the concept of 'imaginal' simply denotes what is made of images, be they real images or not. Furthermore, in contrast to 'imagination' and 'imaginary' as substantives, 'imaginal' can be both the product of a social context and of the free imagination of individuals" (2011a:8). This passage raises several questions: Why should we assume that the imaginary refers to the fictitious and the unreal? As I note later in this introduction, Foucault refers to it as a "mode of actuality" (1986: 70). Can there be such a thing as the free imagination of individuals? This phrasing suggests that all persons everywhere are individuals when that is not actually the case. Even western "autonomous, bounded individuals" are still *social* persons. It should also be considered that "the individual" is not a universally meaningful concept. What does freedom mean here? Is it not related to language and the social? Are there contexts in which the imaginary would not simply signify the "irreal" (in Sartre's terms)? This is a question that Benedict Anderson also considered in *Imagined Communities* (1991). From that tradition it became clear that the imagined, or even the imaginary, can be all too real in the context of nationalism, for example. The imagination of enmity is but another example. Finally, what does it mean for "the imaginal" to be "made of images"? I would not collapse the range of differences between the image and the imagination (differences that have vexed thinking about the imagination at least since Aristotle [see, e.g., White 1990 and Kearney 1991]). For if the image is a visual object, or even only "visual," what happens to affect and the fuller sensorium in relation to the imagination? Ricoeur has convincingly challenged the yoking of the imagination to the image, but his "semantic" definition of the imagination in terms of language in turn raises problems of its own (see Rundell 1994b:9).

18. Mindful of Castoriadis's (1997) views on "the technical" and "the instrumental," I note Snead, Holbraad, and Pedersen's preeminent emphasis on "*technologies of the imagination*"; they "have in mind primarily the diverse manners or indeed styles through which imaginative *effects* are engendered" and they are also inspired by Foucault's concept of "technologies of power" (2009:16, emphasis added). As examples of such technologies, they cite light bulbs in rural Mongolia, Chinese numerological practices, Internet chat rooms, and open source software, among others. These "technologies" have "imaginative *effects*" and have here been arrived at "by means of [a] *means-ends logic*" where "'technologies' count as being 'of the imagination' insofar as they serve to precipitate *outcomes* that they do not fully condition" (2009:16, 24–25, emphasis added). Castoriadis's text critiques precisely such means-ends logics and the reduction of the imagination into "effects" and "outcomes." But because elsewhere the authors refer to

more Kantian views of the imagination, there may be several different conceptions of the imagination at play here.

19. Aristotle, Plato, Hobbes, Descartes, Locke, Hume, and Wittgenstein are among the many who have thought specifically about the problematics of the imagination as a suspect category. See, e.g., White (1990) and Engell (1981).

20. Paul Ricoeur (1994:119) also identifies a persistent newer phenomenon: "The general problem of imagination suffers from the disrepute in which the term 'image' is held following its misuse in the empiricist theory of knowledge. The discredit suffered by 'psychologism' in contemporary semantics . . . also attaches references to imagination. . . . Behaviourist psychology is similarly anxious to eliminate images, which it holds to be private, unobservable mental entities." Likewise, Ricoeur argues that "the zealous pursuit of [a] popular philosophy of creativity" has furthered the discrediting of the imagination.

21. I agree, but would also observe that such intersubjective, dialogical spheres of imagination and experience are actually considered increasingly important to the contemporary "social work" of art, work that can in some ways be useful to ethnography as practice (see Bourriaud 1998; Kester 2004, 2011; Jackson 2011; Bishop 2012; Shenk 2014). Of course, there was also a moment when contemporary artwork began to mimic ethnography (see Hal Foster's *The Return of the Real* [1996]).

22. It is interesting to think of Deleuze (1997) in relation to Ananda Coomaraswamy ([1946] 2007:117), who argues that "in the catholic (and not only Roman Catholic) view of art, *imitation*, *expression*, and *participation* are three predications of the essential nature of art; not three different or conflicting, but three interpenetrating and coincident definitions of art, which is these three in one" (emphasis in the original). Later, he defines the imagination as "the conception of the idea in an imitable form. Without a pattern (*paradeigma*, exemplar), indeed, nothing could be made except by mere chance" ([1946] 2007:118). (But here, too, the imagination is in danger of being yoked too heavily to the image and the visual—and to "art.") Coomaraswamy's ideas regarding imitation, expression, and participation in some respects prefigure more contemporary conceptions and practices of "relational aesthetics" and "dialogical" art (see Bourriaud 1998; Kester 2004; Shenk 2014).

23. It is relevant, too, that the expatriates' accounts were of violence in Africa by Africans. The dismissals by the few remaining Europeans had a dismissive and even racist cast to them (cf. Fassin and Rechtman 2009; see also Malkki 1996).

24. It was recognized by French and other psychologists that after the 1988 Armenian earthquake, "what people really needed was to talk" (Fassin and Rechtman 2009:166). No such understanding was extended, initially, to those caught up in the 1994 genocide in Rwanda or the 1972 genocide in Burundi. Fassin and Rechtman (2009:186) quote an MSF (Médecins Sans Frontières, Doctors without Borders) nurse, "We don't have mental health programs in the refugee camps in Africa. We should. But everyone thinks it's just too complicated—that it's cultural."

25. This was claustrophobic, as I describe in chapter 2.

26. The naïve empiricist suspicion of the imagination parallels distrust of the work

of memory. But out of all this complex and tragic memory, a future had to be imagined in both Burundi and Rwanda. "Practices and experiences of the imagination can have powerful ethical dimensions; they can shape lives and create communities" (Mittermaier 2011:50). But they can also destroy those futures, as has happened again and again in the Great Lakes Region of Central Africa.

27. "Though I want to affirm the Romantic roots of Anthropology; I am not advocating veneration of the irrational, the irreal, the imagination," writes Vincent Crapanzano (2004:18) in parallel fashion. Yet he devotes a whole study to understanding the imagination, calling it a kind of "aura" that accompanies "*all* thought, perception, and experience" (2004:18, emphasis added). I would add affect to that list. And he does go on to cite William James (1992:160) on "sensorial imaginations" (2004:19–20) and Jean Starobinski (1970:173–74) on the role of the imagination in the constitution of reality. But why does Crapanzano link the imagination with "the irrational" and "the irreal"?

28. One should further add, with William James (1992), that the in/visible does not exhaust the being of the imagination; James suggests that its processes are multisensorial (cf. Crapanzano 2004:18). These processes are also affective, as this book will show.

29. See Young (2009:140, 142); see also Deleuze on Kant (1997:33–34, 63).

30. The capacity (or at least the strong desire) to understand and live with something of another's situation is often what anthropologists aspire to do in their professional practice. Here it is productive to seek to understand and imaginatively inhabit another's circumstances, even if momentarily and very partially, but it can be dangerous to develop points of communion between self and other to such a degree that the line between self and other blurs. This danger, and its connection to the situation of the Red Cross workers, is explored at some length in chapter 2.

31. Mittermaier likens this to the Egyptian form of imagination, *al-khayal*, where the imagined is "not inherently unreal, but . . . is present and absent at the same time. It defies the either/or and closure" (2011:18). It is an "in-betweenness" (2011:29).

32. Comparably, Robert Musil distinguished between "the normal relation to experience and the heightened relation to experience that is common to art, religion, and erotic excitement, which he called the 'other condition.' The intensification of experience . . . is characterized by a *weakening of the role of the ego in the social sense*; this expressed Musil's interest in 'a deeper embedding of thought in the emotional sphere, a more personal relation to the experiencing subject.' *Common to all experiences of the other condition is that 'the border between self and nonself' is less sharp than usual. . . .* Whereas normally the self masters the world, in the other condition the world flows into the self, or mingles with it, or bears it'" (Luft 1994:xxvii, emphasis added). In "the other condition," the self becomes utterly vulnerable. Again, I think of this state in relation to Foucault's (1991), Bataille's (see Noys 2000), Blanchot's (1993), Lacan's (see Evans 1996), and others' quest for "limit experiences." To me, fieldwork in Tanzania and sometimes in Finland was "the other condition" where the relation of self to Other, and even self to self, became difficult to manage.

33. Pauline von Bonsdorff writing about Kant (2009:27–28, emphasis added).

34. See artist Jay Koh, cited in Kester 2004:102–3.

1. Professionals Abroad

1. See, e.g., Hancock 1989; Burman 1994; de Waal 1997; Terry 2002; Bornstein 2003; Barnett and Weiss 2008; Bornstein and Redfield 2010; Fassin 2010a, 2010b, 2012; Fassin and Pandolfi 2010; Feldman and Ticktin 2010a, 2010b; Pandolfi 2010; Polman 2011; Ticktin 2011; Redfield 2013, among many others.

2. Only one of the aid workers I interviewed mentioned finding partners or spouses in the field, although the formation of such a relationship would be unsurprising. One administrator in Helsinki observed that long missions sometimes produced very personal, sometimes sexual, relationships. Many aid workers were single, but many also had meaningful partnerships in Finland. Some had been going on international missions for decades, while for others it was linked to a particular phase in life. Yet others left spouse and children at home to go on missions. Many talked critically about "other" colleagues who were too restless for new missions to settle down in Finland.

3. A study of humanitarian motivations by nurse Liisa Riikonen concluded: "The motives for leaving were professional, [a] desire to get experiences, personal [development] and idealistic ones. The field of commission was very large: war and field hospitals, refugee camps, [natural disasters], epidemic areas, war prisons, child and mother health care centers, clinics, and [development] programs. The aim of caring was [to give] humanitarian help and/or to strengthen a national organization of [the] Red Cross or Red Crescent" (Riikonen 1994: n.p., quoted from the thesis abstract originally in English). In the body of the thesis Riikonen clearly stated that the universal motive was the "desire to help" (1994:31).

4. The International Committee of the Red Cross (ICRC) deals with humanitarian intervention in political conflicts, while the International Federation of the Red Cross (IFRC) responds to "natural" disasters. Both are headquartered in Geneva.

5. Julie Livingston (2012) has documented similar practices in Botswana in *Improvising Medicine*; see also Wendland (2010). In surprising contrast, the European staff of MSF (Médecins Sans Frontières, Doctors without Borders) worried instead about the motivations of their national-level colleagues at their mission sites: "Should national staff be involved more directly in decisions? If working for money, would they still exhibit the right humanitarian motivations?" (Redfield 2013:146; see also 238). Peter Redfield points out that the same doubts could of course attach to the "expat volunteers themselves," as several MSF "expats" themselves recognized (Redfield 2013:146).

6. Elsewhere (Malkki 1997:100) I have written about "accidental communities of memory" that may form among people, like aid workers, soldiers, witnesses or survivors of some tragic event, and communities "that have always tended to reach, willy-nilly, over and through categorical identities and pure locations, beyond families and national communities." For the members of these communities—for example, soldiers—it may be impossible to communicate important things to people other than their comrades. The aid workers faced similar problems.

7. The doctor said that even nuns did not often aspire to self-sacrifice anymore: "We

had a nun there, in Goma, a French Canadian in her fifties who had worked in Africa for twenty-five years. She had probably come there with those kinds of ideas [of a religious calling and self-sacrifice] in her mind. She was very vigorous—Roman Catholic and there she was distributing condoms! And she was a really sturdy worker, just like any irreligious person." When I pressed her on the theme of self-sacrifice among humanitarians, she said impatiently: "Self-sacrifice means that when a new patient comes to you, you always find the energy to take them as a new person toward whom you have no negative expectations. You have the energy to *skarpata* [keep at it] night and day. Kindness is self-sacrifice. . . . But it's just the same whether you're somewhere in Africa or here. You have to sacrifice your own importance, and you can't be a boss. The patient has to be on the same level as you—and it has to be that way every single time, and that's why this work is so wearing, I think."

8. This passage is taken from an e-mail originally written in English; slight grammatical changes have been made.

9. An administrator said that these expectations of hard work and Finland's lack of a colonial past, combined with other things—"'good' characteristics like transparency, equality, democracy, good governance, etc."—made them more "capable" than other nationalities of delivering aid to a wider range of places.

10. In marked contrast, in MSF the self-image was much more self-confident. Redfield (2013) mentions, for example: a "rebellious flare" (233), "romance" (61, 101), "flamboyance" (77), a "rebellious humanitarianism" driven to be "restless," "mobile," "combative," and "radical" (98, 59), and a "mythic self-conception" (63). On the other hand, Redfield notes, more recently there has been a movement in MSF toward "pragmatism and professionalism" (60).

11. Often, of course, they worked under both the Red Cross and Red Crescent emblems.

12. It should also be mentioned that spiritual practices of the residents of the sites in which the Red Cross worked often shaped and complicated the day-to-day operations of aid work. This will be especially apparent in chapter 6 but comes up in other chapters as well.

13. In a study examining medical workers' motivations, *Measuring Medical Professionalism* (Stern 2006), the author of the afterword, Fred Hafferty (2006:294), concludes: "Altruism is the 'missing hero' of this book. What once stood as core and definitional has begun to disappear from the professionalism lexicon." Describing his six-year study of the concerns and priorities of medical students, Hafferty notes: "Rather than an ideal and an object of occupational reverence, these students saw altruism as something that would 'tie you to your work,' with altruistic physicians the ones most likely to be 'taken advantage of' by their 'manipulative patients'" (2006:295).

14. Frederick Cooper (1983), cited in Malkki (1994:56, 2002); see also Naumann (1915), Woolf (1916), Lyons (1963), Aranguren (1966), Wittner (1995), Iriye (1997), Calhoun (2002), Englund (2005), Tsing (2005), and Balibar (2006).

15. The Red Cross has 188 National Societies within the Red Cross and Red Crescent Movement (RCRCM) around the world, and works with national governments and su-

pranational organizations. The movement has ninety-seven million staff, volunteers, and members worldwide.

16. The early interviews referred to internationalism; from the late 1990s onward some Red Cross people also referred to the global.

17. The significance of teamwork and solidarity was also evident in the moments of their frustration or even failure. Psychologists who worked on behalf of the Finnish Red Cross with aid workers said that these forms of professional failure, and injured professional pride, were a predominating topic in aid workers' conversations, and bothered people profoundly. One psychologist identified two themes that tended to crop up in her conversations. One had to do with the problematics of human relationships and group dynamics. The other involved problems of team management: strained teamwork, difficult team leaders, the formation of cliques, and otherwise unsupportive work environments. There were also frustrations about some organizations' misuse of resources and "living in luxury." One aid worker said that poor practices like this made her feel like a *lääkärin irvikuva* (a travesty, or distorted caricature, of a doctor).

18. Cf. Berlant (2004) on compassion and attachment.

19. Echoing comparable sentiments, another nurse said: "Everywhere in the world, in every single place, there are people who want to help those in need. In that we are all alike" (Petterson 2013:4). She had been on international Red Cross missions for twenty years.

20. It was also satisfying for aid workers to learn, from many different professionals and volunteers, about the whole collective process of building up a medical system from often unpromising beginnings. One nurse said: "It's also that one gets such a huge *satisfaction* from the work . . . The more miserable the system from which you start [in the field] . . . when you see it grow and develop and then when you go home and leave a functioning system behind . . . and you've helped some to breathe a bit better—then that feeling gratification, it is really . . . !!! And you really have to do *hard work*. Those [institutional] patterns [in crisis zones] are not borne easily. But when you get the local people [to work] together with you, and you get them to build their own things and that, well, that's a good experience."

21. The quotation above appears to conflate resident professional staff and resident volunteers, but the distinction was obvious to Kaarina.

22. Kaarina, another nurse, experienced travel on behalf of the Red Cross as a source of internationalism and far-flung networks of sociality. She said, "You can [also] say that [as a result of your international work] you have all around the world—if not friends, at least people you can ask for advice—or [provided you don't abuse their hospitality!]—you can go and stay with them. Yes, this internationalism is an immense treasure, an immense wealth [*suunnaton aarre, suunnaton omaisuus*]." I heard this view from many people. *It was not just about seeing the world; it was experienced as a more profound and demanding way of being in and of the world. This was cherished.*

23. She was initially referring to the "risks" of breaking with one's routines and encountering difference, but remarked also that the security risks in international aid work had risen markedly since the mid-1990s. Before that she had never been afraid on

missions. Now she, like many of her colleagues, had become much more cautious about accepting missions.

24. Professional rewards abroad, I was told, led to desires for other kinds of personal growth, for example through reading about the societies in which people had worked, even if they had originally been on emergency missions that had allowed for no preparatory reading. Islam and Buddhism kept reappearing as objects of study.

25. Leila's desire to engage with other women's femininities through veils, bangles, and other material and bodily qualities would be condemned as naively superficial and even scandalous (especially in a person in the healing arts) by a preponderance of social theorists, philosophers, and others. Kant wrote at length against the "mere" ornament: "Taste is always still barbaric when it needs the addition of charms and emotions for satisfaction, let alone if it makes these into the standard for its approval" (2006:108).

26. Leila was like a number of my other self-described feminist interlocutors who mentioned that on their missions they kept an eye out for women in particular.

27. Kemijärvi is an unglamorous city in northern Finland.

28. Nurse Kati Partanen talks about the loneliness of being back from a mission: "You have given everything of yourself and been *inside* the site [of aid]. When one has to go, one's state of being is such that, 'I don't belong there in the crisis area anymore, but not yet at home either.' One is very alone with these things" (Hyvönen 2012:15).

29. Sonneveld (2007) writes about "touch hunger: one can be hungry for touching and being touched (Field [2001], and, [as] with the need for food, one can wither when this hunger . . . is not satisfied)." Thank you to Ariana Hernandez-Reguant for this reference.

30. But alienated forms of loneliness were mentioned by the psychologists who worked with the aid workers. One said, "There have been circumstances in which people have been left terribly alone—either because they've been in an [isolating] job, or [an isolated] place or situation, or simply because they have socially drifted into a situation where they have been [too] alone. Particularly if one is in a remote place as the only foreigner and some row or fighting starts—that can be very stressful." This alienated kind of loneliness was mentioned by the therapists but not by the aid workers. Again, while loneliness was problematic, solitude was prized. This was a culturally significant distinction. See chapter 5.

31. In the dictionary, the very next entry is *hävetä*, to feel ashamed, or embarrassed.

32. I think that for many, alcohol did enable the relaxing of a level of shyness and self-discipline that was otherwise very high. But this does not mean that people didn't also work hard or that they forgot their professional responsibilities. Red Cross administrators at the headquarters were prompt to point out that any sign of trouble in that direction would result in the recalling of an aid worker.

33. I do not know whether national-level or international Red Cross work was in question.

34. Much critical work has been done on these topics by Finnish scholars including Alasuutari and Ruuska (1998, 1999:219); Lehtonen, Löytty, and Ruuska (2004); Eide and Nikunen (2010); and Keskinen (2012).

35. At the Finnish Red Cross headquarters in Helsinki, staffers also pointed to "certain 'good' characteristics [like] transparency, equality, democracy, good governance, etc." as being assets in international aid work.

2. Impossible Situations

1. It is of course not just the medical teams that are caught in violence or extreme experiences; so too are the Red Cross people in transportation, logistics, administration, finance, and other areas.

2. It is crucial to recognize, of course, that "professional care-giving is also an inherently political act" (Livingston 2012:96). The politics of the ICRC principle of neutrality will be taken up in chapter 6.

3. One nurse who had worked for the Red Cross in Afghanistan, Kenya, Albania, Kosovo, Iran, Sri Lanka, Pakistan, Iraq, Ethiopia, and North Korea dealt with it by moving to the very north of Finland, to Lapland, where she lived with her dog in a small cottage in the middle of swampland. She had no electricity or running water. "Here it is good to find calm[;] the cottage is far enough away from war and refugee camps" (Petterson 2013:4).

4. Red Cross workers are offered the opportunity to see psychologists as they are leaving for or returning from international missions (see, e.g., Dyregrov 1997). This is not sustained one-on-one therapy but rather a practice known in Finland as "psychic work protection" (psyykkinen työsuojelu). Sometimes this relatively brief engagement acts as a gateway to other, perhaps earlier, psychic issues; the client might then seek a personal therapist. (Crisis work [kriisityö] generally refers to Red Cross work in crises within Finland, and psychologists work with people in those contexts also, along with other first responders [cf. Fassin and Rechtman 2009]. Crisis work entails a complex set of practices in its own right; here I concentrate only on the people who have participated in international missions. See, e.g., S. Saari [2000] on domestic crisis work.)

5. The sites of their interventions were not simply, pace Agamben (2005), chaotic sites of exception.

6. Thank you to Hannah Appel for coming up with the concept of "extraordinary affect" (personal communication, July 2011).

7. I thank Paulla Ebron for a good conversation about institutional affect management. See also Dyregrov (1997).

8. Thank you to Hannah Appel for helping me to phrase this thought. The term affective neutrality has been used by Eva Brann (1991:758), but in a way that differs from mine. She sees affect as "nonrational," "subjective," and having to do with the "soul." It has also been used in a medical context by Frankel (1986).

9. Here Schwenkel acknowledges a debt to Thrift (2004:62), and to Richard and Rudnyckyj (2009:62). She herself insightfully examines how "affective forces" can motivate "political thought and social action" in the specific instance of what she calls "socialist affect" (2013:252).

10. Cf. Ahmed (2004:119), cited in Schwenkel (2013). In her essay "The Turn to Affect:

A Critique," Ruth Leys (2011:443, 451) argues that much recent work on affect would separate it from reason.

11. Again, those I interviewed all emphasized that in their work with the Red Cross at least, they were "psychologists" and *not* "therapists"; a psychologist is perhaps best described here as a first responder especially useful in the initial debriefing of aid workers.

12. See Petterson (2013:4). The Finnish original has been slightly edited for flow.

13. See, e.g., *My War Gone By, I Miss It So* (Loyd 1999); *A Cruel Paradise* (Olson 1999); *The Bang Bang Club* (Marinovich and Silva 2000); *Another Day in Paradise* (Bergman 2003); *War Hospital* (Fink 2003); *Hope in Hell* (Bortolotti 2004); *Where Soldiers Fear to Tread* (Burnett 2005).

14. I do not recall whether I had already mentioned the term *affective neutrality* in our conversations.

15. As mentioned earlier, Red Cross people currently receive psychic and social support not only through counseling help but also at regular debriefings, Red Cross reunions where veterans of many missions meet newer delegates, and the many training sessions and courses run annually by the Red Cross. This, however, needs to be understood, the doctor said, "against a historical background of the neglect of PTSD [posttraumatic stress disorder], et cetera. [After] World War II, vets were neglected and left on their own. They were called 'lazy' and 'sissy.' . . . There was an idea—there still is—that this a tough, *sisu*-based [grit-based] society. You just have to cope. This was carried quite naturally into [institutional] Red Cross thinking." Against this context, he said, the Red Cross reunions often "become therapeutic though they are usually conceptualized as technical . . . [Again,] the emotional and the technical are one."

16. Foucault and others have, in contrast, *sought* the limit experience. Foucault explains: "Nietzsche, Bataille, and Blanchot . . . try through experience to reach that point of life which lies as close as possible to the impossibility of living, which lies at the limit or extreme" (1991:31). See chapter 5.

17. My use of an impasse differs from that of Lauren Berlant, who writes that "the impasse is a stretch of time in which one moves around with a sense that the world is at once intensely present and enigmatic, such that the activity of living demands both a wandering absorptive awareness and a hypervigilance that collects material that might help to clarify things, maintain one's sea legs, and coordinate the standard melodramatic crises with those processes that have not yet found their genre of event" (2011:4).

18. This case was described by an informant to Riikonen (1994:41).

19. I have obscured and omitted some identifying details from this account.

20. Cf. Megan Vaughan's account of how colonial missionaries saw "heathen grandmothers" as "The Last Fortress of Satan" (1991:67).

21. It would likely be wrong to automatically interpret Elina's relationship with Mariama in terms of a "mother complex." She had children of her own in Finland. We did not directly address this issue, however.

22. See Sharika Thiranagama's brilliant writing on attachment: "the forces that make and unmake us are the sites of ceaselessly generative ambivalent attachments" (2011:12).

23. Erica Bornstein and Peter Redfield rightly make the general and important point

that "secular humanitarianism . . . resonates with salvational narratives of rescue" (2010:12).

24. Povinelli (2002) also uses the term *objects-beings*. See also MacGaffey and Harris (1993) on the "ritual personhood of objects," A. L. Moore (2008) on the spiritualization of whales and other charismatic mega-fauna, and Sturken (2007) on teddy bears.

25. The term *jewel in the crown* was used by a senior Red Cross staffer as he tried to explain that aid workers who had survived crises in the field, had returned to Red Cross work, and had developed a certain kind of professional maturity and affective neutrality were invaluable to the organization.

26. Personal details of several other informants were added to Kaisa's story so as to preserve her anonymity. Other features of her story were omitted.

27. I have not heard any others mention "small emergency kits."

28. Kaisa and her Dutch colleague spoke "only school French," she said.

29. And perhaps it in some way strengthened the efficacy of her performative, tactical claim to *political* neutrality. Cf. Redfield (2010:53, 68) on the uses of neutrality by representatives of Médecins Sans Frontières (MSF). On "performative efficacy" see Stanley Tambiah (1985:123–66).

30. There were also other differences. Methodologically, the project in Finland was interview research supplemented by documentary work, while that in Tanzania was ethnographic fieldwork in a fuller sense of the term. The time periods in question are also far apart. I did the fieldwork in Tanzania in the mid-1980s, while the Red Cross research began in 1996 and continued intermittently until 2012.

31. My friend Kate Makuen was kind enough to save my letters from the field and to give them to me on my return.

32. Cf. Lacan (1966) on "the mirror stage," discussed by Silverman (2007:344).

33. See Achille Mbembe's (2001) discussion of "absolute otherness" in Fassin and Rechtman (2009:187). Fassin and Rechtman give a chilling account of how the global media saw the Rwandan perpetrators of the genocide as "monsters" and "beasts," and describe the thinking of a child psychiatrist, Michel Dechambre, who concluded: "I discovered that a white person could have difficulties in understanding a 'black consciousness,' 'black' revelations, and a 'black truth' which is not ours." The authors add that this "articulates a deep truth about humanitarian psychiatry" (187).

34. I discuss these in further detail in Malkki (2002b).

35. I realized in retrospect that nowhere in their accounts of the genocide had the refugees, often themselves wounded, mentioned pain as a distinct ontological presence. Julie Livingston found the same in her ethnography of an oncology ward in Gaborone, Botswana (2012:120).

36. In a historical study of the imagination, James Engell (1981:157) discusses the German term *Einfühlung*, which signifies "in-feeling" and "feeling into" something. *Feeling into* might be a useful term for thinking about aspects of imaginative communion.

37. Both Michael Barnett (2002) and Christopher Taylor (2001) explicitly refer to the sadism of the 1994 torture and killing in Rwanda. See also Orbinski (2008) for a doctor's account.

38. Anthropologist Linda Green writes in a much more extreme situation, after living under a regime of terror in Guatemala: "Gradually I came to realize that terror's power, its matter-of-factness, is exactly about doubting one own perceptions of reality" (1994:231, excerpted by Crapanzano 2004:88).

39. This premonitory imagination did not depend on visualizing *images* of something threatening or dangerous. The linking of the image and the imagination has been a pervasive theme in much of western thought. See Aristotle, Rene Descartes, John Locke, Bishop Berkeley, Immanuel Kant, and David Hume, among others (White 1990:86). See Michael Taussig on "nonvisual imagery" and "the tyranny of the visual notion of image" (1993:57).

40. That isolation made for a sense that anything could happen there and no one would know. That worry was actually articulated to me by the refugees first; they expressed concern that there were no UNHCR legal protection officers to witness anything and that, therefore, "no one would know if something happened." For me, the isolation tended to amplify whatever else was going on and whatever I was learning and thinking. It tended to heighten my affective states and intensities of embodiment.

41. Christopher Taylor (2001:viii) writes about a heartbreaking relationship between a small boy and the dog he lost during the 1994 Rwanda genocide.

42. Despite tracing parallels here, my intent has never been to "absorb" the accounts of the refugees or the aid workers as my own (see Finnström 2008:17, 22).

43. My use of the impasse differs from Lauren Berlant's imaginative use of it (2011:4–6).

44. See also Harri Englund (2011:87–89) on another use of the impasse.

3. Figurations of the Human

An earlier version of this chapter appeared as Malkki 2010.

1. A significant part of the humanitarian representation of children occurs in connection with complex emergencies in the Global South, as Erica Burman points out in her indictment of "the chauvinism of the Northern public and policy makers for whom disaster imagery constitutes a major source of information about the South" (1994:238).

2. John Wall, whose work I have cited extensively in this section, actually concludes his article by foregrounding a variant of this angel-devil tension: "While children share the ambiguity of human good and evil with the rest of us, they do so in a peculiarly sharp way . . . Children experience in a more direct and unmediated way than adults the primordial dimensions of human existence, and the more so the younger the child. It is in this fallen innocence that, at least from the Christian ethical point of view, the true 'mystery' of children's initial being in the world may be said to consist" (Wall 2004:181). Wall concludes that children are productively thought of as "fallen angels."

3. I thank Ramah McKay for this insight.

4. Sharon Stephens, personal communication, 1994.

5. I am indebted to the late Sharon Stephens for this insight (personal communica-

tion), 1994. I have also benefited greatly from conversations with Aila Ferguson about U.S. sentencing laws.

6. In stark contrast, see Nakazawa ([1978] 2004); Yamazaki (1995); and Yoneyama (1999).

7. Noam Chomsky (1999) offers a trenchant analysis of the Vienna Conference.

8. I thank Jess Auerbach for this insight.

9. One popular example of children as seers came on to newsstands in the March 1998 issue of *Life* magazine. The lead story was about children and truth, and on the cover was written: "Kids' Pictures to God: What Children Want God to See" (Adato 1998). A little (white) girl was pictured holding up a nature photograph for God to see. Her truth, as it transcended politics, became neutered and, once again, ritually sealed off in a politically safe and domesticated register. It was not of the here and now, not worldly. Did the "Nature" in the cover photograph stand in for "Peace"?

10. Sharon Stephens, personal communication, 1994.

11. Children's books in this genre include: Nathan Aaseng, *The Peace Seekers: The Nobel Peace Prize* (1987); Ann Durell and Marilyn Sachs, *The Big Book for Peace* (1990); Katherine Scholes, *Peace Begins with You* (1990); Joan Walsh Anglund, *Peace Is a Circle of Love* (1993); Holly Near, *The Great Peace March* (1993); Jennifer Garrison and Andrew Tubesing, *A Million Visions of Peace* (1995); and Sheila Hamanaka, *Peace Crane* (1995).

12. To take only one example, Christina Schwenkel's (2009:138, 149) ethnography of political struggles over the memorialization and monumentalization of "the American war in Vietnam" shows how heroizing war monuments are increasingly being criticized for drowning out other initiatives, like monuments for peace. Here, too, youth are linked with peace. See also Yoneyama (1999).

13. I thank Zhanara Nauruzbayeva for this recollection.

14. When I discussed this research project with an elementary school teacher in an after-school day care program in Irvine, California, he offered the children with whom he worked the opportunity of drawing pictures of war and peace. When I saw the set of drawings a few weeks later, I was startled by their ritual sameness. They were as Nauruzbayeva described, with the difference that the bombs and bomber aircraft were not identified. The potentially perpetual, calculatedly diffuse U.S. "war on terror" might have had something to do with the absence of a named "enemy."

15. One such crease is Naguib Mahfouz's poem "A Prayer" (1997), which begins, "I was less than seven years old when I said a prayer for the revolution" (cited in Shihab Nye 1998:9). Thank you to Chris Dole for this reference.

16. This book is also published under the title *My World/Peace: Thoughts and Illustrations from the Children of All Nations* (1985). It is part of a boxed set in which the other volume is titled *My World/Nature*.

17. Thank you to Laurie Kain Hart for this insight.

18. I thank Harri Englund for this reference.

19. Examples include Kent (1991:1): "Our principal link to the future is our children. What will their lives be like? Our thinking about the future should be informed by concern with the prospects for [those] who will occupy the future." See also Benedek (1990); Chan (1990); Conrad (1990); Children's Express (1993); and O'Connor (1993).

20. I thank Bill Maurer for this insight.

21. Sharon Stephens, personal communication, 1994.

22. Sharon Stephens, personal communication, 1994.

4. Bear Humanity

1. Gleason (2007:176) is here writing about her daughter's stuffed companion rabbit.

2. See Lawrence (1986:66–67) on neotenization and juvenilization in Disney's Mickey Mouse and other fantasy animals. See also Gell (1988:7).

3. See, e.g., www.tightknitworld.net.au/KnittingPatterns/TraumaTeddyPattern.pdf (accessed January 9, 2015); Newby n.d. I thank Jane Ferguson for additional information about the uses of the Trauma Teddies. See also Sturken (2007:132).

4. Marita Sturken (2007:91, 133–35) powerfully demonstrates the presence of "the teddy" at sites of tragedy like Oklahoma City and the Twin Towers.

5. A similar and effective logic was at work with the live "comfort dogs" that were brought to Sandy Hook Elementary School from several different K-9 organizations in the aftermath of the mass killings there (Cunningham and Edelman 2012). The dogs were humanized—"companion species" (Haraway 2008:134) that were there to bring comfort and consolation. They were more than mere dogs, or more than mere animals.

6. Thank you to Jean Comaroff for giving me a Forward Bear and telling me about their histories.

7. Archaeologists have also encountered the challenge of analyzing figures that "blur the boundary between anthropomorphic and zoomorphic representations" (Nakamura and Meskell 2009:227).

8. I have here translated the Finnish original, *henkinen tuki*, as "psychic support," but it could also be rendered as "spiritual support."

9. Slater (2012) details the scientific and industry struggles over various different fire retardants. Some of the compounds in retardants have been studied for their toxic and carcinogenic effects.

10. "Pupujen perheportretti: Apupuputalkoissa syntyneitä lisää," June 11, 2007, accessed February 14, 2008, http://pupukokous.vuodatus.net/.

11. Mustikka, August 18, 2006, accessed February 14, 2008, http://aski.vuodatus.net /blog/category/apupupu.

12. "Maartsi," "006 and the secret weapon," November 28, 2006, accessed May 16, 2008, http://maartsi.vuodatus.net/lue/2006/11/006-ja-salainen-ase.

13. "Maartsi," "007 and a license to hug," December 19, 2006, accessed May 16, 2008, http://maartsi.vuodatus.net/lue/2006/12/007-ja-lupa-halia.

14. Anita, http://anita63.vuodatus.net/blog/archive?m=08&y=2000, accessed February 25, 2008, http://anita63.vuodatus.net/blog/archive?m=08&y=2006.

15. "Hannaliini," "Hannaliinin neuleet," August 29, 2006, accessed February 25, 2008, http://hannaliini.vuodatus.net/blog/219720.

16. Mustikka, August 30, 2006, accessed February 14, 2008, http://aski.vuodatus.net /blog/category/apupupu.

17. Iso Gnu, "Iso Gnu: Apupupu Anselmi lahdössä maailmalle," August 28, 2006, accessed February 14, 2008, http://isognu.blogspot.com/2006/08/apupupu-anselmi-lhdss -maailmalle.html.

18. "Perhoneito," "Apupupu," January 5, 2007, accessed February 25, 2008, http:// perhoneito.blogspot.com/2007/01/apupupu.html.

19. "Rakkautta ja rimakauhua," "Puikot sulmussa vuorostaan," September 18, 2006, accessed February 14, 2008, http://juliaerin.vuodatus.net/lue/2006/09/puikot-sulmussa -vuorostaan.

20. The childhood that is imagined is in fact a very middle-class childhood, unevenly globalized. The utopian belief is that toys and play, like childhood vaccinations and nutritious food, *should* in the future enable children of poor countries to live like their middle-class counterparts in the North (Boyden 1990; Steedman 1995; Stephens 1995).

21. "Eilen, tänään ja huomenna," accessed February 19, 2008, http://www.kolumbus .fi/webweaver/pr.html.

22. Both of my grandmothers did that.

23. I thank Christopher Steiner for this information.

24. Again, Foucault insisted, "The imaginary is "not false . . . nor illusory. *The imaginary is not a mode of unreality, but indeed a mode of actuality*" (Foucault [1954] 1986:70, emphasis added; cf. Deleuze 1997:63; Mittermaier 2011:17–19; see also the introduction).

5. Homemade Humanitarianism

1. Much work of relevance here has been written about the gift; see, e.g., Mauss (1990); Bourdieu (1977, 1990); Parry (1986); Derrida (1994); M. Strathern (1990, 1999); Laidlaw (2000); Bornstein (2001, 2012); Ssorin-Chaikov (2006); and Venkatesan (2011).

2. These rates are similar to those in Belgium, Denmark, India, Ireland, and Singapore; in Sweden and the United States, the figure exceeds 50 percent (Mykrä 2010:7, citing Musick and Wilson 2008:34). Mykrä adds: "According to the first comprehensive study of volunteer activity in Finland (Yeung 2002), Finland is an active voluntary work country, [in contrast to what] is usually thought. Finns' participation in voluntary service is high: almost 2 of 5 (37%) Finns participate in voluntary activity. The level of participation activity does not differ much in different population groups. Women and men, young and old, participate equally on average. Finns use about 18 hours a month in volunteer activity. The young (15–24) and the most aged participate even more, almost 20 hours per month" (2010:7). Andrea Muehlebach (2011) has described similar patterns for Italy; thank you to Christina Schwenkel for directing me to her work.

3. See Allahyari (2000:3) and also her critique of Wuthnow (1991).

4. Making things, and having the skills to make things, are not the exclusive preserve of the few or the specialist in Finland. Neither is work of the hand necessarily marked as rural versus urban, working class versus middle class, young versus old. According to Tilastokeskus, the Finnish center for statistics, *käsityö* (handwork or work of the hand) was the most popular leisure activity for both men and women as measured in the years 1981, 1991, and 2002 (Liikkanen, Hanifi, and Hannula 2005). This is a social pattern of

long standing. Many of these skills are taught in schools. Older generations of Finns saw long periods of poverty, wartime want, and thrift, and were usually good at improvising. These skills are now valued as a source of ecological alternatives and an outlet for creativity. And, whatever else they are, they may be an important sensorial and social palliative for loneliness and isolation in old age.

5. This belittling is akin to the denigration of the "mere" image in other contexts; see the introduction. See also White (1990).

6. This appears to be the case despite the existence of "open" or outpatient services (avopalvelu) such as "home service" (kotipalvelu) and "home nursing" (kotisairaanhoito). The first is run by the state social services (Sosiaalivirasto) and the second by the state health services (Terveysvirasto). Both are spread much too thin.

7. Muehlebach (2012:35–37) has written with deep insight about the "figure of the impoverished old woman living alone" and her place in the new form of "ethical citizenship" in Italy.

8. Espoo is a city contiguous with Helsinki.

9. Talk of what Finnishness means, and, as mentioned earlier, self-stereotyping, are extremely common in Finland, and much written about. The classic book is Väinö Linna's Täällä Pohjan tähden alla (1959), translated into English as Under the North Star (2001). See also Laaksonen and Mettomäki (1996); Alasuutari and Ruuska (1998, 1999); Apo (1998); Lehtonen, Löytty, and Ruuska (2004); Siikala (2006); and Dutton (2010). In her study of Finnish Red Cross nurses on international missions, Riikonen (2005:25–26) also observes that "Finnishness talk" (suomalaisuuspuhe) was a predominant element of how the nurses talked. The most dominant was "nurse talk" (sairaanhoitajapuhe), however.

10. This account—necessarily partial and fragmentary—would not reflect everyday social reality were I not to mention the social fact that, in addition to living in apartments, most middle-class people have (or have access to) a mökki with a sauna, ideally near a lake, a river, or the sea. The mökki is variously a cabin in the woods, a cottage, a hideaway, a getaway; it is often a rundown place to be omassa rauhassa (in your own peace), olla itsekseen (to be on your own), hiljaisuuden keskellä (in the midst of silence), luonnon sylissä (in nature's lap). This kind of solitude is deeply prized, as is "communion" with nature. On summer weekends, the mökki is most often where people go. For urban elders, this "being in nature" (olla luonnon keskellä), or just simply being anywhere outdoors, may also become a painful, frustrated need.

11. In an electronic version of a column in the newspaper Uusi Suomi, Tarja Tallqvist (2009) writes about "elders' suicides, an unspoken shame." She reports a statistical fact: "every other day, a person over 65 commits suicide." She adds, "I am shocked by the fact that this issue has been known about for many years, but it is not very visibly worried about. I haven't seen shocked headlines, or comments by experts. . . . Elders', aged people's, suicides are largely caused by loneliness and the depression caused by that. Children might be living in another [town], and there may be no kin. The spouse may be dead, or in the hospital. One's own enfeebled state, pains that a doctor trivializes. Poverty, every tenth pensioner is poor. The feeling that one is no longer useful in this world

that demands results. From all this, singly or together, follows depression which leads to hopeless agony/anguish [*tuska*]. Self-destroying words and actions. . . . In our welfare state, the suicide-vulnerable elder is left alone" (emphasis added). The first comment to Tallqvist is left on January 2, 2009, by "Timo," who asks: "Why is euthanasia seen as such an ogre?"

12. As I showed in chapter 1 and earlier in this chapter, solitude is sought and prized by many, if not most, Finns. The Red Cross aid workers on international missions found it oppressive not to have solitude, to just be able to be by themselves; yet in other ways they craved and admired others' capacity for sociality. More generally, many Finns would probably recognize similar tensions, whether between solitude and sociality, or, particularly, solitude and loneliness.

13. I disagree with Berlant about genocide necessarily being a "discrete, time-framed phenome[non]" (2011:100). Genocide and its aftermaths go on for generations.

14. The psychic effects of solitary confinement in prisons would make an informative point of comparison here. Indeed, being confined to one's home as an old and sometimes also disabled person has been variously characterized as being in prison. One person has been quoted as saying: "Home can become a prison where the time spent is full of angst [*ahdistus*] and fear, for example about bouts of illness" (Punkka 2014:A3).

15. Yksinäinen lammas, "Kuukausi puhumatta kenellekään, August 30, 2009, blog entry, accessed November 14, 2010, http://keskustelu.suomi24.fi/node/8435785.

16. Nwofrl, "Ei surkastu . . . ," August 30, 2009, blog entry, accessed November 14, 2010, http://keskustelu.suomi24.fi/node/8435785.

17. Anonymous, "lyhyt aika," August 30, 2009, blog entry, accessed November 14, 2010, http://keskustelu.suomi24.fi/node/8435785.

18. Yksinäinen sielultaankin, "Have been," September 5, 2009, blog entry, accessed November 14, 2010, http://keskustelu.suomi24.fi/node/8435785.

19. Harmonia tärkeää, "Tasapaino ehkä tärkeintä," September 9, 2009, blog entry, accessed November 14, 2010, http://keskustelu.suomi24.fi/node/8435785.

20. Rane-R, "Sielun ahdistus siedätyshoidossa," September 7, 2009, blog entry, accessed November 14, 2010, http://keskustelu.suomi24.fi/node/8435785.

21. Of course, one can also be very alone in a relationship, as many researchers have pointed out (see, e.g., Jokinen 2005:9).

22. The Common Responsibility Collection, now an independent organization, is an annual nationwide fund-raising campaign originally organized by the Evangelical Lutheran Church of Finland around categories of people that have included widows, orphans, the unemployed, the homeless, the mentally handicapped, marginalized youth, and lonely elders (see J. Saari, Kainulainen, and Yeung 2005).

23. The 2014 Common Responsibility Campaign works to give more people "a good death."

24. All the phrases quoted in this paragraph are from Saari, quoted in Holopainen (2011:37).

25. My account of the facts of this case comes from the *Helsingin Sanomain Kuu-*

kausiliite, the monthly magazine of the newspaper *Helsingin Sanomat*. Ilkka Malmberg, "Kulkuri: Hanen elamansa kiinnosti vain viranomaisia. Hanen kuolemansa kiinnosti kaikkia," *Helsingin Sanomain Kuukausiliite*, November 2000, 30–39, accessed July 12, 2013, http://www2.hs.fi/extrat/digilehti/kuukausiliite/112000/.

26. There is no statistic for this among "causes of death" in the Tilastokeskus (Center for Statistics), but the Information Gas Station Service (iGS toimitus) of the City of Helsinki Library, having reviewed cases of mummification, found them to involve aged people. See http://igs.kirjastot.fi (or http://www.kysy.fi/). *Mummification* as a search word leads to *Egyptology*; this complicated my search, and that of the research librarians at the City of Helsinki Library. I would like to thank them for their generous and patient help.

27. "Taas muumiolöytö Helsingissä—vainaja kuolleena 8 kuukautta," February 4, 2010, accessed January 28, 2011, http://www.iltasanomat.fi/kotimaa/art-1288335408236.html.

28. Indeed, as I describe in chapter 1, I was initially quite narrowly focused on the Finnish Red Cross professionals who had worked in Central Africa around the 1994 genocide in Rwanda.

29. The projects listed here include one-off events, annual campaigns, regular services, and permanent programs.

30. See, e.g., "Social Services to a Retiree" [Palvelut ja etuudet ikääntyneille], February 18, 2009, Ministry of Social Affairs and Health, accessed, July 12, 2012, http://www.stm.fi/en/social_and_health_services/old people/services_and_benefits.

31. "Tule mukaan ystavaksi," accessed October 19, 2011, http://www.redcross.fi/aktiivit/osastot/helsinki-uusimaa/lansi-vantaa/Ystavatoiminta/fi_FI/Ystavatoiminta/. The other information in this paragraph is drawn from this same source.

32. In this last sense, people were being invited in, to become members of the society of volunteer friends—and, often, of other Red Cross programs.

33. "Ole hyva. Ole ystava," FRC 2011 campaign, accessed October 25, 2011, http://frccampaigns.mearra.com/news?page=1.

34. "Nuoret ystävät valtaavat vanhainkoteja," *Satakunnan kansa*, February 9, 2010, accessed October 27, 2011, http://www.satakunnankansa.fi/cs/Satellite/Kotimaa/1194635561914/artikkeli/nuoret+ystavat+valtaavat+vanhainkoteja.html.

35. The study's title is translated as "The formation of the role of volunteers in the Red Cross Friendship Service."

36. I base this suggestion mainly on everyday comments in my own extended family, as well as on my quite old ethnographic research on the institutionalization of aging in the United States.

37. Muehlebach (2011:68) says of a similar context in Italy: "Volunteers emphasized the intense pleasures and bonds they felt as volunteers. They seldom lingered on the kinds of exclusion that often moved them into these activities in the first place."

38. Certainly, state-provided services were in many ways more institutionalized and durable, a right of citizenship—even if seriously overstretched. There is no reason to suppose that the people in question went without state social services, or that those services afforded *no* occasion for human contact, but that does not mean people were not left very alone nevertheless, and needy for sociality.

39. Povinelli notes the parallel liberal horror over both the "ritual pathology" of aboriginality and the "sexual pathology" of undomesticated gay stranger sociality (2006:62).

40. It has been noted that the state could do more to partner and coordinate with organizations such as the Red Cross; as it is, it is spared significant social expenditure on pressing social problems. Laasanen has calculated that the volunteer hours per annum add up to 2.1 million euros (2011:17; cf. Turja and Engdahl 2008).

41. Cf. "Salon de refuse," discussed by Peter Dormer (1997), quoted in Heinänen (2006:11).

42. Negative Finnish equivalents include *akka, ämmä, muori, mummeli, muija,* and *eukko.* A more respectful expression is *vanha rouva* ("old Mrs."). *Mummi, mummu,* and *mummo* are warm and tender terms. Thank you to Arvi Pihlman for adding to this list.

43. The Swedish term *den glada stressen* (Frankenhaeuser 1999) is translated by Pöllänen (2006:74) as *iloinen stressikokemus.* Cf. also Heikkinen (1997:87).

44. Kant was eloquent, but wrong, in dismissing this work as mere "disagreeable" and "burdensome" drudgery driven by "remuneration" (2006:183).

45. "Ryhdy tekemään Äiti Teresa filttejä! Ohje täällä!," May 26, 2010, accessed October 19, 2011, http://www.seniorinetti.fi/keskustelu/ryhdy-tekemaan-aiti-teresa-filtteja -ohje-taalla. All quotations in this paragraph are from this source.

46. Mummeli6, March 26, 2010, blog entry, accessed October 19, 2011, http://www .seniorinetti.fi/keskustelu/ryhdy-tekemaan-aiti-teresa-filtteja-ohje-taalla.

47. Päikky, "ihania töitä tuossa tupun kuvassa!," March 26, 2010, blog entry, accessed October 19, 2011, http://www.seniorinetti.fi/keskustelu/ryhdy-tekemaan-aiti-teresa -filtteja-ohje-taalla, emphasis added.

48. Vaaka ry, "Toimitetut peitot," updated November 4, 2010, accessed October 26, 2011, http://www.vaaka.org/projektit/tilkkupeitot. All quotations in this paragraph are from this source. Cf. Marttaliitto (2011).

49. The information cited here about the 2010 Vaaka ry tally comes from a list of "delivered blankets" kept by Vaaka ry, dated November 4, 2010. Tallies of blankets and other homemade items are updated regularly.

50. See "Auta Äiti Teresa -työtä kutomalla" [Help Mother Teresa work by knitting], accessed October 19, 2011, http://www.espoonseurakunnat.fi/web/espoonlahti /aiti-teresa-peiton-ohjeet.

51. I thank Jim Ferguson for this insight, 2011.

52. I remember this as a significant worry among the residents of an old-age institution I worked in.

53. Hannapoo, "Ajatuksia käsityöllisestä hyvinvoinnista vanhuksia ajatellen," January 15, 2008, in Pöllänen 2007a.

54. Erkoskel, "Käsityö ja yksilön/yhteisön hyvinvointi," November 19, 2007, in Pöllänen 2007a.

55. Ira, "Käsityö ilon ja tyydytyksen tuottajana," January 24, 2008, in Pöllänen 2007a.

56. A Red Cross volunteer stood in a drizzle in an old plaza in downtown Helsinki.

The Red Cross apron over his duffel coat and his red collection box in hand, he had stood there for six consecutive days, collecting funds in aid of the victims of the 2004 tsunami. Coins had been dropping in at a steady rate. "That morning a man, maybe in his fifties, had come up. He had pushed three or four sandy 50e bills into the box. The man had said that they were 'from there.' 'There?' [the volunteer wondered]. 'In other words from somewhere on the beaches of Thailand? Khao Lak?' He did not go and ask."

57. Fiona Terry (2002:216), for example, argues: "We can never construct the best world in which our compassion can immediately translate into an end to suffering, but we can try to build a second-best world based on hard-headed assessments of needs and options." This is an example of the authorial "we" that so often assumes the power and compassion of building worlds for hapless, suffering others. Terry's work is, of course, part of a large genre. Often those others turn a wry eye on the compassionate ones.

6. A Zealous Humanism and Its Limits

1. The subtitled English-language release was called *Of Gods and Men*—an inversion of the true French original, *Des hommes et des dieux* (Of men and gods).

2. "Common sense thinking contains what Gramsci called the traces of ideology 'without an inventory.' Consider, for example, the trace of religious thinking in a world which believes itself to be secular and which, therefore, invests 'the sacred' in secular ideas" (Hall 1985:111).

3. However, the bounds of the apolitical are being negotiated within the Red Cross Red Crescent Movement, too. In a 2011 workshop on the seven fundamental principles organized by the International Federation of the Red Cross (IFRC), it was debated "whether it was still possible to maintain our Neutrality when relief work turns into development work, requiring stakeholders to tackle the intrinsic causes of inequality and hardship . . . Too often the Fundamental Principle of Neutrality is misunderstood . . . Over time, our interpretation of it has been conditioned and overly restrained into a 'straightjacket' to read like a calling for limited action or abstention. This is not congruent with the Pictet Commentary[,] which explains that the essential characteristic of the RCRC is to act and not to remain passive, or in other words, that neutrality must not be an excuse not to act" (IFRC 2011:2, 5). Moreover, the IFRC workshop suggested that the principle of neutrality should be seen less as a "moral stance" or "ethical principle" and more as a "tactic" (2011:5).

4. "Humanity is *still a sacrosanct Fundamental Principle*" (IFRC 2011:3, emphasis in the original).

5. See Talal Asad on the concept of "religion" as a Christian category (1993; 2003). See also Mahmood (2005).

6. Hansen further writes: "The interest in empathy and sincerity firmed up as rationality became a preeminent public value at the end of the eighteenth century. It was no longer enough to be sincere; *one also had to be rational and commit oneself to higher and more universal truths*. Immanuel Kant added a crucial element to modern convictions: judgment as the essential human capacity that anchors the cool passion of the new

responsible and autonomous self in an interior law, in moral duty and in practical responsibility. . . . With the Kantian ethics it was no longer enough to be sincere and true to oneself. One must reach higher and deeper and reach for *an ethical consistency that also has a more universal and transcendent element*" (2009:12, 13, emphasis added).

7. A comment left by Octavian4 on December 6 on Bradshaw's (2010) review.

8. As Kabir Tambar also points out, "invocations of 'zealotry' in discussions of Islam are usually ways of avoiding the specificity of a political encounter," and of denying the reasonableness of certain demands or the people who make them. "All that gets washed [away] under the generic term, 'zealous'" (personal communication).

While the contemporary ICRC insists on its global status as a secular organization, there has been much debate about its history. In her large tome on the Red Cross movement, Caroline Moorehead writes: "Though the founders were all practicing Christians, the ideas had no religious overtones and clashed with no religious tenets" (1998:51). David Forsythe counters: "But it was a fact that Dunant was an evangelical and fundamentalist Christian, and the origin of the Geneva committee was steeped in notions of Christian charity and good works" (2005:27). See also Hutchinson (1996). The origin question is, however, less interesting than actual practices and their effects.

9. Sanna talked about fairness. There is not an interlocutor in my interviews who did not address this "unfairness," and who was not in some degree motivated by this value to do her Red Cross work. In fact, in a group interview with Finnish Red Cross workers from a variety of sectors, most of the participants together came up with *reiluus* (decency, fairness, fair play) as a term that could be the eighth fundamental principle. They recognized that some elements of *reiluus* are already present in impartiality, but still thought *reiluus* important enough to deserve special mention as a motivator.

10. As a viewer of the film, I thought that they were not all of the same mind, at any point. At times, it seemed to me, Abbott Christian was trying to exert his own will too strongly. The fundamental principles have been translated into the languages spoken in all the member states of the movement worldwide—but of course Pictet meant more than that, appealing to a common humanity understood in his cosmological terms.

11. Red Cross members laugh that once in the organization—whether at the national or the international level—the seven principles are drilled into them so much that they are supposed to become second nature (along with the Geneva Conventions). As one veteran doctor expressed it, it is not enough to believe in the principles; one has to *live* them. He pointed me to Confucius. I think of the doctor's words in relation to the daily devotional practices the Cistercian monks followed; they too *lived* their principles. (See Confucius 2011.)

12. A 1985 article on the ICRC and political prisoners considers it odd that "the vast literature on human rights that has appeared in recent years has hardly touched upon the activities of the [ICRC]. The omission is surprising. Since 1945 the ICRC has paid increasing attention to one of the most fundamental human rights issues—political prisoners—to such an extent that by 1982 the ICRC had visited over 300,000 political detainees in 75 countries" (Armstrong 1985:615).

13. The Kennedy epigraph is from Clerc (2011:139); see also Hertog and Kruizing

(2011). *Neutraalius* is a now widely used neologism to describe Finland as de facto neutral. The old, now widely obsolete term for neutrality, *puoluettomuus*, can be literally translated as "partylessness."

14. Indeed, peacekeeping began to be a very important part of being in the "world community" of the United Nations in the 1960s; by the mid-1990s, fifty thousand Finnish peacekeepers had served under the UN flag (Kallenautio 2005:176). In the Cold War years, economic integration into western Europe was also a way of being in the world with political dimensions (Visuri 2003:99).

15. This Finnish neutrality—in its guise as a philosophy of not meddling in other people's business and wishing to be left alone—has sometimes been shameful. One of its very high moral costs has been not to speak up about Stalin's and the later Soviet Union's persecution of Estonia. This persecution has been searingly detailed in Sofi Oksanen's novels *Stalinin lehmät* (Stalin's cows, 2003) and *Puhdistus* (2008); *Purge* (2010). I thank Ulla Kaarina Nikunen for our conversation about this history, and about Finland's neutrality more generally.

16. I thank Arvi Pihlman for a good 2012 conversation about Finnish neutrality.

17. See J. Rahkonen (2011) on "security identities." See also Visuri (2003:156–58).

18. When in Finland, many were active in antiracist work.

19. Faisal Devji makes a powerful argument for recognizing how the "western" values of humanism, human rights, and humanitarianism act as "planetary ideals" that are in fact shared by the people who have inspired Al-Qaeda, and give inspiration to the "globalization of militancy." He writes, centrally, about "humanity as the ideal that permits terrorism to stake its claim to a global arena in the most powerful way" (2008:x).

20. Rieffer-Flanagan (2009:912), interviewing ICRC's Andreas Wiggen in 2006.

21. Here is this "logic of the one" again expressed: if the suffering of *just one person* has been alleviated, the *entire operation* will have been "worthwhile" (see Redfield 2008:149). I have mentioned this emphasis on "the one" in other chapters. From stories of war, violence, and injustice, from humanitarian and advocacy organizations to corporate advertisers this logic of the one remains potent. Interestingly, a similar logic is to be found in Qur'anic verses: "*Whoever has saved a life, it is as if he has saved the whole of humanity.*"

22. Marianne Fermé (n.d.:18) writes about how easily the "Red Cross" was subverted into the "Rebel Cross" by different, warring parties in Sierra Leone. The highly visible, familiar, legally protected symbol of the Red Cross could often be associated with the kinds of secrecy, discretion, and silence that made the organization suspect. "On the one hand the Red Cross presence and its emblem were visible everywhere in Sierra Leone in countless, repetitive iterations on vehicles, relief supplies, human rights handbooks, and fliers seeking and offering information to track down family members separated by the conflict. On the other hand, the work of compiling virtual databases of names to facilitate the process of reuniting families, the diplomatic mediations to effect the exchange of prisoners, and the logistical support for facilitating dialogue among warring factions was often invisible."

23. Rieffer-Flanagan (2009:899) notes decisive concerns that public ICRC criticism

against the Nazis would provoke Germany to attack Switzerland: "Thus the prevailing view was to avoid offending Germany and to protect Swiss sovereignty. The failure of the ICRC to speak out against war crimes or to press the Nazis privately leads to the conclusion that the ICRC was not neutral or independent in all its activities during WWII."

24. No ICRC personnel apparently left mid-mission—missions usually lasting six months to one year—but when they did end, people were reportedly happy to be out of this ethically troubled position.

25. Epigraph from "Managing Emotions in Medical School," Smith and Kleinman 1989:56.

26. It was Bernard Frankel (1986:515) who pointed out that it was Talcott Parsons who described "affective neutrality as one of the five principles governing the role of the physician."

27. They did not call it affective neutrality; the term *emotional neutrality* originally came from Leif. But the nurses used other terms that served the same purpose.

28. Eeva also pointed out situations in which breaches of neutrality might occur if aid workers' missions stretched into longer stays; this showed in the developing of more multi-layered social, and often sexual, relationships in the field.

29. Karl Marx and Friedrich Engels, "Conservative, or Bourgeois Socialism," in the *Communist Manifesto*, quoted in Barnett and Weiss (2008:16).

30. Nietzsche would likely have appreciated late artist Mike Kelley's large assemblage of found objects of women's "domestic craft": "More love hours than can ever be repaid" (see chapter 5).

31. Coetzee here draws on Plutarch, "Of Eating of Flesh," quoted in Regan and Singer (1989:111).

32. It is also the case that the absolutism and radicalism of Humanity, Neutrality, and the other five Red Cross Fundamental Principles—Universality, Impartiality, Unity, Voluntary Service, Independence—are subject to constant internal discussion at all levels of the Red Cross and Red Crescent Movement.

Conclusion. The Power of the Mere

1. Fred Turner has written a recent, very thoughtful essay on the "Family of Man" exhibition (2012).

2. These particular personal circumstances contributed, it was evident, to her willingness to work even in extremely hazardous conditions.

3. This is not to say that some did not undertake missions at significant cost to their personal lives. Some left small children at home and others found relationships with partners strained by distance and worry.

4. She was mildly uneasy about the old-fashioned, sexist assumptions embedded in what she was saying, and she differed in this respect from most of the other nurses and doctors I interviewed.

5. In gendering, too, the feminine is the mere to the masculine. Kaisa's subjectivity was interesting because it was an atypical comment in my research with the Red Cross

women in its understanding of gender, too. Most aid workers talked about themselves and others mainly as persons or people most of the time, but of course socio-cultural contexts in their mission sites often interpellated them first and foremost as women, even as "ladies" or "white ladies." The sociopolitical and cultural contexts of the work mattered, in other words: these contexts might impose heteronormative femininity where that was not welcomed, and yet had to be accepted, for work to proceed. This was a constant negotiation, if not struggle, in Sanna's work in Afghanistan, for example (chapter 6). The countermove was an insistence on professionalism and a kind of tactical "self-naughting" (Coomaraswamy [1946] 2007:182).

6. See also Ananda Coomaraswamy's essay on "Ornament" (2007:71–83).

7. That is why, said one aid worker, it makes sense—as a private citizen—to complement one's aid work by supporting "political" organizations like Amnesty International. She was hardly alone in this view.

8. Here, as Hugo Slim (2010) and many others (including the Red Cross itself) have emphasized, the Red Cross's wartime effort to deliver neutral medical aid to inmates of concentration camps in Nazi Germany is an indelible moral stain. See chapter 6 on the hazards of neutrality.

References

Aalto, Mauri, and Antti Holopainen. 2008. "Ikääntyneiden alkoholin suurkulutuksen tunnistaminen ja hoito." *Duodecim* 124: 1492–98.

Aaltola, Mika. 2003. *Suomen ulkopolitiikan kielipelejä: Analyysi ulkopolitiikan tutkimuksesta 1970–2003*. Tampere: Tampereen yliopistopaino.

Aalto-Setälä, Pauli. n.d. "Kansalaisaktivismi on in." Accessed November 27, 2010. http://www.aalto-setala.fi/00010019-kansalaisaktivismi-on-in.

Aaseng, Nathan. 1987. *The Peace Seekers: The Nobel Peace Prize*. Minneapolis: Lerner Publications Co.

Adamson, Glenn. 2007. *Thinking through Craft*. New York: Berg.

———, ed. 2010. *The Craft Reader*. New York: Berg.

Adato, Allison. 1998. "Kids' Pictures to God: What Children Want God to See." *Life*, March, 68–80.

Adorno, Theodor. 2010. "Functionalism Today." In *The Craft Reader*, ed. Glenn Adamson, 395–403. New York: Berg.

Agamben, Giorgio. 1998. *Homo Sacer: Sovereign Power and Bare Life*. Trans. Daniel Heller-Roazen. Stanford: Stanford University Press.

———. 2005. *State of Exception*. Trans. Kevin Attell. Chicago: University of Chicago Press.

Ahlström, Salme. 2007. "Iäkkäiden naisten päihteiden käyttö: Kirjallisuuskatsaus." *Yhteiskuntapolitiikka* 72 (5): 562–67.

Ahlström, Salme, and Pia Mäkelä. 2009. "Alkoholi ja iäkkäät Suomessa." *Yhteiskuntapolitiikka* 74 (6): 674–78.

Ahmed, Sara. 2004. "Affective Economies." *Social Text* 22 (2): 117–39.

Ahonen, Viktoria, and Hanna Bukis. 2008. "Vanhusten yksinäisyys: Yli 75-vuotiaiden kotona yksinasuvien palvelukeskuksessa käyvien kokemuksia." Bachelor's thesis, Diakonia-ammattikorkeakoulu, Helsinki.

Alasuutari, Pertti, and Petri Ruuska, eds. 1998. *Elävänä Euroopassa: Muuttuva suomalainen identtiteetti.* Tampere: Vastapaino.

———. 1999. *Post-patria? Globalisaation kulttuuri Suomessa.* Tampere: Vastapaino.

Alfoldy, Sandra. 2007a. "Introduction." In *NeoCraft: Modernity and the Crafts*, ed. Sandra Alfoldy, xiv–xxii. Halifax: Press of the Nova Scotia College of Arts and Design.

———. 2007b. *NeoCraft: Modernity and the Crafts.* Halifax: Press of the Nova Scotia College of Arts and Design.

Allahyari, Rebecca. 2000. *Visions of Charity: Volunteer Workers and Moral Community.* Berkeley: University of California Press.

Allison, Anne. 2004. "Cuteness as Japan's Millennial Product." In *Pikachu's Global Adventure: The Rise and Fall of Pokemon*, ed. Joseph Tobin, 34–49. Durham, NC: Duke University Press.

Alloula, Malek. 1986. *The Colonial Harem.* Trans. Myrna Godzich and Wlad Godzich. Minneapolis: University of Minnesota Press.

Althusser, Louis. 2007. "Ideology and Ideological State Apparatuses (Notes toward an Investigation)." In *Visual Culture: The Reader*, ed. Jessica Evans and Stuart Hall, 317–23. Thousand Oaks, CA: Sage Publications, in association with the Open University.

Amadi, Elechi. 1991. *The Concubine.* London: Heinemann.

Anderson, Benedict. 1991. *Imagined Communities: Reflections on the Origins and Spread of Nationalism.* New York: Verso.

Anglund, Joan Walsh. 1993. *Peace Is a Circle of Love.* San Diego: Gulliver Books, Harcourt Brace & Co.

Apo, Satu. 1998. "Suomalaisuuden stigmatisoinnin traditio." In *Elävänä Euroopassa: Muuttuva suomalainen identtiteetti*, ed. Pertti Alasuutari and Petri Ruuska, 83–128. Tampere: Vastapaino.

Appadurai, Arjun, ed. 1986. *The Social Life of Things: Commodities in Cultural Perspective.* Cambridge: Cambridge University Press.

———. 1996. *Modernity at Large: Cultural Dimensions of Globalization.* Minneapolis: University of Minnesota Press.

Aranguren, José Luis. 1966. "Openness to the World: An Approach to World Peace." *Daedalus* 95 (2): 590–606.

Arendt, Hannah. (1951) 1973. *The Origins of Totalitarianism.* New York: Harcourt Brace Jovanovich.

———. 2006. *Eichmann in Jerusalem.* New York: Penguin.

Ariès, Philippe. 1962. *Centuries of Childhood.* Trans. Robert Baldick. London: Jonathan Cape.

Armstrong, J. D. 1985. "The International Committee of the Red Cross and Political Prisoners." *International Organizations* 39 (4): 615–30.

Asad, Talal. 1993. *Genealogies of Religion: Discipline and Reasons of Power in Christianity and Islam.* Baltimore: Johns Hopkins University Press.

———. 2003. *Formations of the Secular: Christianity, Islam, Modernity*. Stanford: Stanford University Press.

Ashforth, Adam. 2005. *Madumo: A Man Bewitched*. Chicago: University of Chicago Press.

Auther, Elissa. 2010. *String Felt Thread: The Hierarchy of Art and Craft in American Art*. Minneapolis: University of Minnesota Press.

Bachelard, Gaston. 2005. *On Poetic Imagination and Reverie*. Putnam, CT: Spring Publications.

Badiou, Alain. 2001. *Ethics: An Essay on the Understanding of Evil*. London: Verso.

Baitenmann, Helga. 1990. "NGOs and the Afghan War: The Politicization of Humanitarian Aid." *Third World Quarterly* 12 (1): 62–85.

Balibar, Étienne. 1994. *Masses, Classes, Ideas: Studies on Politics and Philosophy Before and After Marx*. New York: Routledge.

———. 1995. "Ambiguous Universality." *differences: A Journal of Feminist Cultural Studies* 7 (1): 49–74.

———. 1996. "Is European Citizenship Possible?" *Public Culture* 8 (2): 355–76.

———. 2006. "Constructions and Deconstructions of the Universal." *Critical Horizons: A Journal of Philosophy and Social Theory* 7 (1): 21–43.

———. 2007. "On Universalism: In Debate with Alain Badiou" (opening statement). Koehn Endowed Event in Critical Theory. University of California, Irvine, CA. Feb. 2. English version revised by Mary O'Neill. Accessed March 25, 2013. http://eipcp.net /transversal/0607/balibar/en.

Balibar, Étienne, and Immanuel Wallerstein. 1992. *Race, Nation, Class: Ambiguous Identities*. New York: Verso.

Barnett, Michael. 2002. *Eyewitness to a Genocide: The United Nations and Rwanda*. Ithaca, NY: Cornell University Press.

Barnett, Michael, and Thomas Weiss. 2008. *Humanitarianism in Question: Politics, Power, Ethics*. Ithaca, NY: Cornell University Press.

Barthes, Roland. (1957) 2013. *Mythologies*. Trans. Richard Howard. New York: Hill and Wang.

———. 2005. *The Neutral*. Lecture course at the Collège de France, 1977–1978. Trans. Rosalind Krauss and Denis Hollier. New York: Columbia University Press.

Bataille, Georges. 2000. *A Critical Introduction*. Ed. Benjamin Noys. London: Pluto Press.

Beauvois, Xavier, dir. 2010. *Des Hommes et des dieux*. Film. France: Mars Distribution.

Becker, Gary. 1981. *A Treatise on the Family*. Cambridge, MA: Harvard University Press.

Beckett, Samuel. 1966. *Imagination Dead Imagine*. London: Calder Publications.

Bellal, Annyssa, Giles Giacca, and Stuart Casey-Maslen. 2011. "International Law and Armed Non-state Actors in Afghanistan." *International Review of the Red Cross* 93 (881): 47–79.

Belting, Hans. 1994. *Likeness and Presence: A History of the Image before the Era of Art*. Chicago: University of Chicago Press.

Benedek, Elissa. 1990. "Response to the Presidential Address: Our Children, Our Future." *American Journal of Psychiatry* 147 (9): 1120–25.

Benjamin, Walter. 1999a. "Old Toys." In *Walter Benjamin: Selected Writings*, Vol. 2, 1927–1934, ed. Michael Jennings, Howard Eiland, and Gary Smith, 98–102. Cambridge, MA: Belknap Press of Harvard University Press.

———. 1999b. "Toys and Play: Marginal Notes on a Monumental Work." In *Walter Benjamin: Selected Writings*, Vol. 2, 1927–1934, ed. Michael Jennings, Howard Eiland, and Gary Smith, 117–21. Cambridge, MA: Belknap Press of Harvard University Press.

Benthall, Jeremy. 2010. "Islamic Humanitarianism in Adversarial Context." In *Forces of Compassion: Humanitarianism between Ethics and Politics*, ed. Erica Bornstein and Peter Redfield, 99–121. Santa Fe: School for Advanced Research Press.

Berggren, Henrik, and Lars Trägårdh. 2006. *Är svensken människa? Gemenskap och oberoende i det moderna Sverige*. Stockholm: Nordstedt.

Bergman, Carol, ed. 2003. *Another Day in Paradise: International Humanitarian Workers Tell Their Stories*. Maryknoll, NY: Orbis Books.

Berlant, Lauren, ed. 2004. *Compassion: The Culture and Politics of an Emotion*. New York: Routledge.

———. 2011. *Cruel Optimism*. Durham, NC: Duke University Press.

Berliner, Paul. 1994. *Thinking in Jazz: The Infinite Art of Improvisation*. Chicago: University of Chicago Press.

Berman, Marshall. 1993. "Children of the Future." *Dissent* 40 (2): 221–25.

Best, Joel. 1990. *Threatened Children: Rhetoric and Concern About Child-Victims*. Chicago: University of Chicago Press.

Bhabha, Homi. 1990. *Nation and Narration*. New York: Routledge.

Biehl, João. 2005. *Vita: Life in a Zone of Social Abandonment*. Berkeley: University of California Press.

Bierens de Haan, Barthold. 1997. "Providing Support for Red Cross Volunteers and Other Humanitarian Workers Following a Security Incident or a Disaster." Report number 318. Geneva: ICRC. Accessed July 7, 2011. http://www.icrc.org/eng/resources/documents/misc/57jnph.htm.

Bishop, Claire. 2012. *Artificial Hells: Participatory Art and the Politics of Spectatorship*. New York: Verso.

Björkbacka, Hannu. 2011. "Jumalista ja ihmisistä. Movie Review." Accessed August 11, 2012. http://www.dvdopas.fi/index.php?udpview=showreview&rid=18942523284e71 1853cb70f8.21305419.

Björkman, Irina. 2010. "Auttaminen tuo onnea." ET 15: 11–14.

Blake, William. (ca. 1826) 1992. *Songs of Innocence and Songs of Experience*. New York: Dover.

Blanchot, Maurice. 1993. *The Infinite Conversation*. Trans. Susan Hanson. Minneapolis: University of Minnesota Press.

Bloch, Ernst. 1986. *The Principle of Hope*. 3 vols. Cambridge, MA: MIT Press.

Boltanski, Luc. 1993. *Distant Suffering: Morality, Media, and Politics*. Cambridge: Cambridge University Press.

Bornstein, Erica. 2001. "Child Sponsorship, Evangelism, and Belonging in the Work of World Vision." *American Ethnologist* 28 (3): 595–622.

———. 2003. *The Spirit of Development: Protestant NGOs, Morality, and Economics in Zimbabwe*. New York: Routledge.

―――. 2012. *Disquieting Gifts: Humanitarianism in New Delhi*. Stanford: Stanford University Press.

Bornstein, Erica, and Peter Redfield, eds. 2010. *The Forces of Compassion: Humanitarianism between Ethics and Politics*. Santa Fe: School for Advanced Research Press.

Bortolotti, Dan. 2004. *Hope in Hell: Inside the World of Doctors Without Borders*. Buffalo: Firefly Books.

Bottici, Chiara. 2011. "From Imagination to the Imaginary and Beyond: Towards a Theory of Imaginal Politics." In *The Politics of Imagination*, ed. Chiari Bottici and Benoît Challand, 16–37. New York: Birkbeck Law Press.

Bottici, Chiara, and Benoît Challand, eds. 2011a. "Introduction." In *The Politics of Imagination*, ed. Chiari Bottici and Benoît Challand, 1–15. New York: Birkbeck Law Press.

―――. 2011b. *The Politics of Imagination*. New York: Birkbeck Law Press.

Bourdieu, Pierre. 1977. *Outline of a Theory of Practice*. Trans. Richard Nice. Cambridge: Cambridge University Press.

―――. 1990. *The Logic of Practice*. Trans. Richard Nice. Stanford: Stanford University Press.

―――. 2000. *Pascalian Meditations*. Trans. Richard Nice. Stanford: Stanford University Press.

Bourriaud, Nicolas. 1998. *Relational Aesthetics*. Trans. Simon Pleasance and Fronza Woods with Mathieu Copeland. Dijon: Les Presses du Réel.

Boutros-Ghali, Boutros. 1993. "Address by the Secretary-General of the United Nations at the Opening of the World Conference on Human Rights." Vienna, June 14. United Nations, Office of the High Commission for Human Rights. http://www.ohchr.org/EN/NewsEvents/Pages/DisplayNews.aspx?NewsID=7906&LangID=E.

Boyden, Jo. 1990. "Childhood and the Policymakers: A Comparative Perspective on the Globalization of Childhood." In *Constructing and Reconstructing Childhood*, ed. Allison James and Alan Prout, 187–210. London: Falmer.

Boyden, Jo, and Joanna de Berry, eds. 2005. *Children and Youth on the Frontline: Ethnography, Armed Conflict and Displacement*. New York: Berghahn.

Bradshaw, Peter. 2010. "Of Gods and Men—Review." December 2. Accessed August 3, 2013. http://www.guardian.co.uk/film/2010/dec/02/of-gods-and-men-review.

Brann, Eva. 1991. *The World of the Imagination: Sum and Substance*. Lanham: Rowman and Littlefield.

Breed, Allen. 1990. "America's Future: The Necessity of Investing in Children." *Corrections Today* 52 (1): 68–72.

Brown, Louise. 2003. "Africa 'Adopts' Lonely European Adults." *Deutsche Welle*, August 3. Accessed July 24, 2014. http://www.dw.de/africa-adopts-lonely-european-adults/a-938260.

Bugnion, François. 1997. "17 December 1996: Six ICRC Delegates Assassinated in Chechnya." *International Review of the Red Cross* 37 (317): 140–42.

Burman, Erica. 1994. "Innocents Abroad: Western Fantasies of Childhood and the Iconography of Emergencies." *Disasters* 18 (3): 238–53.

Burnett, John. 2005. *Where Soldiers Fear to Tread: A Relief Worker's Tale of Survival*. New York: Bantam Books.

Butler, Judith. 1993. *Bodies That Matter: On the Discursive Limits of "Sex."* New York: Routledge.

———. 1997. *Excitable Speech: A Politics of the Performative.* New York: Routledge.

———. 2004. *Precarious Life: The Powers of Mourning and Violence.* New York: Verso.

Caldeira, Teresa P. R. 1996. "Fortified Enclaves: The New Urban Segregation." *Public Culture* 8 (2): 303–28.

Calhoun, Craig. 2002. "Imagining Solidarity: Cosmopolitanism, Patriotism, and the Public Sphere." *Public Culture* 14 (1): 147–71.

———. 2008. "The Imperative to Reduce Suffering: Charity, Progress, and Emergencies in the Field of Humanitarian Action." In *Humanitarianism in Question: Politics, Power, Ethics,* ed. Michael Barnett and Thomas Weiss, 73–97. Ithaca, NY: Cornell University Press.

———. 2010. "The Idea of Emergency: Humanitarian Action and Global (Dis)Order." In *Contemporary States of Emergency: The Politics of Military and Humanitarian Interventions,* ed. Didier Fassin and Mariella Pandolfi, 29–58. New York: Zone Books.

Cameron, Elizabeth. 1996. *Isn't S/he a Doll? Play and Ritual in African Sculpture.* Los Angeles: University of California at Los Angeles Fowler Museum of Cultural History.

Campobasso, Carlo, Rosa Falamingo, Ignazio Grattagliano, and Francesco Vinci. 2009. "The Mummified Corpse in a Domestic Setting." *American Journal of Forensic Medicine and Pathology* 30 (3): 307–10.

Canetti, Elias. (1960) 1984. *Crowds and Power.* New York: Farrar, Straus & Giroux.

Carr, Edward Hallett. 2001. *The Twenty Years' Crisis, 1919–1939: An Introduction to the Study of International Relations.* London: Harper Perennial.

Castells, Manuel. 1977. *The Urban Question: A Marxist Approach.* Cambridge, MA: MIT Press.

Castoriadis, Cornelius. 1997. *The Castoriadis Reader.* Ed. and trans. David Ames Curtis. Malden, MA: Blackwell.

Cerwonka, Allaine, and Liisa Malkki. 2007. *Improvising Theory: Process and Temporality in Ethnographic Fieldwork.* Chicago: University of Chicago Press.

Chan, Stephanie. 1990. "Ambassadors to the Future." *Journal of Nutrition and Education* 22 (5): 240.

Children's Express. 1993. *Voices from the Future: Our Children Tell Us About Violence in America.* Ed. Susan Goodwillie. New York: Crown.

Chomsky, Noam. 1999. *The Umbrella of US Power: The Universal Declaration of Human Rights and the Contradictions of US Policy.* Open Media Pamphlet Series 9. New York: Seven Stories.

Christensen, Terje, and Jon B. Reitan. 1992. "Radiation Risks: Which Types of Risks Are of Significance to Our Children?" In *Children at Risk: Selected Papers,* ed. Karin Ekberg and Per Egil Mjaavatn, 71–78. Trondheim: The Norwegian Centre for Child Research.

Cirtautas, K. C. 1963. *The Refugee.* New York: Citadel Press.

Clerc, Louis. 2011. "The Hottest Places in Hell: Finnish and Nordic Neutrality from the Perspective of French Foreign Policy, 1900–1940." In *Caught in the Middle: Neutrals, Neutrality, and the First World War,* ed. Johan Den Hertog and Samuel Kruizinga, 139–53. Amsterdam: Aksant Academic Publishers.

Coerr, Eleanor. 1977. *Sadako and the Thousand Paper Cranes*. New York: Dell.

Coetzee, J. M. 2001. *The Lives of Animals*. Princeton, NJ: Princeton University Press.

———. 2003. *Elizabeth Costello*. New York: Penguin.

Cohn, Ilene. 1993. *Child Soldiers: The Role of Children in Armed Conflict*. Oxford: Oxford University Press.

Coleman, David. 2009. "Population Ageing: An Unavoidable Future." In *The Welfare State Reader*, ed. Christopher Pierson and Francis Castles, 298–308. Cambridge, MA: Polity Press.

Coleman, Joseph. 2005. "1945 Tokyo Firebombing Left Legacy of Terror, Pain." Associated Press, March 10. Accessed February 6, 2014. http:/www.commondreams.org/headlines05/0310-08.htm.

Coles, Robert. 1986. *The Political Life of Children*. Boston: Atlantic Monthly Press.

Comaroff, Jean, and John L. Comaroff. 1992. "Home-Made Hegemony: Modernity, Domesticity, and Colonialism in South Africa." In *African Encounters with Domesticity*, ed. Karen Tranberg Hansen, 37–74. New Brunswick, NJ: Rutgers University Press.

———. 1999. "Occult Economies and the Violence of Abstraction." *American Ethnologist* 26 (2): 279–303.

Comaroff, John, and Jean Comaroff. 1992. *Ethnography and the Historical Imagination*. Boulder, CO: Westview Press.

Confucius. 2011. *Getting to Know Confucius: A New Translation of the Analects*. Trans. Lin Wusun. Beijing: Foreign Languages Press.

Conrad, John. 1990. "The Future Is Almost Here." *Federal Probation* 54 (1): 62–64.

Coomaraswamy, Ananda. (1946) 2007. *Figures of Speech or Figures of Thought? The Traditional View of Art*. Ed. William Wroth. Bloomington, IN: World Wisdom Press.

Cooper, Frederick, ed. 1983. *Struggle for the City: Migrant Labor, Capital, and the State in Urban Africa*. Beverly Hills: Sage Publications.

Coveney, Peter. 1957. *Poor Monkey: The Child in Literature*. London: Rockcliff.

Coyne, Kelly, and Eric Knutzen. 2008. *The Urban Homestead: Your Guide to Self-Sufficient Living in the Heart of the City*. Port Townsend, WA: Process Media.

Crapanzano, Vincent. 2004. *Imaginative Horizons: An Essay in Literary-Philosophical Anthropology*. Chicago: University of Chicago Press.

Csikszentmihalyi, Mihaly. 1991. *Flow: The Psychology of Optimal Experience*. New York: Harper and Row.

Cunningham, Jennifer, and Adam Edelman. 2012. "Comfort Dogs Help Ease Pain of Mourning Newtown Community." *New York Daily News*, December 17. Accessed July 12, 2013. http://www.nydailynews.com/news/national/comfort-dogs-helping-ease-pain-sandy-hook-tragedy-article-1.1222295.

Da Costa, Peter. 1993. "Securing the Future." *Africa Report* 38 (1): 47–50.

Dangarembga, Tsitsi. 2004. *Nervous Conditions*. New York: Seal Press.

Das, Veena. 1989. "Voices of Children." *Daedalus* 118 (4): 263–94.

De Boeck, Filip. 2004. "On Being *Shege* in Kinshasa: Children, the Occult, and the Street." In *Reinventing Order in the Congo*, ed. Theodore Trefon, 155–73. London: Zed Books.

Deleuze, Gilles. (1962) 1983. *Nietzsche and Philosophy*. Trans. Hugh Tomlinson. New York: Columbia University Press.

———. 1984. *Kant's Critical Philosophy: The Doctrine of the Faculties*. Trans. Hugh Tomlinson and Barbara Habberjam. London: Athlone.

———. 1997. *Essays Clinical and Critical*. Minneapolis: University of Minnesota Press.

DeLillo, Don. 2002. *The Body Artist: A Novel*. New York: Scribner.

———. 2010. *Point Omega*. New York: Scribner.

Delvaux, Denise. 2005. "The Politics of Humanitarian Organizations: Neutrality and Solidarity, the Case of the ICRC and MSF during the 1994 Rwandan Genocide." Master's thesis, Rhodes University, Grahamstown, South Africa.

Derrida, Jacques. 1994. *Given Time*. Vol. 1, *Counterfeit Money*. Trans. Peggy Kamuf. Chicago: University of Chicago Press.

———. 1998. *Of Grammatology*. Trans. Gayatri Chakravorty Spivak. Baltimore: Johns Hopkins University Press.

Devji, Faisal. 2008. *The Terrorist in Search of Humanity: Militant Islam and Global Politics*. New York: Columbia University Press.

DeVries, Dawn. 2001. "'Be Converted and Become as Little Children': Friedrich Schleiermacher on the Religious Significance of Childhood." In *The Child in Christian Thought*, ed. Marcia Bunge, 329–49. Grand Rapids, MI: William B. Eerdmans.

de Waal, Alex. 1997. *Famine Crimes: Politics and the Disaster Relief Industry in Africa*. Oxford: James Curry.

———. 2010. "Emancipatory Imperium? Power and Principle in the Humanitarian International." In *Contemporary States of Emergency: The Politics of Military and Humanitarian Interventions*, ed. Didier Fassin and Mariella Pandolfi, 295–316. New York: Zone Books.

Donini, Antonio. 2011. "Between a Rock and a Hard Place: Integration or Independence of Humanitarian Action?" *International Review of the Red Cross* 98 (881): 141–57.

Dormer, Peter, ed. 1997. *The Culture of Craft*. Manchester: University of Manchester Press.

Douglas, Mary. 2002. *Purity and Danger: An Analysis of Concepts of Pollution and Taboo*. New York: Routledge.

Du Bois, Cora. 1980. "Some Anthropological Hindsights." *Annual Review of Anthropology* 9: 1–13.

duBois, Page. 1991. *Torture and Truth*. New York: Routledge.

Duffield, Mark. 2001. *Global Governance and the New Wars: The Merging of Development and Security*. New York: Palgrave.

Durell, Ann, and Marilyn Sachs, eds. 1990. *The Big Book for Peace*. New York: Dutton Children's Books.

Durkheim, Émile. (1912) 1995. *The Elementary Forms of Religious Life*. New York: Free Press.

———. (1957) 2005. *Professional Ethics and Civic Morals*. 2nd ed. New York: Routledge.

Dutton, Edward. 2010. "Here the Status Symbols Clash: Social Status and Status Expression in Finnish Homes." *Suomen Antropologi: Journal of the Finnish Anthropological Society* 35 (1): 5–22.

Dyregrov, Atle. 1997. "The Process in Psychological Debriefings." *Journal of Traumatic Stress* 10 (4): 589–605.

Dyregrov, Atle, Leila Gupta, and Eugenie Mukanoheli. 2000. "Trauma Exposure and Psychological Reactions to Genocide among Rwandan Children." *Journal of Traumatic Stress* 13 (1): 3–21.

Eaton-Robb, Pat. 2013. "Cards, Gifts Sent to Newtown after Rampage Saved." Associated Press, December 26, 2013. Accessed February 11, 2014. http://bigstory.ap.org/article/cards-gifts-sent-newtown-after-rampage-saved.

Eide, Elisabeth, and Kaarina Nikunen. 2010. *Media in Motion: Cultural Complexity and Migration in the Nordic Region.* Surrey: Ashgate.

Einola-Head, Outi. 2007. *Suomen Punainen Risti Kantaa Huolta Avun Puolueettomuudesta.* Ulkoasiainministeriö: Kehitysviestintä.

El Said, Maria, and Sanna Patja. 2011. "Vapaaehtoisten roolin muotoutuminen Punaisen Ristin ystävätoiminnassa." Master's thesis, University of Jyväskylä, Jyväskylä, Finland.

Elshtain, Jean Bethke. 1994. "Political Children." *Criterion* 33: 2–15.

Engell, James. 1981. *The Creative Imagination: Enlightenment to Romanticism.* Cambridge, MA: Harvard University Press.

Englund, Harri. 2005. "Universal Africa." CODESRIA *Bulletin* 3–4: 11.

———. 2006. *Prisoners of Freedom: Human Rights and the African Poor.* Berkeley: University of California Press.

———. 2011. "The Anthropologist and His Poor." In *Forces of Compassion: Humanitarianism between Ethics and Politics,* ed. Erica Bornstein and Peter Redfield, 71–93. Santa Fe: School for Advanced Research Press.

Evans, Dylan. 1996. *An Introductory Dictionary of Lacanian Psychoanalysis.* New York: Routledge.

Evans, Jessica, and Stuart Hall, eds. 2007. *Visual Culture: The Reader.* Thousand Oaks, CA: Sage Publications, in association with the Open University.

Exley, Richard, and Helen Exley, eds. 1985. *My World/Peace: Thoughts and Illustrations from the Children of All Nations.* Lincolnwood, IL: Passport Books. Also published as *Dear World: "How I'd Put the World Right"—By the Children of over 50 Nations* (New York: Methuen, 1978).

Fabian, Johannes. (1983) 2002. *Time and the Other: How Anthropology Makes Its Object.* New York: Columbia University Press.

Fanon, Frantz. 2008. *Black Skin, White Masks.* New York: Grove Press.

Fassin, Didier. 2005. "Compassion and Repression: The Moral Economy of Immigration Policies in France." *Cultural Anthropology* 20 (3): 362–87.

———. 2006. "L'humanitaire contre l'état, tout contre." *Vacarme* 34: 15–19.

———. 2010a. "Heart of Humaneness: The Moral Economy of Humanitarian Action." In *Contemporary States of Emergency: The Politics of Military and Humanitarian Interventions,* ed. Didier Fassin and Mariella Pandolfi, 269–94. New York: Zone Books.

———. 2010b. "Inequality of Lives, Hierarchies of Humanity: Moral Commitments and Ethical Dilemmas of Humanitarianism." In *In the Name of Humanity: The Government of Threat and Care*, ed. Ilana Feldman and Miriam Ticktin, 238–355. Durham, NC: Duke University Press.

———. 2011. *Humanitarian Reason: A Moral History of the Present*. Berkeley: University of California Press.

———. 2012. *Humanitarian Reason: A Moral History of the Present*. Berkeley: University of California Press.

Fassin, Didier, and Mariella Pandolfi, eds. 2010. *Contemporary States of Emergency: The Politics of Military and Humanitarian Interventions*. New York: Zone Books.

Fassin, Didier, and Richard Rechtman. 2009. *The Empire of Trauma: An Inquiry into the Condition of Victimhood*. Trans. Rachel Gomme. Princeton, NJ: Princeton University Press.

Feldman, Ilana. 2007. "The Quaker Way: Ethical Labor and Humanitarian Relief." *American Ethnologist* 34 (4): 689–705.

———. 2008. *Governing Gaza: Bureaucracy, Authority, and the Work of Rule, 1917–1967*. Durham, NC: Duke University Press.

Feldman, Ilana, and Miriam Ticktin. 2010a. "Government and Humanity." In *In the Name of Humanity: The Government of Threat and Care*, ed. Ilana Feldman and Miriam Ticktin, 1–26. Durham, NC: Duke University Press.

———, eds. 2010b. *In the Name of Humanity: The Government of Threat and Care*. Durham, NC: Duke University Press.

Ferguson, James. 1994. *The Anti-Politics Machine: "Development," Depoliticization, and Bureaucratic Power in Lesotho*. Minneapolis: University of Minnesota Press.

———. 2006. *Global Shadows: Africa in the Neoliberal World Order*. Durham, NC: Duke University Press.

Fermé, Marianne. n.d. "Red Cross/Rebel Cross: Rumors, Visibility, and Secrecy." Unpublished manuscript.

Festa, Lynn. 2010. "Humanity without Feathers." *Humanity* 1 (1): 3–37.

Fichte, Johann-Gottlieb. 1845. *Méthode pour arriver à la vie bienheureuse*. Trans. M. Bouillier. Paris: Ladrange.

Field, Tiffany. 2001. *Touch*. Cambridge, MA: MIT Press.

Filipovic, Zlata. 1994. *Zlata's Diary: A Child's Life in Sarajevo*. New York: Viking.

Fineberg, Jonathan. 1997. *The Innocent Eye: Children's Art and the Modern Artist*. Princeton, NJ: Princeton University Press.

Fink, Sheri. 2003. *War Hospital: A True Story of Surgery and Survival*. New York: Perseus.

Finnström, Sverker. 2008. *Living with Bad Surroundings: War, History, and Everyday Moments in Northern Uganda*. Durham, NC: Duke University Press.

Fisher, Philip. 2002. *The Vehement Passions*. Princeton, NJ: Princeton University Press.

Forsblom, Arja. 1998. *Yksinäisyys ja elämän autius ahdistavat suomalaisia*. Helsinki: Sosiaali- ja terveysministeriö.

Forsythe, David. 2005. *The Humanitarians: The International Committee of the Red Cross*. Cambridge: Cambridge University Press.

———. 2009. "Contemporary Humanitarianism: The Global and the Local." In *Human-*

itarianism and Suffering: The Mobilization of Empathy, ed. Richard Ashby Wilson and Richard Brown, 58–88. Cambridge: Cambridge University Press.

Foster, Hal. 1996. *The Return of the Real: The Avant-Garde at the End of the Century.* Cambridge, MA: MIT Press.

Foster, Robert. 1991. "Making National Cultures in the Global Ecumene." *Annual Review of Anthropology* 20: 253–60.

Foucault, Michel. (1954) 1986. "Dream, Imagination and Existence: An Introduction to Ludwig Binswanger's 'Dream and Existence.'" Reprinted in *Dream and Existence*, ed. Keith Hoeller (Atlantic Highlands, NJ: Humanities Press, 1986), 31–78.

———. 1978. *History of Sexuality: An Introduction.* Vol. 1 of *The History of Sexuality.* New York: Random House.

———. 1986. *The Care of the Self.* Vol. 3 of *The History of Sexuality.* New York: Pantheon.

———. 1988. "Practicing Criticism." Trans. A. Sheridan et al. In *Politics, Philosophy, Culture: Interviews and Other Writings, 1977–1984*, ed. L.D. Kritzman, 152–58. New York: Routledge.

———. 1991. *Remarks on Marx: Conversations with Duccio Trombadori.* Trans. R. James Goldstein and James Cascaito. New York: Semiotext(e).

———.2000. *Power.* Vol. 3 of *The Essential Works of Foucault, 1954–1984.* Ed. James Faubion. New York: New Press.

———. 2003. *Society Must Be Defended: Lectures at the Collège de France, 1975–1976.* Trans. David Macey. New York: Picador.

Frank, Isabelle. 2000. *The Theory of Decorative Art: An Anthology of European and American Writings, 1750–1940.* New Haven, CT: Yale University Press.

Frankel, Bernard. 1986. "Affective Neutrality." *Journal of the American Medical Association* 256 (4): 515.

Frankenberg, Ruth. 1993. *White Women, Race Matters: The Social Construction of Whiteness.* Minneapolis: University of Minnesota Press.

Frankenhaeuser, Marianne. 1999. *Kvinnligt, Manligt, Stressigt.* Stockholm: Brombergsbokförlag AB.

Fustel de Coulanges, Numa Denis. 1980. *The Ancient City.* Baltimore: Johns Hopkins University Press.

Garcia, Angela. 2010a. *The Pastoral Clinic: Addiction and Dispossession along the Rio Grande.* Berkeley: University of California Press.

———. 2010b. "Reading *Righteous Dopefiend* with My Mother." *Anthropology Now* 2 (3): 31–36.

Garrett, J. n.d. "Kant's Model of the Mind: The Concept of the Imagination before Kant." Accessed March 4, 2014. http://www.calstatela.edu/faculty/jgarrett/560/notes-kant.pdf.

Garrison, Jennifer, and Andrew Tubesing. 1995. *A Million Visions of Peace: Wisdom from the Friends of Old Turtle.* Duluth, MN: Pfeifer-Hamilton.

Gaudin, Colette. 2005. "Introduction." In *On Poetic Imagination and Reverie*, by Gaston Bachelard, xxxi–lix. Putnam, CT: Spring Publications.

Geertz, Clifford. 2000. *Available Light: Anthropological Reflections on Philosophical Topics.* Princeton, NJ: Princeton University Press.

Geiss, Robin, and Michael Siegrist. 2011. "Has the Armed Conflict in Afghanistan Affected the Rules on the Conduct of Hostilities?" *International Review of the Red Cross* 93 (881): 11–46.

Gell, Alfred. 1988. "Technology and Magic." *Anthropology Today* 4 (2): 6–9.

———. 1998. *Art and Agency: An Anthropological Theory*. Oxford: Clarendon.

Genosko, Gary. 2005. "Natures and Cultures of Cuteness." *Invisible Culture: An Electronic Journal for Visual Culture* 9. Accessed March 16, 2009. http://www.rochester.edu/in _visible_culture/Issue_9/genosko.html.

Gilliam, Kelly. 2007. "Knitting and Crochet for Charity." Accessed February 17, 2014. http://knittingcrochet.suite101.com/article.cfm/knitting_and_crochet_for_charity.

Gilroy, Paul. 1991. *"There Ain't No Black in the Union Jack": The Cultural Politics of Race and Nation*. Chicago: University of Chicago Press.

———. 2000. *Against Race: Imagining Political Culture beyond the Color Line*. Cambridge, MA: Belknap Press of Harvard University Press.

Gleason, Tracy. 2007. "Murray: The Stuffed Bunny." In *Evocative Objects: Things We Think With*, ed. Sherry Turkle, 171–77. Cambridge, MA: MIT Press.

Goldberg, Arnold. 2007. *Moral Stealth: How "Correct Behavior" Insinuates Itself into Psychotherapeutic Practice*. Chicago: University of Chicago Press.

Goldberg, David Theo, ed. 1990. *The Anatomy of Racism*. Minneapolis: University of Minnesota Press.

Goodwin-Gill, Guy, and Ilene Cohn. 1995. *Child Soldiers: The Role of Children in Armed Conflict*. Oxford: Clarendon.

Gottlieb, Alma. 2004. *The Afterlife Is Where We Come From: The Culture of Infancy in West Africa*. Chicago: University of Chicago Press.

Gould, Stephen Jay. 1979. "This View of Life: Mickey Mouse Meets Konrad Lorenz." *Natural History* 88 (5): 30, 32, 34, 36.

———. 1980. *The Panda's Thumb: More Reflections on Natural History*. Harmondsworth, UK: Penguin.

Green, Linda. 1994. "Fear as a Way of Life." *Cultural Anthropology* 9 (2): 227–56.

Grewal, Inderpal. 1996. *Home and Harem: Nation, Gender, Empire, and the Cultures of Travel*. Durham, NC: Duke University Press.

Grönvall, Ursula. 2005. "Sairaanhoitajat Kaakkois-Aasian katastrofialueella: 'Jos yhtäkin on auttanut, se on ollut sen arvoist.'" *Sairaanhoitaja* 2: 1–2. Accessed March 24, 2013. https://www.sairaanhoitajaliitto.fi/ammatilliset_urapalvelut/julkaisut/sairaanhoitaja -lehti/2_2005/ajankohtaiskirjoitus/sairaanhoitajat_kaakkois-aasiaan/.

Gupta, Akhil. 1992. "The Song of the Non-Aligned World: Transnational Identities and the Reinscription of Space in Late Capitalism." *Cultural Anthropology* 7 (1): 63–79.

———. 2001. "Reliving Childhood? The Temporality of Childhood and Narratives of Reincarnation." *Ethnos* 67 (1): 1–23.

Gupta, Akhil, and James Ferguson, eds. 1997. *Culture, Power, Place: Explorations in Critical Anthropology*. Durham, NC: Duke University Press.

Gutmann, Amy. 1999. "Introduction." In *The Lives of Animals*, by J. M. Coetzee, 3–11. Princeton, NJ: Princeton University Press.

Gutting, Gary, ed. 2007. *The Cambridge Companion to Foucault*. Cambridge: Cambridge University Press.

Hafferty, Fred. 2006. "Measuring Professionalism: A Commentary." In *Measuring Medical Professionalism*, ed. David Stern, 281–306. New York: Oxford University Press.

Hall, Stuart. 1978. *Policing the Crisis*. New York: Palgrave Macmillan.

———. 1985. "Signification, Representation, Ideology: Althusser and the Post-Structuralist Debates." *Critical Studies in Mass Communication* 2 (2): 91–114.

Halonen, Kaisa. 2008. "Kaiken keskellä yksin: Yksinäisyys on ihmisen osa, mutta joillekin sitä on langennut kohtuuttoman paljon." *Vantaan Lauri*. December 18, 2008. Accessed January 17, 2015. http://www.vantaanlauri.fi/arkisto/2008-12-18/kaiken _keskella_yksin.

Hamanaka, Sheila. 1995. *Peace Crane*. New York: Harper Collins.

Hammond, Laura. 2008. "The Power of Holding Humanitarianism Hostage and the Myth of Protective Principles." In *Humanitarianism in Question: Politics, Power, Ethics*, ed. Michael Barnett and Thomas Weiss, 172–95. Ithaca, NY: Cornell University Press.

Hancock, Graham. 1989. *The Lords of Poverty: The Power, Prestige, and Corruption of the International Aid Business*. New York: Atlantic Monthly Press.

Hannerz, Ulf. 1987. "The World in Creolization." *Africa* 57 (4): 546–59.

———. 1989. "Notes on the Global Ecumene." *Public Culture* 1 (2): 66–75.

Hansen, Thomas Blom. 2009. *Cool Passion: The Political Theology of Conviction*. Amsterdam: Vossiuspers Uva.

Haraway, Donna. 1990. *Primate Visions: Gender, Race, and Nature in the World of Modern Science*. New York: Routledge.

———. 2008. *When Species Meet*. Posthumanities. Minneapolis: University of Minnesota Press.

———. 2013. *Simians, Cyborgs, and Women: The Reinvention of Nature*. New York: Routledge.

Harkki, Anu. 2006. *Puikoissa!* Keuruu, Finland: Otava.

Härkönen, Riikka. 1999a. "Yhteisvastuu." Accessed September 28, 2001. http://www .yhteisvastuu.fi/index.php?fid=80.

———. 1999b. *Yhteisvastuun Ajankuvat*. Helsinki: Kirkkopalvelut.

Haskell, Thomas. 1985. "Capitalism and the Origins of the Humanitarian Sensibility (Parts I and II)." *American Historical Review* 90 (2): 339–61 and 90 (3): 547–66.

———. 1998. *Objectivity Is Not Neutrality: Explanatory Schemes in History*. Baltimore: Johns Hopkins University Press.

Haug, Hans. 1993. *Humanity for All: The Red Cross and Red Crescent Movement*. Henry Dunant Institute. Bern: Haupt.

———. n.d. *The Fundamental Principles of the International Red Cross and Red Crescent Movement*. Offprint from *Humanity for All: The Red Cross and Red Crescent Movement*. https:// www.icrc.org/eng/resources/documents/publication/p2116-03.htm.

Head, Bessie. 1990. *A Woman Alone: Autobiographical Writings*. London: Heinemann.

Heikkinen, Kaija. 1997. *Käsityöt naisten arjessa: Kulttuuriantropologinen tutkimus pohjoiskarjalaisten naisten käsityön tekemisestä*. Artefakta 4. Helsinki: Akatiimi Oy.

Heinänen, Seija. 2006. "Käsityö—Taide—Teollisuus: Näkemyksiä käsityöstä taideteollisuuteen 1900-luvun alun ammatti- ja aikakauslehdissä." Jyväskylä Studies in Humanities 52. Jyväskylä, Finland: University of Jyväskylä.

Heiskanen, Tarja, and Liisa Saaristo, eds. 2011. *Kaiken keskellä yksin: Yksinäisyyden syyt, seuraukset ja hallintakeinot*. Juva, Finland: PS-kustannus.

Hertog, Johan Den, and Samuel Kruizinga. 2011. *Caught in the Middle: Neutrals, Neutrality, and the First World War*. Amsterdam: Aksant Academic Publishers.

Herzfeld. 1993. *The Social Production of Indifference*. Chicago: University of Chicago Press.

Hietaniemi, Helena. 2007. "The Finnish Red Cross Secretary General: 'My Work Gives Me Happiness.'" *Kotiliesi*, May 10, 12–15.

Higonnet, Anne. 1998. *Pictures of Innocence: The History and Crisis of Ideal Childhood*. London: Thames and Hudson.

Hill, Leslie, ed. 1997. *Blanchot: Extreme Contemporary*. Warwick Studies in European History. New York: Routledge.

Hirschfeld, Lawrence. 2002. "Why Don't Anthropologists Like Children?" *American Anthropologist* 104 (2): 611–27.

Holopainen, Kimmo. 2011. "Yksinäisten asialla." *Avun Maailma* 2: 36–39.

Holston, James, and Arjun Appadurai. 1996. "Cities and Citizenship." *Public Culture* 8 (2): 187–204.

Huber, Gregory. 2007. *The Craft of Bureaucratic Neutrality: Interests and Influence in Governmental Regulation of Occupational Safety*. Cambridge: Cambridge University Press.

Hung, Shu, and Joseph Magliaro, eds. 2007. *By Hand: The Use of Craft in Contemporary Art*. New York: Princeton Architectural Press.

Hursti, Irene. 2002. *Ystävyyttä yli etnisten esteiden: Tutkimus SPR:n maahanmuuttajien ystävävälityksen ja neuvonnan kehittämisestä*. Diakonia-ammattikorkeakoulun julkaisuja B Raportteja 14. Helsinki: Diakonia-ammattikorkeakoulu.

Hutchinson, John. 1996. *Champions of Charity: War and the Rise of the Red Cross*. Boulder, CO: Westview Press.

Hytönen, Yki. 2002. *Ihminen ihmiselle: Suomen Punainen Risti 1877–2002*. Helsinki: Finnish Red Cross.

Hyvönen, Helena. 2012. "Punainen apu." *Minä/työ/ura* [no. N/A]: 14–15.

Ingold, Tim. 2013. *Making: Anthropology, Archaeology, Art and Architecture*. New York: Routledge.

International Committee of the Red Cross (ICRC). 1996. "The Fundamental Principles of the Red Cross and Red Crescent." Publication Ref. 0513. https://www.icrc.org/eng/resources/documents/publication/p0513.htm.

———. 2010. "Afghanistan: An Uncertain Future for Humanitarian Work." August 18, 2010. Interview with Reto Stocker. Accessed November 1, 2012. http://www.icrc.org/eng/resources/documents/interview/afghanistan-interview-180810.htm.

International Federation of the Red Cross (IFRC). 2011. "Brief Consensus on the Revision of the Pictet Commentary, Fundamental Principles Workshop." December 15–16. Statement developed from meeting attended by author.

Iriye, Akira. 1997. *Cultural Internationalism and World Order*. Baltimore: Johns Hopkins University Press.

Ivy, Marilyn. 1995. "Have You Seen Me? Recovering the Inner Child in Late Twentieth-Century America." In *Children and the Politics of Culture*, ed. Sharon Stephens, 79–104. Princeton, NJ: Princeton University Press.

Jaakkola, Elina. 2009. Photographer for "Pikku koti" advertisement. *Gloria*, no. 122, 42.

Jackson, Shannon. 2011. *Social Works: Performing Art, Supporting Publics*. New York: Routledge.

Jakobson, Max. 1968. *Finnish Neutrality: A Study of Finnish Foreign Policy since the Second World War*. New York: Praeger.

James, Allison. 2004. "Understanding Childhood from an Interdisciplinary Perspective: Problems and Potentials." In *Rethinking Childhood*, ed. Peter Pufall and Richard Unsworth, 25–37. New Brunswick, NJ: Rutgers University Press.

James, Allison, Chris Jenks, and Alan Prout, eds. 1998. *Theorizing Childhood*. Cambridge, MA: Polity Press.

James, Allison, and Alan Prout, eds. 1997. *Constructing and Reconstructing Childhood: Contemporary Issues in the Sociological Study of Childhood*. London: Falmer Press.

James, William. 1992. "Psychology: The Briefer Course." In *Writings, 1878–1899*, 1–443. New York: Library of America.

Järvi, Antti. 2007. "Nauru katosi suomalaisesta romaanista." *Helsingin Sanomat*, June 29, C1.

Jenkins, Janis. 1991. "The State Construction of Affect: Political Ethos and Mental Health among Salvadoran Refugees." *Culture, Medicine, Psychiatry* 15: 139–65.

Jenks, Chris. 1996. *Childhood*. New York: Routledge.

Jokinen, Kimmo, ed. 2005. *Yksinäisten sanat: Kirjoituksia omasta tilasta, erillisyydestä ja yksinolosta*. Nykykulttuurin Tutkimuskeskuksen Julkaisuja 84. Jyväskylä, Finland: Jyväskylän Yliopisto.

Jokinen, Kimmo, and Kimmo Saaristo. 2006. *Suomalainen Yhteiskunta*. Helsinki, Finland: Sanoma Pro.

Kairema, Mirkka. 2000. "75-vuotta täyttäneiden, yksinasuvien, kotihoitoa saavien vanhusten sosiaalinen verkosto." Päättötyö, Sosionomin (AMK) Koulutusohjelma. Diakonia-ammattikorkeakoulu, Alppikadun yksikkö, Helsinki.

Kallenautio, Jorma. 2005. *Suomi kylmän rauhan maailmassa: Suomen ulkopolitiikka Porkkalan palautuksesta 1955 Euroopan Unionin jäsenyyteen*. Helsinki: Suomalaisen Kirjallisuuden Seura.

Kangas, Minna, and Minna Keski-Heroja. 2000. "Ystävänä toimimisen onni ja raskaus: Tutkimus ystävän jaksamisesta." Vaasan ammattikorkeakoulu, Vaasa, Finland.

Kant, Immanuel. 2006. *Critique of the Power of Judgment*. Ed. Paul Guyer. Cambridge: Cambridge University Press.

———. 2008. *Critique of Judgement*. Ed. Nicholas Walker. New York: Oxford University Press.

Kauranen, Anja. 1993. *Ihon Aika*. Helsinki: Otava.

Kearney, Richard. 1991. *Poetics of Imagining: From Husserl to Lyotard*. London: Harper Collins Academic.

Kekkonen, Urho. 1970. *Neutrality: The Finnish Position*. London: Heinemann.

Kelley, Mike. 1991. *In the Image of Man*. Pittsburgh: Carnegie Museum of Art.

———. 2003. *Foul Perfection: Essays and Criticism*. Cambridge, MA: MIT Press.

Kent, George. 1991. "Our Children, Our Future." *Futures* 23 (1): 32–50.

Keskinen, Suvi. 2012. "Limits to Speech? The Racialized Politics of Gendered Violence in Denmark and Finland." *Journal of Intercultural Studies* 33 (3): 261–74.

Kester, Grant. 2004. *Conversation Pieces: Community and Communication in Modern Art*. Berkeley: University of California Press.

———. 2011. *The One and the Many: Contemporary Collaborative Art in a Global Context*. Durham, NC: Duke University Press.

Kirksey, Eben, and Stefan Helmreich. 2010. "The Emergence of Multispecies Ethnography." *Cultural Anthropology* 25 (4): 545–76.

Kjörup, Sören. 2010. "Kant, Art and Craft." Trans. Francesca Nichols. *Norwegian Crafts*, no. 4. Accessed August 7, 2013. http://www.norwegiancrafts.no/magazine/04-2010/kant-art-and-craft.

Kleinman, Arthur, and Joan Kleinman. 1996. "The Appeal of Experience; the Dismay of Images: Cultural Appropriates of Suffering in Our Times." *Daedalus* 125 (1): 1–23.

Kopytoff, Igor. 1986. "The Cultural Biography of Gifts: Commoditization as Process." In *The Social Life of Things: Commodities in Cultural Perspective*, ed. Arjun Appadurai, 64–91. Cambridge: Cambridge University Press.

Korbin, Jill. 2003. "Children, Childhoods and Violence." *Annual Review of Anthropology* 32: 431–46.

Korhonen, Johanna. 2012. "Kunnioitusvaje vie kaiken." *Helsingin Sanomat*, June 13, C1.

Korhonen, Keijo. 1999. *Sattumakorpraali: Korhonen Kekkosen komennuksessa*. Helsinki: Otava.

Kosek, Jake. 2010. "Ecologies of Empire." *Cultural Anthropology* 25 (4): 650–78.

Koskennurmi-Sivonen, Ritva, Annamari Raunio, and Marketta Luutonen. 2009. "Näkökulmia käsityön opetuksen tutkimukseen: Pirkko Anttila 80 vuotta." Anniversary Seminar, May 18. Puheenvuorojen tiivistelmät. Käyttäytymistieteellinen tiedekunta, Kotitalous- ja käsityötieteiden laitos, University of Helsinki, Helsinki.

Kotila, Laura. 2012. "Ompelemalla apua maailmalle: Siitä tulikin mekko!" *Avun maailma* 4: 20–21.

Krause, Elliott. 1996. *Death of the Guilds: Professions, States, and the Advance of Capitalism, 1930 to the Present*. New Haven, CT: Yale University Press.

Kriner, Stephanie. 2001. "President Bush Thanks Children at American Red Cross Headquarters." American Red Cross. Accessed July 4, 2004. http://www.redcross.org/news/ds/0109wtc/011017bush.html.

Kumpula, Kristiina. 2007. "SPR:n Pääsihteeri Kristiina Kumpula: 'Työni antaa minulle onnea.'" *Kodin Kuvalehti* 10 (October 5): 12–15.

———. 2008. "Vapaaehtoiset arvoyhteisönä." *Tiedepolitiikka* 4: 45–49.

———. 2010. "Auttaminen tuo onnea." *ET* 15: 10–14.

Kurz, Kathleen, and Cynthia Prather. 1995. *Improving the Quality of Life of Girls*. New York: United Nations Children's Fund (UNICEF); and Washington, DC: Association for Women in Development (AWID).

Kwon, Miwon. 2004. *One Place after Another: Site-Specific Art and Locational Identity.* Cambridge, MA: MIT Press.

Laaksonen, Pekka, and Sirkka-Liisa Mettomäki, eds. 1996. *Olkaamme siis suomalaisia.* Helsinki: Suomalaisen Kirjallisuuden Seura.

Lääperi, Pirjo. 2007. "Avustustyö ulkomailla tuo haasteita." *Sairaanhoitaja* 3: 1–2. Accessed March 24, 2013. http://www.sairaanhoitajaliitto.fi/ammatilliset_urapalvelut/julkaisut/sairaanhoitaja-lehti/3_2007/muut_artikkelit/avustustyo_ulkomailla_tuo_haaste/.

Laasanen, Juhani. 2011. *Vapaaehtoistyön kansantaloudelliset vaikutukset: Mannerheimin Lastensuojeluliitto, Suomen 4-H Liitto, Suomen Pelastusalan Keskusjärjestö.* Report 70. Helsinki: University of Helsinki and Ruralia Institute.

Lacan, Jacques. 1966. *Écrits.* Paris: Éditions du Seuil.

Laidlaw, James. 2000. "A Free Gift Makes No Friends." *Journal of the Royal Anthropological Institute* 6 (4): 617–34.

Laitalainen, Elina, Satu Helakorpi, and Antti Uutela. 2008. *Eläkeikäisen väestön terveyskäyttäytyminen ja terveys keväällä 2007 ja niiden muutokset 1993–2007.* Helsinki: Kansanterveyslaitoksen julkaisuja B14.

Laqueur, Thomas. 1989. "Bodies, Details, and the Humanitarian Narrative." In *The New Cultural History,* ed. Lynn Hunt, 176–204. Berkeley: University of California Press.

———. 2009. "Mourning, Pity, and the Work of Narrative in the Making of 'Humanity.'" In *Humanitarianism and Suffering: The Mobilization of Empathy,* ed. Richard Ashby Wilson and Richard Brown, 31–57. Cambridge: Cambridge University Press.

Laszlo, Ervin. 1992. "Children and the Future of Humanity." *World Futures* 41 (1–3): 49–53.

Latour, Bruno. 2004. *Politics of Nature: How to Bring the Sciences into Democracy.* Cambridge, MA: Harvard University Press.

———. 2005. *Reassembling the Social: An Introduction to Actor-Network Theory.* Oxford: Oxford University Press.

Lawrence, Elizabeth A. 1986. "In the Mick of Time: Reflections on Disney's Ageless Mouse." *Journal of Popular Culture* 20 (2): 65–72.

Leader, Nicholas. 2000. *The Politics of Principle: The Principles of Humanitarian Action in Practice.* London: Humanitarian Policy Group.

Le Carré, John. 2003. "Foreword." In *Another Day in Paradise: International Humanitarian Workers Tell Their Stories,* ed. Carol Bergman, 9–10. Maryknoll, NY: Orbis Books.

Lehtonen, Mikko, Olli Löytty, and Petri Ruuska, eds. 2004. *Suomi toisin sanoen.* Tampere: Vastapaino.

Leskinen, Tapio. 2011. "Muukalaisten auttaminen: Suomalaiset ja kehitysapu." In *Hyvien ihmisten maa: Auttaminen kilpailukyky-yhteiskunnassa,* ed. Anne Birgitta Pessi and Juho Saari, 91–120. A Tutkimuksia 31. Helsinki: Diakonia-ammattikorkeakoulun julkaisuja.

Levine, Faythe, and Cortney Heimerl. 2008. *Handmade Nation: The Rise of DIY, Art, Craft and Design.* New York: Princeton Architectural Press.

Lévi-Strauss, Claude. 1966. *The Savage Mind.* Trans. Rodney Needham. Chicago: University of Chicago Press.

————. 1971. *Totemism.* Trans. Rodney Needham. Boston: Beacon Press.

Leys, Ruth. 2011. "The Turn to Affect: A Critique." *Critical Inquiry* 37: 434–72.

Liikkanen, Mirja, Riitta Hanifi, and Ulla Hannula, eds. 2005. *Yksilöllisiä valintoja, kulttuurien pysyvyyttä: Vapaa-ajan muutokset 1981–2002.* Helsinki: Tilastokeskus.

Linna, Väinö. 2001. *Under the North Star.* Ed. Börje Vähämäki and Richard Impola. Trans. Richard Impola. 3 vols. Beaverton: Aspasia Books. First published in Finnish in 1959.

Lippard, Lucy. 2010. "Making Something from Nothing: Toward a Definition of Women's 'Hobby Art.'" In *The Craft Reader*, ed. Glenn Adamson, 483–90. New York: Berg.

Livingston, Julie. 2012. *Improvising Medicine: An African Oncology Ward in an Emerging Cancer Epidemic.* Durham, NC: Duke University Press.

Llewellyn, John. 2000. *The HypoCritical Imagination: Between Kant and Levinas.* New York: Routledge.

Löfgren, Orvar. 1999. *On Holiday: A History of Vacationing.* California Series in Critical Human Geography. Berkeley: University of California Press.

Loos, Adolf. (1910) 2000. "Ornament and Crime." Reprinted in *The Theory of Decorative Art: An Anthology of European and American Writings, 1750–1940*, ed. Isabelle Frank, trans. David Britt, 288–94. New Haven, CT: Yale University Press, 2000.

Lorenz, Konrad. 1981. *The Foundations of Ethology.* New York: Simon and Schuster.

Loyd, Anthony. 1999. *My War Gone By, I Miss It So.* New York: Penguin.

Luft, David S. 1994. "Introduction." In *Precision and Soul: Essays and Addresses*, ed. and trans. Burton Pike and David S. Luft, xv–xxviii. Chicago: University of Chicago Press.

Lutz, Catherine. 2001. *Homefront: A Military City and the American Twentieth Century.* Boston: Beacon.

Lyons, F. S. L. 1963. *Internationalism in Europe, 1815–1914.* Leiden: A. W. Sythoff.

MacGaffey, Wyatt, and Michael Harris. 1993. *Astonishment and Power.* Washington: Smithsonian Institution Press.

Machel, Graça. 2002. *The Impact of War on Children: A Review of Progress since the 1995 United Nations Report on the Impact of Armed Conflict on Children.* New York: United Nations.

MacIntyre, Alasdair. 1984. *After Virtue: A Study in Moral Theory.* Notre Dame: University of Notre Dame Press.

Mahmood, Saba. 2005. *Politics of Piety: The Islamic Revival and the Feminist Subject.* Princeton, NJ: Princeton University Press.

Mäkelä, Pia, Heli Mustonen, and Petri Huhtanen. 2009. "Suomalaisten alkoholinkäyttötapojen muutokset 2000-luvun alussa." *Yhteiskuntapolitiikka* 74 (3): 268–98.

Malinowski, Bronisław. (1935) 1978. *Coral Gardens and Their Magic.* Mineola, NY: Dover.

Malkki, Liisa. 1992. "National Geographic: The Rooting of Peoples and the Territorialization of National Identity Among Scholars and Refugees." *Cultural Anthropology* 7 (1): 24–44.

————. 1994. "Citizens of Humanity: Internationalism and the Imagined Community of Nations." *Diaspora* 3 (1): 41–68.

————. 1995a. *Purity and Exile: Violence, Memory, and National Cosmology among Hutu Refugees in Tanzania.* Chicago: University of Chicago Press.

————. 1995b. "Refugees and Exile: From Refugee Studies to the National Order of Things." *Annual Review of Anthropology* 24: 495–523.

————. 1996. "Speechless Emissaries: Refugees, Humanitarianism, and Dehistoricization." *Cultural Anthropology* 11 (3): 377–404.

————. 1997. "News and Culture: Transitory Phenomena and the Fieldwork Tradition." In *Anthropological Locations: Boundaries and Grounds of a Field Science*, ed. Akhil Gupta and James Ferguson, 86–101. Berkeley: University of California Press.

————. 1998. "Things to Come: Internationalism and Global Solidarities in the Late 1990s." *Public Culture* 10(2): 431–42.

————. 1999. "Forgotten Cosmopolitanisms: Movements for World Citizenship in the National Order of Things." *Working Papers in Local Governance and Democracy* 2: 137–43.

————. 2002a. "Die Anatomie der Feindschaft: Gewalt, Entmenschlichung, und rassistische Konstruktionen von Hutu und Tutsi." In *Auf den Spüren des Körpers in einer technogenen Welt*, ed. Barbara Duden and Dorothée Noeres, 103–26. Opladen, Germany: Leske + Budrich.

————. 2002b. "News from Nowhere: Mass Displacement and Globalized 'Problems of Organization.'" *Ethnography* 3 (3): 351–60.

————. 2003. "Beyond Cultural Fundamentalism and Evangelical Imperialism." In *Enjeux éthiques de la mondialisation: Actes du premier colloque national, parrainé par le Projet Ethique de l'Université de Sudbury, 3–5 octobre 2002*, ed. Melchior Mbonimpa and Paolo Biondi, 97–128. Sudbury, Canada: Les Editions Glopro.

————. 2008. "The Heart Monologues: Professionalism and Geographies of Affect in Red Cross Aid Work." Paper presented at the 2008 Annual Meetings of the American Anthropological Association on the panel "Affective Governmentality: Cultivating and Adjudicating Responsibility in the Configuration of the 'Self,'" organized by Tomas Matza, Ramah McKay, and Jocelyn Chua, San Francisco, CA.

————. 2010. "Children, Humanity, and the Infantilization of Peace." In *In the Name of Humanity: The Government of Threat and Care*, ed. Ilana Feldman and Miriam Ticktin, 58–85. Durham, NC: Duke University Press.

Malkki, Liisa, and Emily Martin. 2003. "Children and the Gendered Politics of Globalization: In Remembrance of Sharon Stephens." *American Ethnologist* 30 (2): 216–24.

Marinovich, Greg, and João Silva. 2000. *The Bang Bang Club: Snapshots from a Hidden War*. New York: Basic Books.

Markkanen, Tiina. 2009. "Kannatusta, vastustusta vai varauksellisuutta? Työvoimaviranomaisten suhtautuminen tukityöllistämiseen SPR:n Kontti-kierrätystavarataloissa." Master's thesis, University of Tampere, Tampere, Finland.

Marks, Shula. 1994. *Divided Sisterhood: Race, Class and Gender in the South African Nursing Profession*. London: St. Martin's.

Martin, Emily. 2009. *Bipolar Expeditions: Mania and Depression in American Culture*. Princeton, NJ: Princeton University Press.

Marttaliitto. 2011. "Tilkkupeittojen määrä ylitti kaikki odotukset." Accessed February 20, 2012. http://www.martat.fi/medialle/?x127892=196997793.

Massumi, Brian. 2002. *Parables for the Virtual: Movement, Affect, Sensation*. Durham, NC: Duke University Press.

Matteuzi Bruni, Nancy. 2005. *Political Neutrality and Humanitarian Aid: Practical Implications of Organizational Ideology*. Master's thesis, Duquesne University, Pittsburgh.

Maude, George. 1976. *The Finnish Dilemma: Neutrality in the Shadow of Power*. Oxford: Oxford University Press.

Mauss, Marcel. 1985. "A Category of the Human Mind: The Notion of the Person; the Notion of Self." Trans. W. D. Halls. In *The Category of the Person: Anthropology, Philosophy, History*, ed. Michael Carrithers, Steven Collins, and Steven Lukes, 1–25. Cambridge: Cambridge University Press.

———. 1990. *The Gift: The Form and Reason for Exchange in Archaic Societies*. Trans. W. D. Halls. New York: Norton.

Mazzarella, William. 2009. "Affect: What Is It Good For?" In *Enchantments of Modernity: Empire, Nation, Globalization*, ed. Saurabh Dube, 291–309. New York: Routledge.

Mbembe, Achille. 2001. *On the Post-Colony*. Berkeley: University of California Press.

———. 2006. "Variations on the Beautiful in Congolese Worlds of Sound." In *Beautiful Ugly: African and Diaspora Aesthetics*, ed. Sarah Nuttall, 60–93. Durham, NC: Duke University Press.

McBride, Keally, and Annick Wibben. 2010. "The Gendering of Counterinsurgency in Afghanistan." *Humanity* 3 (2): 199–215.

McClintock, Anne. 1995. *Imperial Leather: Race, Gender, and Sexuality in the Colonial Contest*. New York: Routledge.

McFalls, Laurence. 2010. "Benevolent Dictatorship: The Formal Logic of Humanitarian Government." In *Contemporary States of Emergency: The Politics of Military and Humanitarian Interventions*, ed. Didier Fassin and Mariella Pandolfi, 317–34. New York: Zone Books.

McKay, Ramah. 2012a. "Afterlives: Humanitarian Histories and Critical Subjects in Mozambique." *Cultural Anthropology* 27 (2): 286–309.

———. 2012b. "Documentary Disorders: Managing Medical Multiplicity in Mozambique." *American Ethnologist* 39: 545–61.

Meinander, Henrik. 1999. *Tasavallan tiellä: Suomi kansalaissodasta 2000-luvulle*. Helsinki: Schildts.

———. 2006. *Suomen historia: Linjat, rakenteet, käännekohdat*. Trans. Paula Autio. Helsinki: Werner Söderström Osakeyhtiö.

Melody, Cheryl. 1997. *World Peace: The Children's Dream! A Multicultural Musical for the Whole Family!* Compact disc. Hopkington, MA: Cheryl Melody Productions.

Meskell, Lynn, ed. 2005. *Archaeologies of Materiality*. Malden, MA: Blackwell.

Mindry, Deborah. 1999. "Good Women: Philanthropy, Power, and the Politics of Femininity in Contemporary South Africa." PhD dissertation, University of California, Irvine.

Mitchell, W. J. T. 2001. "Romanticism and the Life of Things: Fossils, Totems, and Images." *Critical Inquiry* 28 (1): 167–84.

Mittermaier, Amira. 2011. *Dreams That Matter: Egyptian Landscapes of the Imagination*. Berkeley: University of California Press.

Moore, Amanda Leslie. 2008. "Whale Stories: An Ethnography of Late Modern Nature." PhD dissertation, University of California, Irvine.

Moore, Sally Falk. 1978. *Law as Process: An Anthropological Approach.* New York: Routledge & Kegan Paul.

Moore, Sally Falk, and Barbara Meyerhoff. 1975. *Symbol and Politics in Communal Ideology.* Ithaca, NY: Cornell University Press.

———. 1977. *Secular Ritual.* New York: Van Gorcom.

Moorehead, Caroline. 1998. *Dunant's Dream: War, Switzerland and the History of the Red Cross.* London: Harper Collins.

Muehlebach, Andrea. 2011. "On Affective Labor in Post-Fordist Italy." *Cultural Anthropology* 26 (1): 59–82.

———. 2012. *The Moral Neoliberal: Welfare and Citizenship in Italy.* Chicago: University of Chicago Press.

Mulvey, Laura. 2009. *Visual and Other Pleasures.* New York: Palgrave Macmillan.

Munir, Muhammad. 2011. "The Layha for the Mujahideen: An Analysis of the Code of Conduct for the Taliban Fighters under Islamic Law." *International Review of the Red Cross* 93 (881): 81–120.

Musick, Marc, and John Wilson. 2008. *Volunteers: A Social Profile.* Bloomington: Indiana University Press.

Musil, Robert. 1994. *Precision and Soul: Essays and Addresses.* Ed. and trans. by Burton Pike and David S. Luft. Chicago: University of Chicago Press.

———. 1996a. *The Man Without Qualities.* Vol. 1, *A Sort of an Introduction and Pseudoreality Prevails.* Ed. Sophie Wilkins and Burton Pike. New York: Vintage.

———. 1996b. *The Man Without Qualities.* Vol. 2, *Into the Millennium and from the Posthumous Papers.* Ed. Sophie Wilkins and Burton Pike. New York: Vintage.

Mykrä, Pekka. 2010. *Kansalaisjärjestötoiminnan ytimessä: Tutkimus RAY:n avustamien sosiaali- ja terveysjärjestöjen vapaaehtoistoiminnasta.* Helsinki: Raha-automaattiyhdistys.

Nairn, Tom. 1977. *The Break-Up of Britain: Crisis and Neo-Nationalism.* London: Verso.

Nakamura, Carolyn, and Lynn Meskell. 2009. "Articulate Bodies: Forms and Figures at Çatalhöyük." *Journal of Archaeological Method and Theory* 16: 205–30.

Nakazawa, Keiji. (1978) 2004. *Barefoot Gen: A Cartoon Story of Hiroshima.* Trans. Project Gen. San Francisco: Last Gasp.

Natarajan, L. 1955. *From Hiroshima to Bandung: A Survey of American Policies in Asia.* New Delhi: People's Publishing House.

Naumann, Friedrich. 1915. *Mitteleuropa.* New York: R. Reimer.

Near, Holly. 1993. *The Great Peace March.* Paintings by Lisa Desimini. New York: Henry Holt.

Newby, Francesca. n.d. "How to Knit a Trauma Teddy." *Notebook Magazine: Home of Hints and How-tos.* Accessed March 12, 2009. http://www.homelife.com.au/how+to/how+to+knit+a+trauma+teddy,4676.

Nietzsche, Friedrich. 1956. *The Birth of Tragedy and the Genealogy of Morals.* Trans. Francis Golffing. New York: Doubleday.

———. 1966. *Beyond Good and Evil: Prelude to a Philosophy of the Future.* Trans. Walter Kaufmann. New York: Vintage.

————. 2005. *The Anti-Christ, Ecce Homo, Twilight of the Idols, and Other Writings*. Ed. Aaron Ridley and Judith Norman. Trans. Judith Norman. Cambridge: Cambridge University Press.

Nihtilä, E., and Pekka Martikainen. 2004. "Ikäihmisten yksinasuminen Suomessa vuosina 1970–2000." *Yhteiskuntapolitiikka* 69 (2): 135–46.

Nissinen, Minna. 2004. "Neulonta on mulle kuin aspiriinia!" Master's thesis.

Nousiainen, Anu. 2005. "Kädestä käteen." *Källor* (January). Accessed January 18, 2015. http://global.finland.fi/Public/default.aspx?contentid=86507.

Noys, Benjamin, ed. 2000. *Georges Bataille: A Critical Introduction*. London: Pluto Press.

O'Connor, Karen. 1993. "They Believe That Children Are the Future." *Billboard* 105 (7): C3.

Okri, Ben. 1993. *The Famished Road*. New York: Anchor.

————. 1996. *Dangerous Love*. London: Phoenix House.

Oksanen, Sofi. 2003. *Stalinin lehmät*. Helsinki: WSOY.

————. 2008. *Puhdistus*. Helsinki: WSOY.

Olson, Leanne. 1999. *A Cruel Paradise: Journals of an International Relief Worker*. Toronto: Insomniac Press.

Omenn, G. 1988. "Healthy Children: Investing in the Future." *Issues in Science and Technology* 5 (1): 106.

Ong, Aihwa. 2006. *Neoliberalism as Exception: Mutations in Citizenship and Sovereignty*. Durham, NC: Duke University Press.

Ophir, Adi. 2010. "The Politics of Catastrophization: Emergency and Exception." In *Contemporary States of Emergency: The Politics of Military and Humanitarian Interventions*, ed. Didier Fassin and Mariella Pandolfi, 59–88. New York: Zone Books.

Orbinski, James. 2008. *An Imperfect Offering: Humanitarian Action for the Twenty-First Century*. New York: Walker.

Ozawa, Martha. 1993. "America's Future and Her Investment in Children." *Child Welfare* 72 (6): 517–30.

Pajunen, Aimo. 1982. "Some Aspects of Finnish Security Policy." In *Neutrality and Non-Alignment in Europe Today*, ed. Hanna Ojanen, 156–64. Vienna: Wilhelm Braumuller.

Paley, Vivian Gussin. 2004. *A Child's Work: The Importance of Fantasy Play*. Chicago: University of Chicago Press.

Palkeinen, Hanna. 2005. "Yksinäisyys iäkkäiden ihmisten kirjoituksissa." *Gerontologia* 3: 111–20.

Palosaari, Teemu. 2011. "The Art of Adaptation: A Study of Finland's Foreign and Security Policy." *TAPRI Studies in Peace and Conflict Research*, no. 96. Tampere: Tampere Peace Research Institute.

Pandolfi, Mariella. 2010. "Humanitarianism and Its Discontents." In *The Forces of Compassion: Humanitarianism between Ethics and Politics*, ed. Erica Bornstein and Peter Redfield, 227–48. Santa Fe: School for Advanced Research Press.

Parker, Rozsika. (1984) 2010. *The Subversive Stitch: Embroidery and the Making of the Feminine*. New ed. London: I. B. Tauris.

Parker, Rozsika, and Griselda Pollock. 1981. *Old Mistresses: Women, Art and Ideology*. New York: Pantheon.

Parry, Jonathan. 1986. "The Gift, the Indian Gift, and the 'Indian Gift.'" Man (n.s.) 21 (3): 453–73.

Parsons, Talcott. 1951. The Social System. New York: Free Press.

Peace Child Foundation. 1987. Peace Child: A Musical Fantasy about Children Bringing Peace to the World. Musical director's score. Music and lyrics by David Gordon. Arrangements by Steve Riffkin. Fairfax, VA: Peace Child Foundation.

Pejic, Jelena. 2011. "The Protective Scope of Common Article 3: More Than Meets the Eye." International Review of the Red Cross 93 (881): 189–225.

Perales, César A. 1988. "Black and Hispanic Children: Their Future Is Ours." Journal of State Government 61 (2): 45–48.

Pessi, Anne Birgitta, and Juho Saari, eds. 2011. Hyvien ihmisten maa: Auttaminen kilpailukyky-yhteiskunnassa. A Tutkimuksia 31. Helsinki: Diakonia-ammattikorkeakoulun julkaisuja.

Peters, Krijn, and Paul Richards. 1998. "Fighting with Open Eyes: Young Combatants Talking about War in Sierra Leone." In Rethinking the Trauma of War, ed. P. Bracken and C. Petty, 76–111. New York: Free Association Press.

Petryna, Adriana. 2002. Life Exposed: Biological Citizens after Chernobyl. Princeton, NJ: Princeton University Press.

Petterson, Maria. 2013. "Sodan jälkeen rauha." Helsingin Sanomat, Thursday insert, August 15, 4–5. Photographs by Sabrina Bqain.

Pictet, Jean. 1979. "The Fundamental Principles of the Red Cross: Commentary." Accessed August 11, 2013. http://www.icrc.org/eng/resources/documents/misc/fundamental-principles-commentary-010179.htm.

Pierson, Christopher, and Francis Castles. 2009. The Welfare State: A Reader. Cambridge: Cambridge University Press.

Pietz, William. 1985. "The Problem of the Fetish, I." RES: Anthropology and Aesthetics 9: 5–17.

———. 1987. "The Problem of the Fetish, II: The Origin of the Fetish." RES: Anthropology and Aesthetics 13: 23–45.

———. 1988. "The Problem of the Fetish, IIIa: Bosman's Guinea and the Enlightenment Theory." RES: Anthropology and Aesthetics 16: 105–24.

Pinder, Mike. 1995. A Planet with One Mind: Stories from around the World for the Child within Us All. Audiocassette. One Step Records, BMI.

Piper, Adrian M. S. 1991. "Impartiality, Compassion and Modal Imagination." Ethics 101 (4): 726–57.

Poikolainen, Mari. 1997. "Towards the Cultural Meaning of Volunteering: The Application of a World View Model in Understanding Volunteering in World Shops." Master's thesis, University of Jyväskylä, Jyväskylä, Finland.

Pöllänen, Sinikka. 2006. "Elämä ilman käsitöitä—mitä se on? Käsityö harrastajien psyykkisen hyvinvoinnin tukena." In Tekstejä ja Kangastuksia: Puheenvuoroja käsityöstä ja sen tulevaisuudesta, ed. Leena Kaukinen and Miia Collanus, n.p. Tampere: Akatiimi.

———. 2007a. "Käsityö ja hyvinvointi: Taide kokonaisvaltaisen elämänhahmotuksen alueena." Accessed October 27, 2011. http://taide.motionforum.net/15-kasityo-ja-hyvinvointi.

————. 2007b. *Käsityö psyykkisen hyvinvoinnin tukena.* Savonlinnan opettajankoulutuslaitos. Joensuu: University of Joensuu.

Polman, Linda. 2011. *The Crisis Caravan: What's Wrong with Humanitarian Aid?* New York: Metropolitan Books.

Povinelli, Elizabeth. 2002. *The Cunning of Recognition: Indigenous Alterities and the Making of Multiculturalism.* Durham, NC: Duke University Press.

————. 2006. *The Empire of Love.* Durham, NC: Duke University Press.

Prashad, Vijay. 1997. "Mother Teresa: Mirror of Bourgeois Guilt." *Economic and Political Weekly* 32 (44/45): 2856–58.

Pratt, Mary-Louise. 2008. *Imperial Eyes: Travel Writing and Transculturation.* 2nd ed. New York: Routledge.

Press, Mike. 2007. "Handmade Futures: The Emerging Role of Craft Knowledge in Our Digital Culture." In *NeoCraft: Modernity and the Crafts,* ed. Sandra Alfoldy, 249–66. Halifax: Press of the Nova Scotia College of Arts and Design.

Price, David H. 2005. *Threatening Anthropology: McCarthyism and the FBI's Surveillance of Activist Anthropologists.* Durham, NC: Duke University Press.

Price, Sally. 1991. *Primitive Art in Civilized Places.* Chicago: University of Chicago Press.

Proudfoot, Malcolm. 1956. *European Refugees, 1939–52: A Study of Forced Population Movement.* Evanston: Northwestern University Press.

Punainen Risti. n.d. "Anna hetki ajastasi—tule ystäväksi." Accessed October 26, 2011. http://oleystävä.fi/content.anna.hetki_ajastasi-tule-ystäväksi.

Punkka, Päivi. 2014. "The Handless as Her Home's Prisoner." *Helsingin Sanomat,* July 7, A3, A18–19.

Pupavac, Vanessa. 2010. "Between Compassion and Conservatism: A Genealogy of Humanitarian Sensibilities." In *Contemporary States of Emergency: The Politics of Military and Humanitarian Interventions,* ed. Didier Fassin and Mariella Pandolfi, 129–52. New York: Zone Books.

Puusaari, Hille. 1993. "Kuolemaan on hyvä saatella." *Mielenterveys* 5: 38–39.

Rahkonen, Juho. 2004. *Nato and Media.* Tampere: Tampere University Press.

————. 2006. "Journalismi taistelukenttänä: Suomen Nato-jäsenyydestä käyty julkinen keskustelu 2003–2004." PhD dissertation, Tampere University, Tampere, Finland.

————. 2011. "Perussuomalaisten ruumiinavaus." *Yhteiskuntapolitiikka* 76(4): n.p.

Rajaniemi, Jere. 2007. *Ikääntyneet järjestö- ja vapaaehtoistoiminnassa: Pääkaupunkiseudun järjestökyselyksen tuloksia.* Raportteja 2. Helsinki: Ikäinstituutti.

Ramos, Alcida. 1997. *Indigenism: Ethnic Politics in Brazil.* Madison: University of Wisconsin Press.

Rancière, Jacques. 2004. *The Philosopher and His Poor.* Durham, NC: Duke University Press.

————. 2011. *Dissensus: On Politics and Aesthetics.* New York: Continuum.

Rastas, Anna. 2007. *Rasismi lasten ja nuorten arjessa: Transnationaalit juuret ja monikulttuuristuva Suomi.* Tampere: University of Tampere Press.

————. 2012. "Reading History through Finnish Exceptionalism." In *Whiteness and Postcolonialism in the Nordic Region,* ed. Kristín Loftsdóttir and Lars Jensen, 89–103. Burlington, VT: Ashgate.

Redfield, Peter. 2006. "A Less Modest Witness: Collective Advocacy and Motivated Truth in a Medical Humanitarian Movement." *American Ethnologist* 33 (1): 3–26.

———. 2008. "Vital Mobility and the Humanitarian Kit." In *Biosecurity Interventions: Global Health and Security in Question*, ed. Andrew Lakoff and Stephen Collier, 147–71. New York: Columbia University Press.

———. 2010. "The Impossible Problem of Neutrality." In *Forces of Compassion: Humanitarianism between Ethics and Politics*, ed. Erica Bornstein and Peter Redfield, 53–70. Santa Fe: School for Advanced Research Press.

———. 2013. *Life in Crisis: The Ethical Journey of Doctors without Borders*. Berkeley: University of California Press.

Redfield, Peter, and Erica Bornstein. 2010. "An Introduction to the Anthropology of Humanitarianism." In *Forces of Compassion: Humanitarianism between Ethics and Politics*, ed. Erica Bornstein and Peter Redfield, 3–30. Santa Fe: School for Advanced Research Press.

Regan, Tom, and Peter Singer. 1989. *Animal Rights and Human Obligations*. Englewood Cliffs, NJ: Prentice-Hall.

Reynolds, Pamela. 1996. *Traditional Healers and Childhood in Zimbabwe*. Athens: Ohio University Press.

Richard, Analiese, and Daromir Rudnyckyj. 2009. "Economies of Affect." *Journal of the Royal Anthropological Institute* 15 (1): 57–77.

Ricoeur, Paul. 1994. "Imagination in Discourse and in Action." In *Rethinking Imagination: Culture and Creativity*, ed. Gillian Robinson and John Rundell, 118–35. New York: Routledge.

Rieffer-Flanagan, Barbara Ann. 2009. "Is Neutral Humanitarianism Dead? Red Cross Neutrality: Walking the Tightrope of Neutral Humanitarianism." *Human Rights Quarterly* 31: 888–915.

Riikonen, Liisa. 1994. "Uskomattomia tarinoita: Etnografinen tutkimus hoitamisesta vieraassa kulttuurissa ja poikkeusoloissa suomalaisten sairaanhoitajien kuvaamana." Master's thesis, University of Kuopio, Kuopio, Finland.

———. 2005. "'Kuran ja kuoleman keskelle sinne sinisten vuorten alle': Sairaanhoitajan ammattitaito poikkeusoloissa ja vieraassa kulttuurissa." Kasvatustieteellisiä julkaisuja, no. 109. PhD dissertation, Joensuun yliopiston, Joensuu, Finland.

Risatti, Howard. 2007. *A Theory of Craft: Function and Aesthetic Expression*. Chapel Hill: University of North Carolina Press.

Ritvo, Harriet. 1985. "Learning from Animals: Natural History for Children." *The Threepenny Review* 21: 4–6.

Robinson, Gillian, and John Rundell, eds. 1994. *Rethinking Imagination: Culture and Creativity*. New York: Routledge.

Roedigger, David. 2007. *The Wages of Whiteness: Race and the Making of the American Working Class*. New York: Verso.

Romulo, Carlos. 1956. *The Meaning of Bandung*. Chapel Hill: University of North Carolina Press.

Roponen, Maria. 2010. "Tuetun työn merkitykset yksilön hyvinvoinnille: Tutkimus työntekijöiden kokemuksista SPR:n Kontti-kierrätystavaratalojen työstä." Master's thesis, University of Tampere, Tampere, Finland.

Rosen, David M. 2005. *Armies of the Young: Child Soldiers in War and Terrorism.* New Brunswick, NJ: Rutgers University Press.

Rosenblum, Robert. 1988. *The Romantic Child: From Runge to Sendak.* The Walter Neurath Memorial Lecture. New York: Thames and Hudson.

Rousseau, Jean-Jacques. (1762) 1978. *Emile: Or, On Education.* Ed. and trans. Allan Bloom. New York: Basic Books.

Ruismäki, Heikki, and Inkeri Ruokonen, eds. 2011a. "Arts and Skills—Source of Wellbeing." *Third International Journal of Intercultural Arts Education.* Research Report 330. Helsinki: University of Helsinki.

———, eds. 2011b. "Design Learning and Well-being." *Fourth International Journal of Intercultural Arts Education.* Research Report 331. Helsinki: University of Helsinki.

Rundell, John. 1994a. "Creativity and Judgement: Kant on Reason and Imagination." In *Rethinking Imagination,* ed. Gillian Robinson and John Rundell, 87–117. New York: Routledge.

———. 1994b. "Introduction." In *Rethinking Imagination,* ed. Gillian Robinson and John Rundell, 1–11. New York: Routledge.

Ruohonen, M. 2003. "Järjestöt vapaaehtoistoiminnan areenoina ja mahdollistajina." In *Hyvinvoinnin arjen asiantuntijat: Sosiaali-ja terveysjärjestöt uudella vuosituhannella,* ed. J. Niemelä and V. Dufva, 40–55. Juva: PS-kustannus.

Saari, Juho. 2009. *Yksinäisten yhteiskunta.* Helsinki: WSOY.

———. 2012. "Yksinäisenä yhteisössä." *Diakonia* 1: 32–52.

Saari, Juho, Sakari Kainulainen, and Anne Birgitta Yeung. 2005. *Altruismi: Antamisen lahja Suomen evankelis-luterilaisessa kirkossa.* Helsinki: Yliopistopaino.

Saari, Salli. 2000. *Kuin salama kirkkaalta taivaalta: Kriisit ja niista selviytyminen.* Helsinki: Otava.

Said, Edward. 1979. *Orientalism.* New York: Random House.

Sartre, Jean-Paul. (1940) 2004. *The Imaginary.* Trans. Jonathan Webber. New York: Routledge.

Sarvimäki, Anneli, Sirkkaliisa Heimonen, and Anna Mäki-Petäjä-Leinonen. 2010. *Vanhuus ja haavoittuvuus.* Helsinki: Edita.

Sarwary, Walid Akbar. 2011. "Interview with Fatima Ghailani." *International Review of the Red Cross* 93 (881): 5–9.

Sass, Louis. 1992. *Madness and Modernism: Insanity in the Light of Modern Art, Literature, and Thought.* New York: Basic Books.

Scarry, Elaine. 1985. *The Body in Pain: The Making and Unmaking of the World.* New York: Oxford University Press.

———. 2001. *Dreaming by the Book.* Princeton, NJ: Princeton University Press.

Scheper-Hughes, Nancy, and Carolyn Sargent, eds. 1998. *Small Wars: The Cultural Politics of Childhood.* Berkeley: University of California Press.

Schmitt, Carl. (1922) 2007. *Political Theology: Four Chapters on the Concept of Sovereignty.* Trans. George Schwab. Chicago: University of Chicago Press.

Scholes, Katherine. 1990. *Peace Begins with You*. Illus. Robert Ingpen. Boston: Little, Brown; San Francisco: Sierra Club Books.

Schweitzer, Albert. 1950. *Denken und Tat*. Ed. Rudolph Grabs. Hamburg: Richard Meiner Verlag.

Schwenkel, Christina. 2009. *The American War in Contemporary Vietnam: Transnational Remembrance and Representation*. Indianapolis: Indiana University Press.

———. 2012. "Civilizing the City: Socialist Ruins and Urban Renewal in Central Vietnam." *positions* 20 (2): 437–70.

———. 2013. "Post/Socialist Affect: Ruination and Reconstruction of the Nation in Urban Vietnam." *Cultural Anthropology* 28 (2): 252–77.

Scott, A. O. 2011. "Between Heaven and Earth: A True Story of Monks in Algeria." *New York Times*, February 24. Accessed August 4, 2013. movies.nytimes.com/2011/02/25/movies/25gods.html?_r=0.

Sendak, Maurice. 1981. *Outside Over There*. New York: Harper Collins.

Sennett, Richard. 2008. *The Craftsman*. New Haven, CT: Yale University Press.

Shenk, Joshua Wolf. 2014. "The End of 'Genius.'" *New York Times*, July 20, 6–7. Sunday Review section.

Shihab Nye, Naomi. 1998. *Fuel: Poems*. Rochester, NY: Boa Editions.

Siikala, Jukka. 2006. "The Ethnography of Finland." *Annual Review of Anthropology* 35: 153–70.

Silverman, Kaja. 2007. "The Subject." In *Visual Culture: The Reader*, ed. Jessica Evans and Stuart Hall, 340–55. Thousand Oaks, CA: Sage Publications, in association with the Open University.

Sjöberg-Uotila, Jaana. 2009. "Kotimaasta kriisialueelle: Sairaanhoitajan tie Punaisen Ristin delegaatiksi." Thesis, Pirkanmaan Ammattikorkeakoulu.

Slater, Dashka. 2012. "Is This the Most Dangerous Thing in Your House?" *New York Times*, September 9, 22–27. Accessed August 9, 2013. http://query.nytimes.com/gst/fullpage.html?res=9903E3D7103CF93AA3575AC0A9649D8B63.

Slim, Hugo. 2001. "Humanitarianism and the Holocaust: Lessons from ICRC's Policy toward the Jews." *International Journal of Human Rights* 5 (1): 130–44.

———. 2010. *Killing Civilians: Method, Madness, and Morality in War*. New York: Columbia University Press.

Smith, Allen C., III, and Sherryl Kleinman. 1989. "Managing Emotions in Medical School: Students' Contacts with the Living and the Dead." *Social Psychology Quarterly* 52 (1): 56–69.

Sneath, David, Martin Holbraad, and Morten Axel Pedersen. 2009. "Technologies of the Imagination: An Introduction." *Ethnos* 74 (1): 5–30.

Sonneveld, Marieke. 2007. "Aesthetics of Tactual Experience: About the Body Language of Objects." PhD dissertation, Technische Universiteit Delft, Delft, The Netherlands.

Sontag, Susan. 2003. *Regarding the Pain of Others*. New York: Farrar, Straus and Giroux.

———. 2007. "The Image-World." In *Visual Culture: A Reader*, ed. Jessica Evans and Stuart

Hall, 80–94. Thousand Oaks, CA: Sage Publications, in association with the Open University.

Spier, Peter. 1980. *People*. New York: Doubleday.

Ssorin-Chaikov, Nikolai. 2006. "On Heterochrony: Birthday Gifts to Stalin, 1949." *Journal of the Royal Anthropological Institute* (n.s.) 12 (2): 355–75.

Stals, José Lebrero. 1997. *Mike Kelley 1985–1996*. Barcelona: Museu d'Art Contemporani de Barcelona.

Standing, Guy. 2011. *The Precariat*. London: Bloomsbury Academic.

Starobinski, Jean. 1970. *La relation critique*. Paris: Gallimard.

Stebbins, Robert, and Margaret Graham. 2004. *Volunteering as Leisure/Leisure as Volunteering*. Cambridge, MA: CABI Publishing.

Steedman, Carolyn. 1995. *Strange Dislocations: Childhood and the Idea of Human Interiority, 1780–1930*. Cambridge, MA: Harvard University Press.

Stenbäck, Pär. 2009. *Kriisejä ja katastrofeja: Poliittinen ja humanitaarinen työni* [*Kriser och katastrofer*]. Trans. Salla Simukka. Keuruu, Finland: Schildts.

Stephens, Sharon. 1995. "Children and the Politics of Culture in 'Late Capitalism.'" In *Children and the Politics of Culture*, ed. Sharon Stephens, 3–48. Princeton, NJ: Princeton University Press.

———. 1996. "Reflections on Environmental Justice: Children as Victims and Actors." *Social Justice* 23 (4): 62–86.

Stern, David, ed. 2006. *Measuring Medical Professionalism*. New York: Oxford University Press.

Stewart, Kathleen. 2007. *Ordinary Affects*. Durham, NC: Duke University Press.

Stoler, Ann. 2004. "Affective States." In *A Companion to the Anthropology of Politics*, ed. David Nugent and Joan Vincent, 4–20. Malden, MA: Blackwell.

Strathern, Andrew, and Pamela Stewart. 2006. "Introduction: Terror, Imagination, Cosmology." In *Terror and Violence: Imagination and the Unimaginable*, ed. Andrew Strathern, Pamela Stewart, and Neil Whitehead, 1–39. Ann Arbor, MI: Pluto Press.

Strathern, Andrew, Pamela Stewart, and Neil Whitehead, eds. 2006. *Terror and Violence: Imagination and the Unimaginable*. Ann Arbor, MI: Pluto Press.

Strathern, Marilyn. 1990. *The Gender of the Gift: Problems with Women and Problems with Society in Melanesia*. Berkeley: University of California Press.

———. 1999. *Property, Substance and Effect: Anthropological Essays on Persons and Things*. London: Athlone Press.

Sturken, Marita. 2007. *Tourists of History: Memory, Kitsch, and Consumerism from Oklahoma City to Ground Zero*. Durham, NC: Duke University Press.

Suhonen, Heikki. 2005. *Elämä on pysähtynyt keinu: Tutkimus ikääntyneistä A-klinikan asiakkaista ja heidän asiakkuudestaan*. A-klinikkasäätiön monistesarja 48. Helsinki: A-klinikkasäätiö.

Suski, Laura. 2009. "Children, Suffering and the Humanitarian Appeal." In *Humanitarianism and Suffering: The Mobilization of Empathy*, ed. Richard Ashby Wilson and Richard Brown, 202–22. Cambridge: Cambridge University Press.

Szymborska, Wislawa. 2001. "The End and the Beginning." In *Miracle Fair: Selected Poems of Wislawa Szymborska*, trans. Joanna Trzeciak, 48–49. New York: W. W. Norton.

Tabassum, Sadia. 2011. "Combatants, Not Bandits: The Status of Rebels in Islamic Law." *International Review of the Red Cross* 93 (881): 121–39.

Tallqvist, Tarja. 2009. "Vanhusten itsemurhat, vaiettu häpeä." *Uusi Suomi*, January 21. Accessed February 17, 2014. http://tallqvist.puheenvuoro.ussisuomi.fi.

Talvitie, Liisa. 2008. "Finland's 10 Best Dressed." Photos by Marica Rosengård. *Gloria*, no. 255, May, 48–51.

Tambiah, Stanley. 1984. *The Buddhist Saints of the Forest and the Cult of Amulets*. Cambridge: Cambridge University Press.

———. 1985. *Culture, Thought, and Social Action: An Anthropological Perspective*. Cambridge, MA: Harvard University Press.

Tammisto, Maarit, and Simo Lahtinen. 1994. *Antakaa minulle ihminen! Ystäväpalvelusta vapaaehtoistyön tukikohdaksi*. STAKES raportteja 159. Jyväskylä: Gummerus.

Tanskanen, Alpo. 2009. "Välinpitämättömyys ja auttamisen ilo." Mielipidekirjoitukset, *Keskisuomalainen*, April 30. Accessed August 9, 2013. http://www.ksml.fi/mielipide /mielipidekirjoitukset/valinpitamattomyys-ja-auttamisen-ilo/822633.

Taussig, Michael. 1991. "Tactility and Distraction." *Cultural Anthropology* 6 (2): 147–53.

———. 1993. *Mimesis and Alterity: A Particular History of the Senses*. New York: Routledge.

Taylor, Charles. 2004. *Modern Social Imaginaries*. Durham, NC: Duke University Press.

Taylor, Christopher. 2001. *Sacrifice as Terror: The Rwandan Genocide of 1994*. New York: Berg.

Terry, Fiona. 2002. *Condemned to Repeat? The Paradox of Humanitarian Action*. Ithaca, NY: Cornell University Press.

———. 2011. "The International Committee of the Red Cross in Afghanistan: Reasserting the Neutrality of Humanitarian Action." *International Review of the Red Cross* 93 (881): 173–88.

Thiranagama, Sharika. 2011. *In My Mother's House: Civil War in Sri Lanka*. Philadelphia: University of Pennsylvania Press.

Thomas, Nigel J. T. n.d. "Imagination." In *Dictionary of Philosophy of Mind*, ed. Eric Hochstein, n.p. Waterloo, Canada: University of Waterloo. Accessed August 9, 2013. http://philosophy.uwaterloo.ca/MindDict/imagination.html.

Thompson, Guy. 1996. "The Rule of Neutrality." *Psychoanalysis and Contemporary Thought* 19: 57–84.

Thompson, Nato. 2012. *Living as Form: Socially Engaged Art from 1991–2011*. Cambridge, MA: MIT Press.

Thrift, Nigel. 2004. "Intensities of Feeling: Towards a Spatial Politics of Affect." *Geografiska Annaler: Series B. Human Geography* 86 (1): 57–78.

Ticktin, Miriam. 2006a. "Medical Humanitarianism in and beyond France: Breaking Down or Patrolling Borders?" In *Medicine at the Border: The History, Culture, and Politics of Global Health*, ed. Alison Bashford, 116–35. New York: Palgrave.

———. 2006b. "Where Ethics and Politics Meet: The Violence of Humanitarianism in France." *American Ethnologist* 33 (1): 33–49.

———. 2011. *Casualties of Care: Immigration and the Politics of Humanitarianism in France*. Berkeley: University of California Press.

Tierala, Lauri. 2006. "'Äläkä luota vieraaseen apuun': Suomen sotilaallinen liittoutumattomuus Euroopan turvallisuus- ja puolustuspolitiikan puitteissa." Master's thesis, University of Helsinki, Helsinki.

Tiikkainen, Pirjo. 2006. "Vanhuusiän yksinäisyys: Seuruututkimus emotionaalista ja sosiaalista yksinäisyyttä määrittävistä tekijöistä." *Studies in Sport, Physical Education and Health* 114. Jyväskylä: University of Jyväskylä.

Tilus, Sirkka. 1998. "Liisa Selänteen Mielestä Vapaaehtoistyö on Enkelitehtävä." *Avun Maailma* 4: 8–9.

———. 2009. "Palkittu kirja kertoo nuorten auttamishalusta." *Avun Maailma* 1: 18–19.

TNS Gallup. 2011. *Ikäihmiset ja teknologia 2011.* Helsinki: Karate.

Truog, Robert. 2012. "Patients and Doctors—The Evolution of a Relationship." *The New England Journal of Medicine* 366 (7): 581–85.

Tsing, Anna. 2005. *Friction: An Ethnography of Global Connection.* Princeton, NJ: Princeton University Press.

Tsuchiya, Yukio. (1951) 1988. *Faithful Elephants: A True Story of Animals, People and War.* Boston: Houghton Mifflin.

Turja, Tuomo, and Lotta Engdahl. 2008. *Suomen Punainen Risti: SPR:n järjestökuva.* Helsinki: Taloustutkimus.

Turkle, Sherry, ed. 2007. *Evocative Objects: Things We Think With.* Cambridge, MA: MIT Press.

Turner, Fred. 2012. "The Family of Man and the Politics of Attention in Cold War America." *Public Culture* 24 (1): 55–84.

Turner, Victor. 1970. *The Forest of Symbols: Aspects of Ndembu Ritual.* Ithaca, NY: Cornell University Press.

United Nations Children's Fund (UNICEF). 1994. *I Dream of Peace: Images of War by Children of Former Yugoslavia.* New York: UNICEF/Harper Collins.

United Nations Organization. 1995. *My Wish for Tomorrow: Words and Pictures from Children Around the World (In Celebration of the Fiftieth Anniversary of the United Nations).* New York: Tambourine Books.

Uotila, Hanna. 2011. "Vanhuus ja yksinäisyys: Tutkimus iäkkäiden ihmisten yksinäisyyskokemuksista, niiden merkityksistä ja tulkinnoista." Acta Universitatis Tamperensis, no. 1651. PhD dissertation, University of Tampere, Tampere, Finland.

Uotila, Hanna, Kirsi Lumme-Sandt, and Marja Saarenheimo. 2010. "Lonely Older People as a Problem in Society—Construction in Finnish Media." *International Journal of Ageing and Later Life* 5 (2): 103–30.

Valentine, Gill. 1996. "Angels and Devils: Moral Landscapes of Childhood." *Environment and Planning D: Society and Space* 14 (5): 581–99.

Van Eys, Jan. 1981. *Humanity and Personhood: Personal Reaction to a World in Which Children Can Die.* Springfield: Charles C. Thomas.

Vaughan, Megan. 1991. *Curing Their Ills: Colonial Power and African Illness.* Stanford: Stanford University Press.

Venkatesan, Soumhya. 2011. "The Social Life of a 'Free' Gift." *American Ethnologist* 38 (1): 47–57.

Viktorin, Mattias. 2008. "Exercising Peace: Conflict Preventionism, Neoliberalism, and the New Military." PhD dissertation, Stockholm University, Stockholm.

Viljanen, Maria. 2010. "Ikääntyminen, alkoholi ja lääkkeet." A-klinikkasäätiö 1–4. Helsinki: A-klinikkasäätiö. Accessed March 27, 2012. http://www.a-klinikka.fi/tiimi/884 /ikaantyminen-alkoholi-ja-laakkeet.

Visuri, Pekka, ed. 2003. Suomen turvallisuus- ja puolustuspolitiikan linjaukset. Helsinki: Otava.

Vittachi, Varindra Tarzie. 1993. Between the Guns: Children as a Zone of Peace. London: Hodder and Stoughton.

Von Bonsdorff, Pauline. 2009. "Mielikuvituksen voima: Ruumiin ja runouden kuvat." In Kuva, ed. Leila Haaparanta, Timo Klemola, Jussi Kotkavirta, and Sami Pihlström, 27–47. Acta Philosophica Tamperensia 5. Tampere: University of Tampere Press.

Walker, Peter. 2005. "Cracking the Code: The Genesis, Use and Future of the Code of Conduct." Disasters 29 (4): 323–36.

Wall, John. 2004. "Fallen Angels: A Contemporary Christian Ethical Ontology of Childhood." International Journal of Practical Theology 8: 160–84.

Ware, Vron. 1992. Beyond the Pale: White Women, Racism, and History. New York: Verso.

Wark, McKenzie. 1995. "Fresh Maimed Babies: The Uses of Innocence." Transition 65 (spring): 36–47.

Weber, Max. (1930) 2000. The Protestant Ethic and the Spirit of Capitalism. New York: Routledge.

Weiner, Myron. 1968. "Neutralism and Nonalignment." In International Encyclopaedia of the Social Sciences, ed. David Sills, 11: 166–72. New York: Macmillan and The Free Press.

Weller, Shane. 2009. "'Some Experience of the Schizoid Voice': Samuel Beckett and the Language of Derangement." Forum for Modern Language Studies 45 (1): 32–50.

Wells, Rosemary. 1996. The Language of Doves. New York: Dial Books for Young Readers.

Wendland, Claire. 2010. A Heart for the Work: Journeys through an African Medical School. Chicago: University of Chicago Press.

White, Alan. 1990. The Language of Imagination. Cambridge, MA: Basil Blackwell.

White, Hayden. 1998. Address to "Histories of the Future" Residential Research Group, University of California Humanities Research Institute, University of California, Irvine.

Whitman. Walt. 2002. Selected Poems. New York: State Street Press.

Williams, Raymond. 1985. Marxism and Literature. Oxford: Oxford University Press.

Wilson, John. 2000. "Volunteering." Annual Review of Sociology 26: 215–40.

Wilson, Richard Ashby. 2010. "When Humanity Sits in Judgment: Crimes Against Humanity and the Conundrum of Race and Ethnicity at the International Criminal Tribunal for Rwanda." In In the Name of Humanity: The Government of Threat and Care, ed. Ilana Feldman and Miriam Ticktin, 27–57. Durham, NC: Duke University Press.

Wilson, Richard Ashby, and Richard Brown, eds. 2008. Humanitarianism and Suffering: The Mobilization of Empathy. Cambridge: Cambridge University Press.

Winnicott, Donald W. (1971) 2005. Playing and Reality. New York: Routledge.

Wittner, Lawrence S. 1995. The Struggle against the Bomb. Vol. 1, One World or None. Stanford Nuclear Age Series. Stanford: Stanford University Press.

Woolf, Leonard. 1916. International Government. London: Allen and Unwin.

Wright, Richard. 1956. The Color Curtain: A Report on the Bandung Conference. New York: World Publishing Co.

Wuthnow, Robert. 1991. *Acts of Compassion: Caring for Others and Helping Ourselves*. Princeton, NJ: Princeton University Press.

Yamazaki, James, with Louis Fleming. 1995. *Children of the Atomic Bomb: An American Physician's Memoir of Nagasaki, Hiroshima, and the Marshall Islands*. Durham, NC: Duke University Press.

Yeung, Anne Birgitta. 2002. *Vapaaehtoistoiminta osana kansalaisyhteiskuntaa—ihanteita vai todellisuutta? Tutkimus suomalaisten asennoitumisesta ja osallistumisesta vapaaehtoistoimintaan*. Helsinki: Sosiaali- ja terveysjärjestöjen yhteistyöyhdistys.

Yle News. 2010. "Vanhus Virui Kolmatta Vuotta Kotonaan." January 27. Accessed August 7, 2013. http://yle.fi/alueet/helsinki/helsinki/2010/01/vanhus_virui_kolmatta_vuotta_kuolleena_kotonaan_1398178.html.

Yoneyama, Lisa. 1999. *Hiroshima Traces: Time, Space, and the Dialectics of Memory*. Berkeley: University of California Press.

Young, Michael. 2009. "Kant's View of the Imagination." *Kant-Studien* 79 (1–4): 140–64.

Zelizer, Viviana. 1994. *Pricing the Priceless Child: The Changing Social Value of Children*. Princeton, NJ: Princeton University Press.

Index